JOURNAL FOR THE STUDY OF THE OLD TESTAMENT
SUPPLEMENT SERIES
47

Editors
David J A Clines
Philip R Davies

Department of Biblical Studies
The University of Sheffield
Sheffield S10 2TN
England

THE
GREEK TEXT
OF
JEREMIAH

A Revised Hypothesis

Sven Soderlund

Journal for the Study of the Old Testament
Supplement Series 47

Published by
JSOT Press
Department of Biblical Studies
The University of Sheffield
Sheffield S10 2TN
England

Printed in Great Britain
by Redwood Burn Ltd.,
Trowbridge, Wiltshire.

British Library Cataloguing in Publication Data

Soderlund, Sven
    The Greek text of Jeremiah : a revised hypothesis.
    —(Journal for the study of the Old Testament
    supplement series. ISSN 0309-0789; v.47)
    1. Bible. O.T. Jeremiah—Criticism, Textual
    I. Title   II. Series
    224′.204   BS1525.2

    ISBN 1-85075-028-9
    ISBN 1-85075-029-7 Pbk

CONTENTS

CHAPTER FOUR

CHAPTER FIVE

PREFACE

This work represents a revision of a doctoral
thesis presented to the University of Glasgow in 1978.
The study was originally supervised by Prof. R. Davidson
to whom I am much indebted. The manuscript was slightly
revised and updated during my sabbatical leave from
Regent College, Vancouver, 1984. I am grateful to the
College for the opportunity for research provided by the
sabbatical, to my wife for much help in typing, and to
JSOT Press for accepting the manuscript for publication.

ABBREVIATIONS

AASF   Annales academiae scientiarum Fennicae

AS   Anatolian Studies

BANE   The Bible and the Ancient Near East: Essays in
         Honor of William Foxwell Albright, ed. G.W.
         Wright, New York, 1961.

BASOR   Bulletin of the American Schools of Oriental
         Research

BDB   Brown, F., Driver, S.R., and Briggs, C.A.
         A Hebrew and English Lexicon of the Old
         Testament, Oxford, edition of 1968.

BETL   Bibliotheca Ephemeridum Theologigicarum
         Lovaniensium

BHS   Biblia Hebraica Stuttgartensia

BibOr   Bibliotheca Orientalis

BK   Biblischer Kommentar

BM   Brooke, A.E. and McLean, N., The Old Testament
         in Greek, Cambridge, 1906-40.

BWAT   Beiträge zur Wissenschaft vom Alten Testament

BZAW   Beiheft zur Zeitschrift für die alttestament-
         liche Wissenschaft

CBQ   Catholic Biblical Quarterly

CCL   Corpus Christianorum, Series Latina

CSEL   Corpus Scriptorum Ecclesiasticorum Latinorum

CHB   Cambridge History of the Bible

DJD   Discoveries in the Judaean Desert of the Jordan

EB   Encyclopaedia Biblica, London, 1889

FSAC   Albright, W.F. From Stone Age to Christianity,
         New York, 2nd ed., 1957.

GCS	Die Griechischen Christlichen Schriftsteller der ersten Jahrhunderte
GGA	Göttingische Gelehrte Anzeigen
GK	Gesenius, W. and Kautzsh, E. Hebrew Grammar, rev. A.E. Cowley, Oxford, 1910.
HAT	Handbuch zum Alten Testament
HJ	Heythrop Journal
HP	Holmes, R. and Parsons, J., Vetus Testamentum Graeceum, Oxford, 1897-1827.
HR	Hatch, E., and Redpath, H.A. A Concordance to the Septuagint, Oxford, 1897.
HSDB	Hasting's Shorter Dictionary of the Bible, ed. J. Hastings; rev. F.C. Grant and H.H. Rowley, Edinburgh, 1963.
HSM	Harvard Semitic Monographs
HTR	Harvard Theological Review
HUCA	Hebrew Union College Annual
IDB	Interpreter's Dictionary of the Bible, New York, 1962
IEJ	Israel Exploration Journal
ILOT	Driver, S.R. Introduction to the Literature of the Old Testament, Edinburgh, edition of 1913.
IOSCS	International Organization for Septuagint and Cognate Studies
ISBE	International Standard Bible Encyclopaedia, 1929
JAOS	Journal of the American Oriental Society
JB	The Jerusalem Bible, 1966
JBL	Journal of Biblical Literature
JCS	Journal of Cuneiform Studies

JJS	Journal of Jewish Studies
JNSL	Journal of Northwest Semitic Languages
JSOT	Journal for the Study of the Old Testament
JSS	Journal of Semitic Studies
JTS	Journal of Theological Studies
LSJ	Liddell, H.G., Scott, R., and Jones, H.S., Greek-English Lexicon, Oxford, 9th ed., 1940.
MSU	Mitteilungen des Septuaginta-Unternehemens zu Göttignen
NAWG	Nachrichten der Akademie der Wissenschaften zu Göttingen
NEB	The New English Bible, 1970
NovTSup	Supplements to Novum Testamentum
NTS	New Testament Studies
PG	Patrologia Graece, ed. J.P. Migne
PL	Patrologia Latina, ed. J.P. Migne
QHBT	Cross, F.M. and Talmon, S. eds. Qumran and the History of the Biblical Text, Cambridge, Mass., 1975.
RB	Revue Biblique
RivStorLettRel	Rivista di storia e letteratura religiosa
RSV	Revised Standard Version, 1952
RV	Revised Version, 1881
SC	Sources Chrétiennes
SMS	Jellicoe, S. The Septuagint and Modern Study, Oxford, 1968
SupVT	Supplements to Vetus Testamentum

TRe	Theologische Revue
TRu	Theologische Rundschau
TU	Texte und Untersuchungen zur Geschichte der altchristlichen Literatur
VT	Vetus Testamentum
ZAW	Zeitschrift für die alttestamentliche Wissenschaft

CHAPTER ONE

INTRODUCTION

I. Scope and Methodology

One of the observable phenomena of OT studies
in the second half of the 20th century has been the
considerable attention devoted to the ancient translation of the Hebrew Scriptures into Greek known as the
Septuagint (LXX). The era has produced an impressive
number of text editions, monographs, theses and essays
probing the LXX from a variety of perspectives. In
the course of these studies the composite and complex
nature of the LXX has been demonstrated many times,
confirming the principle that the translation characteristics and transmission history of this document
must be analyzed one book at a time.

Among the books that have have been closely
examined in this way is that of the prophet Jeremiah
(Jer). Considering the nature and extent of the differences between the LXX and the Masoretic Text (MT)
of this work, as well as the existence of several
problematic inner-Greek phenomena in the LXX, this kind
of scholarly attention is perhaps not surprising. To
some degree, Jer-LXX has attracted notice ever since
Origen wrote in his Letter to Africanus that he had
observed in this book many instances of "disagreement"
(διαφοραν) between the two versions as well as "much
transposition and variation in the readings of the
prophecies" (πολλην μεταθεσιν και εναλλαγην της
λεξεως των προφητευομενων, PG 11, col. 56]). With the
discovery of Jer fragments among the Hebrew MSS at
Qumrân supporting readings both from the LXX and MT
versions, interest in the textual phenomena of this
book has intensified in the post-Qumrân era.

The present work is offered as a further contribution to the ongoing research into the Greek text of
Jer. Specifically, it seeks to evaluate some of the
major studies on this book that have appeared during

1

the last 25 years. The principal works in view are
those of J. Ziegler, Ieremias, vol. 15 of the Larger
Göttingen edition of the LXX (1957; 2nd ed. 1976),
E. Tov, The Septuagint Translation of Jeremiah and
Baruch: A Discussion of an Early Revision of the LXX
of Jeremiah 29-52 and Baruch 1:1-3:8 (1976), and J.G.
Janzen, Studies in the Text of Jeremiah (1973). The
researches of these scholars cover three distinct,
though interrelated, problem areas that emerge in
a study of Jer-LXX, namely those of Greek text,
translator/reviser theories, and relationship to the
Hebrew text. While contributions by other scholars
will also be integrated as relevant, it is the work of
the aforementioned that will provide the background and
organizational structure to the discussion.

     As for methodology, the approach taken is that of
an in-depth analysis of a passage of limited length in
Jer-LXX that is tangent in significant ways to the
problem areas posed. The passage in question is that
of LXX Ch. 29, consisting of the oracles against the
Philistines and Edom (in Rahlf's edition, 29:1-7 and
30:1-16 respectively; in the MT, 47:1-7 and 49:7-22).
While this limitation to Ch. 29 naturally restricts the
scope of the inquiry, it nonetheless provides the most
satisfactory and manageable approach for the kind of
critique envisioned. It gives the investigation a
clear focus and structure while at the same time de-
manding a rigorous attention to detail /1/.

     However, the limitation to Ch. 29 of Jer-LXX has
not been interpreted in an absolute or unreasonable
way. Rather, where the elucidation of a translation or
textual problem in Ch. 29 requires it, the discussion
takes account of material anywhere in the book of Jer
and indeed beyond. For example, in analyzing the
translation of the introductory heading in MT 47:1
אשר היה דבר יהוה אל ירמיהו הנביא אל פלשתים בטרם יכה
פרעה את עזה by the simple Greek phrase επι τους αλλοφυλους in LXX 29:1, this becomes the occasion for
investigating all variants found in the introductory
headings within Jer. Only in this way, when seen as
part of a larger pattern, is it possible to make a
judgement about the nature of the variant headings in
Jer-LXX 29:1 / Jer-MT 47:1 and to asses contemporary
explanations of the phenomenon. Other textual and
translation problems are handled in the same way.

In short, where appropriate, Ch. 29 becomes the spring-
board for a discussion of issues that is comprehensive
for the whole text of Jer.

But it may be asked why LXX Ch. 29 should be taken
as the basis for this critique. What is needed is a
passage that adequately represents each of the problem
areas posed. In this regard, Ch. 29 suits our purposes
admirably. For one thing, the examination of the inner-
Greek text critical problem is well served by this
chapter. The oracles against the Philistines and Edom
contain an abundance of variant readings representative
of all the important textual decisions relevant to the
book. Clearly exemplified also are the groupings of
MSS as well as the editorial characteristics of the
recensions and Minor Greek VSS. As a result, the
chapter can be used with confidence to evaluate the
accuracy and text critical principles of J. Ziegler's
edition.

With respect to the translator/reviser problem,
LXX Ch. 29 occupies a pivotal position. Analysis of
the text shows that the lexical differences between the
two halves of the book begin to appear precisely at LXX
Ch. 29. Moreover, a remarkably high percentage of all
the translation terms on which the translator/reviser
theories are based is illustrated in the Philistine and
Edom oracles. For instance, E. Tov's case for a reviser theory to explain the lexical phenomena of the
second half of Jer as opposed to a multiple translator
theory rests principally on 45 instances of unusual
renditions common to Jer a' (Chs. 1-28) and Jer b'
(Chs. 29-52). As it happens, 12 of the 45 (or 26%) are
found in Ch. 29. Similarly, the number of significant
differences between Jer a' and b' listed by Tov is 51;
of these, 15 (or 29%) appear in Ch. 29. Taken together, these examples provide a solid base for
analyzing Tov's methodology and interpretation of
the data.

As for the Hebrew/Greek problem, it too is
adequately represented in the oracles against the
Philistines and Edom. In the first place it may be
observed that the chapter is part of the section known
as the Oracles Against the Nations (OAN), a collection
of poems located in different positions in the two
texts each with its own internal order, thus drawing

attention to the many transpositions so characteristic
of the book. More important still are the several
variation units in the chapter illustrating all the
major categories of differences between the two texts.
Consequently, the chapter provides a suitable platform
for testing the conclusions of J.G. Janzen with respect
to the priority of the LXX text.

II. Background History

A.   The Greek Text

     Of the three issues investigated in this study,
that of establishing the Greek text is foundational to
the rest of the research. Without a firm text critical
base other inquiries into the nature of the LXX and its
relationship to the Hebrew "schweben in der Luft," as
Paul de Lagarde expressed it (Anmerkungen, p. 2). Research conducted on the basis of an uncertain text is
necessarily vulnerable to interpretative distortions.
This was one of the main conclusions of a 1950 dissertation on Jer-LXX by A.P. Hastoupis, The Septuagint
Text of the Book of Jeremiah (Chs. 1-25). According to
Hastoupis, much of the previous discussion of the
relationship between the two texts was vitiated by the
lack of a prior sifting of the Greek MS evidence.

     But this recognition of the problems posed by the
presence of variant readings in different MSS of the
LXX is of no modern vintage. For some of the earliest
observations on the subject, we need to go back again
to the work of Origen. In his editorial work on the
monumental Hexapla he claims that he often found
"disagreement among the copies of the Old Testament"
(την εν τοις αντιγραφοις της παλαιας διαθηκης διαφωνιαν,
Commentary on Matthew, xv, 14, GCS, Origenes, X, p. 388).
Also in the course of his numerous commentaries on the
books of the Bible, Origen several times had occasion
to remark on the presence of discrepant readings within
the copies of his Greek MSS. An illuminating example
of this is found in one of his homilies on Jer (xiv, 3)
where, commenting on Jer. 15:10 he encountered the
phrase which "in the majority of MSS" (τους πλειστοις
αντιγραφοις) read, "I have not helped, nor has anyone
helped me" (ουκ ωφελησα, ουδε ωφελησε με ουδεις), but
which "in the most accurate MSS and those which agree

with the Hebrew" (εν δε τοις ακριβεστατοις και
συμφωνουσι τοις Εβραικοις) read, "I have not lent on
usury, neither has anyone lent to me on usury" (ουκ
ωφειλησα ουδε ωφειλησε με ουδεις [GCS, Origenes, III,
p. 107]). In this homily Origen felt obliged to ex-
pound both versions, but when he returned to the same
passage in the following homily (xv, 5), in the meantime having had a chance to study the matter more
closely, he decided that the majority LXX reading was
in fact the result of a "scribal error" (γραφικον . . .
αμαρτημα [Origenes III, p. 129]). Other examples of a
rudimentary sort of textual criticism applied to Jer-
LXX in early times may be found in the margins of some
MSS and in the commentaries of certain of the patristic
writers such as Jerome, Theodoret and Olympiodorus /2/.

The modern history of LXX textual criticism began,
it could be argued, as early as the 16th century with
the publication of the first printed editions of the
Greek OT. The Complutensian Polyglot (printed 1514-17,
published 1520), the Aldine (1518) and Sixtine (1587)
editions--the latter of which was destined to become a
kind of textus receptus for generations of LXX readers
/3/--all had to make text critical decisions in the
choice of which MS(S) to use and which readings to
print. When collated against each other, they all
manifest a number of unique readings, some of which
are trivial in nature but others of which are sub-
stantive /4/.

Following the famous 16th century editions of
southern Europe, the next major LXX publication
enterprises took place in England, where, between the
years 1707-20, J.E. Grabe and collaborators produced an
elaborate edition of the oldest British MS at the time,
Codex Alexandrinus. By the use of symbols and different types of print, Grabe sought to communicate his
convictions about the priority of readings and their
relationship to the Hebrew. Collation of MSS began in
earnest with the work of R. Holmes and J. Parson who in
the years 1798-1827 published an edition of the LXX
containing an apparatus of variant readings from nearly
300 MSS, though the base text employed was merely a
reprint of the Sixtine edition. The discovery in the
19th century of the invaluable Codex Sinaiticus
stimulated the production in Leipzig, Germany, of
Tischendorf's seven editions of the LXX, 1850-87

(the last two edited by Eb. Nestle), which while again reprinting a (revised) Sixtine text, contained a useful apparatus of select variants from the main uncials, i.e. Codex Alexandrinus, Codex Sinaiticus (or Codex Friderico-Augustanus, as Tischendorf called it), and Codex Ephraemi.

Within the last century, however, the publication of LXX texts has been associated mainly with two academic centres, those of Cambridge and Göttingen. As early as 1875 F.H.A. Scrivener of Cambridge presented to the Syndics of the University Press a plan for the preparation of a major edition of the LXX, the execution of which was entrusted in 1883 to H.B. Swete and duly announced in the Cambridge University Reporter on March 13th of that year (p. 473). The notice stated that it was the intention of the Syndics of the press to publish "an edition of the Septuagint and Apocrypha with an ample apparatus criticus, intended to provide materials for the critical determination of the text" and that as a preliminary step they hoped to publish a "portable text" of the LXX, "taken from the Vatican MS where this is not defective, with variations of two or three other early uncial MSS." This enterprise bore fruit in the publication between the years 1887-94 of the first edition of Swete's widely distributed three volume work, The Old Testament in Greek (later several times revised and reprinted). When Swete was unable also to assume the responsibility for directing the larger edition--programmatic guidelines for this edition in the meantime having been worked out by F.J.A. Hort--the task was entrusted in 1895 to A.E. Brooke and N. McLean (later, in 1927, officially joined by H. St. J. Thackeray), so that between the years 1906-40 almost the first half of the LXX appeared in this eminent publishing venture /5/.

Meanwhile, the Septuaginta Unternehmen of Göttingen (the well known LXX research centre established there in 1908 by the Akademie der Wissenschaften zu Göttingen) was proceeding with its own program but along different lines from those of Cambridge. Whereas the Cambridge approach was to collate the evidence on the basis of one MS (mainly Codex Vaticanus, or failing that, the nearest standing uncial), the reigning philosophy in Göttingen was to attempt a critically restored text through a comparison and grouping of all

the sources. The inspiration for this project derived
from the encyclopaedic scholar Paul de Lagarde who, in
his work on the LXX, laboured hard to formulate the
text critical principles by which such an edition might
be constructed /6/. Although one peculiar aspect of
his methodology having to do with the prior preparation
of the three ecclesiastical texts of Origen, Lucian,
and Hesychius had to be abandoned, his successors
nevertheless carried on with the preparation of prolegomena and the publication of critical editions
according to the general Richtlinien laid down by
Lagarde. Just as Swete's text preceded the larger
Cambridge edition, so a two volume Handausgabe by
Rahlfs, Septuaginta (1935)--although a private undertaking and published in Stuttgart--demonstrated the
Göttingen approach. The text is an eclectic one,
determined primarily on the basis of the three major
uncials B, S, and A. Rahlfs was also the first to
prepare texts for the larger Göttingen series, Genesis
(1926, likewise published in Stuttgart; since then
superseded by the edition of J.W. Wevers, 1975), and
Psalmi cum Odis (1931). Under a variety of editors
this series continues to appear, to date more than half
of the LXX having been published /7/.

    As for the text of Jer, this is included in all
the editions mentioned so far, with the notable exception of the larger Cambridge series, which regrettably
did not reach the section of the Prophets before the
project ceased publication. In addition, Jer has also
appeared in two independent editions, the critical text
of M.G.L. Spohn (1824) /8/ and that of Eb. Nestle /9/.
The former offers a unique reconstruction of the text
drawing heavily on Hexaplaric material while the second
represents something of a halfway stage between the
Cambridge and Göttingen approaches since its base text
reproduces essentially Codex Vaticanus (albeit corrected at a few points by other MS readings and even by
a few conjectural emendations) but is accompanied by
its own pioneering attempt at grouped readings in the
apparatus.

    Far and away the most important text of Jer
produced hitherto, however, is volume 15 of the Larger
Göttingen series edited by Joseph Ziegler (1957; reprinted 1976). Previously Ziegler had also edited the
texts of Isaiah (1939), the Twelve (1934),

Ezekiel (1952), and Daniel (including Susanna and Bel and the Dragon, 1954), so that as the last of the prophetic books to be edited, the text of Jer enjoyed the advantage of hindsight and expertise gained in the execution of the earlier volumes. In addition to preparing this edition, Ziegler also wrote an accompanying monograph, Beiträge zur Ieremias-Septuaginta (MSU 6, 1958), as well as two articles, "Die Septuaginta Hieronymi im Buch des Propheten Jeremias" (1952) /10/, and "Jeremias-Zitate in Väter-Schriften" (1958) /11/.

The critique of Ziegler's work is to be found in Ch. III of the present study, following an independent documentation of the MS evidence for the oracles against the Philistines and Edom in Ch. II. This sort of detailed critique seems especially necessary in the case of the Göttingen texts since there persists in some quarters a crisis of doubt concerning the validity of a critically reconstructed LXX text. Here and there, both in verbal and written form, one meets with remarks about "the concoction of eclectic texts," a clear preference for the Cambridge one-MS approach being intended /12/. Yet it is strange that one school should be so frequently pitted against the other as though they had in view two radically different objectives. This is manifestly false. The leading spirits in Cambridge no less than in Göttingen had as their ultimate objective a critically restored text. This is clear not only from their explicit statements on the subject /13/, but also from the high esteem in which the Cambridge editors held Lagarde /14/ and his colleagues and the constant friendly exchange of MS and collation material that passed between the two centres. The difference between them lay not in ultimate objective but in the means of getting there. In Cambridge the attitude that prevailed was one of "Not yet" /15/, whereas in Göttingen the question was rather "Why not?" British policy was that all the data should first be collected in published form before being worked over by an editor in the preparation of a reconstructed text. In Göttingen it was believed the process of collating and editing could go hand in hand. Here lay the difference of approach.

The review of the evidence undertaken for this study supports the Göttingen position that the materials for an attempted reconstruction of the text

are in hand. It is also clear that the quality of
Ziegler's work on Jer-LXX is very impressive and
represents a monumental step forward in the textual
analysis of this book. Yet, impressive as it is, it
cannot be allowed to ring down the curtain on further
scholarly inquiry into the textual problems of the
book. As Peter Walter (formerly Katz) has well
described it, the Göttingen project represents a "task
for which there is neither end nor limit: that of an
ever-increasing approximation to the supposed archetype
to which the evidence points" (The Text of the Septuagint, 1973, p. 10). In order that scholarship continue
to advance, it is essential that even Ziegler's text be
subjected to objective critique so that its text critical philosophy can be evaluated, its merits appreciated
and any inaccuracies corrected. Apart from a few gen-
eralized reviews in the journals at the time of publication /16/, it appears that this kind of critique has
not previously been undertaken.

B.   The Translator/Reviser Problem

     While the pursuit of the earliest recoverable text
of the translation is a fundamental and essential task,
the student of Jer-LXX also has to contend with what we
have called the "translator/reviser" problem. As mentioned above (p. 3), analysis of the text makes it
clear that around the middle of the book--specifically
in LXX Ch. 29--certain lexical differences begin to
appear between the first and the second half, the
clearest example of which is the shift from the conventional form of the Messenger Formula ταδε λεγει +
nomen sacrum in first half of the book to ουτως ειπε +
nomen sacrum in the second half /17/. Such peculiari-
ties of the text and the implications of these for a
plurality of translators in the book had been noticed
by scholars working on Jer-LXX already in the 18th and
19th centuries /18/, but it was not till the first
decades of this century that the matter received systematic treatment at the hands of the eminent Septua-
gintalist Henry St. John Thackeray. It was Thackeray
who first noticed that the change in style and vocabulary takes place at a definite point in the book and
who, on this basis, first produced a specific multiple
translator theory to account for the observed phenomena
/19/.

Having "discovered" the multiple translator phenomenon in Jer, Thackeray himself extended the discussion
to other books and found evidence for the same thing
occurring in Ez and Reigns /20/. Other scholars followed him and in turn proposed a plurality of translators for the Pentateuch, Isa, the MP as well as other
books /21/, so that by 1941 H.M. Orlinsky could write
that this phase of LXX study already had a respectable
bibliography /22/. But since arguments used in some of
these works were increasingly exposed to negative criticism and as new explanations for the observed phenomena were proposed on the basis of recently discovered
recensions, enthusiasm for multiple translation theories
waned proportionately /23/. Through the ebb and flow
of popularity for such theories, however, the case for
Jer--the book that had originally sparked the search
for multiple translator explanations--seemed secure and
was accepted as an established datum in most commentaries, introductions, biblical dictionaries and ency-
clopaedias /24/. Even Ziegler who had severely criti-
cized the multiple translation theories for Isa and MP
was much more impressed by the evidence for Jer and
declared himself in basic agreement with Thackeray's
observations, himself employing Thackeray's terminology
of different translators /25/. However, in one short
but important footnote in the Introduction to his
Ieremias text (p. 128, n. 1), Ziegler entered a caveat
on the interpretation of Thackeray's findings. In view
of some of the remarkable agreements between the two
halves of Jer, he suggested, it should be inquired
whether the differences in the second half do not
derive from a reviser rather than a second translator.

Evidently taking his cue from this footnote,
E. Tov has elaborated on Ziegler's suggestion in a
thesis presented in 1973 to the University of Jerusalem
and later published (in revised form) under the title
The Septuagint Translation of Jeremiah and Baruch: A
Discussion of an Early Revision of the LXX of Jeremiah
29-52 and Baruch 1:1-3:8, 1976. In this work Tov has
sought to defend the proposition that a translator-
reviser theory better accounts for the lexical phenomena of the book of Jer than does a multiple translator
theory, though his theory differs in certain respects
from Ziegler's seminal suggestion. Tov's thesis represents a strong challenge to the traditional view on
this issue. Ch. IV of the present study explores

further the nature of the problem and seeks to evaluate
the merits of Tov's counter-theory on the basis of data
provided by the oracles against the Philistines and
Edom, the place where a new hand evidently appears.

C.   The Hebrew/Greek Problem

     The questions having to do with the recovery of
the earliest possible Greek text and the solution of
the intriguing translator/reviser problem are indeed
interesting and important. Yet it is not these matters
that have attracted most attention to Jer-LXX; rather,
it is the relationship of the LXX text to that of the
MT that in the minds of most scholars is the crucial
issue. As is well known, the LXX is considerably
shorter than the corresponding MT text. According to
recent statistical studies by Y.-J. Min, 3097 words of
Jer-MT are unrepresented in Jer-LXX, i.e. approximately
1/7 of the MT text /26/. Additionally there is the
problem of the transpositions of various passages,
mainly--though not exclusively--the OAN section which
in the MT comes in the penultimate position of the book
(Chs. 46-51) while in the LXX it appears in the middle
(25:14-31:44) along with an alternate internal order
/27/. Finally, there are the typical kinds of variants
where the LXX represents a different reading or interpretation in comparison with the MT.

     In the history of the investigation of the shorter/
longer texts of Jer, four theories, broadly speaking,
have been proposed to account for the differences between them. These may be labeled the "abbreviation,"
"editorial," "expansion," and "mediating" theories,
respectively.

     1. The "abbreviation" theory. The most common
approach has been to regard the Greek text as an
abbreviated or mutilated version of the Hebrew. Such
abbreviation has been blamed either on copyists (so
Jerome /28/ and Grabe /29/), or more frequently on the
original translator(s) (e.g. M.G.L. Spohn, J. Wichelhaus, K.H. Graf, C.F. Keil, C. von Orelli). The theory
implies that the LXX was translated from a basically
similar or identical Vorlage to that of the MT;
normally it also holds as original the MT order and
arrangement of the OAN section.

2. The "editorial" theory. The first scholar to
oppose the idea of a deliberately abbreviated LXX was
J.G. Eichhorn who, in the 3rd volume of his Einleitung
in Das Alte Testament (1803, 3rd ed.), took issue with
the views of Jerome and Grabe on the one hand (p. 152),
and those of Spohn on the other (pp. 174-78). Instead, Eichhorn advanced the theory that the two texts
derive from two different editions or recensions of the
book produced by Jer himself, the one an early copy
which became the basis of the LXX translation in Egypt,
the other a reworked copy sent to the exiles in Babylon
and later introduced to Palestine with the returning
exiles (pp. 137ff.). His views were adopted by some,
e.g. L. Bertholdt, but by 1892 A. Kuenan could say that
the theory was then held by hardly anyone (Historisch-
kritische Einleitung, p. 239). Recently, however, the
thesis has been revived, albeit in a modified form by
A. van Selms (VT 26 [1976], esp. 112). Along the same
lines is the view of T.W. Overholt (CBQ 30 [1968],
esp. 43-45) to the effect that some of the divergencies
between the LXX and the MT traditions (e.g. the title
"Nebuchadnezzar my servant") go back to different versions of the material edited by the prophet himself.

3. The "expansion" theory. On this view the LXX
version is the best witness to the text of Jer, the MT
having suffered greatly from expansion, conflation, and
interpolation in the course of transmission. The main
proponents of this position have been F.C. Movers, A.
Scholz, G.C. Workman, and somewhat more moderately,
A.W. Streane.

4. The "mediating" theory. According to this
theory it is impossible to generalize on the relative
priority of the two texts; instead, each reading has
to be evaluated on its own merits, resulting sometimes
in a preference for the MT, sometimes for the LXX. As
representatives of this view though varying considerably among themselves--can be cited F. Hitzig, B. Duhm,
F. Giesebrecht, P. Volz, W. Rudolph, J. Bright, and
J.A. Thompson.

By the middle of the 20th century, the mediating
position seemed firmly entrenched as the consensus
view, particularly as given expression in the commentaries of Rudolph and Bright. However, as a result of
the the Qumrân discoveries, some of which contain

fragments from Jer with a text approximating the presumed Hebrew Vorlage of the LXX, the whole question of
the Hebrew/Greek relationship has of necessity been
reopened. This was forcibly done by G.J. Janzen in the
publication of his Harvard dissertation, Studies in the
Text of Jeremiah, 1973. In this work--which to some
extent represents the documentation of views previously
expressed elsewhere by his supervisor, Frank M. Cross
/30/--Janzen has marshaled evidence for two principal
conclusions, namely that the Greek text was translated
from an already shorter Hebrew Vorlage, and that this
Vorlage represents an earlier and superior tradition of
the Hebrew text of Jer than that contained in the MT.
In effect, Cross and Janzen have returned to the third
theory outlined above, the "expansion" theory. In this
they are followed by E. Tov and Y.-J. Min who have
sought to move beyond the work of Janzen by defining
more precisely the recensional characteristics of the
MT additions /31/. But when it comes to documentation
of the evidence that the LXX does in fact testify to a
shorter Hebrew text, we are everywhere referred to
Janzen's published monograph. When the work first
appeared, it received a number of both positive and
negative reviews /32/. The final chapter of the
present study is devoted to a close analysis of this
influential work, based again on the oracles against
the Philistines and Edom.

     In addressing the above issues it needs to be
emphasized that the investigation has been pursued in
a spirit of positive rather than negative criticism.
Although at points this study arrives at conclusions
different from those recently advanced, the writer
stands in admiration of the quality of scholarship and
academic integrity of those who have wrestled with the
difficult problems surrounding the Greek text of Jer.
Publication of the results of this critique is grounded
in the conviction that our common goal of reconstructing
the transmission history of Jer-LXX and Jer-MT is best
served by a dialectical process of statement and
evaluation. It is my hope that the present work will
contribute to that process.

CHAPTER TWO

THE TEXT CRITICAL PROBLEM (1): AN INDUCTIVE STUDY

OF THE MANUSCRIPT EVIDENCE FOR JER-LXX CH. 29

The purpose of this chapter is to analyze the
textual evidence pertaining to Ch. 29 of Jer-LXX. By
means of an inductive and independent investigation of
the MS variants attested for the oracles against the
Philistines and Edom, the analysis seeks to trace the
various stages of revision and corruption through which
the Greek text of this section has passed back to the
earliest MS witnesses at our disposal. The discussion
will proceed under the headings of I) Description of
the Evidence, II) Collation of the Evidence, and III)
Grouping of the Evidence.

I.   Description of the Evidence

The primary source material for the text critical
study pursued in this chapter is found in A) Greek MSS
containing the oracles against the Philistines and
Edom, B) patristic citations, and C) ancient daughter
versions of the LXX. Of these, by far the most
important are the Greek MSS themselves. The following
is a list of the extant witnesses to the text of Jer 29
employed in this study.

A.   Greek MSS

A total of 39 Greek MSS have been collated for
this investigation /1/. Of these, 5 are uncials and 34
are minuscules. The MS information cited below is
taken primarily from A. Rahlfs' Verzeichnis der griechischen Handschriften des Alten Testaments (1914) and
Ziegler's Göttingen edition, though some of the data in
these sources has been updated or corrected according
to the results of my own research.

1.   Uncials

A   "Codex Alexandrinus" /2/, London, British Museum,
     Royal 1 D.VI; 5th century. Jer 29 is found on
     pp. 347*-48 of the codex /3/.

B   "Codex Vaticanus," Rome, Vatican Library, Vat. gr.
     1209; 4th century. Jer 29 on pp. 1099-1100.

Q   "Codex Marchalianus" /4/, Rome, Vatican Library,
     Vat. gr. 2125; 6th century. Jer 29 on pp. 442-
     46.

S   "Codex Sinaiticus" /5/, London, British Museum,
     Additional MS 43725 (199 leaves); Leipzig, Uni-
     versitäts-Bibliothek, Cod. gr. 1 (43 leaves; this
     part of the codex is technically known as "Cod.
     Friderico-Augustanus"); Leningrad Public Library
     (3 fragments); 4th century. Jer 29 is found in
     the Leipzig portion of the codex, pp. 30-30*
     (pp. 106-106* in Helen and Kirsopp Lake's photo
     facsimile reproduction, Oxford, 1922).

V   "Codex Venetus" /6/, Venice, Biblioteca Nazionale
     Marciana, Gr. 1; 8th century. Jer 29 on pp.
     86*-87.

2.   Minuscules

22   London, British Museum, Royal 1 B. II; 11th-12th
     centuries. Philistine oracle on pp. 241-41*;
     Edom oracle on pp. 245-46 /7/.

26   Rome, Vatican Library, Vat. gr. 556; 10th century.
     Jer 29 on pp. 156-57.

36   Rome, Vatican Library, Vat. gr. 347; 11th century.
     Philistine oracle on pp. 216*-17; Edom oracle
     on pp. 220-21.

46   Paris, Bibliothèque Nationale, Coislin 4; 13th-
     14th centuries. Jer 29 on pp. 359*-60.

48   Rome, Vatican Library, Vat. gr. 1794; 10th-11th
     centuries. Philistine oracle on pp. 249*-50;
     Edom oracle on pp. 253-254.

49   Florence, Biblioteca Medicea-Laurenziana, Plutei
     XI 4; 11th century. Jer 29 on pp. 221*-23.

51   Florence, Biblioteca Medicea-Laurenziana, Plutei
     X 8; 11th century. The Oracles Against the Na-
     tions occur twice in this MS, the first time in
     the usual LXX position and internal order in the
     middle of the book, the second time in the MT
     position and order at the end of the book. In
     the first instance Jer 29 is found on pp. 223*-
     25, in the second part (referred to here as 51s
     [s=supplement]), the Philistine oracle is found
     on pp. 266*-67 and the Edom oracle on pp. 270-
     71*.

62   Oxford, New College, 44; 11th century. Philis-
     tine oracle on p. 97*; Edom oracle on pp. 99-
     99*.

68   Venice, Biblioteca Nazionale Marciana, Gr. 5; 15th
     century. Jer 29 on pp. 197-98.

86   "Codex Barberinus," Rome, Vatican Library, Barbe-
     rini gr. 549; 9th-10th centuries. Jer 29, in-
     cluding commentary of Olympiodorus, on pp. 157-
     59.

87   Rome, Vatican Library, Chigi R. VIII 54 /8/; 10th
     century. Jer 29 on pp. 304-05.

88   "Codex Chisianus," Rome, Vatican Library, Chigi
     R. VII 45 /9/; 10th century. Philistine oracle
     on pp. 94-94*; Edom oracle on pp. 98-99*.

90   Florence, Biblioteca Medicea-Laurenziana, Plutei
     V 9; 11th century. Jer 29 on pp. 170*-71*.

91   Rome, Vatican Library, Ottoboniani gr. 452; 11th
     century. Jer 29 on pp. 168*-69.

96   Copenhagen, Det Kongelige Bibliotek, Ny Kongelige
     Samling, 4 , Nr. 5; 11th century. Philistine
     oracle on pp. 134*-35; Edom oracle on pp. 137*-
     38*.

106 Ferrara, Biblioteca Communale, 187 II /10/; 14th
     century. Jer 29 on p. 94.

122 Venice, Biblioteca Nazionale Marciana, Gr. 6;   15th
century. Jer 29 on pp. 166-67.

130 Vienna, Nationalbibliothek, Theologici gr. 23
/11/;   12th-13th centuries. Jer 29 on pp. 419*-20.

233 Rome, Vatican Library, Vat. gr. 2067;   10th century. Jer 29 on pp. 172-73.

239 Bologne, Biblioteca Universitaria, 2603;   copied
A.D. 1046. Jer 29 on pp. 156-57.

311 Moscow, formerly The Synod Library, Gr. 354;   12th
century. Philistine oracle on p. 222;   Edom oracle
on pp. 224-25.

407 Jerusalem, Patriarchal Library, Ταφου 2;   9th
century. Philistine oracle on p. 335;   Edom oracle
on pp. 336*-37.

410 Jerusalem, Patriarchal Library, Ταφου 36;   13th
century. A palimpset;   Jer 29 on pp. 270-72.

449 Milan, Biblioteca Ambrosiana, E. 3 inf.;   10th-
11th centuries. Jer 29 on pp. 3*-4*.

490 Munich, Staatsbibliothek, Gr., 472;   11th century.
Jer 29 on pp. 209-10.

534 Paris, Bibliothèque Nationale, Coislin 18;   11th
century. Jer 29 on pp. 71*-72.

538 Paris, Bibliothèque Nationale, Coislin 191;   12th
century. Jer 29 on pp. 262*-64.

544 Paris, Bibliothèque Nationale, Gr. 15;   11th century. Jer 29 on pp. 186-88.

613 Patmos, Ιωαννου του Θεολογου 209;   13th century.
Jer 29 on pp. 359-60.

631 Raudnitz, Lobkowitz'sche Bibliothek, VI. E. f. 19.
14th century. Jer 29 on pp. 123-24.

710 Sinai, St. Catharine's Monastery, Cod. gr. 5; 10th
century. Jer 29 on pp. 95-96*.

763   Athens, Μονη Βατοπαιδιου 514;   11th century.
      Philistine oracle on pp. 194*-95;   Edom oracle
      on pp. 195*-96*.

764   Athens, Λαυρα 169;   13th-14th centuries.   Jer 29
      on pp. 147*-49.

770   Athens, Λαυρα 234;   12th century.   Jer 29 on
      pp. 104f.

986   Oxford, Ashmolean Museum, P. Antinoopolis 53;
      6th-7th centuries /12/.

B.   Patristic Citations

The extant evidence from patristic sources for the
text of Jer 29 is found in four commentaries written on
the text of Jer and in several quotations scattered
throughout various works of early Christian literature.

1.   Commentaries

John Chrysostom (d. 407).   All that remains of
Chrysostom's commentary on the text of Jer are those
portions preserved in a few Catena MSS.   These selec-
tions, taken mainly from Vat. 675, Vat. 1204, and
especially from an Altemps Library MS, were collected
by Michael Ghisler in his monumental work, Ieremiam
Prophetam Comentarii (1632).   From there they were
reprinted in Migne PG 64 (= Chr. XIII) but with the
lemma texts taken not from Chrysostom but from some
textus receptus or composed in an ad hoc way.   Also,
citations from within Chrysostom's commentary itself
were not always fully reproduced in Migne.   For these
reasons, collation of Chrysostom's Jer citations must
be based on Ghisler's edition and not on Migne.   According to Ghisler, then, the following verses from Jer
29 are partially or wholly quoted by Chrysostom: 4, 5,
7, 14, 20.

Theodoret of Cyrus (d. 460?).   Theodoret is our
richest source of Jer citations from among the Church
Fathers.   His commentary on Jer has been published in
full by J.L. Schulze, Theodoreti Opera Omnia (Vol. 2,
1770;   Philistine oracle on pp. 592-93;   Edom oracle

on pp. 602-06), reprinted in Migne, PG 81 (Philistine oracle on cols. 716-17; Edom oracle on cols. 728-33). The text is based mainly on two MSS in the Staatsbibliothek of Munich: Gr. 117 from the 16th century (designated "B" by Schulze, from "bavaricus": cf. Schulze, Vol. 2, p. 403, and Rahlfs, Verzeichnis, p. 433, n. 4) and Gr. 472 (= LXX MS 490, see above) from the 11th century (designated by Schulze as "Cod." or "Cod. august[anus]", and from p. 403 onwards, simply as "A"). According to the text of Schulze, all verses except 1, 2, 19, and 22 of Jer 29 are cited either in whole or in part by Theodoret.

Olympiodorus (6th century). The commentary of Olympiodorus is preserved in "Codex Barberinus" (see above MS 86). It was partially published by Ghisler in his compendium and reprinted by Migne, PG 93 (Philistine oracle on col. 705; Edom oracle on cols. 710-12). But because the lemma texts in these editions are not to be trusted, collation must be based on the actual MS, which consists of alternating sections of LXX text and Olympiodorus commentary. Contrary to the impression given by Migne, the commentary follows the order of the Greek text, not the Hebrew. The commentary itself consists of short citations from the text of Jer accompanied by explanatory comments. From Jer 29, parts of the following verses are quoted by Olympiodorus: 2, 5, 6, 8, 9, 11, 12, 13, 15, 17, 19, 20, 23.

Basilius of Neopatrae (9th century). The commentary on Jer of this late and less important Greek Father has never been published. It is extant in two MSS: the 12th century MS 31, in Patmos, and the 12th century. Vatican gr. 1687 in Rome. A collation of the Patmos MS exists in the collation books for Jer at the Septuaginta-Unternehmen in Göttingen.

2.   Miscellaneous Citations

Clement of Alexandria, (d. before 225) quotes from Jer 29:20 in Stromata, Book 2, Ch. 15 (GCS, Clem. II, p. 148; PG 8, col. 1004).

Eusebius of Caesarea (d. 339) cites names from vv. 5, 8, 9, and 20 in Onomasticon (GCS, Eus. III, pp. 38, 80, 90, 102).

Gregory of Nyssa (d. 394) quotes from v. 20 in
Testimonia adversus Iudaeos, Ch. 20 (PG 46 [= Greg.
III], col. 232).

Didymus the Blind of Alexandria (d. 398?) quotes
from vv. 5-6 in In Zachariam (SC 83, p. 380).

Cyril of Alexandria (d. 444) quotes from v. 2 in
his commentary In Sophoniam (PG 71 [= Cyr. IV], col.
984).

Sacra Parallela quotes from vv. 8-9 (PG 96
[= Joannes Damasenus III], col. 348).

Liber de divinis scripturis sive speculum, Ch.
130, quotes from vv. 2-3 (CSEL 12, pp. 677-78) /13/.

C.   Daughter Versions

Six ancient VSS translated directly from the LXX
are included in the collation notes for Jer 29.   In
probable chronological order of translation these are
the Old Latin, the Coptic (Sahidic and Bohairic
dialects), the Syriac, the Ethiopic, the Arabic, and
the Armenian.

1.   Old Latin

The only extant witness to the Old Latin text of
Jer 29 is a fragment in "Codex Sangallensis" 912
containing a passage from 29:13-19.   The collation is
taken from F.C. Burkitt's publication, "The S. Gallen
Fragment of Jeremiah," in Texts and Studies 4 (1896),
79-92, which constitutes an appendix to his article on
"The Old Latin and the Itala" in that journal.

2.   Coptic

The Coptic translation of Jer 29 has been preserved in the Bohairic and Sahidic dialects.   An
edition of the Bohairic was published in 1852 by H.
Tattam, together with a Latin translation: Prophetae
majores, in linguae aegyptiacae memphitica seu coptica,
Oxford, 1852.   The Sahidic of Jer 29 exists in two

papyri fragments. The first contains 28:59-29:4,
published by G. Maspero, Fragments de la version
thébaine de l'Ancien Testament (Mémoires publiés par
les membres de la Mission archéologique française au
Caire, vol. 6, fasc. 1.2), Paris, 1892, p. 239. The
second fragment contains 29:3-23, published by C. Wessely, Griechische und Koptische Texte, theologischen
Inhalts IV (Studien zur Paläeographie und Papyruskunde,
XV), Leipzig, 1914, p. 83.

3. Syriac

    The Syriac version of the LXX (called the Syro-
hexapla because it was translated--in 616/17 by Paul of
Tella--from Origen's Hexaplaric recension), is found in
the 8th century "Codex Ambrosianus," first published,
along with a Latin translation, by M. Norberg in 1787
under the title Codex Syriaco-Hexaplaris Ambrosiano-
Mediolanensis, London/Gothenborg (Philistine oracle on
pp. 236-39; Edom oracle on pp. 248-53). A reprint
of Norberg's Latin translation is found in PG 16, cols.
2299-394. A photographed facsimile copy of the codex
was issued by A.M. Ceriani in Monumenta Sacra et Profana, Vol. VII, Milan, 1874.

4. Ethiopic

    There exists no published edition of the Ethiopic
version of Jer. Of the various Ethiopic MSS, Ziegler
(following J. Schäfers) has determined that the
Ethiopic is best preserved in the Berlin codex, MS
orient. fol. 3067 Geez, designated "B" by J. Schäfers
(cf. Ziegler, Ieremias, p. 30).

5. Arabic

    The collation is taken from Brian Walton's London
Polyglot, 1657, pp. 281-83, accompanied by Latin
translation /14/.

6. Armenian

    The Armenian text is found in J. Zohrabian's

edition, Venice, 1805, from where it was collated by
Ziegler in the Septuaginta-Unternehmen collation notes.

II. Collation of the Evidence

     This section contains my fresh collation of the MS
variants for Jer-LXX Ch. 29. The collation of the four
main uncials A, B, Q, and S has been based on the of-
ficial photographic reproductions of those MSS: Codex
Alexandrinus published by the British Museum (1883);
Codex Vaticanus and Codex Marchalianus published by the
Vatican Library (1907 and 1890 respectively); Codex
Sinaiticus published by the Oxford Press (1922, edited
by Helen and Kirsopp Lake). The collation of the other
Greek MSS is based on photographs or microfilms, most
of which were made available to me at the Septuaginta-
Unternehmen in Göttingen.

     For the patristic sources I have consulted the
standard published editions as cited above, except for
the commentary of Olympiodorus which is based directly
on Codex Barberinus (MS 86). In the case of the Sahidic, Ethiopic, and Armenian VSS I have been entirely
dependent on the Göttingen collation books. For those
of the Bohairic, Syriac, and Arabic VSS I have also
relied heavily on the Göttingen collation notes, but
have been able to check these against the published
texts and accompanying Latin translations. The versional evidence where it diverges from the Greek is
usually cited in Latin form, except for the Syro-
hexapla which, because of its sister relationship to
MS 88, is regularly cited in Greek transliteration.

     The base text is essentially that of the Sixtine
textus receptus (in the edition published by Samuel
Bagster and Sons, London, n.d.), albeit slightly modified at a few points, e.g. when the Sixtine text prints
a reading unique to Codex Vaticanus or the B group, the
majority text has been adopted in the base column so as
not to overload the collation notes. The base text
has, of course, no critical value; its function at
this point is strictly utilitarian as a means of exhibiting in the most practical way the many "variation
units" /15/ within this chapter.

In these collation notes, and generally throughout the document, superscripts are not normally employed. Thus, the designation "86mg" means that the reading is found in the "margin" of MS 86, "Qc" has reference to the reading of a "corrector" of Q, "51s" refers to the "supplement" to MS 51 (see above, p. 16). However, where the juxtaposition of letters makes for an ambiguous formula, e.g. Syhmg, the two parts--MS and qualification--are separated by a slash, e.g., Syh/mg (= margin of Syh), Sa/We (= the portion of the Sahidic VS published by C. Wessely, see above, p. 21), Aeth/B (= "Codex B" of the Ethiopic VS, see above, p. 21), Tht./p (= "part" of the MS evidence for Theodoret), etc. One superscript employed is the asterisk (*), signifying the original--rather than corrected--reading of a MS).

29:1-2

επι τους
αλλοφυλους

επι τους αλλ.: > 106 538* Bo Arm/p; α΄ προς φυλιστιαιους Syh/mg; σ΄ περι των φυλιστιαιων 86mg
pr. ← επι τους αλλοφυλους΄ ※λογος κυριου ος
εγενεθη προς ιερεμιαν τον προφητην΄ Syh Arm
pr. επι τους αλλοφυλους (-λλους 311) ος (ως 62)
εγενετο λογος κυριου προς ιερεμιαν (ιη. 62 449)
τον προφητην 51 62 311 449 770
pr. ※ος εγενηθη λογος κυριου προς ιερεμιαν τον
προφητην 88 = α΄σ΄ Qmg 86mg(om. ※)
+ προ του παταξαι φαραω την γαζαν ※Qmg 51 62 ※88
311 449 770 ※Syh = α΄σ΄ 86mg(om. ※)
+ ος (ως 22*) εγενετο λογος κυριου προς ιερεμιαν
τον προφητην προ του παταξαι φαραω την γαζαν 22
÷36 48 51s 96 407 763

ταδε λεγει
κυριος

v. 2 ιδου
υδατα

αναβαινει

-βεννι A   -βεννει S*   -βενη 26   -βαιννει 62
-βαινη 239   ερχεται Cyr. IV, p. 984

απο

επι 106

βορρα

βορραν S*

και
εσται
εις

και εσται > Spec. p. 677; α΄ και εσονται 86mg
εστε S*

χειμαρρουν

χειμ. κατακλυζοντα: pl. Bo
χι. A   χιμαρρον S*(-ουν Sc)   χειμαρρον 534

κατακλυζοντα
και

και κατακλυσει: α΄ και κυκλωσουσι   86mg

+ δη Cyr. IV, p. 984

29:2-3

κατακλυσει   -κλυσι A S* -κλυζει 46 -καυσει 239 410
                      κλυσει 534

γην   pr. την 449 538

και   > Arm

το πληρωμα   το πλ. αυτης πολιν: et urbem cum plenitude eius
αυτης   Aeth/B
πολιν   πολις S* 544 pl. Arm

και   > Aeth/B

τους κατ-   τους ενοι. A 106
  οικουντας
εν αυτη
και   > Arm Bo Sa/Ma

κεκραξονται   κραξονται S*(-οντη vid.) 62 86c

οι   οι ανθρωποι: universi Spec.
                 > 87
ανθρωποι
και   και αλαλα. παντες: α′ και ολολυξουσι παντες 86mg
αλαλαξουσιν   -ουσι 86 90 233 239 534 613 710   -ονται A
                 αλλαλαξουσι 130(-σιν) 106c Bas.N.
                 ολολυξουσι 22c 36 48c 51-51s 62 96 311 407 763 770
                 ολολυζουσι 22* 48* 449   peribunt Arab

παντες   απαντες B S Q 68 87 88 91 122 130 410 490 538 544
οι κατ-
  οικουντας   -αις S*
την γην
v. 3 απο
φωνης   φων. ορ. αυ.: ιω′ προσωπου οργης θυμου   86mg
                 Qmg(anon.)
ορμης   ορ. αυ.: δρομου ιππων Syh/mg
                 οργης 239

αυτου   pl. Bo

απο   pr. και 22 36 48 51-51s 62 96 311 407 449 763 770
                 Aeth/B   + voce Sa/We,Ma

των   τ. οπλων τ. ποδων: θ′ οπλων αυτου των δυνατων
                 86mg Qmg(δυνατω)
οπλων   armis Syh Aeth Arm Arab Spec.
                 + αυτου 22 36 48 51s 62 96 311 407 763

των   pr. και S*   pr. και απο 106 Spec.(et a)

29:3-4

ποδων   δυνατων 22 36 48 51s 62 96 311 763   δυναμεων 407
                πολλων 130 538

αυτου   ÷86   αυτων 106   + των δυνατων 51 449 770
και απο
σεισμου   σεισ/μου B*   σει/σμου Bc   σισμου S 86c 407
               544(vid.)

των   > Arm

αρματων   ιω´ τεθριππων 86mg

αυτου   αυτων 544 Spec.(eorum)   + et a Spec. Aeth Arm

ηχου   η. τρο. αυτ. > 88; α´σ´ πληθους τροχων αυτου
                pr. και A 22 36 48 51-51s 62 87 90 91 96 106 311
                  407 410 449 490 534 613 763 764 770 Arab Bo
                ηχους 538 α´σ´ πληθους Syh/mg

τροχων   pr. των A 410   τροχου S*
αυτου
ουκ   pr. et Arm

επεστρεφαν   εστρεφαν S*   επεστρεφα 51   απεστρεφαν 239

πατερες   pr. οι 88

επι   εφ B S 68 122 130

υιους   ους 46   υιοις 130
αυτων
απο   pr. εφ 763(vid.)

εκλυσεως   εκκαυσεως 239 BasN.

χειρων   χειαως S*(vid.)   χειρος 239 BasN.

αυτων   αυτου 96 130
v. 4 εν
τη ημερα τη
ερχομενη   επερχομενη B 68 122   > τη ερχ. Aeth/p(hab.Aeth/B)
του
απολεσαι   ¬σε S*   αφανισαι 88 Syh   απολεσθαι 410

παντας   pr. συν 86mg ※88   απαντες 538   > Aeth/B

τους   τους αλλο.: σ´ τους φυλιστιαιους 86mg
               > Tht.

αλλοφυλους   -λλους 48   λαους Tht./p
και αφανιω την
Τυρον   τυρων 538

29:4-5
και
την   > Tht.

Σιδωνα   σειδονα B* σιδωρα 22   σιδονα 130*
                  σειδωνα 68 122 = Sixt.
και
παντας   > Tht.
τους
καταλοιπους   -λυπους S*(vid.)
της   > 239 BasN.
βοηθειας   -θιας S 62 544(vid.)   βοης 106
αυτων οτι
εξολοθρευσει   εξολο. κυριος: tr. Bo Sa/We Arab
                  -λεθρευσει A B* Q 86* 544(-λεθρευσαι)
                  -ωλεθρευσι S*(-ωλεθρευσει Sc)   -ση 91

κυριος   + τους αλλοφυλους 22 36(τ. αλλ. και) 48 51 -51s
                    ※88 96 311(-λλους) 407 449 763 770 Tht. Chr.
                    ※Syh Arm = ο´ ※86mg, α´θ´ ※Qmg

τους   τ. κατα. τ. ωη.: ιω´ τα λειψανα των νησων 86mg
                  τ. κατα.: sing. Bo
                  τας A 49 86 87 90 91 410 490 764

καταλοιπους   + τους αλλοφυλους 62

των νησων   + καψκαππαδοκιας 22 36 48 51 51s 62 88 96 311
                    407 ※449 763 ※770 Tht. Chr. Syh Arm = α´θ´ ※Qmg;
                    οι γ´ + καππαδοκας 86mg

v. 5 ηκει   εκει 407

φαλακρωμα   φαρακλωμα 26
επι
Γαζαν   πασαν κεφαλην 407
                  + και 62 106 410 Bo Aeth/B

απερριφη   απ. ασκ.: α´ ηφανισθη ασκαλων 86mg   σ´ εσιωπησεν
                    ασκ. 86mg
                  -εριφη A B* Q S 62 86 538 544   -ερριφει 91

Ασκαλων   σακλωνα Syh
και   ±86

οι κατα-   οι κατα. Εν.: α´ το καταλιμμα των κοιλαδων 86mg
  λοιποι   τα καταλοιπα A 106   τα λοιπα 22 36 48 51 51s
                  62 86mg 88 96 311 407 449 763 770 Tht. Chr. Syh
                  sing. Bo

Ενακειμ   pr. των 22 36 48 51-51s 62 96 311 407 449 763 770
                  Tht. Chr.
                  -κιμ 22 46 86 87 91 96 407 490   εναμ 534

29:5-7

εν ακημ Chr.   εμακειμ Eus. Onom. p. 90, 1. 13
in aqim Syh Sa/We Arab   ο εβρ΄ κοιλαδες Syh/mg
α΄σ΄ των κοιλαδων Syh/mg, Eus. Onom.

v. 6 εως   εως . . . μαχ.: α΄ εως ποτε εφελκυσθηση ω μαχ.
86mg; σ΄ εως ποτε συστραφησεσθε ω μαχ. 86mg
pr. εως ποτε συστραφησεσθε 22 36 48 51-51s 62 96
311 407 449 763 770 Tht. Syh/mg

τινος   ποτε Didy.

κοφεις   -ψης S*(vid.) 62 87 233 311 534   -ψεται 407
-ψει 410 Tht./txt Olymp.   συνκοψει Tht./B

η   > Olymp.

μαχαιρα   -χερα S

του   > A 88 106 410

κυριου   κυριε 410   θεου 544   + amputabisne Arab
εως τινος
ουχ   ουκ A B* Q 26 68 86 538 544   ου μη S 534

ησυχασεις   συχασις S* (ησυχασις Sc)   ησυχασει 106
ησυχασης 87 233 311 534   εισυχασεις 544
εις
αποκαταστηθι   -καταστηση 544 -καταστης Olym. επιστραφητι Didy.
εις
τον   το 130

κολεον   κουλεον 88 106 613   ξιφοθηκη 26mg
α΄σ΄θ΄ ομοιως 86mg
σου
αναπαυσαι   ανα. και επ.: α΄ ταχυνον και σιωπησον 86mg
-σε S   -σον 62   αναπασαν 449
και
επαρθητι   ησυχασον 22 36 48 51-51s 96 311 407 449 763 770
Tht./B   ησυχασαι 62   επαροντι 122

v. 7 πως   pr. et Aeth/B   > πως ησ. Tht.(vid)

ησυχασει   -σεις A 410   -σι S*   -ση 239

και   οτι 534 Arm   qoud Aeth/B   > Sa/We Bo

κυριος   pr. ου S*(ο Sc)

ενετειλατο   -τιλατο S*(vid.)   συνεταξατο 86mg

αυτη   > Aeth/B

29:7-8

επι   επι τ. Ασκ.: > 534 (post παραθαλασσιους)
την
Ασκαλωνα
και επι
τας   τους 534 613
παρα-
  θαλασσιους   -λασιους 86 130* 538   + και 22 36 46 48 49 51
                51s 62 87 90 91 96 311 407 410 449 490 534 613
                631 763 764 770 Tht. Syh Bo Sa/We Aeth/B
                + και επι την ασκαλωνα 534

επι   επι . . . επεγ.: α'σ' εκει δη συνεταξεν αυτη
                Syh/mg

τας   τας κατα.: sing. Bo
                τους 26 46 130 239 410 534 613 631 BasN.

καταλοιπους   -που A

επεγερθηναι   εγερθηναι 534   πορευθηναι Tht.   > Sa/We Bo

v. 8 τη   τη ιδ.: σ' τω εδωμ 86mg   > 46 106 538txt
                631 Arm/p   pr. verbum propter Sa/We

Ιδουμαια   ιουμεα S*   ιδουμαι 36   ιουδαια 49 90* 534 764

ταδε   ουδε 534
λεγει
κυριος   > Qtxt   + των δυναμεων ※Qmg 22 36 48 51-51s 62 88
                96 311 407 449 763 770 Syh Arm = ο' 86mg

ουκ   ουκ εστιν: α' μη ουκ εστιν Syh/mg   σ' αρα ουκ
                εστιν Syh/mg
                α' μη 86mg   σ' αρα 86mg

εστιν   εστι Tht.

ετι   > 407 Tht. SacPar.   εν 710

σοφια   σοφος Sa/We   α' συνεσις 86mg

θαιμαν   θεμαν S 62 SacPar./p BasN. Bo Arm

απωλετο   επ. A   απο. SacPar./p   pr. et Bo Aeth

βουλη   συμβουλη 22 36 48 51s 96 763

εκ   εκ συνετων: α'σ' εξ υιων   86mg

συνετων   συν/ετων B* συνε/των   Bc   υνετων 62
                + et Bo Aeth/p

29:8-9

ωχετο   ωχ. σο. αυτ.: > 22 36 (> ωχ. . . . βαθυνατε [v. 9])
                     48 51s 62 96 311 763 Tht.
                     α' ηφανισθη Syh/mg

σοφια   pr. η 51 239 407 449 770

αυτων   sing. Arm   + et Bo Aeth/B

v. 9 ηπατηθη   ηπατηθη . . . καθισιν: α' εφυγον απεστραφησαν
                     εβαθυναν κατοικησαι 86mg
                     ηπ. ο τοπ. αυ.: > 106(hap.); σ' εφυγον απ-
                     εστραφησαν Syh/mg
                     επατηθη 87 91 490 Syh Arab (excisus)   επατηθι 239

ο   το S* ※88   > 130 410

τοπος   προς S*

αυτων   αυτον S*   αυτου Tht./txt Arm/txt

βαθυνατε   βαθ. εις κατ.:   α' εβαθυναν κατοικησαι Syh
                     σ' εν οικωθεν βαθει ωκησαν 86mg
                     ιω' καταδυετε εις χασματα οικητωρες 86mg
                     βαθηνατε 233   βαθυ συνετε 534

εις   pr. εαυτοις A Q 36 49 86 90 91 233 239 410 449
                     534 613 710 764 770 Olymp. BasN. Sa/We Bo
                     Aeth/B Arab
                     pr. εν αυτοις 106   pr. εαυτους 87 538 Tht.

καθισιν   -ησιν A 26 36 62 88 91 407 Tht./B   καυχησιν 534
οι
κατοικουντες   -ται S*   κακουντες 86*

εν   > Q txt   ÷86

Δαιδαν   δαιδαμ B 68 122   δεδαν 407 538 544 Arm/txt
                     δεδανω 534   δεδαμ Bo   δαδαν Syh Arb Arm/p

οτι   οτι δυσ. επ.: α'σ' οτι απωλειαν ησαυ 86mg;
                     θ' οτι απωλεσαν ησαυ 86mg

δυσκολα   δυσ. επ. ηγ.: α' απωλειαν ησαυ επηγαγον Syh/mg
                     pr. εις 538   pr. opera Bo

εποιησεν   -σαν 538   + et Aeth/p

ηγαγον   ει γεγονεν 410   ηγαγεν 534

επ   ε/π Bc   > Q 62 Olymp.

αυτον   αυτην 538   pl. Arm

29:9-10

εν χρονω   pr. γαρ Bo   εχθρον εν 407
ω
επεσκεφαμην   ενεσκεφαμην 534

επ   εν S* om. A V 22 48 51-51s 62 86 88 96 239 311
                  407 449 534 538 544 710 763 770 Tht. BasN. Syh
                  Arm

αυτον   αυτην S 26 410 Aeth/B Arab   αυτω 91 490

v. 10 οτι   οτι . . . καταλειφουσι: σ΄ ει τρυγηται επηλθον
                  σοι ουχ αν απελειπον 86mg

τρυγηται   τρυγητε S*   τρυγησται 91

ηλθον   + σοι A Q* V 22 26 36 46 48 51-51s 62 86 88 96
                  130 233 239 311 407 449 534 544 631 710 763 770
                  Tht./txt Olymp. BasN. Arm

οι   > A Q* V 46 86 130 534 544 631 710 Syh Sa/We
                  ο 764   και Tht. Arm

ου   > S* 62 Aeth   ουχ 233 239

καταλειφουσι   -σιν A Q V 22* 26 48 49 51s* 68 96 122 407 534
                  538 710 763 764 BasN.   -λιφουσιν B* S 490 544
                  -λιφουσι 91   εγκαταλειφουσιν 233 239(-σι)

σοι   σε 490   σου 538   > 410 Tht./B

καταλειμμα   -λιμμα B* S 26 91 490 764   -λειμα 106
                  -λειμματα Q* V 46 130 233 538(-λη-) 631 710 Tht./B
                  Sa/We Bo Arm   -λιμματα A Qc 86 544
                  καλαμηματα 22 36 48 51-51s 62 88 96 311 407 449
                  763 770 Syh = ο΄ 86mg
                  α΄σ΄ επιφυλλιδας Syh/mg   ρηγματα 86mg

ως   ωσπερ A 49 87 90 91 106 410 490 613 764
                  ωσει Q V 22 26 36 46 48 51-51s 62 86 88 96 130
                  233 239 311 407 449 534 538 544 631 710 763 770

κλεπται   κεπται S*
εν νυκτι
επιθησουσι   επιθ. χειρα αυτων: ουχ αν ηφανισαν τα ιχανα
                  εαυτοις Syh/mg
                  -σιν B S Q V 26 48 49 51s* 96 122 407 544 763 764
                  επειθησουσιν A   επιθυσουσιν 22 (-θει. 22c)

χειρα   pr. σοι Qmg 22 36 48 51-51s 62 96 311 407 449 763
                  770 Tht./B
                  χειρας A Q S(χι.) 49 87 88 90 91 130(pr.τας) 233
                  239 410 490 613 764 Bo Arm

29:10-11

αυτων   εϕ αυτον 538 Sa/We Bo(super eam) Arm(super eos)
v. 11 οτι εγω
κατεσυρα   κατηραυνησα A

τον Ησαυ   τον Ησαυ ανε.: > Arab

ανεκαλυϕα   ανα. S*   -ϕαν 130   απ. 410 = α΄ 86mg
                     Syh/mg(sub α΄σ΄)   α΄ απεστεγασα 86mg

τα   τε S*

κρυπτα   γλυπτα 86txt 710

αυτων   αυτου 239 Syh Aeth/B Arm BasN.   σου Tht./B

κρυβηναι   pr. και 410 Bo Aeth/B Arm
ου
μη   > 534

δυνωνται   -ονται 26 233 534   -ωντε 544   -ηται Tht. Aeth/B

ωλοντο   ωλοντο δια χειρα: ο΄ ※ ωλετο σπερμα αυτου 88
                     86mg(sub ο΄) Syh Arm(> ※)
                     ωλετο Qc 22 36 48 51-51s 62 86mg 96 106 130 311
                     407 449 763 770 Tht.   ολοντο 544
                     α΄ϑ΄ εταλαιπωρησεν 86mg   σ΄ διεϕθαρη 86mg
                     α΄ επρονομευθη Syh/mg

δια   pr. σπερμα αυτου 51 62 88 311 407 449 770 Tht.
                     pr. το σπερμα αυτου ※Qmg 22 36 48 51s 96 763

χειρα   χιρα S*   χειρος 407 534 Tht./A(-ας Tht./B)

αδελϕου   αδελ. αυτ. κ. γειτ. αυτ.: οι γ΄ και αδελϕου αυτου
                     και γειτονος αυτου 86mg Syh/mg(sub οι λ΄)

αυτου   σου S*   αυτων 534 Arab   > Tht. Arm

και   > B S 68 122 130 Sa/We Bo Aeth/B

γειτονος   γι. A 407 544

αυτου   μου B S 410 Bo Aeth Arab   αυτων 68 122 534
                     > 49 87 90 91 106 490 764

και   και . . . πεποιθασιν: σ΄ και ουκ εστιν ος ερει
                     καταλειπε τους ορϕανους σου και εγω διασωσω και
                     χηραι σου εις εμε μη αμεριμνειτωσαν 86mg
ουκ
εστιν   εσται 233   + ο λεγων 22 36 48 51 51s 62 96 311
                     407 449 763 770 Tht./B   + ο ελεων Tht./lxt

29:12-13

v. 12 υπο-
λειπεσθαι

υπολειπεσθαι . . . πεποιθασιν: α′ καταλειπε
ορφανους εγω ζωωσω σε και χηραι σου επ εμε
πεποιθησουσιν Syh/mg; ιω′ εασον τους ορφανους
τους εν σοι εγω γαρ αυτους διασωσω 86mg;
σ′ κατελιπεν ορφανους και αι χηραι σου εις εμε
ελπισατωσαν Ghisler, II, 861
-λιπεσθαι A B* 26 88 130 544   - λιπεσθε S*
-λειπεσθε 239 407

ορφανον

-ους 22 36 48 51-51s 62 96 311 407 449 763 770
Tht.   ορφανην 631

σου
ινα
ζησηται

> 26 407 538   σοι 239 Bas.N.

ζησεται A B* Q S V 26 46 49 86 87 90 91 239 490
534 538 544 710 764   ζησητε 106
σωθωσι 36 48 51-51s 311 449 763 770 Tht. Sa/We
Syh/mg   σωθωσιν 22 62 96 407

και εγω

και εγω ζη.:> Q V 26 46 86 88 130 233 534 544 631
+ αυτους 22 36 48 51-51s 62 96 311 407 449 763
770 Syh/mg Tht.

ζησομαι

και
αι

-σομε 764   διασωσω 22 36 58 51-51s 62 96 311
407 449 763 770 Syh/mg Tht.

> B Q S V 26 46 86 88 130 534 538 544 631 710
Olymp.

χηραι

επ
εμε

χηρε S   χειρες 62 407   χειρα 68
+ σου 22 36 48 51-51s 62 96 311 407 449 763 770
Tht.   + αυτων Arm

εμοι 613 Tht.

πεποιθασιν
v.13 οτι ταδε
λεγει

πεποιθετωσαν 51-51s 62 407 449 770 Tht.

ειπεν B S 68 122 538

κυριος

pr. ο 538

ους

pr. ιδου Q V 22 26 36 48 51-51s 62 86 88 96 130
233 239 311 407 449 534 544 613 631 710 763 770
Tht. Olymp. Syh Arm

ουκ ην
νομος

α′σ′θ′ κριμα 86mg Syh/mg(sub οι λ′)

πιειν
το ποτηριον
επιον

πιν S*

pr. πιοντες 22 36 48 51-51s 62 ※88 96 311 407 449
763 770 Tht. ※Syh Arm = α′θ′ ※Qmg, οι γ′ ※86mg,
οι λ′ pr. πιονται Syh/mg   pr. hoc Bo   > 534

29:13-14

και   και . . . αθωωθης: α᾽ και συ αυτος καθαρισμω
               καθαρισθηση ου μη καθαρισθεις 86mg
συ
αθωωμενη   αθοω. B* Q S 538   αθωο. 46* 631   αθοου. A V
               86 91 534 544 BasN.   αθωου. 22 36 48 49 51-51s
               62 87 88 90 96 106 130 233 239 407 449 490 613
               710 763 764 770

ου   > 239 407 544   pr. αθωωθηση 22 36 48 51s ※88 96
               311 763 ※Syh Arm = ϑ᾽ ※86mg
μη
αθωωθης   αθοω. A B* S V 86 91 490 538 BasN.   αθοωθηση Q
               αθωωθεις 26   αθωοθεις 534   αθωωθηση 106 233
               239 407(-ωο.) Tht./B

οτι   οτι πινων πιεσαι: > B S 106 410 538 La/Sg Sa/We
               Bo Aeth/B Arab

πινων   πιων Q 26 544 BasN.   πινοντι 534   πινουσα 22
               36 48 51-51s 62 96 311 407 449 763 770 Tht.
               πιουσα 88 Syh

πιεσαι   πιη 22 36 48 51-51s 62 96 311 407 449 763 770 Tht.

v. 14 οτι   > A

κατ   κατ . . . κυριος: σ᾽ επ αυτον γαρ ωμοσα φησι
               κυριος 86mg

εμαυτου   + enim La/Sg

ωμοσα   ωμωσα 613
λεγει κυριος
οτι   οτι εις αβατον: α᾽ οτι εις χερσειαν Syh/mg; nemo
               pertransiet La/Sg

εις   pr. εις αφανισμον και 22 36 48 51-51s 62 88 96
               311 407 449 763 770 Syh Tht. Arm = ο᾽ 86txt

αβατον   σαββατον 534   ονειδισμον 22 36 48 51-51s 62 88
               96 311 407 449 763 770 Syh Tht. Arm

και   > 410

εις   > 91 106 410 490 710 Tht.

ονειδισμον   ονιδισμον A S 544   αβατον 22 36 48 51-51s 62
               88 96 311 407 449 763 770 Syh Tht. Arm
               α᾽ + και εις ρομφαιαν Syh/mg

και   και . . . πασαι: > 410

29:14-15

εις   επι   86mg

καταρασιν   -αραν   A S V 49 87 90 91 106 239 490 538 544
               613 764   καταπαυσιν 46 631   επικαταραν 88
               επικαταρασιν 22 36 48 51-51s 62 96 311 407 449
               763 770 Chr. Tht.

εση   εση εν μεσω αυτης: οι γ′ εσται βοσορα 86mg
               Syh/mg(sub οι λ′)
               εσει 239   > 710   ⇒ Syh;   + βοσορ 22 36 48 51-51s
               62 96 311 407 449 763 770 Chr.(-ωρ) Tht.(-ωρ)

εν   εμ A 91 544;   εν μεσω: in parte La/Sg

μεσω   μεση 233   μετω 490   ο′ μερει 86mg
               + μερη 88 Syh   + μερους 22 36 48 51-51s 62
               96 311 407 449 763 770 Chr. Tht. Arm

αυτης   tua La/Sg   + συνημμενας Chr./comm.
και

πασαι αι   πασε ε S*

πολεις   πολις S*   civitates La/Sg

αυτης   αυτων 534 Arb Arm   tuae Sa/Sg

εσονται   εσονται . . . αιωνα: α′σ′ εσονται εις ερημιας
               αιωνιους 86mg
               εσοντε S*

ερημοι   ερημοι εις αιωνα: > 407

εις   εις αιωνα: εως αιωνος 22 36 48 51s 62 96 311
               763 Tht.(εως του αιωνος)

αιωνα   pr. τον A Q 49 87 90 91 233 410 490 538 613 764
               Arab;   αιωνας 51 88 449 770 Syh
v. 15 αχοην   > 410
ηκουσα παρα
κυριου   pr. του 22 36 48 51s 62 96 311 407 763

και   και . . . απεστειλε: α′ περιοχη εν τοις εθνεσιν
               απεσταλη 86mg;   σ′ και πρεσβευτης εις εθνη
               απεσταλη Syh/mg;   > 410
               ÷86
αγγελους εις
εθνη   pr. τα V 239 538 Tht./comm. BasN.

απεστειλε   -λεν A B Q Sc(-τιλεν) 22* 26 48 51ς* 86 87 88
               91c(-λα 91*) 96 233 239 311 407 449 490 544 710
               763 770 BasN.   -λαν 62
               εξαπεστειλεν 49 90(-λε) 534 613(-λε) 764

29:15-17

συναχθητε   pr. dicen La/Sg;   συναχθηναι   S* 407(+ τε)
                   συναχθηται Sc 534

και
παραγενεσθε   -θαι A S 26 86 407 534 544
                   -γινεσθε 106 239 538 BasN.

εις   εις αυτην: εν αυτη 62;   > 407
                   επ 22 36 48 51-51x 96 311 449 763 770 Tht.
                   La/Sa(adversum) Aeth/B Syh/mg
αυτην
αναστητε   pr. και 22 36 48 51 62 88 96 106 311 449 534
                   763 770 Tht. Bo Aeth/B Arm/M   > 407

εις πολεμον   + επ αυτην 22 36 48 51-51s 62 96 311 407 449
                   763 770 Tht. Syh/mg

v. 16 μικρον   pr. ιδου A Q V 22 36 48 51-51s 86 96 130 233 239
                   311 407 449 534 544 613 710 763 770 Tht. Olymp.
                   pr. οτι ιδου 62 88 ⊗Syh Arm(+ ego)   pr. et Aeth
                   α΄σ΄ ⊗ οτι μικρον 86mg

εδωκα   δεκωκα A 22 26 36 48 51-51s 62(δεδο.) 96 233 311
                   407 449 763 770 Tht.   εδωκας 239 544 BasN.

σε   > 239 544 BasN.

εν   εν . . . ανθρωποις: α΄ εν τοις εθνεσιν
                   εξουδενομενον εν ανθρωποις 86mg

εθνεσιν   -σι 88 90c 239 410 613 BasN.
ευκατα-
  φρονητον   pr. και A 49 87 88 90 91 239 410 490 613 764
                   BasN. Syh Arab   -φρονιτον 86
                   > 763   α΄σ΄ εξουδενωμενον Syh/mg

εν   > 311

ανθρωπους   + ευκαταφρονητον 763

v. 17 η   η . . . σου: α΄ αλαζοσυνη σου επηρεν σε 86mg;
                   σ΄ αλαζονια σου επηρεν σε 86mg Syh/mg
                   > 311

παιγνια   πεγ. S*   α΄θ΄ υπερηφανια Syh/mg

σου   pr. της καρδιας 51 449 770

ενεχειρησε   -σεν A B Q S(-χιρ. Sc) V 49 91 233 490 538 544 764
                   επεχειρισεν 26 534(-ρησεν)   ενεχειρισε 22c 36
                   46 51-51s 88 106 239 311 449 613c 770 Syh
                   ενεχειρισεν 22* 48 51s* 87 96 407 710 763

29:17

σου   + ταυτα   22 36 48 51-51s 62 ※88 96 311 407 449
             763 770 Tht. Syh/mg Arm;   hoc tibi La/Sg

ιταμια   ιταμια . . . υψηλου: α′σ′ υπερηφανια της καρδιας
             σου κατασκηνουντας εν οπαις των πετρων επιλαμ-
             βανομενους υψους βουνου 86mg
             pr. η 51 88 233 239 311 407 449 770 BasN.
             ιταμιαν Q   ηταμια 106 490   ιταμοτις 534
             ιταμιον 544   πι ταμιεια αυτης 62
             και η ατιμια 22 36 48 51s 96 763
             duritia Bo   stultitiam La/Sg   ιματια Aeth
             α′ θλιψις Syh/mg

καρδιας   pr. της 22 36 48 51 96 311 407 449 763 770 Tht.
             καρδια V 68 106 122 239
σου
κατελυσε   κατελυσε . . . πετρων: α′ κατασκηνουντες εν οπαις
             Syh/mg; σ′ επιλαμβανομενοι της πετρας Syh/mg;
             κατελυσεν εν τρυμαλιαις πετρων Syh/mg
             -σεν A B Q S V 22 26 36 48 49 51s 62 86 87 88 91
             96 311 407 490 544 710 763 764 Tht.
             κατελιπε 239

τρυμαλιας   -λειας A   τρυμμ. 26   -ματειας 534
             εν τρυμαλιαις 22 36 48 51s 62 88 96 311 407 763
             Tht. La/Sg(in cavernis)
πετρων
συνελαβεν   -λαβε 239 BasN.   -λαβον 22* 48 407 763 Tht./B

ισχυν   ισχυν . . . υψηλου: θ′ υψος βουνου Syh/mg;
             ÷86;   επι 407;   munitionem La/Sg

βουνου   βουνου υψηλου: pl. Bo

υψηλου   ÷86, ομοιως οι γ′ 86mg;   + σου Arm
οτι
υψωσεν   υψωσας 49 87 90 91 106 490 764 La/Sg(exaltasti)
             Aeth/B Arab   εαν υψωσεις A 26 86mg 239
             εαν υψωσης Q V 22 36 46 48 51-51s 62 86txt 88
             96 130 233 311 407 449 534 544 613 710 763 770

ωσπερ   ως 106 233 538 Tht.
αετος
νοσσιαν   -ειαν B*   νοσιαν 62 88 534   pl. Bo

αυτου   σου A 22 36 48 51-51s 62 88 96 106 239 311 407
             449 763 770 86mg Tht. La/Sg(tuum) Aeth/B Syh
             Arab Arm   εαυτου S 534

εκειθεν   εκειθεν καθελω: εκει ο θς καθελη 534
             εκιθεν S*   pr. et Arm

29:17-19

σε   σαι A   + φησι κυριος 22(-σιν) 36 48(-σιν) 51-51s
            62 88 96 311 407(-σιν) 449 763 770 Syh Arm
            = o´ 86mg   + λεγει κυριος Tht.

v. 18 και
εσται   εστε S*

η   > 46 631

Ιδουμαια   ιουμαια S*   ιουδομαια 68

εις   εις αβατον: sine vestigio La/Sg

αβατον   βατον S*

πας   pr. και Q Bo Arab Arm   pr. quia Aeth/B

ο   > 26
παραπορ-
  ευομενος πορευομενος 311 410

επ   επ αυτην: δι αυτης 534   per eam La/Sg
            την 239

αυτην   αυτη 51 311 407 449 770

συριει   εκστησεται και συριει επι παση τη πληγη (πασαν
            την πληγην Q 239 613 BasN.) αυτης Q V 22 26 36
            46 48 51-51s 62 86 88 96 233 239 311 407 449 534
            544 613 631 710 763 770 Syh
            + εκστησεται και συριει επι (εν 87txt) παση τη
            πληγη αυτης 49 87 90 91 490 764

v. 19 ωσπερ ως V 22 26 36 46 48 51-51s 62 86 88 96 233 311
            407 449 534 544 631 710 763 770
κατεστραφη
Σοδομα και
Γομορρα   -ορα 88 239

και   και . . . παντοκρατωρ: α´ και ε(αι/c) γειτονες
            αυτης ειπε κυριος 86mg

αι   αι παροικοι αυτης: vicinae eius civitates La/Sg
            ε S* 62   88 613

παροικοι   -οικιαι 106

αυτης   + sic subvertam te La/Sg

ειπε   -εν A B Q S V 22* 26 48 49 62 86 87 88 90 96 233
κυριος   311 407 449 490 534 544
παντοκρατωρ ÷ Q 88   ÷ 86 Syh   > Arm

29:19-20

ου   pr. et Aeth Arm

μη   > 26

καθισει   καθιση B Q S 22 46 48 51-51s 62 86 87 88 90 96
                130 311 407 410 449 490 538 544 613 631 710 763
                764 770   καθηση 36 68 122* 534
                καθησει 26 91   κατοικησει A

εκει   εκει ανθρωπος: tr. 613
                εκι S*

ανθρωπος   αθρωπος S*
και ου μη
κατοικησει   καθειση A   ενοικησει B Sc(-σι S*) Olymp.
                ενοικηση Q 130 239 538 613 BasN.
                κατοικηση 22 36 46 48 49 51-51s 86 87 88 90 96
                106 311 407 410 449 534 544 631 710 763 764 770

εκει   εκι S*   > 88 Syh/txt
υιος ανθρωπου
v. 20 ιδου
ωσπερ   ως 22 36 48 51-51s 62 88 96 311 407 449 763 770
                Chr. GregNyss. III, p. 232
λεων αναβησεται
εκ   εκ . . . ιορδανου: α' εκ φρυγματος του ιορδανου
                86mg; σ'α' απο της δοξης 86mg(del. α' 86mg/c)
                Syh

μεσου του   μεσου του ιορδανου: του υδατος S*
Ιορδανου
εις   εις . . . Αιθαμ: α' επι το κατοικητηριον το
                αρχαιον 86mg; ιω' επι το κατοικητηριον το
                ωχυρωτατον 86mg; α' προς ευπρεπειαν στερεαν
                Syh/mg; σ' επι το κατοικητηριον των αρχων Syh/mg

τοπον   pr. τον A 538

Αιθαμ   ηθαμ A   εθαμ 62 544 Chr.   αιμαθ 36c 49 88
                90 91 490 613 764 Syh(חמת)   εμαθ 87
                α' στερεαν   σ' αρχαιαν Eus., Onom. p. 38
                α' στερρον   σ' αρχαια Ghisler, II, p. 862
                το εβρ' εθαμ Chr./comm.

οτι   οτι . . . επιστησατε: α' οτι κατασπευσω αυτον
                τροχασω αυτον επανωθεν αυτης και τις εκλεκτος
                προς αυτην επισκεφομαι   86mg; σ' εξαιφνης
                δραμειν ποιησω αυτον επανωθεν αυτης και τινα
                εκλεκτον επ αυτην επιστησω Syh/mg

ταχυ   ταχυ εκδιωξω: ταχυς και διωξω 22 36 48 51s 96 311
                763

<u>29:20-21</u>
εκδιωξω αυτους
απ αυτης   > 239 BasN.   Bo

και   και . . . επιστησατε: +86;   και τις εκλεκτος προς
                    αυτην επισκεφομαι 86mg(sub ο′) 88 Syh/txt Arm;
τους
νεανισκους
επ   > S* 106*

αυτην   αυτης S Qtxt   +86mg

επιστησατε   -σεται A   -ται 764   -σω 86mg Syh/mg
                    + και τις εκλεκτος προς(επ 62)αυτην επισκεφομαι
                    22 36 48 51-51s 62 96 311 407 449(sub ✳) 763
                    770(sub ✳)

οτι   οτι . . . μου: α′ οτι τις ομοιος μου και τις
                    υποστησεται μου 86mg
τις
ωσπερ   ωσπερ . . . μου: α′σ′ ομοιος μου και τις υπο-
                    στησεται μου Syh/mg
                    ως 538
εγω και τις
αντιστησεται   -ετε S*

μου   μου . . . στησεται: > Clem.
                    μου 26

και   > 233 Tht.
τις
ουτος   est Bo

ποιμην   pr.ο S 130 410 Tht. Bo Arab

ος   ο A   ως V   οστις 26 538

στησεται   στησται B*   συστησεται 538
κατα προ-
σωπον μου
v. 21 δια
τουτο ακουσατε
βουλην   pr.την 22 36 48 51-51s 62 96 311 407 449 763
                    770 Tht.
κυριου ην
εβουλευσατο   fecit Sa/We
επι την
Ιδουμαιαν   -μεαν S* Bo

και   και. . . . αυτου: α′σ′ και τους λογισμους αυτου
                    86mg
λογισμον
αυτου   > Sa/We

29:21-22

ον
ελογισατο   -γεισατο S
επι τους
κατοικουντας
θαιμαν   θεμαν 87 Bo Aeth/B Arm   θαμαν   Arab
                   pr. in Bo Sa/We   α΄θ΄ θημαν   86mg
εαν
μη   > V 544

συμφησθωσι   συνφηφισθωσιν A 51 88 (-σι) 311 407 449 490
                   538 (-σι) 544 770   συνφηθωσιν B*
                   συμφηθωσι Bc 130   συμφηφισθωσιν Q 46
                   51s/c 62 (συμφι.) 106 (-σι) 613 (-σι) 631 (-σι)
                   συνωσιν S 410 (-σι) Sa/We   συνφισθωσιν V 91 (-σι)
                   534 (-σι)   συμφησθωσιν 22 26 36 48 49 51s* 87
                   96 763 764   σ΄ συμφησωσιν αυτους   86mg
                   + ※αυτω Qmg   + αυτων   22 36 48 51-51s 62 96
                   311 407 449 763 770 86mg

τα ελαχιστα   τα . . . προβατων: των ελαχιστων προβατα 106;
                   α΄ ελαχιστα του ποιμνιου   Syh/mg
των
προβατων   σ΄ ποιμενων 86mg
εαν μη
αβατωθη   βατωθη 239

επ   επ αυτους: > Sa/We Arm

αυτους   αυτη A   αυτην B S* 106 130 410 538 Bo Aeth
                   αυτης Sc 26

καταλυσις   -σεις 544
αυτων
v. 22 οτι   οτι . . . αυτων > 62
                   > Q V 22 26 46 48 51-51s 86 88 96 233 311 407 449
                   534 544 631 710 763 770 Syh Arm
απο φωνης
πτωσεως   ιππεων 130   α΄ σεισμου   Syh/mg
αυτνω   sing. Arm

εφοβηθη   εσισθη A 407 544   εσεισθη Q V 22 26 36 46 48
                   51-51s 62 86 87 88 90 91 96 130 233 239 311 449
                   490 534 613 631 710 763 764 770

η γη   + αυτων Bo

και   και . . . ηκουσθη: > 538
                   > Q V 22 26 36 46 48 51-51s 62 86 88 96 130 233
                   311 407 449 534 544 631 710 763 770 Syh Sa/We Arm

κραυγη   pr. η 49 87 90 91 106 239 410 490 613 764 BasN.
                   κραυη S*

29:22-23

σου   σου εν: εουαι   544
                   > B S Aeth/B   ητις 534   αυτων   Bo

εν   > B S Aeth/B

θαλασση   pr. τη 87
                   θαλασσης B S Aeth/B   + ερυθρα   22 36 48
                   51c-51s 62 88 96 311 407 449 763 770 Syh Arm
                   = οι γ' ο' 86mg

ηκουσθη   pr. ουκ B S Aeth/B   εξηκουσθη   V 22 26 36 46 48
                   51c-51s 62 88 96 311 407 449 544 631 763 770 Syh
                   + φωνη σου   22 36 48 51s 96 763
                   + η φωνη σου   51 62 311 407 449 770 Syh/mg Arm
                   + η φωνη αυτης   88 Syh/txt

v. 23 ιδου
ωσπερ
αετος   αετος αετος   449   + qui Aeth/B

οφεται   -ετε S* V   αναβησεται   22 36 48 51-51s 62 96
                   311 407 449 763 770 = α'σ'   86mg Syh/mg
                   + και επιστησεται   22 36 48 96 311 763
                   + και επιπτησεται   51-51s 62 (-σσεται)⁂88 407 449
                   770 ⁂Syh Arm = σ' ⁂86mg

και
εκτενει   εκτενι   A S*   εκτεινει   B*   εκτενη   544
                   εκτενις   710

τας
πτερυγας   χειρας 544 Arab   + αυτον   22 36 48 49 51-51s
                   62 87 90 91 96 311 407 449 490 534 613 763 764
                   770 Syh Bo Aeth/B Arab Arm

επ   επ οχυρωματα: επι βοσορα   86mg; α'σ' επι βοσρα
                   Syh/mg
                   επι   22 36 48 51-512 62 96 311 407 449 763 770
                   απ   490

οχυρωματα   pr. τα   22 36 48 51-51s 62 96 311 407 449 763 770
                   -μασιν   534   -μα 233 710

αυτης και
εσται   -τε   S*
η καρδια
των   τνω . . . καρδια: > 22

ισχυρων   > Qtxt   εχθρων   534
της Ιδουμαιας
εν τη ημερα
εκεινη   εκινη S*
ως καρδια
γυναικος   γυναικος ωδινουσης   pl. Arm

ωδινουσης   ωδει.   B*

III. Grouping of the Evidence

Collation of all the manuscript, patristic and versional evidence in the preceding pages has revealed a host of variant readings for Jer 29. While initial survey of these pages might present a very confused picture, further study soon reveals the existence of certain patterns of attestation within the variants which reduces the apparent confusion considerably. Of prime importance is the fact that some MSS consistently group together in bearing witness to the same reading. This phenomenon of the grouping of MSS has long been recognized as a foundational principle in the work of textual criticism. In the case of LXX studies it goes back at least to the works of A.M. Ceriani (Monumenta sacra et profana, ex codicibus praesertim bibliotheca Ambrosiane, II, 1863, xxiv), J. Wellhausen (Der Text der Bücher Samuelis, 1871, pp. 223f.) and Paul de Lagarde (Librorum Veteris Testamenti canonicorum pars prior Graece, 1883, p. xvi) /16/. In our analysis of Jer 29 the several groupings of MSS provide both a practical way of organizing the discussion as well as a useful means of surveying the textual history of this chapter of the book of Jer, and by extension--with certain modifications /17/--of the whole book. The following six groups are found to exist in Jer: A) The O Group, B) The L Group, C) The C Group, D) The Q Group, E) The A Group, and F) the B Group.

A.   The O Group (or Hexaplaric Recension)

The text critical analysis of the oracles against the Philistines and Edom is most conveniently approached through the MSS attesting the recension of Origen, i.e., the text which derives ultimately from the fifth column of Origen's monumental Hexapla, hence also called the Hexaplaric recension /18/. What makes the study of this recension especially suitable as a point of departure is the fact that it is firmly anchored historically, and thanks to Origen's own comments on his modus operandi in revising the LXX, its readings are often readily identified /19/. A key passage explaining the principles underlying this recension is found in Origen's Commentary on Matthew (xv, 14), where in a discussion of Mat 19:19, he says:

Great differences have arisen in the
transcripts, from the carelessness of some of
the scribes, or from the recklessness of some
persons, or from those who neglected the emendation of the text, or else from those who
made additions to the text or omissions from
it, as they thought fit. With the help of
God's grace I have tried to repair the dis-
agreements in the copies of the Old Testament
on the basis of the other versions. When I
was uncertain of the Septuagint reading because the various copies did not tally, I settled the issue by consulting the other versions and retaining what was in agreement with
them. Some passages did not appear in the
Hebrew; these I marked with an obelus as I
did not dare to leave them out altogether.
Other passages I marked with an asterisk to
show that they were not in the Septuagint but
that I had added them from the other versions
in agreement with the Hebrew text /20/.

Three relevant facts emerge from the above passage: 1) Origen purposed to amend the LXX by bringing
it into conformity with the Hebrew; 2) he used other
Greek versions to settle points of inner-Greek corruption in existing LXX MSS as well as to supply passages
he considered missing in the LXX; 3) he employed a
conventional system of critical signs to indicate omissions and additions in the LXX vis-à-vis the Hebrew:
the obelus to mark a reading found in the LXX but not
in the Hebrew, the asterisk to draw attention to a
reading missing in the LXX but added by him from the
other versions /21/.

Of the three points mentioned here, the use of the
critical signs is the most arresting feature of Origen's
work, providing us frequently with a visual means
of identifying the readings that belong to his recension /22/. For the prophetical books in general and
for Jer in particular the most frequent carriers of the
critical signs are the following four MSS: Codex Chisianus
(MS 88), Codex Ambrosianus, containing the text
of the Syro-hexapla (Syh), Codex Barberinus (MS 86),
and Codex Marchalianus (Q). Of these four, a unique
pair is formed by 88 and Syh; various factors combine

to demonstrate not only their sister relationship but
also their Hexaplaric origin.

The common ancestry of 88 and Syh is shown in at
least five ways. Both attest the same unusual order of
the prophetical books: Jer, Dan, Ez, Isa. Only these
two MSS transmit the LXX text of Dan (where all others,
apart from some fragments in the Chester Beatty papyri,
give Theodotion's version), and place the story of
Susanna and of Bel and the Dragon <u>after</u> the canonical
part of Dan (an arrangement found elsewhere only in MS
62). In Jer only they, together with most of the MSS
of the L group, follow the Hebrew text in the matter of
the location and internal order of the oracles against
foreign nations. Finally, the similar (sometimes identical) colophons are strong witness to their common
background.

It is to the colophons, too, that we owe specific
information concerning the Hexaplaric origin of 88 and
Syh. For instance, the colophon for Lam reads as follows: Θρηνοι (pr. τετελονται Syh) Ιερεμιου εγραφη εκ
των εξαπλων εξ ων και παρετεθη. Whether by the phrase
εγραφη εκ των εξαπλων is meant that the text was originally copied out of the Hexapla autograph or from some
transcript of the fifth column (whether by Origen himself or by his friends Pamphilus and Eusebius) cannot
be determined. In the case of the Syh, internal evidence shows that this was translated from a Greek MS
almost identical to the forerunner of 88 (cf. their
mutual agreement in the omission of several asterisks).
By the phrase εξ ων [i.e. των εξαπλων] και παρετεθη is
probably meant that the text was provided with the
Origenic signs. Although no colophon exists for Jer
(Ziegler thinks it may have dropped out by accident,
cf. <u>Ieremias</u>, p. 67), we may assume that what is said
concerning Lam applies equally to Jer. Since the history of these two MSS is so clearly related and since
their common readings and signs unequivocally place
them in the Origenic camp, their mutually attested
readings may legitimately be cited under the symbol O
(= Origen) /23/.

There is one major difference between 88 and the
Syh, namely that in addition to its fifth column text,
Syh also has numerous readings in its margins taken
mainly--though not exclusively--from the other columns

of the Hexapla and identified by the symbols α´, σ´,
ϑ´, ιω´, οι λ´. In this respect Codex Marchalianus (Q)
and Codex Barberinus (86) resemble the Syro-hexapla;
for while the text itself of these MSS does not derive
from Origen's recension, their margins are nevertheless
rich sources of Hexapla readings, including some from
the fifth column text. MS 86 also contains a number of
critical signs (especially obeli) in the body of its
text, but as we shall see, many of these are unreliable
/24/.

With the above modicum of background information
in hand it becomes possible to proceed with a detailed
examination of the Hexaplaric recension of Jer 29. The
goal in view is to isolate those readings which can
with reasonable certainty be attributed to Origen's
recension as secondary additions or alterations and to
disqualify such from a restored archetype text of Jer
29. The material will be dealt with according to the
following outline:

      1. Obelized Readings
         a. Agreeing with MT
         b. Conflicting with MT
      2. Asterized Readings
         a. Agreeing with MT
         b. Conflicting with MT
      3. Unmarked Readings
         a. Supported by Hexapla Readings
            i.   Additions
            ii.   Synonymous Substitutions
            iii. Double Readings
         b. Unsupported by Hexapla Readings
      4. Significance of Data

1. Obelized Readings

There are altogether nine obelized readings in our
extant MS evidence for the oracles against the Philistines and Edom. The obeli appear in three different
forms: ÷, ⊤, ⇔ /25/. Using MT as the comparative
base, six of the obeli agree with Origen's known working principles while three disagree.

a.   Obelized Readings Agreeing with MT

29:1   επι τους αλλοφυλους] pr.⟶επι τους αλλοφυλους´
※λογος κυριου ος εγενηθη προς ιερεμιαν τον προφητην´ Syh
pr. επι τους αλλοφυλους ος εγενετο λογος κυριου προς
ιερεμιαν τον προφητην 51 62 311 449 770

MT 47:1 אשר היה דבר יהוה אל ירמיהו הנביא אל פלשתים

The Syh (followed by minuscules 51 62 311 449 770)
reproduces the phrase επι τους αλλοφυλους twice, once
as a title in common with all other LXX MSS, and once
as part of the longer introductory formula corresponding to MT. It may well be that Syh has preserved the
right Hexaplaric tradition here, namely that when Origen
came to the LXX title επι τους αλλοφυλους he merely
obelized this and proceeded to add from the Minor VSS
the words missing in the LXX (contrast 88 which has the
title επι τους αλλοφυλους preceded only once by the
phrase ος εγενηθη λογος κυριου προς ιερεμιαν τον
προφητην, see below p. 49).

29:5   και οι καταλοιποι] ÷και οι κατα.   86

The MT שארית also omits the article.

29:9   εν δαιδαν] ÷εν δαι.   86;   om. εν Qtxt

The MT דדן also omits the preposition.   The
omission of εν in Qtxt is probably accidental.

29:17   ισχυν βουνου υψηλου]÷ ισχυν βουνου ÷υψηλου   86

MT 49:16 מרום גבעה

It is not clear how the two obeli in the above example are to be explained; probably only one goes back
to Origen. The Greek translation equivalence furthest
removed from the Hebrew is ισχυν and may therefore have
been the word obelized by Origen. An interesting note
in 86mg /26/ comments with reference to υψηλου, "ομοιως
οι γ´," perhaps intended as a scribal remark defending
the retention of the word.

29:19   κυριος παντοκρατωρ]או. ÷παντοκρατωρ   Q O 86

MT has only יהוה.

29:20   και τους νεανισκους επ αυτην επιστησατε] ÷86;
om. 88-Syh/txt. Cf. MT 49:19 ומי בחור אליה אפקד

The phrase sub obeli in 86 has been entirely
suppressed in 88-Syh/txt and replaced by a phrase
which better corresponds to MT (see below, pp. 54-55).

b.   Obelized Readings Conflicting with MT

The above six readings have confirmed the general
correspondence between MT and Origen's Hebrew text. In
the following three examples of obelized readings conflicting with the MT we have to reckon with a Hebrew
text differing from the MT or with incorrectly transmitted obeli.

29:3   ποδων αυτου] πο. ÷αυτου 86. Cf. MT 47:3 אבירו

The obelus before αυτου is a problem since the MT
also has the third person singular suffix. A different
Hebrew Vorlage is a technical possibility, but it may
be that the obelus originally stood before ποδων since
this word in no way agrees with the Hebrew; in O ποδων
was replaced by δυνατων (see below, p. 58). These
facts may mean that in the fifth column both words were
present (i.e., ποδων and δυνατων), the first one sub
obeli, the second sub asterisco, only the latter of
which (minus the asterisk) has survived in O /27/.

29:14   εση]   Syh. Cf. MT 49:13 תהיה

It is doubtful that this obelus is correctly preserved in Syh since εση exactly corresponds to תהיה and
it is unlikely that the Hebrew sentence would have been
composed without the verb. Ziegler (Ieremias, p. 79)
may well be right in suggesting that the obelus originally stood before the phrase which immediately follows
εση, namely εν μεσω. In O this phrase constitutes the
first part of a double reading εν μεσω/μερη (see below

p. 58). In the fifth column εν μεσω would presumably
have been <u>sub obeli</u> and μερη <u>sub asterisco</u>.

29:15   και αγγελους] ÷και αγγ. 86. Cf. MT 49:14 וציר

Since both the LXX and the MT have the conjunction, the obelus is enigmatic. Perhaps the conjunction
was missing in Origen's Hebrew <u>Vorlage</u> and the obelus
is then correctly transmitted. Alternatively, the obelus
may be intended to apply to both words, και αγγελους,
thus drawing attention to the discrepancy between the
Greek plural and the Hebrew singular.

Remarks

The best attested obelus in our chapter is παντοκρατωρ in 29:19 (found in Q O 86). This word was certainly present in the pre-Origenic text. This is an
illustration of the function of a true obelus for the
modern text critic, namely that it guarantees that
reading for the pre-Hexaplaric text.

Six of the nine obelized passages are attested
only by MS 86, and at least two of these are open to
question. The preponderance of obeli in 86 is a phenomenon of that MS in Jer (cf. <u>Ieremias</u>, p. 76); the
presence of several anomalous obeli is also characteristic of that MS (cf. <u>Ieremias</u>, p. 78).

Only in one case (29:20) has an obelized reading
been entirely suppressed in some other MS. This low
frequency of elimination is in conformity with a general reluctance on the part of scribes to omit altogether Origen's obelized passages.

2. Asterized Readings

Fourteen asterized readings have been preserved in
the extant MSS of Jer 29. Eleven of these agree with
the MT, while three conflict with MT.

In this section the relevant data for the asterized
readings is set out in columns in the following

manner: In the centre of the page, straddling the two
columns, is found the lemma text from the collation
notes. In the left-hand column is cited the asterized
reading in question, followed by the corresponding
Hexapla readings under appropriate translator symbols
(where available). In the right-hand column, for comparison purposes, are listed those Greek MSS containing
the same (or very similar) readings as those which in
the left-hand column are under asterisk.

a. Asterized Readings Agreeing with MT

29:1 επι τους αλλοφυλους

pr. ⮌ επι τους αλλοφυλους‹
※λογος κυριου ος εγενηθη
προς ιερ. τον προφητην‹ Syh

pr. ※ος εγενηθη λογος
κυριου προς ιερεμιαν τον
προφητην 88

+ ※προ του παταξαι φαραω
(※88) την γαζαν Qmg 88-
Syh

+ ος εγενετο λογος κυριου
προς ιερεμιαν τον προφητην
(+ επι τους αλλοφυλους 51
62 311 449 770) προ του
παταξαι φαραω την γαζαν
22 36 48 51-51s 62 96 311
407 449 763 770

α΄σ΄ pr. ※ος εγενηθη
λογος κυριου προς ιερ.
τον προφητην Qmg

α΄σ΄ pr. ※ος εγενηθη
λογος κυριου προς ιερ.
τον προφητην επι τους
αλλοφυλους (α΄ προς
φυλιστιους Syh/mg;
σ΄ περι των φυλιστιαιων
86mg) προ του παταξαι
φαραω την γαζαν 86mg

MT 47:1   אשר היה דבר יהוה אל ירמיהו הנביא אל פלשתים
בטרם יכה פרעה את עזה

The long introductory formula in MT is represented
in the LXX only by the phrase επι τους αλλοφυλους.

Aquila and Symmachus, however, supplied the missing parts before and after the short title corresponding to the Hebrew, from where it was taken over by Origen and placed sub asterisco.

The asterized additions in 88 and Syh are identical except for the transposition of the opening phrase ος εγενηθη / λογος κυριου. The order in 88 is undoubtedly original to the Hexaplaric recension as it agrees with α'σ' and with MT. In that part of the asterized addition following the title (προ του παταξαι φαραω την γαζαν), 88-Syh are joined anonymously by Qmg. But since the additions in Qmg preceding the title are under the symbols α'σ', it is likely that the addition following the title is to be regarded as a continuation of the reading under the same symbols, i.e. α'σ'. The additional asterisks in 88 before τον προφητην and την γαζαν are of uncertain significance.

29:4   παντας

pr. ※συν 88   pr. συν 86mg

MT 47:4   את כל

The preposition συν is a telltale sign of Aquila's translation. In that version συν renders the Hebrew nota accusativi whenever the latter is followed by the Hebrew article or by כל (as here); otherwise the Greek article alone is used (cf. Reider, Prolegomena, p. 16, n. 33). The appearance of the asterized συν in 88 raises the question to what extent Origen adopted Aquila's fastidious rendering in the fifth column of the Hexapla. If 88 is to be trusted, he did so rather frequently (115 times in Jer according to Ziegler, Ieremias , p. 72) /28/.

29:4   τους καταλοιπους (2°)

pr. ※τους αλλοφυλους O   pr. τους αλλοφυλους 22 36
                                 36(+ και) 48 51-51s 62(tr.
                                 τους αλλ. /τους καταλ.)
_____   96 311 407 449 763 770

α'θ' pr. ※τους αλλοφυλους
Qmg

ο΄ pr. ⁂τους αλλοφυλους
86mg

MT 47:4 את פלשתים שארית

    The correspondence between MT and O is exact.

29:4   των νησων

+ ⁂και καππαδοκιας 449   + και καππαδοκιας O 22 36
770   48 51-51s 62 96 311 407
                                763

α΄ϑ΄ + ⁂και καππαδοκιας
Qmg

οι γ΄ + καππαδοκας 86mg

MT 47:4 כפתור אי

    Although the asterisk in 449 770 is found in the
margin of these MSS, it is clear from a comparison with
other MSS that it applies to και καππαδοκιας in the
body of the text. It is true that this addition generally corresponds to the Hebrew כפתור, but two things
must be noted: "Cappadocia" is not a correct translation of כפתור, nor does the Hebrew have the conjunction. How are these discrepancies to be explained?

    With regard to the absence of the conjunction in
the Hebrew, it is interesting to note the reading of
The Three (καππαδοκας) in 86mg which also omits the
article and may therefore represent the better tradition from the Hexapla, in contrast to the witness of
Qmg according to which Aquila and Theodotion attests
the conjunction (but καππαδοκας [pl. acc.] in 86mg
must be wrong since the sense definitely requires a
genitive; the loss of the <u>iota</u> may be accidental).
The reading of the Younger VSS would then have been
των νησων καππαδοκιας, "the islands of Cappadocia."
But whence then the και in Qmg and O . . . 770? Possibly it entered the text at a later stage to correct
the geographical absurdity of the phrase "the islands
of Cappadocia," Cappadocia neither being an island nor
having any! (The correct designation of כפתור is

probably Crete). By the simple addition of a και, geographical credibility is restored to the verse: "the Lord will destroy the rest of the islands and (the rest of) Cappadocia."

29:8 κυριος

+ ※των δυναμεων Qmg

+ των δυναμεων O 22 36 48 51-51s 62 96 311 407 449 763 770

_____

ο´ + των δυναμεων 86mg

MT 49:7 יהוה צבאות

The correspondence between the Greek additions and the MT is exact.

29:11 ωλοντο δια χειρα

※ωλετο σπερμα αυτου δια χειρα O

cf. ωλετο δια χειρα Qc 86mg 106 130

ωλοντο] + ※το σπερμα αυτου Qmg

ωλετο σπερμα (pr. το 22 36 48 51s 96 763) αυτου δια χειρα 22 36 48 51-51s 62 96 311 407 449 763 770

_____

ο´ ※ωλετο σπερμα αυτου 86mg

MT 49:10 שדד זרעו

Since the common LXX reading ωλοντο δια χειρα misrepresents the Hebrew שדד זרעו (mainly on account of the confusion of זרוע, "arm," and זרע "seed"), Origen sought to correct the mistranslation. In place of δια χειρα he wrote σπερμα αυτου and in place of the plural ωλοντο he placed the singular verb ωλετο. Since no reading of the Minor VSS has survived at this point, unfortunately we do not know the source of Origen's reading.

According to Origen's stated rules one would have expected the asterisk to have been placed in front of

σπερμα αυτου since that alone represents the <u>addition</u>
of the LXX, ωλετο being a qualitative change. It is of
course possible that the asterisk was moved in the
process of transmission from a hypothetically original
position preceding σπερμα to that preceding ωλετο, but
this is less likely in view of the stable position of
the asterisk in both O and 86mg. If then the asterisk
is correctly transmitted before ωλετο, this would tend
to support the view that Origen occasionally used an
asterisk to designate a qualitative as well as a quantitative change /29/.

A further point of interest is the fact that in O
the majority text reading of δια χειρα has been
retained <u>along</u> <u>with</u> the asterized alteration and
addition. We have here, therefore, a clear case of a
double reading. Presumably in Origen's LXX column δια
χειρα would have been <u>sub</u> <u>obeli</u>, but the obelus at some
point has disappeared and both readings have been
preserved side by side /30/.

29:13 επιον

pr. ※πιοντες O

pr. πιοντες 22 36 48 51-
51s 62 96 311 407 449 763
770

α΄θ΄ pr. ※πιοντες Qmg

οι γ΄ pr. ※πιοντες 86mg

οι λ΄ pr. πιονται Syh/mg

MT 49:12 ישתו שתו

The Hebrew absolute infinitive was often rendered
in the LXX by the juxtaposition of a cognate participle
and finite verb. This model had been followed by The
Three in the translation of שתו ישתו (the minor discrepancies in attestation are of little consequence)
and was in turn taken over from them by Origen.

29:13   αθωωμενη

+ ※αθωωθηση O   + αθωωθηση 22 36 48 51s
                                 96 311 763

ϑ′ + ※αθωωθηση 86mg

MT 49:12 נקה תנקה

    Whereas in the previous example the LXX lacked the
participle in the translation of the Hebrew infinitive
absolute, this time it was missing the finite verb.
The verb was accordingly added by Origen from Theodotion.

29:16   ιδου μικρον

pr. ※οτι⌐ 88(om. signs)   pr. οτι 62
-Syh

α′σ′ ※οτι μικρον 86mg

MT 49:15 כי הנה קטן

    The correspondence between the O addition and MT
is exact.

29:20   και τους νεανισκους επ αυτην επιστησατε

÷86; om. 88-Syh/txt;   και τις εκλεκτος προς
hab. Syh/mg   αυτην επισκεφομαι 88-
                                 Syh/txt

+ ※και τις εκλεκτος προς
αυτην επισκεφομαι 449 770   + και τις εκλεκτος προς
                                 αυτην επισκεφομαι 22 36
                                 48 51-51s 62 96 311 407

α′, ο′ και τις εκλεκτος
προς αυτην επισκεφομαι 86mg

MT 49:19 ומי בחור אליה אפקד

This is another case where the asterisk has been preserved only in MSS 449 770 (cf. 29:4 ※και καππαδοκιας above, p. 51). The above data is to be interpreted along the following lines: The LXX reading τους νεανισκους επ αυτην επιστησατε (which is obelized in 86 and altogether missing in 88-Syh/txt) has been replaced in 88-Syh/txt by the reading from Aquila τις εκλεκτος προς αυτην επισκεψομαι which more closely approximates the Hebrew. In MSS 22 . . . 770 the new reading has been added to the old LXX reading, resulting in a double reading in those MSS. The old LXX reading is also preserved in Syh/mg. The history of the passage, therefore, is probably as follows: The reading in Origen's Greek <u>Vorlage</u> was και τους νεανισκους επ αυτην επιστησατε. Since this phrase did not correspond to the Hebrew it was obelized by Origen (cf. the obelus in 86); at the same time he added the asterized correction και τις εκλεκτος προς αυτην επισκεψομαι from Aquila.

29:23 οψεται

+ ※και επιπτησεται O

cf. αναβησεται και επιστησεται (επιπτησεται 51 -51s 62 407 449 770) 22 36 48 51-51s 62 96 311 407 449 763 770

σ´ + ※και επιπτησεται 86mg

MT 49:22 יעלה וידאה

The LXX translation οψεται was occasioned by the misreading of ד for ר in וידאה; the LXX has no corresponding word for יעלה. By adding επιπτησεται from Symmachus (the latter's translation of וידאה), Origen has succeeded in making his Greek text quantitatively equivalent to the Hebrew, but certainly not qualitatively equivalent, for the Hebrew יעלה remains untranslated. The example illustrates the frequently noted tendency of Origen to strive more for quantitative agreement between the Hebrew and the Greek than qualitative agreement /31/.

b. Asterized Readings Conflicting with MT

29:9 ο τοπος αυτων

※ο 88(-Syh) /32/   om. ο Sc 130 410

MT 49:8 הפנו

    The reading ο τοπος αυτων in the majority of LXX
MSS for MT הפנו is one of the textual conundrums of the
chapter. If the asterisk prior to the Greek article is
authentic to Origen's recension, it points to a pre-
Origenic reading τοπος αυτων (cf. 130 410) to which
Origen added the article, perhaps in conformity with
the Hebrew ה of הפנו, even though the rest of the
Hebrew word in no way corresponds to τοπος αυτων. It
has been argued that the words τοπος αυτων could in
their turn be an inner-Greek corruption of an earlier
reading το προσωπον αυτων (see discussion below,
pp. 145ff.). On the other hand, the asterisk may be
faulty or employed as a scribal index to draw attention
to a phrase which does not correspond to the Hebrew.

29:17 σοι

+ ※ταυτα 88   + ταυτα 22 36 48 51-51s
                               62 96 311 407 449 763
MT 49:16 אתך   770 Syh/mg

    The addition of ταυτα does not correspond to MT
and the asterisk is not to be trusted as a genuine
Origenic sign. For reasons to be explained later (see
below, p. 72, "Readings of L Supported by Syh/mg"), the
reading probably comes from MSS 22 . . . 770.

29:21 συμφησθωσι

+ ※αυτω Qmg   + αυτων 22 36 48 51-51s
                               62 96 311 407 449 763
                               770 86mg
_____

σ´ + αυτους 86mg

MT 49:20 יסחבום

It is doubtful that the Qmg reading αυτω derives
from Origen's recension. As in the previous example,
the reading probably comes from MSS 22 . . . 770, the
<u>nun</u> of αυτων having dropped out (cf. a similar loss of
a final <u>nun</u> in Qmg at 29:3 in connection with the
Theodotionic reading δυνατω[ν]).

Remarks

The Hexaplaric origin of the 11 asterized readings
above which agree with MT is virtually certain. Not
only do they agree with MT, but 10 of the 11 are also
supported by readings from the various columns of the
Hexapla (the only exception, 29:4 συν 88, p. 50, we
know on other grounds to derive from the Hexapla).

This section also gives the <u>internal</u> proof for the
Hexaplaric origin of 88-Syh (in addition to the external evidence cited above p. 44). Of the 11 asterized
additions agreeing with MT, 6 are asterized in 88-Syh,
one is asterized in 88 alone (29:4, p. 50), another is
asterized in Syh alone (29:16, p. 54). The other three
additions, while not asterized in 88-Syh (29:4, p. 51;
29:8, p. 52; 29:20, p. 54) are nevertheless also
attested by them (the asterisks, we assume, had already
dropped out of their common ancestor).

On the question of the reliability of the signs,
we note again (on the basis of the asterisks conflicting with MT) that not every sign is to be automatically trusted.

Four readings from 86mg marked o´ are of special
interest to us (29:4 o´ ※τους αλλοφυλους /33/, 29:8
o´ των δυναμεων, 29:11 o´ ※ωλετο σπερμα αυτου, 29:20
o´ και τις εκλεκτος προς αυτην επισκεφομαι). The correspondence in each case between the o' reading and 88-
Syh makes it clear that the symbol o´ (= οι εβδομη-
κοντα) has reference to Origen's revised version of the
LXX, specifically the fifth column text of the Hexapla.
This conclusion is reinforced by five additional such
correspondences detailed in the next subsection.

3.   Unmarked Readings

In this section our attention focuses on readings in 88-Syh suspected of being Origenic but for which no signs have been preserved anywhere in the MS tradition. However, some of these unmarked readings do find support in the Minor VSS as preserved in 86mg and Qmg. Others do not even enjoy this kind of collateral attestation but can still be judged Hexaplaric by inferential means.

a.   Supported by Hexapla Readings

   i.   Additions

   29:14 εις αβατον και εις ονειδισμον (tr. εις αβ./ εις ον.) O 22 36 48 51-51s 62 96 311 407 449 763 770 = MT)] pr. εις αφανισμον O 22 36 48 51-51s 62 96 311 407 449 763 770 = ο´ 86mg = MT

   29:17 καθελω σε] + φησι(ν)κυριος O 22 . . . 770 = ο´ 86mg = MT

   29:22 εν θαλασση] + ερυθρα O 22 . . . 770 = οι γ´, ο´ 86mg = MT

   ii.   Double Readings

   29:14 εση εν μεσω] + μερη O (μερους 22 . . . 770); cf. μερει ο´ 86mg; cf. MT תהיה בצרה

   iii.   Synonymous Substitutions

   29:3 ποδων] δυνατων O 22 . . . 770 = θ´ 86mg Qmg; cf. MT אביריו

   29:10 καταλειμμα] καλαμηματα O 22 . . . 770 = ο´ 86mg; cf. MT עוללות

The frequent correspondence in the above examples between O and ο´ in 86mg (5x) is noteworthy. Such double attestation secures those readings for the Hexaplaric recension beyond doubt. In the case of the synonymous substitutions it is likely that no signs were ever employed for these.

b. Unsupported by Hexapla Readings

29:14 εις αβατον και εις ονειδισμον] tr. αβατον/
ονειδισμον Ο 22 . . . 770 = MT

29:22 ηκουσθη] εξηκουσθη η φωνη (+ σου 22 . . .
770 ≠ MT) Ο 22 . . . 770 = MT

The above two examples repeat the same pattern of
agreement between O and MT as observed previously.
These readings are almost certainly Hexaplaric.

It does not follow, however, that these O readings
necessarily exhaust the unmarked Hexaplaric readings
present in our two oracles. Any O reading which
approximates MT or stands out against a majority of
other Greek witnesses must be considered a candidate
for Hexaplaric origin, though certain controls on this
criterion will be discussed below, pp. 86-87. Some
readings which fit into this category, but for a
variety of reasons are more difficult to determine
(e.g. O may in some instances have been influenced by
other MSS) are the following:

29:4   απολεσαι] αφανισαι 88(-Syh)

29:5   οι καταλοιποι] τα λοιπα 88(-Syh) 22 . . . 770
       86mg

29:14 εις αιωνα] εις αιωνας Ο 51 449 770; cf. εως
       αιωνος 22 36 48 51s 62 96 311 407 763

29:15 αναστητε] pr. και 88 22 . . . 770 106 534 = MT

29:17 ενεχειρησεν] -ισεν 88(-Syh) 22 . . . 770 46 87
       106 239 613c 710

29:17 νοσσιαν αυτου] νο. σου Ο 22 . . . 770 A 106 239
       86mg = MT

29:23 πτερυγας] + αυτου Syh 22 . . . 770 534 613 = MT

4. Significance of the Data

The foregoing discussion has given ample proof of
Origen's labours on the Greek text of Jer. While we

cannot claim to possess a perfect copy of his revised
text, yet the remarkable correspondences between Origen's known textual principles and many of the readings
in 88-Syh, 86mg, and Qmg suggests that in these sources
we have at least reasonably reliable witnesses to what
the fifth column text of the Hexapla must have looked
like. Many problems remain unresolved with regard to
both the purpose and extent of Origen's revision, e.g.
why he let some obvious mistranslations stand while
correcting others less significant. But for our
present purposes the really important question lies
elsewhere, namely, in the extent to which Origen's
revision has affected other MSS or text traditions. Is
it true, as Jerome suggests, that there hardly exists a
Greek MS of the LXX which has not been affected by the
Hexaplaric recension /34/? To what extent can Origen's
influence be observed in the extant MS evidence for
Jer, specifically in LXX Ch. 29?

    For the moment, this question can be answered only
with regard to the confirmed Hexaplaric readings noted
above. In the case of the unmarked O readings (i.e.
those without critical signs) we do not possess as yet
the criteria or a sufficiently broad base for deciding
in every case the origin of these /35/. But as for the
assured Hexaplaric readings, a review of the previous
pages shows that, apart from one persistent group of
MSS, Origenic readings are rarely supported by other
MSS. The exception is the group of MSS 22 36 48 51-51s
48 62 96 311 407 449 763 770 which over and again support the same or similar reading as the Hexaplaric
recension, so much so, in fact, that were it not for
other considerations one might have thought that these
MSS formed another witness to that recension. It is
therefore to this group of MSS that our attention must
turn next.

B.   The L Group (or Lucianic Recension)

    This section pursues the discussion of MSS 22 36
48 51-51s 62 96 311 407 449 763 770 referred to above
(since 449 and 770 are practically identical, henceforth the combined witness of 449-770 will be referred
to as 449'). That these MSS constitute a homogeneous
group (with some qualifications, see below pp. 72-74)

is clear not only from their frequent attestation of Hexaplaric readings, but also and especially on account of their several unique readings. It is of interest, therefore, to inquire more closely concerning their character and provenance.

The method of approach in this section, however, is the exact reverse of that pursued in the discussion of the Hexaplaric recension. There the analysis moved from Origen's known recensional principles to the identification of MSS exhibiting those principles. Here the analysis begins with a description of the characteristic readings of MSS 22 . . . 763 and only at the end considers the question of probable origin. The difference in approach is necessitated by the difference in the kind of historical and MS information--or lack of it--that is available for the two groups /36/.

All MSS of this group are mediaeval cursives containing the writings of the prophetical books only, the earliest (407) from the 9th century, the latest (311) from the 12th century. With the exception of three MSS (51 449-770), they all have this in common in Jer that they follow the Hebrew (and Hexaplaric) internal order and position of the OAN section. MSS 51 and 449' follow the normal Greek order and position of the oracles by placing them in the middle of the book, though 51 is a special case since it repeats these oracles in the Hebrew order at the end of the MS (in our notes the supplemental section is always referred to as 51s, see above, p. 16). The united attestation of all MSS in this group to a particular reading will be subsumed under the symbol L /37/. The material is arranged according to the following outline:

1. Readings Common to O and L
   a. Readings Identical in O and L
   b. Readings Slightly Different in O and L
2. Readings Common to the Minor Greek VSS and L
   a. Readings Identical in the Minor Greek VSS and L
   b. Readings Slightly Different in the Minor Greek VSS and L
3. Readings Unique to L
   a. Additions
      i.   Of Articles
      ii. Of Conjunctions

1. Readings Common to O and L

Below are catalogued those readings which are
attested only in O and L. Usually these readings are
found in identical form in both traditions, but sometimes they appear in a slightly modified or supple-
mented way in L. Most of the examples have been encountered in the discussion of the Hexaplaric recension, but there are also some new ones.

a. Readings Identical in O and L

29:4   τους καταλοιπους (2°)] pr. (add 62) τους αλλο-
        φυλους (+ και 36) ※O L = α΄θ΄ ※Qmg, ο΄ ※86mg
        = MT

29:4   των νησων] και καππαδοκιας O L(※449΄)
        = α΄θ΄ ※Qmg, οι γ΄(καππαδοκας) 86mg = MT

29:8   κυριος] + των δυναμεων O L ※Qmg = ο΄ 86mg
        = MT

29:10   καταλειμμα] καλαμηματα O L = ο΄ 86mg

29:10   ηλθον] + σοι O L = σ΄ 86mg

9:11   δια χειρα] pr. το (om. το O 51-62-311-407-449')
        σπερμα αυτου ❋O L❋Qmg = ο´ ❋86mg

29:13   επιον] pr. πιοντες ❋O L = α´ϑ´ ❋Qmg, οι γ'
        ❋86mg, οι λ´ Syh/mg(πιονται) = MT

29:13   αϑωωμενη] + αϑωωϑηση ❋O L/-51-62-449' /38/
        = ϑ´ ❋86mg = MT

29:14   εις αβατον και εις ονειδισμον] εις αφανισμον
        και εις ονειδισμον και εις αβατον O L = MT;
        cf. pr. ο´ εις αφανισμον 86mg

29:17   καϑελω σε] + φησι(ν) κυριος O L = ο´ 86mg
        = MT

29:20   και τους νεανισκους επ αυτην επιστησατε] και
        τις εκλεκτος προς αυτην επισκεφομαι 88-Syh/txt
        = α´, ο´ 86mg = MT; + και τις εκλεκτος προς
        (επ 62) αυτην επισκεφομαι L (lectio duplex)

29:22   εν ϑαλασση] + ερυϑρα O L = οι γ´, ο´ 86mg
        = MT

b. Readings Slightly Different in O and L

29:1   επι τους αλλοφυλους] pr. ❋ος εγενηϑη λογος
        κυριου προς ιερεμιαν τον προφητην O (tr. ος
        εγ./λογ. κυ. Syh); + ος εγενετο λογος κυριου
        προς ιερεμιαν τον προφητην (+ επι τους αλλο-
        φυλους 51-62-311-449') L

        The change from the aorist passive εγενηϑη to the
aorist middle εγενετο is frequently found in the L
group of MSS. The introduction of an aorist passive
form -ϑην instead of the middle -ομην on deponent verbs
was a feature of the Koine (cf. Thackeray, Grammar, pp.
238-239). According to Mayser (Grammatik der Griechischen Papyri, I.2, 2, p. 157), the passive forms
were used increasingly in the third century B.C. But
the Atticists objected to this form and preferred the
middle (cf. Phrynichus, Eclogae nominum et verborum
Atticorum, ed. Lobeck, p. 108, "ο αττικιζω γενεσϑαι
λεγετω"). The frequent preference in L for the middle
is probably to be explained in terms of this Atticizing
tendency.

29:13   αθωωθης] + οτι πιουσα πιεσαι O; οτι πινουσα
         πιη L; + οτι πινων (πιων Q 26 544; πινοντι 534)
         πιεσαι A Q V 26 46 86 130 233 239 534 544 613

It will be argued below (pp. 85-86) that the
Hexaplaric form οτι πιουσα πιεσαι is a slight
modification of a pre-Origenic addition οτι πινων
πιεσαι. The L reading οτι πινουσα πιη is a further
modification of the Hexaplaric form, the change from
the indicative future πιεσαι to the more stylistic
subjunctive πιη in the translation of the Hebrew
infinitive absolute being especially noteworthy.

29:14   εση εν μεσω αυτης] εση εν μεσω μερη αυτης O;
         εση βοσορ εν μεσω μερους αυτης L

The phrase μερη αυτης in O has been changed in L
to μερους αυτης in order to correct the lack of agreement of case in O. For discussion of the addition of
βοσορ (= MT) in L see below, pp. 66-67.

29:14   εις αιωνα] εις τον αιωνα A Q 49 87 90 91 233
         410 490 538 613 764; εις αιωνας O 51-449';
         εως αιωνος L/-51-449'

The expressions εις αιωνα and εις αιωνας are both
anomalous since in biblical Greek the phrase is almost
invariably found with the article (as in A Q 49 etc.
εις τον αιωνα). However, in the construction with εως
the article is generally omitted. The L text has
adopted this more conventional Greek form.

29:22   ηκουσθη] εξηκουσθη η φωνη αυτης O = MT;
         εξηκουσθη η (om. η L/-51-62-311-407-449') φωνη
         σου L

The reading of the majority of Greek MSS prior to
the addition in O and L of the phrase (η) φωνη αυτης is
και κραυγη σου εν θαλασση ηκουσθη. The addition of the
phrase found in O η φωνη αυτης (= MT) makes no sense at
all in the Greek. However, by changing the pronoun
αυτης to σου, L has effectively put the phrase
in apposition to the previous phrase κραυγη σου, thus
restoring some logic to the Greek sentence.

29:23   οφεται] + ※και επιπτησεται O; αναβησεται και
        επιστησεται (επιπτησεται 51-51s-62-407-449') L;
        cf. MT יעלה וידאה

As noted above (p. 55), the LXX translation
was occasioned by a misreading of ד for ר in MT וידאה.
Origen's addition of και επιπτησεται (originally Symmachus' rendition of וידאה) left יעלה without Greek
equivalent (a lack supplied in L by taking αναβησεται
from α'σ'). Some MSS of the L group, reflecting
Hexaplaric influence (see below, p. 74), retain επιπτησεται, while others have altered επιπτησεται to
επιστησεται, perhaps as a more suitable Greek parallel
for αναβησεται (even though further removed from the
Hebrew) /39/.

It can be seen from the above six examples that
modifications of O readings in L often go against the
Hebrew but always in favour of better Greek grammar and
logic. Conformity to the Hebrew was obviously no
guiding principle in the formation of the L text.

2.   Readings Common to the Minor Greek VSS and L

Sometimes L has gone even further than O in
adopting readings from the Minor Greek VSS. Some
of these are reproduced identically in L, some are
slightly altered.

a.   Readings Identical in the Minor Greek VSS and L

29:2   αλαλαξουσιν] ολολυξουσι (-λυ ζ. 22*-48*) L
        = α' 86mg

29:3   οπλων των ποδων αυτου] οπλων αυτου των δυνατων
        L = ϑ' 86mg Qmg ≠ MT

29:6   εως τινος κοψεις] pr. εως ποτε συστραφησεσθε
        L Syh/mg = σ' 86mg

29:12   ορφανον] ορφανους L = α' Syh/mg, σ', ιω'
        86mg, σ' Ghisler II, p. 861 = MT

29:17   καρδιας] pr. της L = α'σ' 86mg

29:23   οφεται] αναβησεται L = α'σ' 86mg Syh/mg = MT

b.   Readings Slightly Different in the Minor Greek
     VSS and L

29:6   επαρθητι] ησυχασον (-σαι 62) L = MT; cf. α'
       σιωπησον 86mg

In this case L has either replaced Aquila's translation with a synonym, or else has borrowed a reading
from Symmachus not preserved for us. The latter alternative is quite possible since L has already employed a
phrase from Symmachus in v. 6, namely εως ποτε συστραφησεσθε, see p. 65 above). ησυχαζω is the common LXX
translation of שקט, the Hebrew word used here.

29:12   υπολειπεσθαι] pr. ο λεγων L; cf. σ' pr. ος
        ερει 86mg

Symmachus perhaps read ואן אמר instead of MT
ואיננו and thus translated και ουκ εστιν ος ερει. This
has been modified in L to και ουκ εστιν ο λεγων. In
both cases the new phrase has the effect of making
v. 12 a direct quote, contrary to its function in MT.

29:12   ινα ζησηται και εγω ζησομαι] ινα σωθωσι(ν) και
        εγω αυτους διασωσω L Syh/mg; cf. ιω' εγω γαρ
        αυτους διασωσω 86mg; σ' εγω διασωσω 86mg

The phrase ινα ζησηται και εγω ζησομαι is a double
reading for MT אני אחיה (see below, pp. 86, 138-39). L
has taken over, with a slight alteration, the translation of ιω' /40/. With the addition of αυτους, the
new translation makes explicit what is probably implicit
in the Hebrew אחיה; it also makes for better Greek.

29:14   εση εν μεσω αυτης] εση εν μεσω μερη αυτης O;
        εση βοσορ εν μεσω μερους αυτης L; cf. οι γ'
        εσται βοσορα 86mg Syh/mg(sub οι λ')

The phrase εν μεσω μερη(O)/μερους(L) constitutes a double reading in O and L for MT בצרה (see
above, pp. 47f., 53). The addition of βοσορ (= MT) in

L constitutes a triple reading in that group. The
spelling has been slightly altered (Hellenized) in
comparison with The Three.

29:21   συμφησθωσι] + αυτων L 86mg;   cf. σ΄ συμφησωσιν
        αυτους 86mg;   + ※αυτω Qmg

The addition of the pronoun is in conformity with
the Hebrew plural suffix ‏סם‎- of ‏יסחבום‎.

The heavy reliance of L upon the Minor Greek VSS
is quite evident in the above examples. Any approximation to the Hebrew in the new variants comes merely as
a by-product of the use made of these VSS rather than
as a result of independent scrutiny of the Hebrew on
the part of L. Not infrequently L chooses a reading
that moves away from MT. The conclusion reached in the
previous subsection, namely that the Hebrew text was
not a determining factor in the L revision, is confirmed again. By contrast, a smoother and more coherent Greek style was clearly an important factor in the
choice of new readings.

3.   Readings Unique to L

In addition to the readings in L which are modifications of O or the Minor Greek VSS, this group (or
members of it) also attests several other readings
entirely without support elsewhere in the Greek MS
collection.

a.   Additions

     i.   Of Articles

     9:5   Εναχειμ] pr. των L

     29:11 δια χειρα] pr. (※O ※Qmg) σπερμα (το σμερμα
            Qmg L/-51-62-311-407-449') αυτου O L Qmg

     29:15 κυριου] pr. του L/-51-449'

     29:21 βουλην] pr. την L

     29:23 επ οχυρωματα] επι τα οχ. L

ii. Of Conjunctions

29:3   απο (2°)] pr. και L ≠ MT

29:17 ιταμια] και η ατιμια L/-51-62-407-449' ≠ MT

29:20 εκδιωξω] και διωξω L/-51-62-407-449' ≠ MT

iii. Of Pronouns

29:10 επιθησουσι] + σοι L Qmg ≠ MT

29:12 χηραι] αι χηραι (χειρες 62-407) σου = MT

iv. Of Prepositional Phrases

29:15 αναστητε εις πολεμον] + επ αυτην L Syh/mg
       ≠ MT

b.   Omissions

29:8   ωχετο σοφια αυτων] om. L/-51-407-449'

c.   Word Substitutions

29:8   βουλη] συμβουλη L/-51-62-311-407-449'

29:15 εις αυτην] επ αυτην L/-62-407   Syh/mg = MT;
       εν αυτη 62;   om. 407

29:15 ιταμια] η ατιμια L/-51-62-407-449' ≠ MT

29:15 οτι ταχυ εκδιωξω] οτι ταχυς και διωξω L/-51-62
       -407-449'

d.   Form Substitutions

29:12 πεποιθασιν] πεποιθετωσαν 51-51s-62-407-449'

29:17 συνελαβεν] -βον 22*-48-407-763 ≠ MT

29:18 επ αυτην] επ αυτη 51-311-407-449'

The above examples confirm yet again the conclusions of the previous two sections, namely that
readings unique to L bear no consistent relationship to
the MT. In fact, where judgements can be made, they
appear to go against MT more frequently than they
approximate MT. On the other hand, the same readings
do manifest a definite interest in the improvement of
Greek style and sense. A good example of the latter is
v. 17 ιταμια καρδιας] και η ατιμια της καρδιας. In
this case, the interchange of one letter, α for ι,
provides the phrase with a familiar and meaningful word
in the context instead of a rare word, unattested
outside Jer and of uncertain meaning. The change in
29:20 from οτι ταχυ εκδιωξω to οτι ταχυς· και διωξω may
also have been motivated by a desire to improve on the
Greek, giving the sense "for (he is) swift, and I will
chase them from her," instead of "for I will quickly
drive them from her." However, the change could also
be explained as a scribal correction of a faulty uncial
MS /41/.

4.   Readings of L Supported by Chrysostom and Theodoret

The L Group readings are most frequently supported
by the Antiochean Fathers Chrysostom (d. 407) and
Theodoret (d. 466). This may be clearly seen from the
following examples.

a.   Readings Identical in O and L Supported by Chrysostom and Theodoret

29:4   τους καταλοιπους] pr. (add. 62; ※O) τους
          αλλοφυλους O L Chr. Tht.

29:4   των νησων] + και καππαδοκιας O L Chr. Tht.

29:5   οι καταλοιποι] τα λοιπα O L 86mg Chr. Tht.

29:11   ωλοντο] ωλετο O L Qc 86mg 106 130 Tht.

29:11   δια χειρα] pr. (※O Qmg) (το) σπερμα αυτου O L
          Qmg Tht.

29:13   επιον] pr. (※O) πιοντες O L Tht.

29:14   εις αβατον και εις ονειδισμον] εις αφανισμον
          και εις ονειδισμον και εις αβατον O L Tht.

29:17   σου] + ταυτα 88(sub ※) L Syh/mg Tht.

29:17   τρυμαλιας] εν τρυμαλιαις 88 L/-51-449' Syh/mg
          Tht.

29:17   καθελω σε] + φησι(ν) κυριος O L Tht.(λεγει κ.)

29:20   ωσπερ (1°)] ως O L Chr.

    Although the above readings are of Hexaplaric
origin (except for the addition of ταυτα and the variant εν τρυμαλιαις in v. 17 which are probably original
with L), they have nevertheless been incorporated as an
integral part of the L text.

b.   L Modifications of O Readings Supported by
      Chrysostom and Theodoret

29:13   αθωωθης] + οτι πιουσα πιεσαι O; οτι πινουσα
          πιη L Tht.

29:14   εση εν μεσω αυτης] εση εν μεσω μερη αυτης O;
          εση βοσορ εν μεσω μερους αυτης L Chr. Tht.

29:14   εις αιωνα] εις αιωνας O 51-449'; εως αιωνος
          L/-51-449' Tht.(εως του αιωνος)

    The above readings are of special interest since
they show that when O and L part company, Chr./Tht. go
with L.

c.   L Readings Derived from the Minor Greek VSS
      Supported by Chrysostom and Theodoret

29:6   εως] pr. εως ποτε συστραφησεσθε L Syh/mg Tht.
          = σ´ 86mg

29:6   επαρθητι] ησυχασον (-σαι 62) L Tht./p   /42/

29:12   υπολειπεσθαι] pr. ο λεγων L Tht.(ο ελεων Tht./p)

29:12   ορφανον] -ανους L Tht.

29:12   ινα ζησηται και εγω ζησομαι] ινα σωθωσι(ν) και
        εγω αυτους διασωσω L Syh/mg Tht.

29:17   καρδιας] pr. της L Tht.

d.   Readings Unique to L Supported by Chrysostom and
     Theodoret

29:5   Ενακειμ] pr. των L Chr. Tht.

29:8   om. ωχετο σοφια αυτων L/-51-407-449' Tht.(vid.)

29:10   επιθησουσιν] + σοι L Qmg Tht./p

29:12   χηραι] αι χηραι (χειρες 62 407) σου L Tht.

29:12   πεποιθασιν] πεποιθετωσαν 51-51 s-62-407-449'
        Tht.

29:15   εις αυτην] επ αυτην L/-62-407   Syh/mg Tht.

29:15   πολεμον] + επ αυτην L Syh/mg Tht.

29:17   ιταμια] και (om. και 311) η ατιμια L/-51-62-407
        -449' Tht.

29:17   συνελαβεν] -βον 22*-48-407-763 Tht./p

29:21   βουλην] pr. την L Tht.

     As can be seen, the agreements between L and
Chr./Tht. are striking and consistent. The significance of these agreements for identifying the L text
are discussed below, pp. 75f. /43/.

5.   Readings of L Supported by Anonymous Readings in
     Qmg, 86mg, Syh/mg

     In addition to the clearly identified readings of
the Minor Greek VSS such as those of Aquila, Symmachus
and Theodotion, the margins of Q, 86, and Syh also
contain a number of anonymous readings. Many of
these agree with the L group and were probably taken
from L MSS. Sometimes the anonymous marginal readings
support a variant attested in both the O and L groups,

in which case it is difficult to determine whether O or
L was the original source of the reading; but the
number of unique L readings supported by these margins,
especially Syh/mg, indicate that the L text was by no
means the least important of these sources.

a.   Readings of L Supported by Qmg

29:10   επιθησουσι] + σοι L Qmg ≠ MT

29:11   δια χειρα] pr. (※Qmg) σπερμα (το σπερμα
         L/-51-63-311-407-449' Qmg) αυτου O L Qmg

b.   Readings of L Supported by 86mg

29:5   οι καταλοιποι] τα λοιπα 88(-Syh) L 86mg

29:21   συμφησθωσιν] + αυτων L 86mg (cf. + ※αυτω Qmg)

c.   Readings of L Supported by Syh/mg

29:6   εως τινος κοφεις] pr. εως ποτε συστραφησεσθε
         L Syh/mg

29:12   ινα ζησηται και εγω ζησομαι] ινα σωθωσιν και
         εγω αυτους διασωσω L Syh/mg

29:15   εις αυτην] + επ αυτην L/-62-407   Syh/mg; εν
         αυτη 62;   om. 407

29:15   πολεμον] + επ αυτην L Syh/mg

29:17   σοι] + ταυτα 88(sub ※) L Syh/mg

29:17   τρυμαλιας] εν τρυμαλιαις 88 L/-51-449   Syh/mg

29:22   ηκουσθη] εξηκουσθη η φωνη αυτης O;
         φωνη σου L Syh/mg

6.   Subdivisions Within L

     Our documentation of the L group in Jer 29 has
revealed several occasions where a few MSS have

defaulted from supporting the reading of the group.
Among these defaulters, 51-449' form a special pair.

29:3   οπλων των ποδων αυτου] + των δυνατων 51-449';
        οπλων αυτου των δυνατων L/-51-449'; οπλων των
        δυνατων αυτου O

29:14   εις αιωνα] εις αιωνας O 51-449'; εως αιωνος
        L/-51-449'

29:15   κυριου] pr. του L/-51-449'

29:17] παιγνια] + της καρδιας 51-449'

29:17   τρυμαλιας] εν τρυμαλιαις 88 L/-51-449'   Syh/mg

        This pair of MSS differs from the rest of the L
group in another important aspect as well, in that they
follow the usual LXX position and internal order of the
OAN section in the middle of the book (to be contrasted
with 51s which is a repeat of the OAN section at the
end of the MS according to the MT internal order of the
oracles).

        Frequently 51-449' are joined by a few other
members of the larger group, especially 62, 407 and
sometimes 311.

29:1   επι τους αλλοφυλους] + ος εγενετο λογος κυριου
        προς ιερεμιαν τον προφητην (+ επι τους αλλ. 51-
        62-311-449') προ του παταξαι φαραω την γαζαν L

29:8   βουλη] συμβουλη L/-51-62-311-407-449'

29:8   ωχετο σοφια αυτων] om. L/-51-407-449'

29:8   σοφια] pr. η 51-407-449'   239

29:9   βαθυνατε] + εαυτοις 36-51-449'   et al.

29:11   ωλοντο] ωλετο σπερμα (το σπερμα L/-51-62-311
        -407-449') αυτου O L

29:12   πεποιθασιν] πεποιθετωσαν 51-51s-62-407-449'

29:13   αθωωμενη] + αθωωθηση Ο L/-51-62-449'

29:17   ιταμια] και (om. και 311) η ατιμια L/-51-62-407
        -449'

29:18   επ αυτην] επ αυτη 51-311-407-449'

29:20   ταχυ εκδιωξω] ταχυς και διωξω L/-51-62-407-449'

29:21   συμφησθωσι] συνφηφισθωσι 51-62(συμφι.)-311-407
        -449'   et al.

29:23   ηκουσθη] εξηκουσθη φωνη (pr. η 51-62-311-407
        -449' = O) σου L

29:23   οφεται] αναβησεται και επιστησεται (επιπτησεται
        51-51s-62-407-449' = O) L

        The above readings show that when 51-62(-311)-407
-449' depart from the L group they join either the common LXX reading (e.g. 29:8 βουλη) or the corresponding
O reading (e.g. 29:14 εις αιωνας O 51-449'; 29:11 om.
το O 51-62-311-407-449'; 29:23 η φωνη O 51-62-311-407
-449'). On a few occasions they attest a new reading
altogether (e.g. 29:17 της καρδιας 51-449'; 29:18 επ
αυτη 51-311-407-449'). Such facts suggest that these
particular L MSS have undergone a late revision in
favour of the common LXX text and the Hexaplaric recension. With regard to 51 and 51s it is interesting to
note that it is regularly 51 that departs from the main
group whereas 51s generally stays with it.

7.   Significance of the Data

        It is clear on the basis of the foregoing analysis
that the special readings associated with the L text
are not of the type that "just happen" in MS transmission. Rather they are of the kind that must have
originated in a deliberate re-working of the Greek
text. Underlying this work of revision can be discerned certain guiding principles. One of these was to
revise in favour of a more acceptable and coherent
Greek; another was a preference for certain Atticistic
rather than Hellenistic forms; yet a third principle,
judging by the several double readings present /44/ and

the almost total lack of any omissions /45/, was to
preserve and combine as much as possible of the extant
textual heritage.

As to method, the evidence shows that the text was
created out of a variety of sources, including the
Hexaplaric recension, the Minor Greek VSS and independent alterations. Conspicuous by its absence in this
list of sources is the Hebrew text, which seems to have
played no role at all in the work of revision. What we
have, therefore, is a situation the exact reverse of the
Hexaplaric recension. There the concern was to produce
a text approximating the Hebrew as closely as possible
(at least quantitatively) without much regard to Greek
syntax or coherence, and to eliminate (or at least call
attention to) all that was not in agreement with the
Hebrew. In the case of the L group, the editorial
concern is rather for Greek readability with no eye to
the Hebrew and with as much as possible of the textual
tradition included. But even though the principles of
revision are drastically different, it is obvious that
there is as much deliberate intervention in the formation of the one text as in the other. For this reason
we are amply justified and even compelled to call the L
group a "recension."

But where did this recension originate? Helpful
clues in localizing a text are often obtained through a
correlation with citations of the Church Fathers. When
this criterion is applied to Jer it is found--as we
have seen above--that the Antiochean Fathers Chrysostom
and Theodoret quote from a text almost identical to L.
This in turn means that the L recension must have circulated in those areas where Chrysostom and Theodoret
lived, i.e., in and around Antioch and Constantinople.

These observations have implications for views
regarding the authorship of the L recension. In the
absence of explicit information in the L MSS themselves, conclusions on this subject have to be inferential and tentative, but a key witness in the case is
obviously Jerome who, in his famous reference to the
trifaria varietas of texts which flourished in the
Eastern Mediterranean Church of his day, affirms that
the rendering which held the field in the area from
Constantinople to Antioch was that of "Lucian the mar-
tyr" /46/. It is assumed that this Lucian is the same

Lucian otherwise known as Lucian of Antioch or Lucian
of Samosata (his birthplace), a presbyter and leading
exponent of the Antiochean exegetical school, martyred
under Maximin in 311/312. Since the late 19th century,
Jerome's statement has formed the cornerstone of Lucian
Forschung /47/, but recently the traditional connection
between Lucian and the text associated with his name
has been put in question. In a vigorous challenge, D.
Barthélemy has denied that the "Lucianic recension" is
either a recension or Lucianic /48/. To settle the
controversy lies beyond the scope of this study, though
it does seem that Barthélemy is unnecessarily skeptical
of the historical tradition surrounding Lucian (he
calls it a myth). In the absence of any definitive
evidence to the contrary, therefore, we will continue
to speak of the L text as "Lucianic" and at least for
Jer we must insist on calling it a "recension."

But whether the text be called "Lucianic,"
"Antiochian" (G.F. Moore), "Syrian" (M.L. Margolis) or
anything else, what is of real importance to the text
critic is the realization that the special readings
transmitted by this text are the result of a revision
generally introduced from late sources /49/. Such
readings are therefore secondary and can have no place
in a restored LXX archetype.

C.   The C Group (or Catena Text)

There is a third group of MSS attesting the text
of Jer-LXX that closely hang together and point to
a common source. These are the Catena MSS 49 87 90 91
490 764 /50/, so called because of the "chains" of
patristic commentaries strung together in their margins.
This type of copying was practiced in the Byzantine
church in the declining phase of the patristic period
(6th to 9th centuries), when scholarly activity was
expended on the preservation of the old rather than in
the creation of new theological learning. Although the
preservation of the writings of the Greek Fathers was
an invaluable service to future generations and is in
itself an important object of study, our present
concern is not so much with the catena commentaries as
with the biblical text around which the commentaries
were placed.

Of the six Catena MSS collated for Jer, four (49 87 90 91) are of the type that M. Faulhaber has called "Rahmen catene," where the patristic passages form a crowded but neat frame around the continuous biblical text (Die Propheten-Catenen nach römischen Handschriften, IV, Freiburg, 1889, p. 2, n. 2). The other two MSS (490 764) contain the same type of biblical text, but with the patristic passages omitted from the margins. Apart from 764, these MSS all come from the 10th or 11th centuries; 764 is later and hails from the 13th to 14th centuries.

The Catena text draws its readings from various sources. This can be seen by the way it shares readings with diverse textual traditions and by the relative lack of any new readings of its own. The united witness of this group of MSS is conveniently represented by the symbol C. The material will be surveyed under the following headings:

1. Readings in Common with O/L
2. Readings in Common with Various Minuscules
3. Readings in Common with Various Uncials
   a. In Common with A
   b. In Common with B-S
   c. In Common with Q-V
   d. In Common with Combinations of Uncials
4. Subdivisions Within C
5. Significance of the Data

1.   Readings in Common with O/L

29:7   επι (2°)] pr. και Syh L C 46 410 534 613 ≠ MT

29:9   ηπατηθη] επατηθη Syh C/-49-90-764 ≠ MT

29:19   κατοικησει] -ση O L C 46 86 106 410 534 544

29:20   Αιθαμ] αιμαθ 36c 613 O C ≠ MT

2.   Readings in Common with Various Minuscules

29:6   αναπαυσαι] pr. και C 613 ≠ MT

29:8   τη ιδουμαια] ιουδαια C/-87-91-490   534 ≠ MT

29:11   αυτου (2°)] om. C 106 ≠ MT

29:15   απεστειλεν] εξαπ. C/-87-91-490) 534 613

29:17   υψωσεν] -σας C 106 = MT

29:22   κραυγη] pr. η C 106 239 410 613 ≠ MT

3.   Readings in Common with Various Uncials

    a.   In Common with A

    29:4   τους (2°)] τας A C 86 410

    29:10   ως] ωσπερ A C 106 613

    29:12   χηραι] pr. αι A C 106 233 239 410 613 ≠ MT

    29:13   αθωωθης] + οτι πινων πιεσαι A C 46 86 130
              233 239 613 = MT

    29:16   ευκαταφρονητον] pr. και A C O 239 410 613
              ≠ MT

    b.   In Common with B-S

    29:10   ηλθον B-S C Qc 106 410 538 613] + σοι rel.
              = MT

    29:10   οι B-S C Qc O L 26 106 233 239 410 538
              613] om. rel. = MT

    29:10   καταλειμμα B-S C 26 106 239 410 534 613]
              καταλειμματα A Q-V 46 86 130 233 538 544
              710; καλαμηματα O L

    29:16   μικρον B-S C 26 46 106 410 538] pr. ιδου A
              Q-V 86 130 233 239 534 544 613 710 O L/-62
              = MT

    c.   In Common with Q-V

    29:18   συριει] εκστησεται (pr. συριει C) και
              συριει επι παση τη πληγη (πασαν την πληγην
              Q 239 613) αυτης Q-V C O L 26 46 86 233
              239 534 544 613 710 = MT

29:21   αυτους Q-V C 46 86 233 239 534 544 613 710
        = MT] αυτην B-S* 106 130 410 538; αυτης Sc
        26; αυτη A

d. In Common with Combinations of Uncials

29:9   βαθυνατε] + εαυτοις A Q C

29:9   επ (2°) B Q S C] om. A V

29:10   χειρα] -ας A Q S C

29:12   και εγω ζησομαι A B S C] om. Q-V

29:13   οις A B S C] pr. ιδου Q-V

29:14   καταρασιν] καταραν A S V C

29:14   αιωνα] pr. τον A Q C

29:22   οτι A B S C] om. Q-V

29:22   και A B S C] om. Q-V

29:22   εν θαλασση A Q V C] θαλασσης ουκ B-S

The above documentation of C readings in combination with uncial readings shows that C is not very
loyal in any of its attachments. However, it may be
observed that in section d, in all examples except one
(29:9 επ), C goes with the combination of uncials in
which A is to be found, suggesting a slight favouritism
for the A text (cf. Ziegler, Ieremias, p. 96).

4. Subdivisions Within C

Although on the whole the Catena MSS form a very
closely knit group, on occasion they subdivide into two
groups: 87-91-490 and 49-90-764.

29:2   απαντες 87-91-490] παντες 49-90-764

29:5   Ενακειμ 49-90-764] ενακιμ 87-91-490

29:8   ιδουμαια 87-91-490] ιουδαια 49-90*-764

29:9   ηπατηθη 49-90-764] επατηθη 87-91-490

29:15   απεστειλε 87-91c-490] εξαπεστειλε(ν) 49-90-764

MSS 91-490 are especially closely linked:

29:9   αυτον (2°)] αυτω 91-490

29:10   καταλειφουσι(ν)] καταλιψ. 91-490

29:10   καταλειμμα] -λιμμα 91-490-(764)

29:13   αθωωθης] αθοωθης 91-490

29:14   εις (2°)] om. 91-490

     Certain orthographic features such as the pre-
ference for -ι- as opposed to -ει- forms in (87)-91-490
suggests that this is the earlier of the two subdivisions, hence the "Hauptgruppe" (cf. Ziegler, Ieremias,
p. 93).

5.   Significance of the Data

     The general cohesion of the Catena MSS is an
established fact, but how are we to describe the nature
of the text and how has it come about? To be sure, we
cannot call it a recension in the sense that the Hexaplaric and Lucianic groups are recensions. It is practically impossible to discern in its readings any consistent editorial policy. Approximation to the Hebrew
was certainly no factor in the formation of the text;
indeed, most of its readings go contrary to the Hebrew.
A slight preference for more stylistic Greek is discernible, but not nearly on the same scale as in the
Lucianic recension.

     At the same time, it is equally clear that the
text presupposes some form of editorial intervention.
We have seen that in our test passage of Jer 29 all of
its readings are attested in earlier MSS and family
groupings. This suggests that the text was constructed
as a synthesis of existing textual traditions. As such
it is the "mixed text" par excellence.

Although this form of the Greek OT no doubt served the needs of the time and may even have become a type of textus receptus in the Greek mediaeval church, its shifting loyalties make it almost impossible to classify and render it practically valueless in our search for the earliest recoverable text form of the LXX of Jer.

D.   The Q Group

Turning from the Hexaplaric, Lucianic and Catena groups, the next three sections will be organized around the five uncial codices which contain the text of Jer. These divide into three groups: Q-V, A, and B-S. Around each there clusters, in turn, different sets of more less faithful minuscules.

By the term "The Q Group" is meant that group of MSS of which it can be said that the 6th century Codex Marchalianus (Q) stands as the chief representative, even though that codex itself may not always support the reading of the group. In the previous sections we have often documented readings from the Minor Greek VSS found in the margins of Q; here we examine the text proper of Q. Frequently allied with Q is the 8th century Codex Venedig (V), hence the designation Q-V. On a number of occasions Codex Alexandrinus (A), with or without its congeners 106-410, joins Q-V against the remaining two uncials, but other considerations (see next section, E) go to show that A does not properly belong to the Q group.

Of the minuscules, the following associate themselves more or less regularly with Q: 26 46 86 233 534 544 613 710 (since 86 and 710 are almost identical, henceforth 86' = 86-710). MSS 130, 233 and 538 also join the group on occasion. The minuscules of the Q group range in date from as early as the 9th to 10th centuries (86), to as late as the 13th to 14th centuries (46, 613).

The material will be dealt with according to the following outline:

1. Readings of Q-V+ /51/
2. Readings of Q-V+ A
3. Readings of V+
4. Significance of the Data

1.   Readings of Q-V /52/

29:10   ως] ωσπερ A 106 410 613; ωσει Q-V-26-46-86'-130
        -233-239-534-538-544 O L

29:12   και εγω ζησομαι] om. Q-V-26-46-86'-130-233-534
        -544 O

29:13   οις] pr. ιδου Q-V-26-46-86'-130-233-239-534
        -544-613 O L = MT

29:18   συριει] εκστησεται και συριει επι παση τη πληγη
        (πασαν την πληγην Q-239-613) αυτης Q-V-26-46
        -86'-233-239-534-544-613 O L = MT

29:21   επ αυτους Q-V-46-86'-233-239-534-544-613 O L
        = MT] επ αυτην B-S*; επ αυτη A

29:22   οτι] om. Q-V-26-46-86'-233-534-544 O L = MT

29:22   και] om. Q-V-26-46-86'-130-233-534-544 O L = MT

        The above examples demonstrate the considerable
cohesion that exists among the members of the group Q-
V-26-46-86'(-130)-233(-239)-534-544-(613). It is clear
that they must reflect some common background. Also of
significance is the fact that each of the above readings is supported by O/L (L is missing once, 29:12)
and, where a judgement can be made, each constitutes
an approximation to MT. The implications of this will
be discussed below in subdivision 4.

2.   Readings of Q-V+ A

29:3   εφ] επι Q-V-26-46-86'-233-239-534-544-538-613
        A 106 410 O L

29:9   επ αυτον (2°)] om. επ V-86'-239-534-538-544 A
        O L/-36 = MT

29:10   ηλθον] + σοι Q-V-26-46-86'-130-233-239-534-544
        A O L = MT

29:10   οι] om. Q-V-46-86'-130-534-544   A Syh = MT

29:10   καταλειμμα] καταλ(ε)ιμματα Q-V-46-86'-130-233
        -538-544   A; καλαμημματα O L

29:11   γειτονος] pr. και Q-V-26-46-86'-233-239-534-538
        -613   A 106 410 O L = MT

29:11   γειτονος μου] γ. αυτου Q-V-26-46-86'-233-239
        -534-538-613   A 106   O L = MT

29:13   λεγει Q-V-26-46-86'-130-233-239-534-544-613
        A 106 410   O L] ειπεν B-S 538

29:13   αθωωθης] + οτι πινων (πιων Q-26-544; πινοντι
        534; πιουσα O) πιεσαι Q-V-26-46-86'-233-239
        -534-544-613 A O = MT; + οτι πινουσα πιη L = MT

29:16   μικρον] pr. ιδου Q-V-86'-130-233-239-534-544
        -613 A L/-62; pr. οτι (οτι sub ※ Syh)
        O 62 = MT

29:17   υψωσεν·] εαν υψωσης (-σεις A 26 239 86mg) Q-V
        -26-46-86'-130-233-239-534-544-613   A 106   O L

29:22   εφοβηθη] εσ(ε)ισθη Q-V-26-46-86'-130-233-239
        -239-534-544-613   A 106 410   O L = MT

29:22   κραυγη σου εν θαλασση Q-V-26-46-86'-130-233
        -239-534-538-544-613   A 106 410   O L] κραυγη
        θαλασσης ουκ B-S

As can be observed from the above examples, when A
joins Q-V the same general pattern of O/L support and
approximation to MT prevails.

3.   Readings of V+

Twice in our chapter a similar pattern holds true
even when V is the sole uncial in the group:

29:19   ωσπερ] ως V-26-46-86'-233-534-544   O L

29:22   ηκουσθη] εξηκουσθη V-26-46-544   O L

4. Significance of the Data

The readings of the Q group (often jointed by A)
highlighted above have revealed a fairly consistent
pattern of approximation to MT, together with regular
support from the Hexaplaric and Lucianic recensions.
Considering what is already known about the proclivity
of the O (sometimes L) text to approximate the Hebrew,
one might be tempted at first sight to attribute most
of the above readings to the influence of that tradition on Q. But this theory, plausible as it might
appear, does not stand up to scrutiny.

It is remarkable, first of all, that even though
the readings in this section are generally supported by
O/L, none of these is a Hexaplaric reading supported by
an Origenic sign in some other MS or by a reading of
one of the Minor Greek VSS found in the margins of Q,
86 or Syh. Conversely, the confirmed Hexaplaric readings (i.e. those incorporated by Origen from the Minor
Greek VSS--see section A above, pp. 48ff.), are nowhere
supported by the Q group. Therefore, if we wish to say
that the above readings originated with the Hexaplaric
/Lucianic recensions and were adopted from there by the
Q text, then we must admit that the creators of the
latter text proceeded in a strange way indeed. For in
the process of adopting the alleged "Hexaplaric" readings listed above for which we have found no external
Hexaplaric support, they just as studiously avoided
adopting all readings which elsewhere we have found to
possess such external support. But this would be a
bizarre procedure and it is quite absurd to think that
anything like it should ever have happened, especially
considering the high esteem in which the Hexaplaric
text was held in the early centuries.

It is plain, therefore, that we must look for
another explanation. The most likely is that the
readings jointly attested by the Q and O/L texts stem
from a common source, and that this common source must
have been a pre-Hexaplaric revision of the Greek text
towards the Hebrew /53/. The MSS embodying this revision were known to Origen and used by him. In fact,
the evidence suggests that the proto-Q text became

Origen's Greek <u>Vorlage</u>, probably chosen deliberately because it most closely approximated the Hebrew. This explains why the readings common to Q and the O/L recensions are nowhere marked with Hexaplaric signs: they were adopted by Origen <u>from existent MSS</u> and were not introduced by him. A pair of examples will help to clarify the difference in attestation between a typical Q reading and a genuine Hexaplaric reading:

29:4   τους καταλοιπους (2°)] pr. (※O) τους αλλο-
           φυλους O L = α´ϑ´ Qmg, ο´ 86mg = MT

29:8   κυριος] + (※Qmg) των δυναμεων O L Qmg
           = ο´ 86mg = MT

29:13   αϑωωϑης] + οτι πινων (πιων Q-26-544;
           πινοντι 534) πιεσαι A Q-V-26-46-86'-233
           -239-534-613 = MT; + οτι πιουσα πιεσαι O
           = MT; + οτι πινουσα πιη L = MT

29:18   συριει] εκστησεται και συριει επι παση τη
           πληγη (πασαν την πληγην Q-239-613) αυτης
           Q-V-26-46-86'-233-239-534-544-613 O L = MT

In the first two examples both additions enjoy unequivocal Hexaplaric support. Both are asterized and both constitute approximations to MT. Their Hexaplaric origin is beyond question. They were taken over verbatim in the Lucianic recension.

In the second pair of readings neither addition is asterized nor supported by a Hexaplaric symbol; instead, each reading is supported by O/L and the Q group. The difference in attestation is to be explained as follows: the second pair of readings already existed at the time of Origen's revision and was simply incorporated by him unmarked in his LXX column, whereas the first pair of readings was not in existence at the time of Origen's work and was introduced by him.

In the reading from v. 13 we can see how an original Q reading has been taken over by the O and L recensions, but in slightly modified forms. The pre-Hexaplaric addition probably read οτι πινων πιεσαι (with scribal variants of πιων and πινοντι in some MSS). Origen, however, changed the masculine participle πινων to the feminine πιουσα in conformity with

the preceding participle αθωωμενη. Later still, the
Lucianic text changed Origen's 2nd aorist feminine
participle to the present feminine participle πινουσα
and altered the indicative πιεσαι to the subjunctive
πιη.

Other modifications seem to have taken place in
the following two examples:

29:10　　καταλειμμα] καταλ(ε)ιμματα A Q-V-46-86'
　　　　　-130-233-538-544; καλαμηματα　O L

29:16　　μικρον] pr. ιδου A　Q-V-86'-130-233-239
　　　　　-534-544-613　L/-62;　pr. οτι (οτι sub ※
　　　　　Syh) ιδου O 62 = MT

It is strange that in the second example the L
text does not support O in the addition of οτι (except
for 62 which does have it). This failure to support O
may be due to οτι being a post-Hexaplaric approximation
to the Hebrew and hence not present in L's Hexaplaric
Vorlage, or else to the reluctance of L to transcribe
such unidiomatic Greek as οτι ιδου.

In 29:12 we have the interesting case where the Q
text (followed by O) has eliminated a double reading in
the Old Greek (see discussion below Ch. III, pp. 138-39):

29:12　　ινα ζησηται και εγω ζησομαι] om. και εγω
　　　　　ζησομαι Q-V-26-46-86'-130-233-534-544 O

The evidence of this section also helps us to formulate a rule for determining whether approximations to
MT unsupported by either critical signs or Hexaplaric
symbols derive from Origen or not (see discussion
above, pp. 59-60). There are two criteria: internal
character and external attestation. If an unmarked
reading is to be deemed Hexaplaric its internal character must first be such as to harmonize with Origen's
known text critical principles. Secondly, it must be
attested only within the limits of O/L (possibly in
company with a few straying minuscules), but not by O/L
plus the Q group. If the reading is attested unmarked
by O/L and the Q text, it probably derives from the
pre-Hexaplaric revision /54/. Again two examples will
explain the rule:

29:14   εις αβατον και εις ονειδισμον] tr. αβατον
         /ονειδισμον O L = MT

29:22   ηκουσθη] εξηκουσθη η φωνη αυτης (σου L
         ≠ MT) O L = MT

The two variant readings above constitute correct
approximations to MT. However, they are nowhere supported by external Hexaplaric signs or symbols. Yet
they must derive from Origen because they are attested
only within the limits of O/L. Had they also been
attested by the Q text they would undoubtedly have
derived from that particular pre-Hexaplaric revision.

If we now wish to inquire more closely into the
origins of the Q text, there is regrettably very little
hard data available on the subject. However, it is
necessary to consider briefly the not infrequently
mooted proposition that the Q text represents the Hesychian recension, the third text mentioned by Jerome in
his Preface to Chronicles: "Alexandria et Aegyptus in
Septuaginta suis Hesycium laudat auctorem." According
to a widespread opinion, this Hesychius is to be identified with the Egyptian bishop of the same name mentioned by Eusebius and said to have been martyred along
with Phileas, Pachymius and Theodorus, presumably during the Diocletian persecution, c. 311 (HE VIII, 13.7).

The thesis that the Q text contains the Hesychian
recension was suggested as early as 1890 by the Italian
scholar Ceriani, following the same line of approach as
that employed in his identification of the Lucianic
recension. He argued that there existed a close affinity between Q and the text presupposed by the Egyptian
daughter VSS and the citations of Cyril of Alexandria
(d. 444) /55/. Since then the identification has been
restated several times /56/.

But what is the evidence for this identification
in Jer? As for the Egyptian versions, these definitely
do not support Q. The Arabic consistently goes with
the A text, whereas the Bohairic and Sahidic follow B.
With regard to the citations of Cyril, these are notoriously erratic and cannot be classified with any text
type of Jer. The sole example in Jer 29 is typical:

29:2   υδατα αναβαινει] δη υδατα ερχεται Cyr.

But even more damaging to the Hesychian theory—at
least to the Hesychius of popular identification—is
the chronological factor. The traditional Hesychius is
post-Origen, whereas the revision behind Q is unques-
tionably pre-Origen. Of course, the link between the
Hesychius of Jerome and the one mentioned by Eusebius
is extremely tenuous at best and may not be the correct
identification at all. Even so, we still do not have
any positive reason for associating Jerome's Hesychius
with our Q text /57/.

Having said this, however, we may still point out
the likely Egyptian provenance of the Q text. There
are at least three indicators which favour this view.
First, there is the consideration that since the text
was used by Origen it is likely to have circulated in
Egypt prior to his time. Secondly, it is known that
Codex Marchalianus, the chief representative of the Q
group, was copied in Egypt /58/. Thirdly, whenever
there is a split in the evidence, the citations of the
Egyptian commentator Olympiodorus (d. 510) often line
up with Q. The following are the relevant examples
from Jer 29:

29:9   βαθυνατε] + εαυτοις A 106 410   Q-86'-233
        -239-538-613   36-51-449   Olymp.

29:9   επ αυτον (1°)] om. επ Q 62 Olymp.

29:16   μικρον] pr. ιδου A Q-V-86'-130-233-239-534
        -544-613   L/-62   Olymp.

29:19   κατοικησει] ενοικησει(-ση) B-S Q-130-239
        -538-613 Olymp.

The above data tend to confirm the view that the Q text
was "at home" in Egypt, and may even have been produced
there. But further than saying that it probably represents a very early Egyptian attempt to bring the Greek
in line with the Hebrew, we may not go. Whether this
reworking of the LXX text should be styled a "recension" is also an open question. Because so little is
otherwise known of its background and guiding principles, we prefer to call it simply a "revision" rather
than a full-fledged "recension."

E.   The A Group

It was observed in the previous section that Q
readings were on several occasions supported by Codex
Alexandrinus, the latter being sometimes joined by the
minuscules 106 and 410. Though relatively few and
loosely knit in comparison with previous groups, these
three MSS constitute yet another MS cluster in the
textual evidence for Jer. Each of the three MSS has
its own highly individualistic traits, but enough
occurrences remain where they bear witness to a common
tradition. This tradition alternatively supports Q,
B-S, O/L, or goes its own way entirely, sometimes
joined by a few straying minuscules.

Theories concerning the date of copy for Codex
Alexandrinus range from the late 4th century to the 6th
century, but most often it is assigned to the 5th
century--at least a century earlier than Codex Marchalianus (Q). Its two congeners, 106 and 410, stem from
the 14th and 13th century respectively. MS 106 (BM "p")
is the only minuscule of those collated for Jer (except
for 68 and 122 which are dependent on B) to contain the
entire Bible. In Jer this minuscule is also unique for
its order of the OAN section. Generally it follows the
MT internal order (though in the LXX position in the
middle of the book) except that the Edom oracle follows
that of the Philistines, as in the rest of the LXX
tradition, and the Elam oracle is missing altogether.
The MS is further noteworthy for its absence of titles
in the OAN section (along with 538txt and sometimes
46), the same phenomenon being observed in Isa of this
particular MS. Of all MSS, 410 has been the hardest to
read, being a palimpset and copied by an unusually
sloppy hand.

The discussion will proceed according to the
following outline:

    1.   Readings Unique to Codex Alexandrinus
    2.   Readings in Common with Isolated Minuscules
    3.   Readings in Common with O/L
    4.   Readings in Common with Q-V
    5.   Readings in Common with B-S
    6.   Significance of the Data

1.   Readings Unique to Codex Alexandrinus

29:2   αλαλαξουσιν] -ονται A

29:8   απωλετο] επ. A

29:11   κατεσυρα] κατηραυνησα A

29:14   οτι (1°)] om. A

29:19   καθισει] κατοικησει A

29:19   κατοικησει] καθεισῃ A

29:20   Αιθαμ] ηθαμ A

29:20   επιστησατε] -σεται A

29:21   επ αυτους] επ αυτη A

     This codex contains a relatively high number of
unique readings, some of which may be copyist errors,
but others of which are evidently intentional and revisional. It is noteworthy that in the above list not
one of the unique A readings constitutes an approximation to MT /59/.

2.   Readings in Common with Isolated Minuscules

29:2   κατοικουντας] ενοικ. A-106
               cf. 33:9 κατοικουντων] ενοικ. A-410
                   8:16 κατοικουωτας] ενοικ. 410

29:3   τροχων] pr. των A-410

29:4   τους καταλοιπους] τας καταλ. A-410   86

29:5   οι καταλοιποι] τα καταλοιπα A-106
               cf. 23:3 τους καταλ.] το καταλοιπον A
                   50:15 τους καταλ.] τους λοιπους A
                         -106-410

29:6   μαχαιρα του κυριου] om. του A-106-410(κυριε) 88

29:7   ησυχασει] -σεις A-410 = MT, cf. 6

29:10   ως] ωσπερ A-106-410   613; ωσει   Q-V+

When A is joined by minuscules only, it is clear
that 106-410 form its most frequent allies. The special readings of the A group so far noted concern minor
variants of Greek synonyms, articles, conjunctions and
similar items. The only case of an approximation to
the Hebrew (v. 7) may be explained as a scribal assimilation to the same verb employed in the previous line.

3.   Readings in Common with O and/or L

29:3   ηχου] pr. και A-106-410   534 613 L ≠ MT

29:12   χηραι] pr. αι A-106-410   233 239 613 L

29:16   εδωκα] δεδωκα A 26 233 L = par. passage Ob 2

29:16   ευκαταφρονητον] pr. και A-410   239 613 O ≠ MT

29:17   αυτου] σου A-106 239 86mg O L = MT = Ob 4

When A stands alone against the other uncials, it
is seldom supported by O L. In fact, it is possible
that none of the above readings derive from the Hexaplaric recension. Since the addition of και in v. 16
does not conform to the Hebrew, its Hexaplaric origin
is immediately in doubt. The readings δεδωκα (v. 16)
and σου (v. 17) appear to be assimilations to the
parallel passage in Ob 2,4. The other instances of L
support for A may be coincidental.

4.   Readings in Common with Q-V

For this list of 13 readings see above, pp. 82-83.

5.   Readings in Common with B-S

29:12   και εγω ζησομαι A-106-410   B-S-239-538   C-613]
        om. rel.

29:13   οις A-106-410   B-S-538   C] pr. ιδου rel.

29:18   συριει A-106-410 B-S-130-538] εκστησεται (pr.
         συριει C) και συριει επι παση τη πληγη (πασαν
         την πληγην Q-239-613) αυτης rel. = MT

29:21   επ αυτην(αυτη A) A-106-410 B-S-130-538] επ
         αυτους rel. = MT

29:22   οτι A-106-410 B-S-130-239-538 36 C-613] om.
         rel. = MT

29:22   και A-106-410 B-S-239-538 C-613] om. rel. = MT

It is noteworthy that when the A group joins B-S
against Q-V it stands on the side which does not
approximate the Hebrew.

6.   Significance of the Data

The findings of this section clearly show the
idiosyncratic nature of the A group. Its penchant for
numerous odd, though mostly minor, variations from the
main Greek tradition is revealed in subsections 1 and
2. Subsection 3 at first sight appears to demonstrate
a degree of Hexaplaric and Lucianic influence on the
text, but further examination shows that the shared
readings may be coincidental. Subsections 4 and 5
indicate that A more frequently joins the Q group
(hence strongly influenced by the pre-Hexaplaric revision) than the B group, but its vacillating tendency
sets it apart from either. These facts taken together
suggests that A, like the Catena group, is an eclectic
text, composed of elements from various strands, but
(in contrast to the Catena group) also incorporating a
strong dose of its own innovations. The early date of
Codex Alexandrinus and composite nature of its text
hold out the possibility that among its component parts
is preserved much ancient material, but at the same
time its erratic behaviour demands great care in
separating the grain from the chaff.

F.   The B Group

The final group of MSS with which we have to deal
consists of the two remaining uncials, Codex Vaticanus

and Codex Sinaiticus, sporadically followed by minuscules 130 239 538 and sometimes by 106 410. Whereas
the grouping of minuscules in the Hexaplaric, Lucianic
and Catena texts was relatively clear-cut, the lines of
demarcation between one group and another become increasingly blurred in these final three sections. This
has reference especially to the minuscules, several of
which are notoriously "mixed." At this stage, therefore, grouping of MSS becomes more a matter of degree
and tendency than firm cohesion. Just as 106 and 410
were shown in certain readings to favour Codex Alexandrinus, so here 130, 239 and 538 side with Codex Vaticanus and Sinaiticus in a number of crucial places /60/.

As is well known, Codex Vaticanus and Codex Sinaiticus are our oldest codices of the Greek Bible, both
stemming from the 4th century. Of the minuscules, 239
is the earliest, being copied in A.D. 1046. 130 and
538 hail from the 12th to 13th centuries. The following brief outline will apply:

1. Readings of B-S+
2. Readings of B-S+   A
3. Readings of B-S+   Q/V
4. Significance of the Data

1.   Readings of B-S+

29:3   εφ B-S-130] επι rel.

29:10   ηλθον B-S-538   106-410   Qc   C-613] + σοι rel.
         = MT

29:10   ως B-S] ωσπερ A-106 613; ωσει rel.

29:11   γειτονος B-S-130] pr. και rel. = MT

29:11   μου B-S-410] om. 106; αυτου (-των) rel. = MT

29:13   λεγει] ειπεν B-S-538

29:13   αθωωθης B-S-538   106-410] + οτι πινων πιεσαι
         (with variations) rel. = MT

29:16   μικρον B-S-538   106-410   C   26-46] pr. ιδου
         rel. = MT

29:17   υψωσεν B-S-538   410] υψωσας 106 C = MT; εαν
         υψωσης/-σεις rel.

29:19   κατοικησει(-ση)] ενοικησει B-S; ενοικηση   130
         -239-538   Q-613; καθειση   A

29:21   επ αυτους Q-V+ = MT] επ αυτην B-S*(αυτη   Sc)
         -130-538   106-410

29:22   εφοβηθη B-S-538] εσ(ε)ισθη rel.

29:22   κραυγη σου εν θαλασση] κραυγη θαλασσης ουκ
         B-S

2.   Readings of B-S+   A

29:12   και εγω ζησομαι B-S-239-538   A-106-410   C-613]
         om. rel.

29:13   οις B-S-538   A-106-410   C] pr. ιδου rel.
         = MT

29:18   συριει B-S-130-538   A-106-410] εκστησεται (pr.
         συριει C) και συριει επι παση τη πληγη (πασαν
         την πληγην Q-239-613) αυτης rel. = MT

29:22   οτι B-S-130-239-538   A-106-410   C-613   36] om.
         rel. = MT

29:22   και B-S-239-538   A-106-410   C-613] om. rel.
         = MT

3.   Readings of B-S+   Q/V

29:2   απαντες B-S-130-410-538   Q-544   O   C]
         rel.

29:13   αθωωμενη Bc 311 26 46 410] αθοωμενη B*-S-538 Q;
         αθωουμενη/αθο. rel.

29:14   καταρασιν B-130   410   Q-26-46-86'-233-534]
         καταραν S-239   A-106   V-538-544   C-613; επι-
         καταραν L

29:14   εις αιωνα B-S-106-130-239   V-26-46-86'-534-544]

εἰς τον αιωνα A-410   Q-233-538-613   C; εἰς
αιωνας O 51-449'; εως αιωνος L/-51 449'

29:21   συμφησθωσι(ν) B-130-239 V-26-86'-534] συμφη-
φισθωσι(ν)/συν. A-106   Q-46-544-613   88   51-62
-311-407-449'   490   538

4. Significance of the Data

The evidence of the above subsections is almost
the exact reverse of the lists contained in the analysis of the Q group. When the B group stands alone
against the other uncials it consistently supports the
readings furthest from the MT. The same pattern holds
true even when it is joined by A. When the B group is
supported by Q/V+ it is usually only in matters of
inner-Greek incidentals.

We may therefore make the following generalizations on behalf of the textual patterns that have
emerged in Jer: When the authentic Hexaplaric and
Lucianic elements have been eliminated, together with
the mixed Catena text, there remain two firmly established textual traditions, the B group on the one hand
and the Q group on the other, with A oscillating between the two. In the light of what has already been
demonstrated regarding the revisional character of the
Q group, it is clear that B must represent the purer
tradition of the two. The latter has not been affected
seriously (or at all) by the pre-Hexaplaric revision Q,
nor apparently by the later Hexaplaric and Lucianic
recensions. With regard to Jer at least, therefore,
Jerome's comment noted above (p. 60, n. 34) appears to
be an exaggeration. On the whole, then, B group readings are to be preferred, unless cogent reason can be
found to the contrary. When the A text joins B-S
against Q-V, that reading must be deemed virtually
certain as representing the Old Greek, for in such
cases A reinforces the unrevised tradition. By the
same token, when B and Q groups agree against A, their
readings are also to be preferred in the light of the
mixed and idiosyncratic nature of A.

This is not to say, however, that the B group must
be preferred in every instance or at any cost; it is
by no means sacrosanct. It contains its own share of

unique and improbable readings which have likely crept
in at a later stage or through scribal carelessness.
Some of these corruptions in the B group may have had
the effect of pushing it away from MT where originally
it was closer to MT; likewise, a Q reading need not
automatically be considered a revised one; it may
simply perpetuate an ancient original reading lost to
B.   When it is impossible to decide between two or more
conflicting readings on the basis of the relative superiority of the textual traditions involved, then other
factors have to be invoked (e.g. relevance to immediate
context, translation pattern in the rest of the book,
etc.).   But where the B text makes tolerable sense and
no reason can be given for it having suffered corruption or revision, its readings must weigh as a strong
witness to the earliest recoverable text form for this
book.

CHAPTER THREE

THE TEXT CRITICAL PROBLEM (2):

A CRITIQUE OF J. ZIEGLER'S CRITICAL EDITION OF JER-LXX

As is well-known and was mentioned in Ch. I above (p. 5), it was the Sixtine edition of 1587 which for generations held the field as the standard text of the LXX. For the book of Jer this was not an entirely unhappy event since the Sixtine text is essentially an edited version of Codex Vaticanus, the backbone of the B group which, as has been shown in Ch. II (pp. 92-96), contains on the whole the best available witness to the archetype text of Jer. With this may be contrasted the situation in Isa where the B text is heavily Hexaplaric but is nevertheless the text printed in the Sixtine edition. Or one might consider what the situation would have been like if the highly individualized text of the Complutensian Polyglot had gained prominence instead of the Sixtine edition /1/.

Yet simply to perpetuate the printing of edited copies of Codex Vaticanus was obviously not the way forward, neither in Jer nor in any other book. The various editions and revisions of the Sixtine text that did appear amounted simply to cosmetic touchups involving different sets of compromises between the readings of B* and Bc (= B corrector). The same judgement must be passed even on Swete's text /2/. However good in a general way Codex Vaticanus might be in Jer, neither B* nor Bc could possibly hope in every detail to represent the earliest text. Far from it, almost every page of the codex gives evidence of the kind of scribal errors and ailments that all MSS are heir to. Even if we allow some of its unique readings and orthography to be corrected by its larger group, we cannot simply assume without further ado that the B group always preserves the best reading either. What is needed is a thorough analysis of all the textual evidence available for all the readings.

This was the task assigned to J. Ziegler, the
fruits of his scholarly investigations being embodied
in the Jer edition of the Göttingen series as well as
in his own satellite studies /3/. In this chapter we
shall be concerned to describe and evaluate the text
critical principles operative not only in the constitution of Ziegler's reconstructed text but also in the
format and content of the critical apparatuses, for it
is clear that important editorial decisions have been
made in each of these areas. The material will therefore be discussed according to the following three-
point outline:

    I.   Critique of Ziegler's First Apparatus
        A. Format
        B. Selectivity
        C. Reliability
   II.   Critique of Ziegler's Second Apparatus
        A. Format
        B. Selectivity
        C. Reliability
  III.   Critique of Ziegler's Reconstructed Text
        A. Editorial Miscellanea
           1. Chapter and Verse Divisions
           2. Punctuation and Capitalization
           3. Orthography and Accentuation
        B. Choice of Readings
           1. Choice of B Group Readings
           2. Choice of Other MS Readings
           3. Choice of Conjectural Emendations

I.   Critique of Ziegler's First Apparatus

It could be argued that in a critical edition of
an ancient document the apparatus of variant readings
is as important as—possibly even more important than
—the reconstructed text. The editor must at every
point make known the choice of readings available to
him in the MSS and communicate this information in as
clear and systematic a way as possible. Format, selectivity and reliability are, therefore, the main ingre-
dients by which an apparatus must be judged. The first
apparatus of the Göttingen editions is intended to
present the variants to the text of the LXX proper;
the second apparatus is reserved for readings attested
by other Greek VSS.

A.   Format

In the case of the LXX, an editor is responsible
for documenting three main sources of variants to the
adopted text: Greek MSS, patristic citations and daughter VSS. But opinions differ over which is the preferred order of notation. Ziegler's apparatus (in
conformity with the then reigning Göttingen policy)
follows the order of Greek MSS, daughter VSS, and
patristic citations; however, this has the disadvan-
tage of driving a wedge between the two main bodies of
Greek evidence, i.e., the MSS and the patristic citations. By contrast, in the 1974 edition of Genesis
prepared by J.W. Wevers, the Greek patristic evidence
is now placed ahead of the VSS so that all the Greek
witnessses are grouped together (cf. Wevers, _Genesis_,
p. 64); there is much to be said for this sequence
/4/.

Of the three possible sources of variants, the
most important are the Greek MSS themselves. Following
the recommendation by Lagarde (_Pars Prior_ p. xvi;
"Noch einmal," _Mitteilungen_, III, p. 230), and in
conformity with general practice in classical studies,
Göttingen policy is, as far as possible, to cite variant readings by groups rather than by individual MSS.
As Ch. II of this investigation has shown, the existence of such groups among the MSS of Jer is a given
fact so that the group method is eminently suited for
documenting the variants in this book.

Where the cohesion among the members of a group is
particularly firm, such groups may be represented by a
single symbol, e.g. O, L, C, from which any deviating
MSS may be conveniently indicated by superscripts (or,
as in this work, a slash followed by the MSS in question e.g. L/-51-449'(see above, p. 63, n. 38). Even
subgroups within the main groupings can be accommodated
to this system so that in Jer Ziegler indicates the
members of the Lucianic "Hauptgruppe" by L, the "Untergruppe" by l and the combined witness of L and l by L'
(similarly in the Catena group, C + c = C') /5/. For
groups less stable in composition Ziegler's policy is
to cite all the attesting MSS in numerical and hyphen-
ated sequence e.g. Q-V-26-46-86'-534-544-613.

Moreover, the established groupings are cited

according to a consistent order: the B group, the A
group, the Q group, the O group, the L group, and
finally the C group. The B group naturally heads the
list as the generally most reliable pre-Hexaplaric
text. This is followed by the A group which stands
logically between the B and Q groups whose readings it
alternatively supports. The Hexaplaric and Lucianic
recensions follow in their chronological order, and the
list is completed by the Catena group, that late
textual synthesis which draws its readings from previous traditions.

The above pattern for recording the LXX MS evidence forms a useful model by which to arrange the
material and guide the reader. Unfortunately, the
classification of the evidence does not always fit
into neatly prearranged categories, so that in practice
various modifications of the format have to be resorted
to. Particularly problematic are a number of the minuscules which frequently change their loyalties and are
therefore difficult to classify. Some might easily
qualify for the designation "codices mixti," except for
the fact that Ziegler is reluctant to employ any special category for "codices mixti" and prefers instead
wherever possible to associate them with some established group /6/. This association is again communicated by the extensive use of hyphens, by which means
Ziegler gives expression to his critical judgement
regarding the interdependence of as many readings as
possible in the apparatus.

A few examples will illustrate the way this system
works. In the previous chapter (pp. 92ff.) it was
determined that the minuscules most commonly associated
with the B group are 130, 239 and 538. Not infrequently, however, these MSS support the reading of
another group or groups. In such instances they are
variously joined in Ziegler's text to the Q group, the
Lucianic group (except 239), or the Catena group (239
only).

Examples where 130 239 538 are joined to the Q
group abound:

29:9   βαθυνατε] + εαυτοις (τους 87 538; εν αυτοις
        106) A-106' Q-86'-233-239-538-613

29:10   καταλειμμα] καταλ(ε)ιμματα A Q-V-46-86'
         -130-233-538-544

When 130 does not support the B group it is always
linked in Ziegler's text to the Q group, the only
exception being in Chs. 1-9 where it is under Lucianic
influence (via 311, cf. Ieremias, p. 83); consequently
in those chapters 130 is linked to L in cases where it
neither supports B nor Q:

6:27   με (2°)] σε Syh L'-130'-613

Whenever 239 supports a reading attested by both the Q
and C groups (but not by B), then preference is given
to the Q group as claiming the stronger loyalty:

29:9   βαθυνατε] + εαυτοις A-106'   Q-86'-233-239
         -538-613   36-51-449 C'

But sometimes 239 shows stronger Catena influence and
is then joined to that group (cf. Ieremias, p. 94):

29:12   χηραι] pr. αι A-106' C'-239-613   233

Whenever 538 supports a reading attested by both the Q
and L groups (but not by B), then preference is given to
the L group as the stronger influence (cf. Ieremias,
p. 83):

29:9   επ αυτον (2°)] om. επ A   V-86'-239-534-544
         O L/-36/-538

    MSS 106 410 (106-410 = 106') are properly clas-
sified with the A group, but sometimes they support the
B group instead. In such cases they are cited as integral members of the B group:

29:10   ηλθον B-S-106'-538 . . . .

When 106 and 410 support neither the A nor the B groups
they are usually left to stand alone or are sometimes
joined to the Q group; no example exists for Ch. 29,
but compare the following from Ch. 28:

28:56   ανταποδιδωσιν αυτοις] ο ανταποδιδων Sc V-26
         -46-86*-106-534-538-544-710   O-233

As for 233 it is classified in Ziegler's text
either with the Hexaplaric recension, the Q group, or
on occasion with the L group. On the basis of many
passages where 233 attests readings <u>sub</u> <u>asterisco</u> in
the Hexaplaric recension or eliminates readings <u>sub</u>
<u>obelo</u> in the Hexaplaric recension, Ziegler prefers
wherever possible to link 233 to the O group, as in
the following example:

    29:22 om. οτι Q-V-26-46-86'-534-544 <u>O</u>-233

Where 233 has a different reading from O then it is
normally joined to the Q group (sometimes, though not
in Ch. 29, to the L group):

    29:9 εαυτοις A-106' Q-86'-233-239-538-613

But with 233 there is a special problem in that its
character seems to change precisely in the OAN section.
Whereas outside this section 233 frequently supports O
readings under an asterisk or eliminates readings under
an obelus, there does not appear to be a single instance of this phenomenon in Chs. 25-31 of Jer-LXX.
Here 233 supports an O reading only if that O reading
is in turn supported by the Q group, the pre-Hexaplaric
revision. The conclusion seems inescapable that in
this section 233 is a witness to the Q group and should
accordingly be linked with the former, in contrast to
Ziegler's preference to link it with O.

    MS 613 is classified with the Q group, but not in-
frequently it follows the C group instead (cf. <u>Ieremias</u>,
p. 94):

    29:3 ηχου] pr. και <u>C</u>'-613

Where 613 supports a reading attested by both the Q and
C groups then Ziegler always gives the preference to
the Q group:

    29:9 βαθυνατε] + εαυτοις A-106' Q-86'-233-239
        -538-613 36-51-449 <u>C</u>'

Sometimes, though not in Ch. 29, it is linked (along
with 239) to the L group (cf. <u>Ieremias</u>, p. 83).

Another problem has to do with MS 51. As has
already been mentioned (pp. 16, 73), this MS contains
the OAN section twice, once in the usual LXX position
and order in the middle of the book, and once in the MT
order at the end of the book (the latter referred to as
51s). This fact is nowhere pointed out in Ziegler's
edition, either because it was thought not worthwhile
mentioning or, as seems more likely, that it was unknown to Ziegler since only the first section had been
collated in the Unternehmen's special collation books.
The matter is of some interest since the two sections
of the MS contain a slightly different text. Ziegler
has classified 51 with the Lucianic "Hauptgruppe," but
in the OAN section at least it is only 51s that belongs
to the "Hauptgruppe," 51 being definitely allied with
449' and the "Untergruppe" /7/.

The only circumstances under which Ziegler will
permit a miscellaneous collection of minuscules to
stand independently is where no group exists with which
the individual MSS may be classified, e.g. 29:2 αλλαξ-
ουσι(ν) 46 106* 544, or if a group does exist, there is
nevertheless no precedent for associating a particular
minuscule with the group in question; in such cases
the minuscules are relegated to the end of an entry,
listed simply in their numerical order of ascendancy,
e.g. 29:17 ενεχειρισεν O L/-62 87 46 106 239 613c 710
(in the latter example, the minuscules listed have no
history of being under Hexaplaric or Lucianic influence; the reason why 87 precedes the others in the
list is to be explained by the fact that it represents
one of the firm groups, in this case C). Some of the
decisions when to associate a straying minuscule with a
group and when not to do so are necessarily subjective
and the editor's reasoning is not always immediately
clear /8/. However, of one thing we may be sure, that
the arrangement of the MSS in the apparatus is not
arbitrary but is intended to reflect the editor's
judgement on the interdependence of readings among the
various MSS, in so far as this is possible. Rarely do
Ziegler's judgements fail to command respect and a high
degree of credibility.

The principle of grouping by the use of symbols
and hyphens is reserved in the Göttingen texts for Greek
MSS only, yet a natural extension of this method might
have been to apply it to the patristic citations and

daughter VSS as well. For instance, at 29:5 instead of
simply listing the witnesses for the reading τα λοιπα
as L' Chr. Tht., why could these not be joined by hyphens, since the readings of Chrysostom and Theodoret
are clearly dependent on the Lucianic recensions? Similarly the patristic evidence could have been linked to
the MS readings in the following instances:

29:5   των Εναχ(ε)ιμ L'-Chr.-Tht.

29:6   εως ποτε συστραφησεσθε L'-Syh/mg-Tht.

29:14   βοσορ L'-Chr.-Tht.

The same principle of extension could apply to the
VSS. The Latin, Coptic and Ethiopic VSS usually support the B group, the Arabic follows the A group, and
the Armenian joins the O group. Thus instead of the
notation at 29:11 (το) σπερμα αυτου O-Qmg L' Arm Tht.,
this could be better represented as O-Qmg-Arm L'-Tht.
Likewise we could have the following entries:

29:12   χαι εγω ζησομαι B-S-239-538-Co-Aeth
        A-106'-Arab

29:13   οις B-S-538-Co-Aeth A-106'-Arab

29:14   εις αφανισμον χαι εις ονειδισμον χαι εις
        αβατον O-Arm L'-Tht.

29:17   ταυτα 88(sub ※)-Arm L'-Syh/mg-Tht.

Admittedly the patristic and versional evidence is
often quite erratic and the underlying Greek reading
difficult to discern so that the attempt at grouping
these might involve more trouble than it is worth, but
in principle at least there is no reason why the group
method should not also be extended to these.

Another device employed by the Göttingen apparatus
to indicate relationships among the readings of various
MSS--or the lack of such relationships, as the case may
be--is that of spacing. Sometimes, indeed, it is not
obvious whether a particular manner of spacing is due
to the mechanics of typesetting or whether it was

deliberately intended by the editor. But close inspec-
tion of the apparatus suggests at times at least the
intentional use of spacing. In general, main groups of
MSS are separated by a relatively large space, whereas
isolated minuscules, the VSS, and patristic citations
at the end of an entry are closely spaced, as in the
following example:

29:17   σου A-106   O-86mg   L'   239 La/Sg Aeth
         Arab Arm Tht.

Occasionally, however, the spaces are expanded or
contracted apparently according to the editor's interpretation of the degree of independence or dependence
among the various witnesses. Three examples will illustrate the process.

At 29:12 the reading the adopted for the critical
text is ζησηται (over against the majority reading
ζησεται). The evidence for ζησηται is cited as follows,
Bc   O-233 106(-σητε)-410 130 613, with an unusually
long space between Bc and O-233. Perhaps by this
means the editor intends to convey the message that
he sees no connection between the identical reading
in Bc and the Hexaplaric recension. Rather, he thinks
the true reading has been preserved in O-233 and some
other minuscules, while the form of the verb has been
secondarily corrected in B independent of these sources.

At 29:16 the reading μικρον is supported by B-S
-106'-538 C'   26 46, with C' being placed abnormally
close to the B group while the minuscules 26 46 are
separated from the first cluster of MSS. The interpretation to be placed on this spacing is probably that
the C' group reading μικρον (rather than ιδου μικρον as
in most other MSS) is directly dependent on the B group.

At 29:23 the reading πτερυγας αυτου is supported
by Syh L C'-613   534, this time with an uncommonly
narrow space between the L' and C' groups. Here the
message may be that the C' group reading at this point
has been influenced by the L' recension.

We see, then, that the net effect of this use of
spacing is to engage the reader in a kind of running
commentary on the editor's view of the interdependence
which exists among several variants in the apparatus.

It is another technique which enlivens the presentation
of a very technical and complicated body of information.

    In addition to citing variant readings in the
manner described above, Ziegler skillfully uses the
first apparatus to communicate much other information
needful for a better understanding of the text and its
variants. Cross references to other VSS, editions,
parallel passages and grammars are an important feature
of this supplementary information. For example, agreements between the variants and the MT are clearly
indicated, e.g. 29:1✗ ος εγενηθη λογος κυριου προς
ιερεμιαν τον προφητην 88 = MT↓, the downward pointing
arrow being an internal cross reference to the second
apparatus drawing attention to agreements with the
readings of other Greek VSS. When the Greek variant is
similar to but not identical with the MT this is indicated by the use of the abbreviation "cf.", e.g. 29:22
ηκουσθη] + (η) φωνη σου L' Arm; cf. MT [the MT in the
example cited has קלה, not קלך]. Similarly, agreements
with the Peshitta text and with the Complutensian,
Aldine, and Sixtine editions are carefully noted, e.g.
29:18 πας] pr. και Q Bo Arb Arm = Pesh, and 29:3 πολλων
130 538 = Compl. To these sources could now be added
the agreements with the Qumrân MSS. Thus at 29:4 the
apparatus might note that και αφανιω corresponds to
והכרתי of 2QJer (see below, p. 216).

    Valuable, too, are the cross references to other
Greek passages, whether in the book of Jer or in some
other biblical book. In the oracles against the Philistines and Edom, 36 variants are cross indexed in
this way. For instance, at 29:2 the variants την γην,
πολις, and ενοικουντας are each cross indexed to 8:16
where we find a parallel passage to 29:2 containing
some of the same type of variants. These cross references are extremely useful in helping to form a picture
of the patterns that often exist among certain variants
and MSS. For example, the variants for κατοικουντοι
/ενοικουωτοι are as follows (showing that the A group
evidently had a preference for the ενοικουντοι form):

    8:16   κατοικουντας] ενοικουντας   410 C̲

    29:2   κατοικουντας] ενοικουντας   A-106

    33:9   κατοικουντων] ενοικουντων   A-410

Indirectly this method of cross reference also has the advantage of helping the reader to identify many of the parallel passages which exist both within and outside the book of Jer (in addition to 29:2b//8:16b see several points of comparison in the apparatus between 29:15-17 and Ob 1-4, 29:18 and 19:8, 29:19-21 and 27:40, 44-45). A notable omission among the cross references is the lack of any mention of the intriguing phenomenon in certain MSS (especially 106 and 538txt) which omits the titles in the OAN section and elsewhere. Further examination reveals that this pattern extends even into the book of Isa, a feature that might well have been noted in the apparatus /9/.

The first apparatus also contains several cross references to Thackeray's <u>Grammar</u> for elucidation of various grammatical forms. Thus for an explanation of the variant middle form αλαλαξονται at 29:2 in A (in contrast to the majority text reading αλαλαξουσιν) we are referred to p. 231 of Thackeray's <u>Grammar</u>. These references could now be profitably expanded by making use of Walter's more up-to-date study, <u>The Text of the Septuagint</u> (1973). Hence Ziegler's adoption at 29:13 of the form αθωωμενη rather than αθοωμενη as in the majority of MSS could be supported by a reference to Walters, p. 75.

Yet other miscellaneous information contained in the apparatus includes the citation of patristic comments on the existence of early variant readings (see above, p. 5, n. 2), and the source of a conjectural emendation, e.g. 29:3 ιππων Schleusner II 845. Some emendations not adopted by Ziegler are also included in the apparatus when these are considered worthy of mention, e.g. 27:8 δρακοντες] τραγοι Cappelus apud Schleusner I 641; αρχοντες Spohn.

Certain features of the apparatus are evidently designed to conserve space. Thus while it would have been ideal to cite all the evidence both for the "variants" as well as for the adopted reading or "lemma text" (as Ziegler himself acknowledges, <u>Ieremias</u>, p. 138), the general rule adopted for the Jer edition --with certain exceptions /10/--is to cite the evidence for one side of the equation only, leaving the reader to deduce the MSS relevant for the other side if interested, these MSS being often subsumed under the

convenient abbreviation "rel." But this policy imposes
heavy demands on the reader. In order to determine at
any one point exactly which witnesses support a particular reading not detailed in the apparatus, he has to
subtract all those MSS and VSS which have been cited
from the total number of witnesses attested for that
book, a task which is complicated by the fact that some
witnesses are extant for certain portions only /11/.
What is absolutely essential, therefore, is a clear and
full reckoning on each page of precisely which MSS and
VSS have been collated for the passage covered on that
page. This type of MS "heading list" or <u>Kopfleiste</u>
inserted between the text proper and first apparatus
has been introduced in the latest editions of the
Göttingen series and it is a welcome and useful aid
(cf. Wevers, <u>Genesis</u>, pp. 63-64). If this had been
done for Jer, every page of Ch. 29 would have had the
following <u>Kopfleiste</u>: B-S-130-239-538 A-106' Q-V
-26-46'-86'-233-534-544-613 <u>O</u> <u>L</u> <u>C</u>' verss.

Sometimes the first apparatus saves space by
omitting the lemma text altogether, e.g. 29:8 επωλετο
A. This type of notation can be used only sparingly
and under special circumstances where there can be no
confusion as to what word the variant refers to (in
29:8 επωλετο is clearly a variant of απωλετο), though
vertical lines used as division markers between
variant readings help to avoid confusion. Finally, the
apparatus saves space by not separating the variants
for different verses into paragraph divisions. But
this is counter-productive as the reader is frequently
frustrated by not being able to locate quickly his
desired reading in the apparatus. In the new editions
of the Göttingen series this problem has been corrected
by the use of paragraph units in the apparatuses, thus
facilitating quick location of the documented variants.

B. Selectivity

A comparison between the collation notes above
(pp. 22-41) and the first apparatus of Ziegler's text
shows that many variant readings found in the MSS are
not included in the critical apparatus. This is not
surprising, since the abundance of mere scribal or
clerical variants demands that some form of selectivity

be exercised in the choice of readings to be included
in the main apparatus lest it become overloaded and
unwieldy. The policy followed for the first apparatus
is to record only the kind of readings that could be
called variants of substance, such as different words
or significantly different forms of a word with respect
to number, tense, mood or case. A sampling of the
typical kind of orthographic variants found in the MSS
is reserved for a special section of the "Einleitung"
(pp. 109-25) of Ziegler's edition, keyed to Thackeray's <u>Grammar</u>. To demonstrate the method of selection
adopted in the first apparatus we will compare the variants contained in the collation notes of 29:2 with
those included in the printed apparatus as well as
those found in the orthographic section of the "Einleitung."

υδατα αναβαινει

    For this "variation unit" we find the following
alternative readings:

		υδατα αναβεννι	A
		" -βεννει	S*
		" -βενη	26
		" -βαιννει	62
		" -βαινη	239
δη	"	ερχεται	Cyril of Alexandria

Since the different forms attested for the verb αναβαινει all constitute variations in scribal spelling
without changing the tense, mood or number of the verb,
they are not included in the main apparatus. However,
the forms αναβεννι A, αναβεννει S*, and αναβαιννει 62
of 29:2 are listed in the section of the "Orthographika" under the subheading of the interchange of νν
and ν (p. 120). The vocalic variants αναβενη and
αναβαινη of 26 and 239 respectively are nowhere mentioned in Ziegler's text. By contrast, however, Cyril
of Alexandria's phrase δη υδατα ερχεται is of a different order altogether containing a true vocabulary
alternative (ερχεται) with the addition of a particle
(δη). This is the only phrase, therefore, which is
included in the main apparatus as a real variant of
υδατα αναβαινει.

απο

The reading επι in 106 is a different preposition from that contained in the other MSS and is therefore included in the apparatus.

βορρα

For this word there is only one variant spelling attested, namely βορραν in S*. This is not included in the apparatus, but on p. 123 we find the comment, "Der Genetiv βορρα ist in S* gewöhnlich βορραν geschrieben: 13:20 16:15 23:8 25:9 27:9,41 29:2."

και εσται

The words are missing in the Latin work Speculum while S* has the itacistic variant εστε. Neither is deemed sufficiently important to merit mention in the apparatus.

χειμαρρουν

The Greek variants attested for this word are χι-μαρρουν A, χιμαρρον S* (-ρρουν Sc), and χειμαρρον 534. Since these forms are merely orthographic in nature with no possible change in meaning they are excluded from the main apparatus. However, two of the variants, those of S* and 534, are listed on p. 112 of the "Ein-leitung" as illustrative of the interchange of ου-ο /ο-ου in the MSS. The Bohairic VS has the plural variant "torrentes" but this is not deemed worthy of notation in the apparatus.

κατακλυσει

For this word the following variants are attested: κατακλυσι A S*, κατακλυζει 46, κλυσει 534, and κατα-καυσει 239 410. The form in A S* is another case of itacism and consequently not recorded in the apparatus; however, a note on p. 112 informs that the interchange of ι-ει and ει-ι is very common in the MSS, especially in S and A, exactly as we find in 29:2. The reading

κατακλυζει of 46 represents a different tense of the
verb and is on that account included in the apparatus,
as is the simplex form of the verb found in 534. κατα-
καυσει in 239 410 constitutes an entirely different verb
and must likewise be listed in the apparatus.

και

There are altogether five instances of the conjunction και in 29:2. The first και is attested by all
witnesses, the second is omitted by 407, the third by
the Armenian VS, the fourth by the Ethiopic VS, and the
fifth by the Coptic and Armenian VSS. Of these the
first apparatus notes only the omission of the fifth
conjunction in the Coptic and Armenian VSS. It is not
obvious why the editor made an exception in the case of
the fifth conjunction, unless it was felt that the combined witness of the two VSS, one of these being the
relatively important Coptic (= Sahidic + Bohairic),
made it noteworthy. In the case of the other omissions, these are clearly inconsequential.

γην

In 449* and 538 γην is preceded by the article
την. This must be recorded in the apparatus since the
presence or absence of the article in Jer-LXX constitutes a special problem (in the parallel passage of
8:16 the article is attested by B-S-538 A-106' V-86'
-198-544 36 c).

πολιν

For this word the variant πολις is found in S*
and 544, though Ziegler is undoubtedly correct in suggesting that the intended form in S* 544 is the accusative plural πολεις, the -ις form being a case of itacism, cf. 29:14 πολεις] πολις S*. In either case,
whether the variant form is taken to be nominative
singular or accusative plural, it correctly deserves
mention in the apparatus. The presence of the plural
form in the Armenian VS could also have been mentioned.

κατοικουντας

     The only variant form for this word is ενοικουντας
in A 106; the same kind of variants are found in 8:16
and 33:9 (cf. p. 106 above) and these are always recorded in the apparatus.

κεκραξονται

     The simple (rather than reduplicated) middle fu-
ture form κραξονται is found in S* 62 86c. The apparatus records only S* 62, even though the same form is
clearly found in 86 as a correction over a previous
erasure and should have been included (cf. p. 115, n.
12). The reduplicated middle future form was standard
in Attic and generally throughout the LXX, whereas the
simple middle future appears as variants in the LXX
(cf. Thackeray, Grammar, p. 273); in Jer these are
found in various MSS at 22:20, 30:3, 31:20, 32:20, on
each occasion fully documented in Ziegler's apparatus.

οι ανθρωποι

     The article οι is omitted in 87, obviously by
scribal lapse, but the omission is nonetheless noted in
the apparatus. Speculum attests the reading universi,
a minor but nonetheless real variant and hence included
in the apparatus.

αλαλαξουσιν

     The variant αλαλαξονται in A is the middle future
form of the same verb as in the main text (cf. Thackeray, Grammar, p. 231); the variants αλαλαξουσι(ν) in
46 106* 544 and ολολυξουσι (λυς. 22*-48-449) of L' constitute different verbs altogether. All are correctly
noted in the apparatus.

κατοικουντες

     S* has the common itacism -ταις so characteristic
of this codex; obviously it does not merit mention in
the main apparatus.

Review of the above examples well illustrates how
the first apparatus seeks to distinguish between im-
material and material variants, only the latter of
which are recorded; the former may be listed in the
"Einleitung" or not mentioned at all. It is true, of
course, that the distinction between significant and
insignificant variants cannot be made in an absolute
manner. A scholar studying scribal habits and
orthographic patterns in the MSS would find the term
"insignificant" applied to such variants offensive.
But for the general reader they are certainly secondary
and if included in the main apparatus would tend to
confuse rather than aid in his understanding of the
text. While one has to admire the diligence with which
Swete, for instance, recorded all the minute variants
attested by the uncials collated by him, it needs also
be said that much of his apparatus served no useful
purpose for most readers. The function of the text
critic is surely to use his expertise in weighing the
MS information and in deciding what is relevant and
what is not, lest other users lose their way in a
forest of meaningless clerical mistakes and scribal
idiosyncrasies.

On occasion even the Göttingen text includes in
its apparatus forms which are purely orthographic, i.e.
forms which do not change the meaning of a word in any
way. Thus at 29:13 we have the entry αθωωμενη Βc 311
26 46 410 Tht.; αθοωμ. Β*-S-538 Q; αθωουμενη (vel.
αθοουμ.) rel. In the light of the predominant αθο.
spelling in the MSS, the editor evidently considered
this orthographic variant worthy of mention in the apparatus. But he appears to be inconsistent in not mentioning the same kind of variants to αθωωθης later in
the verse where Β*-S-538 A 86 91-490 have αθοωθης.
Whether the notation was really necessary in the
first place may be disputed (it probably should have
been reserved for the section of the "Orthographika,"
especially since other examples of αθοων/αθωων are
mentioned there, p. 112), but it goes to show that even
the Göttingen apparatus probably includes more rather
than less of what is absolutely essential.

When a decision has been made to enter a certain
word in the apparatus, normally all the attesting Greek
MSS are cited. Occasionally, however, especially in
the case of minor variants, the designation "alii" is

employed to signify additional miscellaneous minuscules, e.g. 29:6 ηουχασεις] -σης 87 alii (the "alii"
here include 233 311 534).

In the case of the daughter VSS the Göttingen
apparatus is much more selective in what it includes as
compared with the Greek MSS. Often, for instance, the
VSS add or omit conjunctions and particles, change the
number of a noun or pronoun, inadvertently omit or
transpose words and phrases. Such variants are usually
ignored unless they happen also to be attested by a
Greek witness. For instance, in 29:3 we find the entry
ηχου] pr. και A-106' L' C'-613 534 Bo Arab; pre. et a
Aeth Arm Spec. But the very next word τροχων is also
followed by a conjunction in the Bohairic and Armenian
VSS; this, however, is not recorded. Sometimes one
feels versional evidence that has been omitted could
profitably have been included. For example, at 29:3
the word οπλων can be read either as ὁπλῶν (from ὁπλή,
"hoof") or ὅπλων (from ὅπλον, pl. "arms"). The context
clearly requires the meaning "hoofs," yet it is significant that the Ethiopic, Syriac, Arabic and Armenian
VSS all read "arms," as did Speculum. Regrettably this
failed to be noted in the apparatus.

The Greek patristic evidence is generally cited in
full. It is sometimes cited for the lemma text even
when the rest of the Greek evidence for it is not provided, cf. the entry at 1:19: λεγει Cyr. Tht.] ειπε(ν)
B-S-239-538 V-26-46-410-534-544 O-233 C'. The mention
of Cyril and Theodoret with the lemma text does not
mean that they alone attest the λεγει reading; rather
it means that λεγει is found in all Greek MSS not mentioned for ειπε(ν), plus the Fathers Cyril and Theodoret. Documentation of the Latin citations, e.g.
Speculum, is less consistent. The readings of the late
Church Father Basilius of Neopatrae are seldom noted in
the apparatus. Nor is it important that they should
be; Basilius attests a text almost identical to 239.

C. Reliability

My independent collation of the MS evidence for
Jer 29 has confirmed the general reliability and
accuracy of the Göttingen apparatus. Nevertheless, the
investigation also revealed numerous instances where

the collators of the Unternehmen's special collation
books failed to record or incorrectly recorded certain
readings. Those readings which I found to bear
directly on material contained in the first apparatus
were communicated to the Unternehmen, and several of
these corrections or additions were adopted in the 1976
reprint of the book /12/. The 1976 edition of Ieremias
is otherwise not a thoroughgoing revision of the text
or the apparatus; rather it is essentially a reprint
of the 1957 edition with miscellaneous alterations
which had come to the attention of the Unternehmen
incorporated where the mechanics of typesetting allowed
for this without major reworking /13/.

Documentation of patristic evidence continues to
accumulate and be refined as well, thanks especially to
the Centre d'Analyse et de Documentation Patristiques
at Strassburg. Now available in published form are the
two volumes of Biblia Patristica (1975, 1977) covering
the first three centuries (except Origen). However,
for Jer-LXX 29 only two remote allusions by the Latin
authors Pseudo-Cyprian and Victor Poetovius were listed
in those volumes which are not referred to in the
Göttingen text (see above, p. 20, n. 13). In private
correspondence the Strassburg Centre provided me from
their as yet unpublished files two additional allusions
/citations, one from Origen (in Latin translation) and
one from Didymus the Blind, only the latter of which
has any significance for our collation (cf. p. 20). In
an updated apparatus Didymus' variants from v. 6 might
well be included (ποτε instead of τινος, and επι-
στραφητε instead of αποκαταστηθι). In addition, there
are now individual studies available such as the one by
Otto Wahl (1965) on the text of Sacra Parallela prepared especially to provide the Göttingen editors with
further reliable patristic material. But the yield
from Sacra Parallela to Jer-LXX 29 is minimal: the
omission of ετι in v. 8 (along with 407 and Tht.), and
in the same verse, the vocalic interchanges θεμαν for
θαιμαν and απολετο for απωλετο (Wahl, p. 557).

The daughter VSS have been collated on the basis of
the available published editions, some of known inferior quality (Ethiopic is a significant exception).
Ideally all VSS would have been based on actual MSS or
good critical texts, but to have undertaken this im-
mense preparatory work for what is in the final

analysis only secondary evidence would hardly have
been proportionate to the effort expended. In time,
no doubt, good critical editions for most of these VSS
will appear in their own right (see, for example, the
work being done on the Armenian VS: M.E. Stone, "The
Old Armenian Version of Isaiah: Towards the Choice of
the Base Text for an Edition," Textus 8 [1973],
107-23), and the material can then be reviewed and
corrected as necessary.

In summary, therefore, we can say that with regard
to the Greek MS and patristic evidence at least, the
first apparatus of Ziegler's critical edition can be
relied upon with considerable confidence, allowance
being made for a small margin of error. There is no
reason to doubt that the same judgement applies to the
versional evidence, though the latter can only be as
good as the available published editions.

II. Critique of Ziegler's Second Apparatus

"Eine Ausgabe der Septuaginta ohne vollständige
Aufnahme des sogennanten hexaplarischen Materials halte
ich für unwissenschaftlich," said Paul de Lagarde in
1889 ("Noch einmal," Mitteilungen, III, 234), an opinion which today is taken as axiomatic. Nonetheless,
Rahlfs' 1926 edition of Genesis contained no documentation of the Hexapla readings. The first Göttingen
edition to incorporate this material was Ziegler's
Isaias (1939), where the policy was adopted of employing two separate apparatuses, one for the variant
readings of the LXX (including recensions such as O and
L) and one for the readings of other Greek VSS, principally those deriving from the various columns of the
Hexapla and preserved in the margins of a few LXX MSS
and the Syh (cf. Isaias, pp. 111-15).

There can be little doubt that the two-apparatus
structure is of great practical value in arranging the
complex body of material at hand, yet the underlying
presuppositions of this model need to be examined.
In effect, the two-apparatus model serves to emphasize
the editor's view that readings in the second apparatus
are not properly variants of the LXX but constitute
readings from other Greek translations to be compared
with the LXX. In the latest editions of the Göttingen

series this distinction has been sharpened even further
by providing all readings in the second apparatus with
accents and breathings just as in the critically restored LXX text (cf. Wevers, Genesis, p. 60).

Yet the postulate of a sharp dichotomy between the
LXX and other ancient Greek VSS has recently been questioned. In his seminal and revolutionary study, Les
Devanciers d'Aquila, D. Barthélemy argued that, far
from being an entirely new translation, even a literal
text like that of Aquila represents the end product of
a long process of revision of an original text, antecedents of which were discovered in the so-called Kaige
recension (according to Barthélemy, to be traced even
in certain readings added to Jer-LXX, Devanciers, p.
44). Similar claims have been made for the translation
of Exodus, cf. the monograph by Kevin G. O'Connell, The
Theodotionic Revision of the Book of Exodus (1972).
The net effect of these and other studies is to put in
question the traditional hard and fast distinction
between recension and version, and instead to underline
the interdependence among the various forms of the
Greek texts current in the early centuries. If this
new orientation to the early history of the Greek OT
were to gain widespread credibility, the formal dif-
ferentiation implied in the Göttingen two-apparatus
structure may come under increasing pressure (cf. the
review of Wevers' Genesis edition by O'Connell in CBQ
39 [1977], 119ff.).

In the meantime, however, all must acknowledge
the convenience and practical utility of the adopted
structure in helping the editor to arrange a host of
technical MS data.

A. Format

In general, the rule adopted for Ziegler's edition
is to include in the second apparatus only such readings as are found in the margins of LXX MSS under the
conventional symbols of the Minor Greek VSS, e.g. α´,
σ´, θ´, οι γ´, οι λ´, and--in Jer--ιω´, while unidenti-
fied or anonymous marginal readings are left in the
first apparatus (necessarily marked by the superscript
"mg"). But it is difficult always to be consistent in
applying this rule. On occasion an anonymous marginal

reading is assigned to the second apparatus if it is
felt that it can with reasonable certainty be attributed to one of the other VSS, cf. the reading of
Syh/mg at 29:10 ουκ αν ηφανισαν τα ικανα εαυτοις which,
although anonymous in Syh/mg, is nevertheless attributed by Ziegler to Symmachus and hence documented in
the second apparatus (but with the presumed source
put in angular brackets, indicating that this is a
conjecture on the part of the editor). There are even
some marginal readings which, while more difficult to
identify as to source, are nevertheless included in the
second rather than the first apparatus, cf. the reading
<?> συνεταξατο of 86mg at 29:7, the question mark in
angular brackets highlighting the editor's uncertainty
as to original source of the reading. Editorial decisions such as these illustrate some of the strains
placed on the two-apparatus system, though an editor's
close familiarity with the style and general character
of the different VSS can facilitate calculated guesses.

    But Ziegler has chosen to exercise this kind of
"source criticism" not only on the anonymous marginal
readings but also on many of the readings transmitted
under the name of one of the established VSS. Sometimes an identical (or similar) reading is found in the
margin of two separate MSS but under different name.
In such cases Ziegler weighs the evidence and makes a
judgement on what he considers the most probable original source to be. Sometimes he feels a transmitted
symbol must be wrong and seeks to identify the correct
source. This kind of editorial intervention is predi-
cated on the knowledge that all MS material has been
transmitted through fallible scribal hands and that in
the process many errors have crept in. The editor
therefore has assumed the responsibility for weighing
the reliability of the MS evidence and for proposing
changes where he feels this is demanded. This procedure
is in keeping with Göttingen policy that a critical
text and apparatus should reflect an editor's considered judgement rather than a mere documentation of
the raw MS material (see Ziegler's discussion of this
policy, Isaias, p. 113). The method will become clear
through a comparison of the actual symbols found in the
MSS and the way this information is annotated and
sometimes modified in the second apparatus.

In the tables below, all readings come from the
<u>margins</u> of the MSS cited. For example, "29:8 α′
συνεσις 86" should be understood as referring to
the reading of Aquila as found in 86mg.

	MS Readings	Second Apparatus
29:3	προσωπου οργης θυμου Q ιω′ -------- " -------- 86	ιω′ προσωπου οργης θυμου Q (anon.) 86
29:4	α′θ′ ✱τους αλλοφυλους Q ο′ ✱------"-------- 86	α′θ′✱τους αλλοφυλους Q 86 (sub ο′)
29:4	α′θ′ ✱και καππαδοκιας Q οι γ′ ✱καππαδοκας 86	α′θ′ ✱καππαδοκιας Q(και καππαδ.) 86 (οι γ′ καππα- δοκας sic)
29:7	συνεταξατο 86	<?> συνεταξατο 86
29:8	α′ συνεσις 86	α′ (leg. σ′) συνεσις 86
29:9	α′σ′ οτι απωλειαν ησαυ 86 α′ απωλειαν ησαυ επηγαγον Syh	α′σ′ οτι απωλειαν ησαυ επ- ηγαγον 86 (om. επηγαγον Syh (sub α′; om. οτι)
29:10	ουκ αν ηφανισαν τα ικανα εαυτοις Syh	<s'> ουκ αν ηφανισαν τα ικανα εαυτοις Syh
29:11	α′ απεκαλυφα 86 α′σ′ ----"---- Syh	α′ απεκαλυφα 86 Syh (sub α′σ′)
29:13	α′θ′ ✱πιοντες Q οι γ′ ✱---"--- 86	α′<σ′>θ′ ✱πιοντες Q 86 (sub οι γ′)
29:14	οι γ′ εσται βοσορα 86 οι λ′ -----"------ Syh	οι γ′ εσται βοσορα 86 Syh (sub οι λ′)
29:20	σ′α′ απο της δοξης 86* σ′ ------"------ 86c σ′ ------"------ Syh	σ′ απο της δοξης 86 (sub σ′α′ sed α′ del./c) Syh
29:20	α′ οτι τις ομοιος μοι και τις υποστησεται μοι 86 α′σ′ ομοιος μοι και τις υποστησεται μοι Syh	α′σ′ οτι τις ομοιος μοι και τις υποστησεται μοι 86 (sub α′) Syh (om. οτι τις)
29:22	α′ σαλου (s. σεισμου) Syh	α′ (leg. σ′) σαλου (s. σεισ- μου) Syh
29:23	επι βοσορ 86 α′σ′ επι βοσρα Syh	α′σ′ επι βοσορ 86 (anon.) Syh (επι βοσρα)

Decisions on the most probable source of a particular reading cannot in the nature of the case be
definitive. Yet the proposed modifications in the
above list are seldom without plausible reason. By
way of illustrating the method we may take the two
instances in 29:8 and 29:22 where Ziegler proposes an
altogether different source from that indicated in the
MSS.

At 29:8 where the LXX has σοφια, 86mg attests the
reading συνεσις under the symbol α´ for Aquila. But
Ziegler proposes Symmachus instead as the source of
this reading. His reasoning presumably runs something
like this: since Aquila's normal rendering of חכמה is
in fact σοφια (cf. Reider-Turner, p. 219), it is doubtful that he would have changed the LXX word at this
point, especially since συνεσις is used by Aquila to
translate another Hebrew word altogether, namely תבונה
(cf. Reider-Turner, p. 228); on the other hand, since
it is characteristic of Symmachus to vary his vocabulary,
he is the more likely translator responsible for this
reading.

A similar reasoning may underlie the documentation
of a versional variant to the LXX reading πτωσις in
29:22. According to Syh/mg, Aquila translated the Hebrew at this point with σαλος (or σεισμος depending on
which Greek word is thought to underlie the Syriac);
Ziegler, however, thinks that this word (i.e. σαλος
/σεισμος) must also originate with Symmachus. He
probably reasoned that since Aquila regularly rendered
the root נפל with derivatives of πιπτω (cf. Reider-
Turner, pp. 293-94), it seems unlikely that he would
have departed from his common practice on this occasion; Symmachus may, however, have sought deliberately
to vary his semantic equivalents.

When we turn from examining the source of a reading to the actual reading itself, we observe that the
second apparatus proceeds in much the same way. Again,
Ziegler is not content merely to reproduce a MS reading
undigested, but cognizant of the cumulative effect of
scribal error, he often proposes a different reading or
spelling from that found in the MSS; sometimes this
even involves addition of words (indicated in the
apparatus by the use of angular brackets).

Below is a list of the changes proposed by Ziegler for Jer 29:

MS Readings	Second Apparatus
29:2 α′ και κυκλωσουσιν 86	και κατακλυσουσιν (κυκλω- σουσιν cod.)
29:3 α′ δρομου ιππων Syh ιω′ προσωπου οργης θυμου Q (anon.) 86	⟨απο φωνης⟩ δρομου ιππων ⟨απο⟩ προσωπου οργης θυμου
29:4 α′θ′ ※ και καππαδοκιας Q οι γ′ ※ καππαδοκας 86	※ καππαδοκιας Q (και καππαδ.) 86 (οι γ′ καππαδοκας sic)
29:5 α′ το καταλιμμα . . . 86	το καταλ⟨ε⟩ιμμα . . .
29:9 α′ . . . εβαθυναν κατ- οικησαι 86	. . . εβαθυναν ⟨του⟩ κατ- οικησαι
29:11 α′θ′ εταλαιπωρησεν 86 σ′ διεφθαρη 86 α′ επρονομευθη Syh	εταλαιπωρησεν ⟨σπερμα αυτου⟩ διεφθαρη ⟨το σπερμα αυτου⟩ επρονομευθη ⟨σπερμα αυτου⟩
29:12 σ′ καταλειπε ορφανους . . . 86	καταλειπε ορφανους ⟨σου⟩
29:12 σ′ κατελιπεν ορφανους σου φησι . . . Ghisler	κατελιπεν ορφανους σου [φησι]
29:12 σ′ . . . μη αμεριμνει- τωσαν 86	. . . [μη] αμεριμνητωσαν (-νειτ. cod.)
29:14 σ′ επ αυτον . . . 86	επ ⟨εμ⟩αυτον
29:14 α′ μερει 86	⟨εση εν⟩ μερει ⟨αυτης⟩
29:15 α′ περιοχη . . . 86	⟨και⟩ περιοχη
29:16 α′σ′ ※ οτι μικρον 86 α′ εν τοις εθνεσιν εξουδενομενον . . . 86	※ οτι⟨ιδου⟩ μικρον εν τοις εθνεσιν εξουδενωμενον (-νομ. cod.)
29:17 σ′ αλαζονια . . . 86 Syh	αλαζονεια (-νια 86) . . .
29:20 σ′ απο της δοξης 86	απο της δοξης ⟨του ιορδανου ⟩
29:20 ιω′ . . . ωχυρωματον 86	. . . οχυρωματον (ωχ. cod.)
29:20 σ′ . . . αρχαια Ghisler	αρχαια⟨ν⟩
29:20 σ′ εξαιφνης δραμειν . . . Syh	εξαιφνης ⟨γαρ⟩ δραμειν . . .

A number of the proposed corrections, it will be observed, are of a mere orthographic nature, e.g. itacisms and otacisms. The more substantial changes are proposed corrections in favour of the Hebrew text. Thus in v. 2 the editor suggests that Aquila must have used the same verb κατακλυζω as is employed elsewhere in the LXX to translate the Hebrew verb שטף, only that he (Aquila) changed it from the LXX third person singular to the third person plural corresponding to the Hebrew ישטפו; the witness of 86mg which assigns the verb κυκλοω to Aquila, Ziegler believes must be a scribal error. In the same way the readings at 29:4 και καππαδοκιας Q and καππαδοκας 86 are rejected in favour simply of the genitive καππαδοκιας without conjunction because this alone corresponds with MT כפתור. The examples of additions and deletions in the above list follow the same pattern of approximation to the Hebrew MT. Implicit in this procedure is the assumption that the Hebrew text of the Minor Greek VSS was identical with the MT, a premise which one feels is sometimes taken too much for granted--notwithstanding the well established proximity of the 2nd century Hebrew text to the MT. But as in the case of the proposed "source" emendations (above, p. 119), so here, too, the MS evidence is always clearly presented alongside the proposed corrections; as a result the reader is free to make up his own mind on the original form or spelling of a versional reading.

In addition to the careful sifting and documentation of the evidence, the second apparatus also contains many useful cross references to different passages in Jer and to other biblical books, much as the first apparatus, cf. 29:2 και κατακλυσει] α´ και κατακλυσουσιν (κυκλωσουσιν cod.) 86; cf. Is. 28:16 Dan.11:10,26 Iob 14:19.

B. Selectivity

The second apparatus--as distinct from the first--strives for comprehensive rather than selective treatment. This becomes clear from a careful check of all the marginal readings found in MSS attesting the oracles against the Philistines and Edom. According to my examination, the apparatus does not miss a single reading relevant for these two oracles. The significance

of this achievement can only be appreciated against the
background of previous collations of the same material,
e.g. those of Spohn, Field, Swete and Nestle-Dahse.

In the "Notae criticae" to his reconstructed text
of Jer, Spohn documented many readings of the Minor VSS
found in the margins of the Syh, as well as some from
"Cod. Ies." (i.e. Q--see above, p. 15, n. 4). While
useful as far as it goes (especially with regard to the
Syh), the treatment is nonetheless only partial.

The standard collection of Hexapla readings since
1875 has been that of F. Field, <u>Origenis</u> hexaplorum <u>quae</u>
<u>supersunt</u> . . . <u>fragmenta</u>. Yet for the oracles against
the Philistines and Edom in Jer, Field's collation is
so incomplete and inaccurate as to be considered almost
useless. The most important and plentiful of all sources for Hexapla readings in Jer is 86mg, yet this MS is
only infrequently cited by Field; the readings of the
new version under the symbol ιω´, for instance, are
never mentioned, along with many other omissions. On
the other hand, Field often cites from MS 88, but most
inaccurately. This is due to the fact that Field's
collation of 88 was based not on the original MS but on
a previous collation by Bernado Stephanopoli of an
inaccurate copy of the original codex transcribed in
the 17th century. Only "Cod. Jes." (= Q) and the Syh
seem to be collated with any degree of fidelity, though
again incompletely.

Swete in his apparatus included a certain amount
of Hexapla material but only from the margin of Q, one
of the uncials available for his collation of the
Prophets. Swete's collation of Qmg is generally
reliable, though not without mistakes, e.g. at 29:3
Swete assigns the reading προσωπου οργης θυμου in Qmg
to Symmachus whereas, in fact, the Qmg reading is
anonymous (in 86mg the reading is found under the
symbol ιω´).

The Jer edition of Nestle-Dahse also contained a
Hexapla apparatus, but again of inferior quality.
Apart from its strange and cumbersome format and the
almost unbelievable omission of MS number or letter for
a particular reading (except for the occasional reference to Q), it does not seem to represent a fresh collation but is rather an extraction of readings from

earlier publications. Comparison with Field shows it
to be even less complete than that collection; one
positive point, however, is that it omits the blatant
errors of Field's references to 88.

In short, for the only complete list of Hexapla
readings for Jer we must have recourse to Ziegler's
second apparatus.

C. Reliability

Our investigation has confirmed the fact that in
the oracles against the Philistines and Edom, Ziegler's
second apparatus is as accurate as it is complete. One
possible source of confusion is the way certain readings are inserted in the middle of a quotation, e.g.
29:1 α´σ´ ος εγενηθη λογος κυριου προς ιερεμιαν τον
προφητην επι τους αλλοφυλους (α´ προς φυλιστιαιους Syh;
σ´ περι των φυλιστιαιων 86) προ του παταξαι φαραω την
γαζαν 86. Unless one is familiar with the editor's
habit (explained in <u>Isaias</u>, p. 114 as a space-saving
device), a question may arise whether the whole clause
ος εγενηθη . . . την γαζαν was present in Syh or
merely the phrase προς φυλιστιαιους of Aquila, as is
in fact the case (cf. the similar type of possible
confusion in 29:16 and 29:17). Another minor point is
the misleading impression at 29:4 ※καππαδοκιας Q(και
καππαδ.) 86(οι γ´ καππαδοκας sic) that the readings
both in Q and 86 are <u>sub asterisco</u> whereas this is true
only for the former. The lemma text at 29:3 should not
read απο των οπλων των ιππων αυτου but simply οπλων των
ιππων αυτου. But on the whole, when tested against the
actual MSS, Ziegler's apparatus bears eloquent testimony to the editor's concern for accuracy and complete-
ness. When compared with previous collations, it so
far outstrips these as to be quite <u>sans pareil</u>.

III. Critique of Ziegler's Reconstructed Text

As important as the apparatuses are, it is nonetheless the critical text that represents our ultimate
concern. Having abandoned the expedient of simply
reproducing one MS as his text, the editor is faced
with a host of decisions regarding which particular
reading, spelling and punctuation to choose. In this

section we will evaluate Ziegler's reconstructed text
under two main headings: A) Editorial Miscellanea, and
B) Choice of Readings.

A.   Editorial Miscellanea

     By the expression "Editorial Miscellanea" we mean
those matters pertaining to the constitution of the
critical text apart from the actual choice of words.
Here we shall discuss three such items: 1) Chapter and
Verse Divisions, 2) Punctuation and Capitalization, and
3) Orthography and Accentuation. Our interest is in
determining and illustrating the methodology employed
by Ziegler in each of these areas.

1.   Chapter and Verse Divisions

     The citation of chapter and verse in Jer-LXX is
complicated by the different arrangement of many passages in the MT and LXX texts. Wherever the numbering
in the two texts is different, the Göttingen edition
always gives both references, the MT being put in par-
enthesis. Also on p. 147 of the "Einleitung" Ziegler
has provided two very helpful comparative lists giving
the MT chapter and verse in terms of the LXX and vice
versa.

     A more serious problem in citing the text of Jer-
LXX however, concerns the conflicting numbering systems employed in different editions of the LXX. This
can be illustrated with reference to the oracles
against the Philistines and Edom. A system of chapter
divisions was first introduced in the Sixtine text of
1587; in this edition Ch. 29 consisted of the Philistine and Edom oracles. The Sixtine precedent for chapter divisions remained standard up until the publication of Rahlfs' Septuaginta (1935) where Rahlfs
frequently broke with previous convention in an effort
better to conform the MT and LXX numbering systems.
This policy had a direct bearing on the oracles against
the Philistines and Edom in Jer. In the MT the oracle
against the Philistines constitutes a chapter by itself, i.e., Ch. 47; Rahlfs followed suit and limited
the Philistine oracle to one chapter as well, i.e., LXX
Ch. 29. This meant that in Rahlfs' edition the Edom

oracle now commenced with Ch. 30, followed by the
oracles against the Ammonites, Kedar and Damascus (in
the Sixtine text and those editions dependent on that
tradition, Ch. 30 had consisted of the last three of
these only).

     The verse divisions are no less confusing. These
were introduced into the Greek text at least as early
as Walton's London Polyglot (1657), generally following the Hebrew order. But for the OAN section of
Jer this order again presented problems. Since in the
Hebrew text the Philistine oracle was numbered vv. 1-7
and the Edom oracle in another chapter was numbered vv.
7-22, there was an overlap at v. 7 where these two
oracles were juxtaposed, as happens in the LXX. Thus
in the early editions of Jer-LXX 29, v. 7 contained
both the last verse of the Philistine oracle as well as
the first verse of the Edom oracle, a practice which
was perpetuated until the first edition of Tischendorf's LXX which numbered the verses of the Edom oracle
8-23 instead of 7-22. This system was, in turn, taken
over by Swete (in Rahlfs' text, as noted above, the
Edom oracle became 30:1-16).

     Rahlfs' chapter and verse divisions had indeed
much to commend them as an attempt to facilitate cross
references between the MT and LXX texts. But the
Septuaginta-Unternehmen made it a policy decision to
follow the traditional chapter and verse divisions,
using Swete's latest edition as its model (cf. Duodecim
prophetae, p. 133). In the event, therefore, Rahlfs'
worthwhile attempt to ease the lot of the reader who
needed to consult both the Hebrew and Greek texts was
aborted; ironically, this has resulted in greater confusion than ever owing to the wide circulation enjoyed
by Rahlfs' text. In citing from Jer-LXX, therefore,
it is absolutely essential to make quite clear which
edition is being used. For instance, depending on
which text is being used, the first verse of the Edom
oracle may be referred to as 29:7 (Walton, Field,
Bagster, HR concordance), 29:8 (Tischendorf, Swete,
Ziegler), or 30:1 (Rahlfs).

     As for paragraph divisions, Ziegler has made
limited used of these; where they occur they conform
to Rahlfs' divisions.

2.   Punctuation and Capitalization

Punctuation is probably the most effective tool
that a modern editor has at his disposal for com-
municating his interpretation of a given passage from
antiquity. By the deliberate use of commas, periods,
semicolons, question marks, and quotation indicators he
seeks to secure a particular interpretation of a passage at the exclusion of other interpretations. In
this area, however, Ziegler's text does not appear to
represent a fresh contribution, being content for the
most part to follow Rahlfs' lead. For an illustration
of the difference that punctuation can make in the
interpretation of a passage, we may compare 29:2b-4a in
the editions of Swete and Rahlfs/Ziegler:

Swete	Rahlfs/Ziegler
και κεκραξονται οι ανθρω- ποι, και αλαλαξουσιν απαντες οι κατοικουντες την γην **v.** 3 απο φωνης ορμης αυτου, απο των οπλων των ποδων αυτου και απο σεισμου των αρματων αυτου, ηχου τροχων αυτου. ουκ επεστρεφαν πατερες εφ υιους αυτων απο εκλυσεως χειρων αυτων, **v.** 4 εν τη ημερα τη επερχομενη του απολεσαι παντας τους αλλοφυλους.	και κεκραξονται οι ανθρω- ποι, και αλαλαξουσιν απαντες οι κατοικουντες την γην. **v.** 3 απο φωνης ορμης αυτου, απο των οπλων των ποδων (ιππων Zi.) αυτου και απο σεισμου των αρματων αυτου, ηχου τροχων αυτου ουκ επεστρεφαν πατερες εφ υιους αυτων απο εκλυσεως χειρων αυτων **v.** 4 εν τη ημερα τη ερχομενη του απολεσαι παντας τους αλλοφυλους.

In Swete's text the phrase απο φωνης ορμης αυτου,
απο των οπλων των ποδων αυτου και απο σεισμου των αρματων
αυτου, ηχου τροχων αυτου is punctuated in such a way as
to constitute the reason for the shouting and wailing
of the earth's inhabitants, whereas in Rahlfs' and
Ziegler's texts the same phrase, by virtue of different
punctuation, becomes the reason why the fathers do not
return to their sons. On this occasion one feels
Swete's punctuation makes for better sense and is to
be preferred.

In the matter of capitalization the three texts
of Swete, Rahlfs and Ziegler are practically identical,
all following the normal Greek practice of using

capitals only for proper names, for the commencement of
larger units and for the introduction of direct speech.
However, in the case of the divine title κυριος the
texts part company, Swete employing upper case <u>kappa</u>
and Rahlfs/Ziegler using lower case (both, however, use
lower case for θεος).

3. Orthography and Accentuation

As we have seen, the MS evidence manifests a bewildering variety of orthographic variants. This was
to be expected, considering the diverse origins in time
and place of our MSS. Nonetheless, the many conflicting spellings impose on an editor the difficult task of
deciding which form to adopt for his critical text.

An important discussion of this subject is found
in P. Walter's book, <u>The</u> <u>Text</u> <u>of</u> <u>the</u> <u>Septuagint</u>, where
on pp. 19ff. he outlines three options available to
the editor of a LXX text: 1) the editor may decide to
present his text in its "traditional" spelling, the
method chosen by the printed editions of the 16th century and their successors; 2) he may seek to reproduce
the spelling of a certain standard MS, the "documentary" approach chosen for the Cambridge editions; or
3) he may deliberately attempt to prefer such spellings
as can be expected for the translator's period, what
might be called the "contemporary" approach, the one
generally preferred by the Göttingen editors /14/.

This third way, that of considering corrupt whatever spelling cannot be justified by the standards of
language contemporary with the author, was pioneered
for the Göttingen texts by Alfred Rahlfs. In this
task he was aided by a vast amount of papyri and in-
scriptional material discovered in modern times
covering both the Ptolemaic period in which the LXX
was translated as well as the Imperial and Byzantine
periods during which it was frequently copied. By
means of this new knowledge Rahlfs sought to eliminate
from his edition of the LXX many spellings which he
reckoned could not go back to the original translators.
Comparison between Ziegler's and Rahlfs' texts shows
that Ziegler has generally reproduced Rahlfs' orthography, much as he took over Rahlfs' punctuation /15/.

    The rationale for this orthographic methodology is
the consideration that if in the area of true vocabulary variants it is desirable to recover the earliest
possible approximation to the original translation, the
same ought to be true for the orthographic variants.
But the two issues are not quite the same. There is
namely the disconcerting fact that the original trans-
lators/authors of the LXX, in common with all writers
of antiquity, were quite inconsistent in their habits
of spelling, conventions of this sort being a relatively modern phenomenon. Faced with the problem of
heterogeneous spelling even in the autographs, how then
should the modern editor proceed? Should he seek to
reflect the lack of standardization in the original
documents as far as this can be determined, or should
he seek to impose some sort of standardization of his
own? The editors of the Göttingen series have chosen
to follow the latter course. They apparently reason
that since the original spelling is inaccessible to us
anyways--by reason of the caprice of scribes--some form
of standardization is inevitable, the best available
being the dominant Attic form.

    In effect, the policy adopted makes a fundamental
distinction between the value of the MS evidence in
determining the actual word employed by the translators
and the way it is to be spelled. In the former case
the MS witness is of primary importance, in the latter
case it is of secondary relevance. Thus, while the
spelling adopted by Rahlfs/Ziegler sometimes follows
the earliest MS evidence against the popular spelling
in the bulk of the minuscules and printed editions
(e.g., the spelling εξολε̱θρευσει at 29:4 in B* A Q
versus εξο̱λοθρευσει elsewhere, including the printed
editions, cf. Thackeray, Grammar, pp. 87-88), more
often they leave aside the spelling of the earliest
codices in favour of what is considered the more proper
form (e.g., the preference for the spelling συμφησ̱θωσι
at 29:21 against that of συν̱ψηθωσιν B* or συμ̱ψηθωσιν Bc
130--Thackeray, Grammar, p. 221). In fact, Walters
specifically states that the editor's task in not to
decide what the authors actually wrote (for at the time
of writing a particular translator may already have
been misled by influences such as itacism), but what is
the normal spelling which best expresses what was in
the author's mind, if not in his pen (Text, p. 27).
Although Walters was never an editor in the Göttingen

series, it seems clear that at this point he is representing a common viewpoint. No doubt one can sympathize with the need for some kind of standardization,
but one also feels that in the sharp distinction which
the Göttingen texts make between variants of substance
and variants of orthography there resides a tension
that has not been entirely resolved or fully justified
/16/.

A special problem has to do with the transcription
of proper names, the orthography of which is notoriously erratic in ancient MSS. Here again standardization plays a vital role in the Göttingen editions;
in fact, in this area Ziegler sometimes goes beyond
Rahlfs, apparently following the lead of Walters.
Ziegler himself says that in the matter of proper names
he has subjected Rahlfs and Katz (Walters) to a new
appraisal, the result of which is embodied in Ch. 2 of
Beiträge. In several instances the determinative norm
here tends to be the Hebrew spelling of the MT. Two
examples from Jer 29 will illustrate the procedure.

29:9   Δαιδαν/Δεδαν

The Hebrew name דדן is found twice in the book of
Jer: 29:9(49:8) and 32:9(25:23). The MS evidence for
Jer-LXX is as follows:

  29:9   δεδανω 534; δεδαν   407 538 544; δαιδαμ B;
          δαιδαν rel.

  32:9   δεδαν S 407; δαιδα 62; δαιδαν   rel.

Ziegler's choice whether to print Δαιδαν or Δεδαν is
determined by the principle, "Wenn ʾ im Hebr. steht,
dann ist ι zu schreiben wie Αιλαμ, Αιθαν," whereas
"Wenn ʾ fehlt, dann muss ε stehen." i.e. "für den
Übersetzer war das ʾ entscheidend" (Beiträge, p. 67).
The spelling Δεδαν had already been proposed by Katz
in his Cambridge thesis, p. 22 (p. 133 of the book,
Text). In adopting the Δεδαν form Ziegler is able to
cite as support MSS 407 538 544 at 29:9 and S 407 at
32:9. However, it is doubtful that the spelling of the
MSS cited goes back directly to the original translation. Rather, Δεδαν in 407 538 544 is probably a
scribal itacistic variant of the archetype spelling

Δαιδαν. This in itself does not rule out the possibility that the original spelling might still have been with ε, but it does suggest that we do not have any MS evidence reaching directly back to that spelling.

One also wonders about the principle that for the translator "war das ﬡ entscheidend." After all, other influences may also have been at work on the translator, such as euphony, the existence of an already Hellenized form of the name, not to mention the possibility of a different spelling in the translator's Vorlage. Consequently, it does not seem convincing to ignore the almost consistent Greek spelling Δαιδαν of the MSS here. Rather, it would be better to print the standard MS form of the name (as did Rahlfs) in preference to a small minority reading in the MSS which happens to conform to the MT. In his review of the Göttingen text of Ezekiel (RB 59 [1952], 609) Barthélemy called attention to Ziegler's over-reliance on the MT as a norm in the restoration of proper names. On the basis of this criticism Ziegler undertook to restudy the proper names of Jer (cf. Beiträge, p. 59). Regrettably Δαιδαν/Δεδαν was not one of those places changed. It is interesting to note that in his edition of Genesis, Wevers has retained the spelling Δαιδαν, cf. Gen. 25:3.

29:20   Αιθαμ/Αιθαν

The Hebrew word אֵיתָן is found in the OT both as an adjective with the meaning "strong"/"enduring" as well as a proper name for person and place. In Jer-MT 49:19 its function is that of an adjective describing a noun ("a strong sheepfold" RSV). In the LXX translation of the passage, however, it was taken as a proper name. The question is, How should it be spelled? Most witnesses have the spelling Αιθαμ (though curiously the Hexaplaric and Catena texts have αιμαθ). Ziegler, nevertheless, prefers the spelling Αιθαν, not at all attested for 29:20 though found in MSS 46 86 233 at 27:44. How valid is this proposal?

There is no doubt that there was frequent interchange of ν and μ in the transmission of the proper name under consideration (as well as in other names, cf. Δαιδαμ/Δαιδαν in 29:8). For illustration we may

cite the most important witnesses to the variants attested for this name in 1 Chr:

	Αιθαμ	Αιθαν
2:6	B	AN
2:8	B	AN
6:42(47)	c$_2$	BAN
6:44(29)	B	AN
15:17	S	BAN
15:19	im	BSAN

In Rahlfs' edition the name is spelled Αιθαν on
each of its occurrences in 1 Chr. But this levelling
of the MS evidence in favour of the Hebrew may not be
felicitous. L.C. Allen has shown that the A group in
Chr (of which N is a member) is heavily recensional
(i.e. Hexaplaric) while the B group (of which c and S
are members) represents the best witnesses to the Old
Greek, much as in Jer (The Greek Chronicles, I, 1974).
The consistent spelling Αιθαν in the A group, therefore, is highly suspect as an approximation to the MT
in 1 Chr. It is possible that the same explanation
accounts for the spelling Αιθαν in Jer. In any event,
standardization on the basis of the MT appears to be a
questionable policy. If there is to be any standardization in the spelling of the word under consideration,
it should be on the basis of the most common and best
attested Greek form, i.e. Αιθαμ (this is also the
spelling adopted in the GCS edition of Eusebius'
Onomastica, p. 38).

Closely related to orthography is the matter of
accentuation. In this area Ziegler again tends to
follow Rahlfs, departing from his predecessor only in
a few instances on the recommendation of P. Katz
(Walters) (cf. Ieremias, p. 110). With respect to
proper names and other transliterations, Ziegler's
procedure is to provide with accents only those forms
which happen to terminate with a natural Greek ending
while leaving "barbarous" words unaccented. This
expedient was also taken oven directly from Rahlfs,
though the practice appears to go back to Lagarde's
edition of Pars Prior (1883). In contrast to this
procedure, Swete accented all Greek names, and this

policy has now been adopted for the latest edition of
the Göttingen series (cf. Wevers, Genesis, p. 62).

Summarizing our observations on the "Editorial
Miscellanea" of Ziegler's edition of Jer, we conclude
that in these matters the text is heavily dependent on
previous editions. In the case of chapter and verse
divisions it follows the edition of Swete over against
Rahlfs, but in the matter of punctuation and orthography the reverse is true. Proper names are assimi-
lated to the MT more than in previous editions.

B.   Choice of Readings

Ultimately the most important decisions that face
an editor of a critical text have to do with his actual
choice of readings to be adopted in the text itself.
In these decisions he is guided by his overall aim and
by the application of specific text critical principles.

The overall aim of the Göttingen enterprise has
been explained as the reconstruction of the LXX "in
seiner ältesten erreichbaren Gestalt" /17/, a deliberately guarded formulation that leaves open the question to what extent the "ältesten erreichbaren Gestalt"
is also supposed to represent the actual text that came
from the hands of the translators. In 1953 Ziegler
wrote, "Richtig ist, dass man sich niemals einbilden
darf, den 'Urtext' der Septuaginta herstellen zu
können" (Biblica 34 [1953], 435);   nevertheless, the
ideal of the Göttingen editors is surely the recovery
of the "Urtext" even though it will always remain an
unattainable ideal in every detail. A reading of
Ziegler's supplementary monograph to the critical
edition of Jeremiah, Beiträge zur Ieremias-Septuaginta,
makes it clear that the discussion is carried on at the
level of what the original translator(s) may or may not
have written. For all practical purposes, therefore,
the goal remains to reach back to the original text,
"the text which the translators brought into being" (to
use Orlinsky's phrase, "Current Progress and Problems,"
p. 144).

To achieve this goal it is necessary to follow
sound text critical principles, a constant concern of
Paul de Lagarde and his successors in Göttingen.

Lagarde insisted that the standard methods employed in
the editing of classical texts should also be applied
to the LXX with certain additional provisions suited to
the translation status of most of its books (cf. p. 7,
n. 6 above). According to classical methodology there
are two principal steps in the restoration of an ancient text, the recensio and the emendatio (or examin-
atio, the term preferred by P. Maas, Textual Criticism,
1958, p. 1), the former being the selection of the most
trustworthy witnesses on which a text is to be based,
the second being the task of deciding which of the
competing readings best represents the original. Decisions of the latter kind--as Westcott and Hort so
clearly taught--are influenced by external considerations such as the date and group relationship of the
witnesses and by internal factors such as transcriptional probability (having to do with a knowledge of
scribal habits and mistakes) and intrinsic probability
(having to do with a knowledge of the author's style
and vocabulary). In cases where none of the transmitted readings can be accepted as representing the
original, a third step, that of divinatio or conjecture
may be resorted to.

     All of the above criteria have been employed by
Ziegler in his reconstruction of the main text. We
will evaluate the success of his enterprise according
to the following outline: 1) Choice of B Group Readings, 2) Choice of Other MS Readings, and 3) Choice of
Conjectural Emendations.

1.   Choice of B Group Readings

     The analysis of the available MS evidence for Jer
(Ch. II above) has revealed that the generally most
reliable witness to the earliest text of this book is
the B group, consisting at its fullest of B-S(-106')
-130-239-538. In keeping with this data, Ziegler's
stated policy is to prefer a reading of the B group
unless it can be shown in some way to be secondary or
corrupt (Ieremias, p. 125). In Jer 29 we can document
several instances where this policy has been carried
through. We note first those places where Ziegler has
preferred a narrowly transmitted B group reading over
against some other widely distributed readings:

29:3   εφ B-S-130] επι rel.

29:10   ως B-S] ωσπερ A-106' C-613; ωσει rel.

29:13   αθωωθης B-S-106'-538] οτι πινουσα πιη L Tht.;
        + οτι πινων (πιων/πιουσα/πινοντι) πιεσαι rel.
        = Rahlfs = MT

29:17   υψωσεν B-S-410-538] -σας C 106 = MT; εαν
        υψωσης (-σεις A 26 239 86mg) rel.

29:21   επ αυτην B-S*-106'-130-538] επ αυτη A; επ
        αυτης Sc 26; επ αυτους rel. = MT

29: 22 εφοβηθη B-S-538] εσ(ε)ισθη rel. = Rahlfs

It is interesting to observe that on two occasions
in the above examples Ziegler has followed the B group
even where Rahlfs opted for the majority text reading.

Sometimes the MS evidence splits right down the
middle; here, too, we can show that Ziegler frequently
sides with the reading supported by the B group:

29:2   απαντες B-S-130-410-538 Q-544 O C/-49-90
        -764] παντες rel.

29:9   βαθυνατε B-S-130 V-26-46-534-544 O L/-36-51
        -449] + εαυτοις(-τους 87 538 Tht.; εν αυτοις
        106) A-106' Q-86-233-239-538-613 36-51-449 C

29:9   επ αυτον (2°) B-106-130 Q-46-233-613 36
        C/-91-490] επ αυτην S 26 410; επ αυτω 91-490;
        om. επ A V-86'-239-534-544 O L/-36/-538 = MT

29:10   ηλθον B-S-106'-538 Qc C-613] + σοι rel. = MT

29:10   οι B-S-106'-239-538 Qc-26-233-613 88 L C]
        om. A Q*-V-46-86'-130-534-544 Syh = MT

29:13   οις B-S-538 A-106' C] pr. ιδου rel. = MT

29:14   καταρασιν B-130-410 Q-26-86'-233-534] καταραν
        S-239 A-106 V-538-544 C-613; επικαταρασιν L
        Tht.; επικαταραν 88; καταπαυσιν 46

29:14 εις αιωνα B-S-106-130-239 V-26-46-86'-534-544]
εις αιωνας O 51-449; εις τον αιωνα A-410 Q-233
-538-613 C; εως αιωνος L/-51-407-449

29:18 συριει B-S-130-538 A-106'] εκστησεται (pr.
συριει C) και συριει επι (εν 87txt) παση τη
πληγη (πασαν την πληγην Q-239-613) αυτης rel.
= MT

29:19 ωσπερ B-S-130-239-538 A-106' Q-613 C] ως V
-26-46-86'-233-534-544 O L

29:21 συμφησθωσι(ν) B-130-239 V-26-86'-233-534 Syh
L/-51-51s-62-311-407-449 C/-490] συμφηφισ-
θωσι(ν) A-106 Q-46-544-613 88 51-51s-62-311
-407-449-538 490; συνωσιν S 410

29:22 οτι B-S-130-239-538 A-106' 36 C-613] om.
rel. = MT

29:22 και B-S-239-538 A-106' C-613] om. rel. = MT

2. Choice of Other MS Readings

While it is true that Ziegler has laid the B group
as his foundational text, on several occasions he has
nevertheless rejected the B group in favour of another
MS reading. We will list and evaluate in turn the
relevant instances for Jer 29.

29:4 επερχομενη B] ερχομενη rel.

The reading επερχομενη in the phrase εν τη ημερα
τη επερχομενη (על היום הבא) is found only in Codex
Vaticanus, so that strictly speaking it is not a B
group reading. Such unique readings in an ancient
codex--even when that codex happens to be Vaticanus--
stand little chance of going back to the original, and
the reading has rightly been rejected by Ziegler. The
similar Hebrew phrase ימים באים is uniformly translated
ημεραι ερχονται in all 13 of its occurrences in Jer-LXX.
The tendency in later Greek to prefer compound in place
of simplex forms of the verb may account for the
scribal change here.

29:10   καταλ(ε)ιμμα B-S-106'-239   26-534-613 C
(-ατα A Q-V+)] καλαμηματα O L

The problem in this verse concerns the translation
of the word עוללות in the phrase לא ישארו עוללות which
in the majority of the Greek tradition is rendered οι
ου καταλειφουσι σοι καταλειμμα(-ατα). Somewhat surprisingly Ziegler has opted for the variant καλαμηματα
attested by the Hexaplaric and Lucianic recensions
only. In defense of this choice Ziegler appeals to the
translation of עלל in Jer 6:9 by καλαμασθαι and explains the form καταλειμμα(-ατα) as conscious or sub-
conscious scribal assimilation to the immediately preceding Greek verb καταλειφουσι (Beiträge, p. 48). But
in the process Ziegler has to by-pass the weighty MS
evidence of the majority Greek tradition and adopt a
reading from two groups of known recensional character.

A priori it is not impossible that an original
reading should have been preserved in the O and L
recensions alone while corrupted in the rest of the MS
tradition. But it is questionable whether in this case
the internal considerations cited (i.e. the single
translation equivalent at 6:9 and the explanation of
transcriptional assimilation in καταλειμμα[-ατα]) are
sufficiently convincing to set aside the strong external MS evidence of the B group and majority Greek tradition. The noun καλαμημα is not attested in the Greek
literature outside its occurrence here in O/L and in
Theodotion's translation of the parallel passage in Ob
5 (where LXX has the standard translation equivalence
επιφυλλιδες/עוללות). If Theodotion used the word καλαμηματα for עוללות in Ob 5, the likelihood is that he
did the same in the Edom oracle of Jer; consequently,
this this may well be the source of the O/L reading at
29:10. Since there is no firm translation pattern in
the rest of the LXX with regard to the use of κατα-
λειμμα(-ατα) there appears to be no reason why it could
not have been used here to render עוללות /18/. Rahlfs
opted for καταλειμματα with A Q-V+, but this has the
appearance of being a case of Greek refinement. In the
end, therefore, we are led back to the B group reading
καταλειμμα as the preferred reading for the critical
text.

29:11 γειτονος μου   B-S] και γειτονος αυτου
= majority text

As a translation of the Hebrew phrase שדד זרעו
ואחיו ושכניו the B-S text has ωλοντο δια χειρα αδελφου
αυτου, γειτονος μου whereas Ziegler's text reads ωλοντο
επιχειρα αδελφου αυτου και γειτονος αυτου. For discussion of the conjectural emendation επιχειρα see
below pp. 147-49. The B-S omission of the conjunction
και is additionally supported by 130 Co Aeth while the
B-S reading μου (as opposed to αυτου) finds further
support in 410 Bo Aeth Arab. The phrase και γειτονος
αυτου, in preference to the B-S reading γειτονος μου,
was adopted initially in Rahlfs' text and has apparently been taken over from there by Ziegler. Is this
critical choice justified?

It is true that the reading και γειτονος αυτου
corresponds to the MT ושכניו and appears to make better
sense in the Greek /19/. But precisely for those
reasons one could argue for the B-S reading as the
lectio difficilior and as the one most likely to have
been amended in the pre-Hexaplaric revision of the Q
group. The tension, as often, is between the weight of
the external witnesses versus internal consistency.
Ziegler and Rahlfs have opted for the latter. An
equally defensible policy would have been to adopt the
earliest MS reading at our disposal--γειτονος μου of
B-S--and let the apparatus speak for any alternative
possibilities.

29:12 και εγω ζησομαι   B-S-239-538   A-106' C-613]
και εγω αυτους διασωσω L; om. Q-V+ O

Where the MT reads אני אחיה the majority Greek
text has ινα ζησηται (-εται) και εγω ζησομαι. It seems
clear that we are dealing here with a double reading in
the Greek. Ziegler has followed the Q and O groups in
omitting και εγω ζησομαι from his critical text and
cites three additional instances from the latter half
of Jer where the double reading is attested by B-S A
(C) while one half is missing in Q-V O L (C) (Beiträge,
p. 102). What cannot be determined with certainty is
whether the Q revision (followed by O) eliminated an
existing double reading or whether the double reading
in B-S A C (cf. L) crept in after the Q revision. If

the Q revision eliminated one half of an existing
double reading it is surprising that it would have
suppressed the reading closest to the MT אני אחיה. At
any rate, Ziegler is justified in omitting και εγω
ζησομαι with Q-V+ O since this has all the marks of a
secondary addition to harmonize with the Hebrew.

29:13   ταδε ειπεν B-S-538] τ. λεγει rel.

        The above variant represents a particularly thorny
problem since the choice between ειπεν and λεγει in the
translation of the MF כה אמר יהוה is related to the
translator/reviser problem to be discussed in the next
chapter. While the common translation of the said
messenger formula in the first half of the book, up to
and including 29:8, is ταδε λεγει κυριος the corresponding rendition in the second half commencing with
30:1 is ουτως ειπε κυριος. In between, at 29:13 in
B-S-538, we find the hybrid form ταδε ειπεν. Here
again the editor is faced with a difficult choice
between the witness of the generally best external
evidence versus the internal evidence of translation
pattern. Rahlfs opted for the former alternative,
Ziegler for the latter. However the situation is complicated by the fact that two translation patterns meet
at this very point. Whereas the ταδε λεγει pattern
occurs up till 29:13 in the majority of MSS, other
considerations suggest that the second hand commenced
his work before rather than after 29:13 (e.g. the use
of απολλυμι in 29:4, pp. 170-71 below). In view of
this, a case could also be made for the B-S-538 ειπεν
form at 29:13 /20/.

29:19   ενοικησει B-S (-ση Q-130-239-538-613)]
κατοικησει V 26 62 91 (-ση 88 L/-62); καθεισῃ A

        In the choice between the verbs ενοικεω and κατ-
οικεω Ziegler has preferred the former which is attested by B-S-130-239-538 Q-613. But in the choice
between the future -σει (B-S) and the aorist subjunctive -ση (Q-130-239-538-613) Ziegler prefers the latter
since the verb in question follows the emphatic ου μη.
The interchange between -ει and -ῃ is probably nothing
more than an orthographic variant so that Ziegler is
justified in following the conventional rule of Greek
grammar in preferring the aorist subjunctive.

Concluding Remarks

As we read Ziegler's critical text, not only in Jer 29 but throughout the book, and compare it with the apparatus we are frequently aware of the opposing claims on the editor's loyalty: on the one hand there is the hard evidence of the MSS and the generally best MS group; on the other hand there is the question of internal considerations such as translation pattern and suitability to context. To resolve the tension created by these (sometimes) opposing forces is no easy task and Ziegler in effect treads a path of compromise between them, sometimes preferring one, sometimes the other in accordance with what he considers the relative merits of each new case.

In adopting this policy Ziegler has avoided the polar positions of NT textual criticism represented on the one hand by Westcott and Hort's reliance on the criterion of the best MS and on the other hand by Prof. Kilpatrick's advocacy of the criterion of internal fitness, the approach labeled "rational" or "rigorous criticism" /21/. If we had to describe Ziegler's text critical posture in current NT terminology, we might call it a "modified rational eclecticism," by which we mean that his approach is decidedly eclectic in that it deliberately seeks to choose the most appropriate reading from a host of competing witnesses, but his choices are frequently tempered by a greater allegiance to the "best MS" tradition than is characteristic among the proponents of "rigorous eclecticism." While there is reason for placing great confidence in Ziegler's ability and sobriety of judgement, both the method chosen and the actual textual decisions made nevertheless invite constant reappraisal. In fact, in one of his earlier volumes Ziegler had himself invited such reappraisal /22/. For our part we would like to see an even greater--though not necessarily exclusive--reliance on the B group readings for the reconstruction of the archetype text than that reflected in Ziegler's edition. While many of Ziegler's proposed improvements on the B group readings are plausible enough, few are decisively convincing--such is the nature and ambiguity of the textual evidence available. In these cases it seems preferable to print the reading of the generally best attested form of the pre-Hexaplaric text, namely the B group, and leave the variants in the apparatus.

3. Choice of Conjectural Emendations

In the field of classical studies, the <u>recensio</u>
and <u>examinatio</u> have often led to <u>divinatio</u>—the adoption of a conjectured reading. In NT textual criticism, by contrast, modern editions of the text rarely,
if ever, incorporate a conjectured reading into the
text, though a few may be included in the apparatus
/23/. The reason for this difference in approach between classical and NT studies is generally attributed
to the fact that whereas most of the classics are preserved only in relatively few and late MSS, the text of
the NT is attested in a superabundance of MSS, many of
them quite early, so that the need for conjectural
emendation does not arise in the latter in the same
way as in the classics /24/.

What should be the policy on the adoption of
conjectural emendations in a critical text of the LXX,
considering the fact that the LXX stands somewhere
between the classics and the NT both with regard to the
wealth and date of the material available? In answer
to this question, LXX text critical scholarship offers
no consensus. Some have contended that a conjectural
emendation should never be adopted into the body of a
critical text (cf. H.S. Gehman, <u>VT</u> 3 [1953], 400);
Ziegler, however, holds that this rule is too strict,
though he agrees that only such emendations should be
admitted into the text as have the highest degree of
probability, while most should be confined to the
apparatus (<u>Beiträge</u>, p. 8; <u>Ieremias</u>, pp. 128-29).

In Jer 29 Ziegler has on four occasions (five if
we count the conjectural spelling Αιθαν discussed
above, pp. 131-32) admitted into his text a conjectured
reading which he feels better represents the original
than any preserved MS reading. In the following pages
I have sought thoroughly to evaluate the <u>Beweiskraft</u> of
these emendations. In the process I have come to the
negative conclusion that they do not convince sufficiently to be retained in the body of the text. This
leads to the further recommendation that in the editing
of the LXX—as in the case of current NT practice—it
is better, except in rare cases, to print only attested
readings. Conjectured readings which attempt to go
behind the archetype should be confined to the
apparatus.

The four emendations to be discussed are ιππων in 29(47):3, το προσωπον in 29:9(49:8), επιχειρα in 29:11 (49:10), and εν θαλασση Σουφ in 29:22(49:21). These and other emendations are briefly commented upon by Ziegler in Ch. 1, "Konjekturen und umstrittene Textlesarten in der Ier.-LXX," Beiträge, pp. 17-58. In the discussion below, each conjectural emendation is introduced by an extract of text from Ziegler's edition containing the conjectured word or phrase, accompanied by an apparatus giving the relevant MS readings.

29(47):3 ιππων

απο φωνης ορμης αυτου   מקול שעטת
απο των οπλων των ιππων αυτου   פרסות אביריו

ιππων Zi.] δυνατων O L/-51-407-449; δυναμεων 407; πολλων 130 538; ποδων rel.

The majority text of 29:3 contains the reading ποδων αυτου, difficult to reconcile with the MT אביריו. Ziegler, following Schleusner, II, p. 845 (approved by Coste, p. 29 [not p. 23 as in Ziegler, Beiträge, p. 27] and Katz, TLZ 61 [1936], 280), has adopted the conjectural emendation ιππων αυτου as representing the Old Greek. But the suggestion is beset with a number of difficulties. The following points apply:

1. Schleusner originally proposed the emendation with the remark, "Fortasse scribendum est ιππος quam notionem אביר haud raro habet" πους. But on that basis the emended reading also stands condemned, for nowhere else in the LXX nor in the Minor Greek VSS is אביר ever rendered by ιππος either. In such a case, the transmitted unique rendition is preferred to the conjectured unique rendition.

2. Apart from 1 Sam 21:8 אביר is found only in poetry, and although its root meaning is well established as "strong" or "mighty," its specific meaning in any given instance can be determined only from the context /25/. The renditions of אביר in the LXX fall into three groups:

a) those instances where the translators simply employed the base meaning of אביר apparently

without much consideration of context /26/, e.g.
δυναστης Gen 49:24, δυνατος Jud 5:22 (A text),
ισχυς Isa 10:13, 49:26, ισχυρος Jud 5:22 (B
text), Lam 1:15, ισχυω Isa 1:24.

b) those instances where context played the
primary role in the interpretation of אביר, e.g.
θεος Ps 131(132):2,5, Isa 60:16, αγγελος Ps 77
(78):25, ταυρος /27/ Ps 21(22):13, 49(50):13, 67
(68):31, Isa 34:7, Jer 27(50):11, ιππασια /28/
Jer 8:16, μοσχος /29/ Jer 26(46):15.

c) those instances of entirely unpredictable
translations, e.g. νεμω 1 Re 21:7(8), ασυνετος
Ps 75(76):6, αδυνατος Job 24:22, 34:20,
Isa 46:12 /30/.

In the light of the great variety of translation
equivalents, there is no guarantee what the translation
might have been in any given instance. Certainly it
would be presumptuous without further evidence to
assume that at 29(47):3 the translator successfully
found the right equivalent according to our modern
exegesis of the context.

3. The translation of אביר in 29(47):3 by ιππος
is made less certain still by the appearance of other
Hebrew/Greek discrepancies in the same verse; in fact,
analysis of the Greek suggests that the translator
found the entire phrase in which אביר appears difficult
to handle. For one thing, the word ορμη (probably in
the sense "assault" or "attack") is a guess at the
meaning of the Hebrew hapax legomenon שעטה*, in the
English VSS rendered "stamping" in conformity with the
understanding of the entire passage, "the stamping of
the hoofs of the stallions" (RSV). Then, assuming
identical Hebrew Vorlage to MT, there was the failure
to connect שעטת with פרסות, and this apparently led the
translator to see in the phrase מקול שעטת פרסות אביריו
two parallel phrases rather than one continuous phrase.
This in turn demanded further changes: the possessive
ορμης αυτου does not correspond to the construct שעטת,
nor is the second απο represented in the Hebrew.

Since in the Greek reading of the phrase, אביר is
parallel to the hapax שעטה*, it is understandable that
the translator would have had difficulty making sense

of אביר, too. Nor is there anything in the entire
oracle preceding אביר which would have prepared him for
any easy solution to the problem or demanded a translation such as ιππος. It is true that the verse goes on
to speak about "chariots" (αρματα/רכבות) and "wheels"
(τροχοι/גלגלים), but this is still not of the order of
parallelism in which, for instance, the meaning ταυρος
was obtained in other contexts where אביר is mentioned
in conjunction with other animals (cf. p. 143, 2b).
Even the correct equivalence οπλοι/פרסות in our verse
does not demand that the translator followed this word
with ιππος. After all, although the phrase οπλων των
ποδων αυτου, "the hoofs of his feet," is rather redun-
dant, perhaps even technically wrong, it is not so
absurd as to be thought entirely impossible.

4. The proposed emendation assumes that an original ΙΠΠΩΝ was later corrupted to ΠΟΔΩΝ. Although there
is some orthographic resemblance between the two forms,
both are simple and common words, and it is not easy to
see (as admitted by Ziegler, Beiträge, p. 27) how the
one would be confused with the other. Transcriptional
probability, therefore, is not in favour of the reading
ΙΠΠΩΝ either. Rudolph (ZAW 48[1930], 277) has suggested that the original Greek reading was ΠΟΛΛΩΝ (attested by 130 538 Compl.) instead of ΠΟΔΩΝ, the Δ and Λ
being easily interchanged. On this reading, the phrase
could be translated "the hoofs of his multitudes."
However, one suspects the direction of corruption was
from Δ to Λ rather than vice versa.

5. Ziegler comments, "Trotz aller Schwierigkeiten
steht fest, dass ποδων verderbt ist. Wenn man ändert,
dann hat ιππων den Vorzug" (Beiträge, p. 28). But if
the case is as uncertain as Ziegler admits and as the
above review had demonstrated, is it not preferable to
let the best attested MS reading stand in the text and
assign the conjecture to the apparatus? For it is
clear that the conjectured reading raises as many problems as the MS reading, and, as B. Metzger has pointed
out, "an emendation that introduces fresh difficulties
stands self-condemned" (Text of the New Testament,
p. 185, n. 1). Metzger's further remarks are also
apropos: "The conjecture does not rise from a certain
level of probability ('a happy guess') to the level of
certainty, or approximate certainty, unless its fitness
is exact and perfect. The only criterion of a

successful conjecture is that is shall approve itself
as inevitable. Lacking inevitability, it remains
doubtful" (Text, p. 183). In short, since nothing is
gained by replacing one doubtful reading with another,
it seems advisable to stay with the best MS reading.

29:9(49:8)   το προσωπον αυτων

ωχετο σοφια αυτων   נסרחה חכמתם
ηπατηθη το προσωπον αυτων   נסו הפנו

το προσωπον αυτων Zi.] το προς αυτον S*; ο (ο sub ※ 88;
om. ο Sc 130 410) τοπος αυτων rel.

Regarding the divergent readings ηπατηθη ο τοπος
αυτων ("their place has been deceived") in most LXX MSS
and נסו הפנו ("flee, turn back") in MT, Spohn (p. 377)
curtly declares, "Nullo modo Graeca hebraicis respondent." The complete lack of correspondence between the
two versions has given rise to a variety of suggestions
for emending the texts. Spohn himself proposed επατηθη
(from πατεω) ο τοπος αυτων, but considered this phrase
an "explicatio verborum sequentium," the LXX having
neglected to translate נסו הפנו, either deliberately or
because the phrase was already missing in its Hebrew
Vorlage. Hitzig (p. 366) retained Spohn's επατηθη but
retroverted the phrase בסו מכנו. Schwally (p. 201, n.
1) carried the speculation further by taking נסו הפנו
as a doublet unrepresented in the Greek, with επατηθη ο
τοπος αυτων corresponding to נדרכה מכונתם (נרמסה Giesebrecht p. 242), which in turn was taken as a variant of
MT נסרחה חכמתם. Duhm (p. 354) poked fun at such fanci-
ful conjecture ("Die Reversion ist also vorsichtig zu
behandeln, sonst macht sie Kunststücken wie ein
Kasperle") and preferred to stay as close as possible
to the MT; in his view ηπατηθη . . . αυτων translated
נסות כנו (post-biblical use of סות).

The reading which we find in Ziegler's text,
ηπατηθη το προσωπον αυτων derives from a suggestion
made by Wutz (p. 34) and endorsed by Katz in correspondence with Ziegler. Wutz's theory is that the reading
of S* (Wutz incorrectly wrote A*), namely το προς
αυτον preserves the remnant of an original το προσωπον
αυτον (Ziegler, Beiträge, p. 28, assumes that Wutz
meant to write αυτων). This Greek phrase may then have

been derived from the Hebrew נסות פנו (cf. Duhm above).
While on first encounter the conjecture appears to have
much to commend it, further investigation reveals a
number of unanswered problems.

1. There is first the danger of relying too much
on S* /31/. While it is true that S is a member of the
B group and hence frequently a witness to the earliest
text, it is also true that this MS--particularly the
portion in which Jer occurs--contains a bewildering
variety of unique variants and scribal errors, as a
glance at Swete's apparatus (or even the collation
notes above, pp. 23-41) will quickly show. Hence it
is just as easy to explain the nonsense phrase το προς
αυτον as a corruption of ο τοπος αυτων (ΟΤΟΠΟΣΑΥΤΩΝ
--→ ΤΟΠΡΟΣΑΥΤΩΝ as it is to regard it as the remnant
of an original το προσωπον αυτων.

2. The above view is reinforced by the consideration that if το προς αυτον is taken as a corruption of
το προσωπον (ΤΟΠΡΟΣΩΠΟΝ --→ ΤΟΠΡΟΣΑΥΤΟΝ) this still
leaves out of account the word αυτων. Either it has to
be assumed that αυτων dropped out of S* or else that
the fragment -ωπον of προσωπον dropped out and the
original αυτων was changed to αυτον in conformity with
the required case of the preposition προς. Either way,
it is essential to see that the S* reading does not
lead automatically to the emended reading.

3. A further factor to take into account is the
problem of explaining why or how the reasonable reading
ηπατηθη το προσωπον αυτων would have been changed to
the more difficult ηπατηθη ο τοπος αυτων. From an
inner-Greek point of view one would have to favour the
transmitted reading on the principle of lectio difficilior potior.

4. The Greek equivalence of הפנו /32/ is only
half of the problem. No attempt has been made to
explain how ηπατηθη is to be deduced from נסו, a point
recognized by Ziegler ("Allerdings ist die Wiedergabe
des Verbums auch nicht durchsichtig"), though Wutz and
Duhm had proposed נסות (the ת corresponding to the ה of
הפנו). But it is highly unlikely that we are to postulate another Vorlage here. The juxtaposition of נוס
and פנו is found three times elsewhere in the OAN
section of Jer (MT 46:5,21 49:24). Streane (p. 281)

speculated that the translator read נסו but saw in it
the root נשא--perhaps as reasonable a theory as any.
Interestingly enough, however, נסו was correctly
rendered by φευγετε a few lines further down,
30:8(49:30).

Thus we have to admit that what we have here is a
textual conundrum of more than ordinary complexity in
which we are thrown back to Spohn's original comment,
"Nullo modo Graeca hebraicis respondent." Ziegler
attempts to emend half of the problem passage by
changing it in favour of a particular reading of the
Hebrew that he thinks the Greek translator had in mind.
The attempt is not without its merits, but the other
problems will not go away. Since we must plead igno-
rance on how ηπατηθη relates to נסו, it seems best to
do the same with ο τοπος αυτων /הפנה and print instead
the transmitted reading. The conjecture belongs in the
apparatus.

29:11(49:10) επιχειρα

ωλοντο επιχειρα αδελφου αυτου   שדד זרעו ואחיו

επιχειρα Zi.] δια χειρα (-ρος 407 534 Tht.[-ρα /p])
omni MSS; pr. (⋇O-Qmg) σπερμα (το σπ. Qmg L/-51-311)
αυτου O-Qmg L Arm Tht.

As may be observed, no part of the Greek phrase
corresponds exactly to the MT (שדד is singular where
ωλοντο is plural; the Greek has no conjunction corresponding to ו in ואחיו), but the root problem with the
LXX translation of this phrase was the misreading of MT
זרעו as deriving from זְרוֹעַ ("arm") instead of זֶרַע
("seed"). In conformity with Origen's principle of not
wanting to eliminate anything from the LXX, he "corrected" the Greek by placing σπερμα αυτου before his
LXX reading, thus resulting in a <u>lectio</u> <u>duplex</u> in the
Hexaplaric recension at this point.

But in addition to the Greek/Hebrew problem,
Ziegler thinks it likely that we also have here an
inner-Greek corruption. While nearly all the MSS read
δια χειρα (407 534 Tht. modify the case to the more
natural χειρος), Ziegler prefers επιχειρα as the original LXX (<u>Beiträge</u>, pp. 28-29; cf. E. Tov, <u>The Text</u>-

Critical Use of the Septuagint in Biblical Research,
1981, pp. 94-95, 149). The suggestion comes from
Rudolph (ZAW 48 [1930], 278), whose reconstruction is
based on the observation that "das blosse χειρ ist
nirgends in LXX Übersetzung von זְרֹעַ" while the word
זרוע is translated by επιχειρον in 31(48):25 and
34:4(27:5). As before, the conjecture is attractive,
but the following considerations must be weighed
against its adoption in the critical text.

1. As already pointed out (p. 142), a unique LXX
translation is in itself not sufficient ground for
emendation. After all, the translation of זרוע by
αντιληψις in Ps 82:8(83:9) is also a unique and odd
rendition.

2. It should be noted that there is a significant
difference in number between the proposed επιχειρα of
29:11 and επιχειρον in 31:25 and 34:4. The singular
form επιχειρον with meaning "arm" is not attested in
Greek literature outside Jer 31:25 and 34:4, while the
plural form is well attested with the meaning "wages,"
"reward," or in the pejorative sense of "punishment."
If the LXX translator (or reviser, see below pp. 174-75)
employed the singular form in 31:25 and 34:4, why would
he use the plural form in 29:11 with the common meaning
"wages"/"reward," especially since there is nothing in
the Hebrew which demands the plural? To do so would
have been both inconsistent on his part and misleading,
since the plural presumably already had an established
meaning.

3. The emendation fails to explain how an original επι was changed to δια. Did it arise as a result
of scribal error (there is no orthographical similarity
between them) or deliberate change (for what reason?)?

4. Although the genitive of χειρ might have been
expected (as in 407 534 Tht.), the phrase ωλοντο δια
χειρα αδελφου αυτου gives reasonable sense in the Greek
and is consistent with the idea of the destruction of
Edom by her neighbours (cf. v. 10 ως κλεπται εν νυκτι
επιθησουσι χειρα αυτων [MT aliter] and further Ob 18-
21). According to the reading ωλοντο επιχειρα αδελφου
αυτου the sense would have to be that Edom's neighbour
has also perished, which is certainly in line with the
Hebrew but ought not to constitute a reason for

emending. In fact, earlier commentators, e.g. Schwally
(p. 201), Giesebrecht (p. 242), and Duhm (p. 355)
preferred the LXX reading δια χειρα in favour of the MT
on the grounds that the phrase can only speak of Edom's
destruction, not that of her neighbours. They may
have been wrong in that judgement, but perhaps the LXX
reading ωλοντο δια χειρα αδελφου αυτου reflects a
similar reasoning.

    5. If δια χειρα is the original reading in 29:11,
it may be significant that both the immediately preceding and following occurrences of χειρ in Jer-LXX
also derive from mistranslations of the Hebrew (cf.
29:10[49:9] from דים--presumably as a result of actual
or imagined metathesis---and 31[48]:26 from בקיאו).
These facts point either to a poorly copied Hebrew
<u>Vorlage</u> or to a loose handling of the text.

    6. Since Ziegler himself admits that "Man könnte
den überlieferten Text halten und ihn erklären in
Abhängigkeit von v. 10 επιθησουσι χειρα αυτων" and
since the conjectural emendation is not without its own
disadvantages, it is necessary once more to urge that
the critical text stay with the best MS reading and
that the conjectured reading be referred to the
apparatus.

29:22(49:21)   εν θαλασση Σουφ

και κραυγη εν θαλασση Σουφ   צעקה בים סוף
ηκουσθη   נשמע

εν θαλασση Σουφ Zi.] θαλασσης ουκ B-S; σου εν θαλασση
(+ ερυθρα O L) rel.

    The conjectural transliteration Σουφ/סוף was first
proposed by Grabe in his "Prolegomena" to the prophetical books of the LXX (III, 1720). It was thereafter
approved by J.L. Schulze in his edition of the commentary of Theodoret (II, 606, n. 82, 1770), by Spohn (II,
390), Streane (p. 284), Wutz (p. 29), and Rudolph (<u>ZAW</u>,
p. 278). However, the exact form of the phrase in
which Σουφ was restored varied slightly among these
commentators. Grabe /33/ and Spohn recommended κραυγη
εν θαλασση Σουφ as the original reading, whereas
Schulze, Wutz, and Rudolph based the emendation on the

text of B, hence κραυγη θαλασσης Σουφ. Ziegler's reference in the critical apparatus to Wutz, and in Beiträge, p. 68, to Spohn, Streane, Wutz and Rudolph as all substantiating the reading κραυγη εν θαλασση Σουφ is slightly misleading. Only Grabe and Spohn proposed the phrase in that form.

In favour of the conjectured reading Σουφ as representing the original LXX we may cite the following points:

1. There is a well attested affinity for transliteration in Jer-LXX, particularly in the latter half of the book, e.g., Αιθαμ(-αν)/איתן (pp. 131-32 above). Since the transmission of proper names is especially vulnerable to scribal corruption, it is quite possible that an original transliteration has been obscured in the extant MS evidence of 29:22.

2. Once elsewhere in the LXX ים סוף has been transliterated, namely in the B text of Jud 11:16 (θαλασσης Σιφ vs. the A text reading θαλασσης ερυθρας = the conventional LXX rendering of ים סוף /34/).

3. The Greek corruption θαλασσης ουκ in the B text could be easily explained by haplography of Σ (with further slight modification of Φ --→ K to read ΟΥΚ.

The question remains whether this conjecture should be adopted into the critical text. The following considerations need to be weighed:

1. If Σουφ is to be accepted as the original Greek here, we would prefer the emendation on the basis of the B text rather than the A text. In other words, we should prefer θαλασσης Σουφ to εν θαλασση Σουφ. The A Q O L reading εν θαλασση is more likely to be a pre-Hexaplaric approximation to the Hebrew בים. Also it is easier to explain the reading θαλασσης ουκ as a corruption of θαλασσης Σουφ (see above #3), than it is to explain the corruption σου εν θαλασση from a presumed original εν θαλασση Σουφ. The latter explanation involves a major dislocation of Σουφ from a position following θαλασση to a position preceding it, the φ dropping out in the process.

2. Other explanations of the B reading θαλασσης
ουκ have been offered. Coste (p. 31) suggested that ουκ
could be traced to a loose translation of סוף read as
סוֹף, i.e. "finis." Streane, who saw in σου of the A
text the remnant of an original Σουφ, nevertheless had
another explanation for the appearance of ουκ in B. He
discovered numerous instances of the translator's apparently arbitrary handling of the negative in the
Greek, sometimes inserting it, sometimes omitting it
without correspondence to the Hebrew /35/. The presence of an unexplained ουκ in 29:22 need not be seen as
a novelty, therefore. Although Coste's proposal is not
persuasive (cf. Ziegler: "Coste . . . kommt nicht in
Frage"), Streane's documentation of the loose handling
of the negative needs further consideration. In short,
the B reading could be referred back to the translator
himself, and Spohn's blanket condemnation, "lectio Cod.
Vat. ουκ absurda" may be too strong.

3. On the principle that the safest way to edit a
critical text of the LXX is to print only hitherto
attested MS readings, we propose that the text should
follow B and read κραυγη θαλασσης ουκ ηκουσθη. If an
attempt is made to reach behind the archetype then it
can be said that the conjectured reading Σουφ is the
most persuasive of the five emendations adopted by
Ziegler in the text of Jer 29. Even so, the reading
should be θαλασσης Σουφ following B, rather than εν
θαλασση Σουφ following A.

Concluding Remarks

In the above proposed emendations we are again
aware of a text critical tension, this time between the
Greek witness on the one hand (sometimes a uniform
Greek witness) and the witness of the Hebrew MT on the
other. The discussion of these emendations in the
accompanying monograph, Beiträge zur Ieremias-
Septuaginta, is usually carried on with reference to
how the Greek translator would have rendered the Hebrew
that lay before him, and the net effect of Ziegler's
decisions is usually to bring the LXX text more in line
with the MT. Methodologically the procedure is open to
some question since the discussion is based largely on
the present MT text; furthermore, even where the translator's Hebrew Vorlage can be equated with the MT it is

always precarious to assume how the translator may have proceeded with regard to his text. If and where it is deemed essential to incorporate a conjectural emendation into the body of the text one would at least like to see the reader alerted to its status as a conjecture by the use of some typographical means such as being placed within daggers or appropriate symbols /36/. It is true that the corresponding MS evidence is always cited by Ziegler in the apparatus, but it is a laborious thing to read a text always with an eye on every detail in the apparatus. The conjectures in this edition are never extreme (Walters, for instance, wanted to go much beyond him /37/), and we may be grateful to Ziegler for proposing readings other than those contained in the MSS which may lie behind the present archetype /38/. Nonetheless, the conclusion which this study has led us to is that the text would be improved if conjectural emendations were reduced even further; at the very least, such emendations should be clearly marked in the body of the text.

CHAPTER FOUR

THE TRANSLATOR/REVISER PROBLEM:

A CRITIQUE OF E. TOV'S CHALLENGE

TO THE MULTIPLE TRANSLATOR THEORY FOR JER-LXX

Discussion of the text critical problem of Jer 29
in Chs. II and III of this work have shown that an
archetype text for the oracles against the Philistines
and Edom from which all extant witnesses have descended
can be posited and restored within a reasonable margin
of probability. But once restored, what does this
archetype text represent: the original translation, a
later textus receptus, or a revision? As we have seen,
the question was not directly addressed by Ziegler,
though indirect comments in Beiträge suggest that his
text is intended to represent the closest possible
approximation to the original translation as it left
the hand of the translator(s).

But at this point a complicating factor emerges.
As noted in Ch. I (p. 9), it is precisely at Jer 29
that certain lexical differences between preceding and
subsequent chapters in Jer begin to appear. The standard explanation for this phenomenon since the days of
Thackeray has been to attribute the differences to the
work of two distinct translators /1/. But in a thesis
presented in 1973 to the Hebrew University in Jerusalem
and published in 1976 under the title The Septuagint
Translation of Jeremiah and Baruch: A Discussion of an
Early Revision of the LXX of Jeremiah 29-52 and Baruch
1:1-3:8, Emanuel Tov has questioned the consensus view
and proposed instead a translator/reviser theory for
the book of Jer.

Essentially Tov's hypothesis proceeds from the
observation that there exist in the two major parts of
Jer not only important differences but equally important similarities, especially such as mark Jer off from
the rest of the LXX ("distinctive" similarities as Tov

calls them). Thackeray had also noticed some of these similarities but tended to accord them a secondary status. Tov believes that it is Thackeray's failure to take seriously these unique similarities which undermines the multiple translator explanation for Jer and invites instead the substitution of a translator /reviser theory.

As observed earlier, the stimulus for Tov's investigation was provided by a footnote in the "Einleitung" to Ziegler's Göttingen text, where the editor noted his general agreements with Thackeray's statistics but at the same time posed the question "ob wirklich zwei Übersetzer beteiligt waren oder bloss ein Redaktor am Werk war, der den einen Teil nur überarbeitete" (p. 128, n. 1); however, Ziegler himself never followed through exploring the implications of his proposal nor integrating it into his discussion /2/. It is the merit of Tov's work that he has carefully explored this suggestion and sought documentation for a creative and potentially useful hypothesis.

The theory ultimately adopted by Tov differs somewhat from Ziegler's original proposal. Whereas Ziegler mooted the possibility of a reviser for the second half of Jer only, Tov envisages an original revision for the entire book (Jer-R), including Bar. 1:1-3:8; at a later stage (according to this theory) when the book came to be copied in codex form, two different MSS were inadvertently chosen, one containing the first half of the book from the unrevised tradition or Old Greek (Jer-OG) and the second half from the revised tradition. This hybrid form then became the archetype for all subsequent recopyings of the book with the result that the second half of the original Jer along with the first half of the revised Jer have been altogether lost to us /3/. Like Thackeray, Tov extended his analysis to the book of Baruch and other prophetical books for further elaboration and support for the theory.

In the subsequent pages we propose to illustrate the problems involved in the multiple translator and translator/reviser theories and on the basis of the data provided by the oracles against the Philistines and Edom evaluate the strengths and weaknesses as we perceive them of Tov's counter-proposals. The discussion will be organized under the following headings:

I.   Similarities Between Jer a' and Jer b'

II. Differences Between Jer a' and Jer b'

III. Conclusions

I.   Similarities Between Jer a' and Jer b'

The key chapter for Tov is his discussion of the semantic similarities between Jer a' and b' (Ch. II, pp. 19-40). If there is going to be a new approach to the problem of the relationship between the two halves of Jer, it will have to come through a new appreciation of the similarities between the two parts. As for the differences between the two parts, Tov acknowledges that these are as amenable to a two-translator theory as they are to a translator/reviser theory. A great deal depends, therefore, on the effectiveness of Tov's arguments in Ch. II of his book.

It is with Ch. II, then, that we are concerned in this section. That chapter considers two types of similarities: the first has to do with unique and rare renditions found in Jer a' and b' (#1-30, pp. 24-32), the second deals with rare (i.e. "rare" to the LXX) Greek words common to both parts (#31-45, pp. 32-36). Both categories are well represented by examples from Jer 29 and these will be analyzed below in their order of appearance in the LXX text. References in parentheses at the commencement of each new word discussed are to Tov's book. Thus in the first example below dealing with the word αλαλαζω, the reference in parentheses to II 6, p. 25 means that αλαλαζω is discussed in Ch. II of Tov's book, the 6th example, found on p. 25. Our concern throughout is with testing the validity of the examples brought forward in defense of Tov's theory and in exploring the possibility of alternate explanations where such may exist.

29(47):2 αλαλαζω   (II 6, p. 25)

και αλαλαξουσιν απαντες   וחילל כל
οι κατοικουντες την γην   יושב הארץ

The translation equivalence αλαλαζω/ה180 which is
found in Jer b' at 29(47):2, 30(49):3, 32:20(25:34),
and possibly at 31(48):39 (a conjectural emendation in
Ziegler's text), occurs once also in Jer a' at 4:8.
This translation is unique to Jer and hence is cited by
Tov as strong support for the theory that the same
translator was responsible for both parts.

At the heart of the problem is the question whether the equivalence αλαλαζω/הׁ180 is to be regarded too
exceptional for it to have originated independently in
two different translators. In evaluating this proposition the following points need to be kept in mind. The
most frequent translation of הׁ180 in the LXX generally
is ολολυζω, a near homonym to αλαλαζω (an equivalence
also found twice in Jer b' at 31[48]:20,31). Since
the two words are very similar both in sound and meaning (both have to do with crying aloud in various
contexts /4/), it seems not unreasonable to think that
either word might have suggested itself to different
translators as a suitable rendition of הׁ180。 This
argument is somewhat weakened by the practice of Aquila
who regularly reserved αλαλαζω for the translation of
the hiphil of רוע while using ολολυζω for the hiphil of
ללי (cf. Reider-Turner, pp. 11, 171), but few, if any,
were as consistent as Aquila in their choice of translation equivalents. On the other occasion in which
הׁ180 occurs in Jer a', for instance, it is rendered
by θρηνεω (28[51]:8). We conclude that the sole occurrence of αλαλαζω in Jer a' and the three occurrences in
Jer b' is ambiguous evidence for the identity of translators in Jer a' and b'.

29(47):2　αππας　(II 19, p. 29)

και αλαλαξουσιν απαντες　　　　　　　　　　　　כל והיל
οι κατοικουντες την γην　　　　　　　　　　　　יושב הארץ

The standard translation of כל in the LXX is
simply the appropriate form of πας. However, there are
also a number of instances where the alternate form
απας occur. According to Thackeray (Grammar, p. 138),
the use of this form was occasioned by a regard for
euphony, i.e., a concern to avoid the harsh juxtaposition of consonants at the close of one word and at the
beginning of the next. The converse of this is that

απας should not be used following a word ending with a
vowel.

Tov has compiled statistics on the use of απας in
both parts of Jer in comparison with its frequency in
the rest of the LXX and on the basis of these statistics has concluded that "the original translator (or
first scribe?) of Jer thus used απας more than his
fellow translators." This observation is given as
another example where it is assumed Jer a' and b' share
a common trait over against the rest of the LXX. The
totals which Tov gives from HR and MS B are as follows:

	Jer a'	Jer b'	Elsewhere
HR	9	16	35
MS B	3	11	17

These totals need to be modified as follows: The
listing in HR of the second απας in 16:10 is a mistake
in that concordance, thus reducing the actual number
for Jer a' to 8. Also in HR there are 15 rather than
16 occurrences of απας listed for Jer b'. In MS B
there are 4 rather than 3 occurrences of απας in Jer a'.

But the real question concerns the usefulness of
the above lists from HR and Codex B. HR merely give an
aggregate of the occurrences found in the major uncials
A B S and the Sixtine text. As for Codex B we can
affirm its special importance, but are equally aware of
its fallibility. A very different picture emerges if
we turn to the critical texts of Rahlfs and Ziegler
where one expects the MS evidence to have been digested
and evaluated. The adjusted totals when the four sources (HR, Codex B, Rahlfs, Ziegler) are compared look as
follows:

	Jer a'	Jer b'	Elsewhere
HR	8	15	35
Codex B	4	11	17
Rahlfs /5/	6	11	20
Ziegler /6/	3	6	--

Using Ziegler's statistics for Jer a' and b', the
frequency of απας in Jer is only marginally greater
than in other books. However, what may be of even more

significance is the fact that no matter what set of
calculations is used, Jer b' always has a higher frequency of occurrences than Jer a' (on the average,
twice as high), an observation that could be taken as
an argument for the <u>difference</u> rather than for the
similarity between <u>the</u> two parts.

29(47):5 απορριπτω (II 2, p. 24)

απερριφη Ασκαλων   נדמתה אשקלון

        In the LXX of Jer 8:14(2x), 28(51):6, 29(47):5,
Hos 10:7,15(2x) and Ob 5, the Hebrew verbs דמה ("to
cease, cut off, destroy") and דמם ("grow dumb, silent,
still") are unexpectedly rendered by forms of απορριπτω
(once also by the simplex form ριπτω in Jer 27[50]:30).
Tov sees in this common rendition at Jer 8:14, 28:6
and 29:5 his second most persuasive example for the
identity of translators in Jer-OG /7/.

        The equivalence απορριπτω/דמה(דמם) can be ex-
plained as reflecting variants from the root רמה ("to
throw, shoot"). However, Tov does not believe that the
translator's parent text actually contained the variant
letter ר; rather he regards this as a "pseudo-variant,"
by which he means that the translator for the purposes
of translation only read the word with a <u>resh</u> rather
than a <u>daleth</u>, presumably because he was uncertain
about the meaning of the Hebrew דמם/דמה or because the
word רמה made more sense to him in the context. In a
separate article in <u>JSS</u> 20 (1975), 165-77, Tov has
developed this interesting concept of "pseudo-variants"
further with several examples, including the one pres-
ently under consideration (pp. 172-73; see also <u>The
Text-Critical</u> <u>Use</u> <u>of</u> <u>the</u> <u>Septuagint</u>, p. 106).

        However, it is not clear that the translation of
נדמתה by απερριφη in 29:5 represents convincing evidence for a unity of translators in Jer a' and b'. For
one thing, απορριπτω is not the only translation of
דמה/דמם in Jer; additionally we find το υψος σου 6:2,
διαλειπω 14:17, πιπτω 30:15(49:26), επαιρω 29(47):6 and
παυομαι 31(48):2, 32:23(25:37). While the translations
το υψος σου, διαλειπω, πιπτω and επαιρω may be interpreted as reflecting uncertainty with regard to the
meaning of the Hebrew /8/--and hence provide indirect

support for Tov's case--the translation by παυομαι in
31(48):2 and 32:23(25:37) is a reasonably correct one.
This translation is not referred to in Tov's monograph
but is dealt with in a footnote in the JSS article
(p. 172, n. 4). The explanation given there for the
correct translation at two points in Jer b' is that
παυομαι must represent examples of correction by the
postulated reviser of the book; the reviser's failure
to correct at 29:5 is merely a matter of inconsistency.
If this conjectural solution is not convincing to us,
Tov invites us to consider the coexistence of correct
and incorrect translations of the same Hebrew word in
other translation units, e.g., the widely divergent
translations of the Hebrew in Isa 38:2 and 38:7.

It is important to note that Tov's case for
identity of translators at 8:14, 28:6 and 29:5 depends
on the assumption that the translation απορριπτω was
occasioned by the same mental process on the part of
the translator (deliberate substitution of ר for ד).
If the scribal variant already existed in the translator's Vorlage--not an impossible scenario given the
frequent interchange of these letters--then the matter
would be very different. There is no way of resolving
this question at present, but the ambiguity does illustrate the inferential and hypothetical nature of the
evidence. The same thing must be said about Tov's
"reviser" explanation of the correct rendition of
παυομαι at 31:2 and 32:23 (as given in the JSS article
referred to above). In short, the translation equiva-
lences under consideration are beset by several problems which are not convincingly resolved by an appeal
to a translator/reviser theory.

29:8(49:7) οιχομαι   (II 25, pp. 30-31)

ωχετο σοφια αυτων   נסרחה חכמתם

The verb οιχομαι is found a total of 21 times in
the translated books of the LXX, almost half (9) of
these occurrences being confined to the book of Jer (3
in Jer a': 9:10[9], 16:11, 27[50]:6; 6 in Jer b':
31[48]:11, 35[28]:11, 48[41]:10,12,15,17). In all of
these instances except one, οιχομαι translates the verb
הלך, one of nearly 90 different words employed in the
LXX to render this common Hebrew verb. The exception

to the otherwise constant equivalence οιχομαι/הלך in
Jer is 29:8(49:7) /9/ where οιχομαι renders the niphal
of the root סרח (a form found only here).

The rate of occurrence of οιχομαι in Jer is admittedly high in comparison with the rest of the LXX (9x
in Jer versus 11x elsewhere) and could conceivably
point to a special preference for this verb by the
presumed single translator of Jer-OG. On the other
hand, it may be questioned whether the equivalence
οιχομαι/הלך can legitimately be called rare (as Tov
does) since outside Jer it occurs 3 times in Gen, twice
in Job and once in 2 Chr. What is "rare" indeed is the
use of οιχομαι for the niphal of סרח, but then this may
not be overly significant either since the root סרח was
rendered by a different Greek word on each of the 7
occasions where it occurred in the OT. Looking at the
distribution of οιχομαι in Jer from another perspective, one could--as in the case of απας above--with
equal justification point out that οιχομαι appears
twice as often in Jer b' and hence call attention to
the differences between the two parts.

29:17(49:16)   εγχειρεω   (II 31, p. 32)
      "   ιταμια   (II 36, p. 34)
      "   τρυμαλια   (II 41, p. 35)

η παιγνια σου ενεχειρησε σοι   תפלצתך השיא אתך
ιταμια καρδιας σου   זדון לבך
κατελυσε τρυμαλιας πετρων   שכני בחגוי הסלע

In 29:17 Tov notes three examples of words common
to Jer a' and b' which recur rarely, if at all, elsewhere in the LXX. These are εγχειρεω, ιταμια and
τρυμαλια, the first of which is given pride of place in
Tov's list of "Rare Greek Words Common to Jer a' and
b'" (pp. 32ff.). We will examine each of these in
turn.

εγχειρεω is found in the LXX only at 2 Chr 23:18
and Jer 18:22, 28:12, 29:17. Yet it is difficult to
know how to evaluate the significance of this kind of
data. Since the word occurs in 2 Chr it is not unique
to Jer-LXX (contra Tov, p. 33). Moreover, the word
itself is not an uncommon Greek verb (cf. LSJ) so that
its appearance 3 times in Jer should perhaps not

surprise us too much. As for the strange equivalence
εγχειρεω/השיא in 29:17(49:16) this is explained by the
confusion of the hiphil of נשׁא with the qal of נשׁא
(similarly in 44[37]:9), and since the qal of נשׁא was
translated in the LXX by some 90 different Greek words
(cf. E.C. dos Santos, An Expanded Index for the Hatch-
Redpath Concordance to the Septuagint, p. 137), one has
the right to expect almost anything as a translation of
this verb.

However, it must be acknowledged that the unique
use of the derivative noun εγχειρημα in the parallel
passages of Jer-LXX 23:20 and 37(30):24 is noteworthy.
Taken together we have five instances of the word group
εγχειρεω/εγχειρημα in Jer-LXX over against the sole use
of εγχειρεω outside Jer in 2 Chr 23:18. This phenomenon is striking and the words in question understand-
ably head up the list of "Rare Greek Words Common to
Jer a' and b'." How to account for the phenomenon is
less clear, however. Admittedly, if there were many
instances of this kind of commonality, the case for a
translator/reviser theory would be greatly strengthened.
It is partly the lack of a consistently convincing
pattern of this type in the rest of the book that makes
us look to other explanations even for the appearances
of εγχειρεω/εγχειρημα in the two halves of Jer. Sheer
coincidence, harmonization of parallel passages (though
discounted by Tov, p. 33), cooperation and cross consultation among translators may be listed among such
possibilities.

ιταμια is a word hitherto attested nowhere else in
Greek literature except in Jer 29:17 and the majority
text of 30(49):4, though rejected in the latter instance by both Ziegler and Walters in favour of ατιμια
(see Walters, Text, p. 76, n. 88). The adjective
ιταμος on the other hand, which in the LXX is found
only in the parallel passages of Jer 6:23 and
27(50):42, is otherwise widely employed in ancient
Greek.

For our purposes the question is whether the use
of ιταμος in Jer a' to translate אכזרי in 6:23 and
27(50):42, along with the use of ιταμια in Jer b' to
translate זדון at 29:17(49:16), can be taken as
evidence for a single translator of both parts of the
book, as Tov suggests. It is not surprising that the

Hebrew אכזרי is rendered in the same way (ιταμος) in
6:23 and 27(50):42 given that the verses are both
found in the first half of the book and in addition
constitute parallel passages. But is the use of the
hapax ιταμια to translate an entirely different Hebrew
word in 29:17(49:16) a testimony to the work of the
same translator? This is a much more tenuous argument.
The explanation is not impossible, but it is hardly of
the same order of persuasion as the use of εγχειρημα in
the parallel passages of 23:20 and 37(30):24 mentioned
in the previous example. The word was noticed by
Thackeray in his JTS article as one of those common to
both parts of the book without it affecting his
multiple translator theory.

        τρυμαλια is likewise a word attested only within
biblical Greek, though of more frequent occurrence than
ιταμια. It is a synonym for τρυμη, the more common
word for "hole." In Jer 13:4 and 16:16 it is employed
to render נקיק while in 29:17(49:16) it translates
חגו. Outside Jer it is found in the LXX only 3 times
in the B text of Judges, namely at 6:2 (for מנהרה; A
has the transliteration μανδρα) and 15:8,11 (for סעיף
A has σπηλαιον and ο η respectively). Outside the LXX
proper it is found further in Symmachus' translation at
Isa 51:1 and in Mark's "eye of the needle" passage, Mk
10:25. Thus the word is not without precedent and its
use in both halves of Jer may be without special significance. Not surprisingly, it comes close to the end
of Tov's list of "Rare Greek Words Common to Jer a' and
b'."

29:19(49:18) παντοκρατωρ   (II 26, p. 31)

ειπε κυριος παντοκρατωρ   אמר יהוה

        In this verse we have the interesting case of a
prophetic formula being longer in the LXX than in the
MT (the reverse of the general tendency in Jer). Why
this should be so is a problem in its own right (see
the discussion in the next chapter, pp. 212-14), but
what concerns us for the present is the recognition
that throughout Jer παντοκρατωρ is the standard translation of the divine name צבאות (whether or not that
word was actually present in the translator's Hebrew

Vorlage at 29:19[49:18]). Including its use at 29:19,
the name παντοκρατωρ is found in Jer altogether 14
times, 7 times in Jer a' and 7 times in Jer b'. Other
renditions of יהוה צבאות in the LXX are κυριος των
δυναμεων and the transliteration κυριος σαβαωθ. A
table summarizing the relevant statistics appears as
follows /10/:

	σαβαωθ/11/	παντοκρατωρ/12/	των δυναμεων/13/
Josh	1	–	1
1-2 Re	5	4	2
3-4 Re	–	2	5
1 Chr	–	3	–
1 Esd	1	–	–
Pss	–	–	15
Sir	–	1	–
MP	–	101	–
Isa	54	–	–
Jer	–	14	–
Bar	–	2	–

     On the basis of these statistics, Tov makes the
observation that "only in Jer and the MP is the phrase
[יהוה צבאות] rendered exclusively by κυριος παντοκρατωρ, the implication being that both parts of Jer and
MP were rendered by the same translator (see further,
Tov, p. 141, #33). Tov's observation on παντοκρατωρ to
the effect that only in Jer is צבאות rendered exclusively by this term needs to be modified slightly since
the appearance of the phrase κυριος παντοκρατωρ in 1
Chr (3x) and Sir (1x) also fits into the same category.
However, it certainly is true that the major concentration of occurrences of παντοκρατωρ is found in Jer and
MP, a fact which may point to some interdependence
among these books--including the two halves of Jer--but
whether this interdependence is best understood in
terms of a single translator is another question.
Again Thackeray was aware of the common rendition of
παντοκρατωρ running through Jer and MP (Jewish Worship,
p. 33).

     If one were to invoke a single translator to
explain the above phenomena one would also have to
account for the anomaly that the literal minded reviser
of Jer b' did not alter παντοκρατωρ--the most idiomatic
rendition of צבאות in the LXX--to the more literal

translations των δυναμεων or των στρατιων. The fact
that παντοκρατωρ was a good candidate for revision can
be seen by the preference on the part of the Younger
Greek translators/revisers for the forms δυναμεων
(Theodotion, Origen, Symmachus) and στρατιων (Aquila,
Symmachus). The failure to revise παντοκρατωρ in Jer
b' can only be explained on this theory as another
example of the reviser's inconsistency.

29:20(49:19)   εκδιωκω   (II 29, p. 32)

        "   ανθιστημι   (II 30, p. 32)

        In 29:20(49:19) there occur two translation
equivalents εκδιωκω/הרי   and ανθιστημι/הועיד) which
are found elsewhere only in Jer 27(50):44 (and in the
case of ανθιστημι/הועיד also in Job 9:19). The two
verses 27(50):44 and 29:20(49:19) are in fact almost
identical parallels which it will be useful to
reproduce for comparison purposes:

            27(50):44   29:20(49:19)

ιδου ωσπερ λεων αναβησεται   ιδου ωσπερ λεων αναβησεται
            הנה כאריה יעלה   הנה כאריה יעלה

εκ μεσου του Ιορδανου εις   απο του Ιορδανου εις Αιθαμ
τοπον Αιθαμ
      מגאון הירדן אל נוה איתן   מגאון הירדן אל נוה איתן

οτι ταχυ εκδιωξω αυτους   οτι ταχεως εκδιωξω αυτους
απ αυτης   απ αυτης
      כי ארגיעה אריצנו מעליה   כי ארגעה ארוצם מעליה

και τους νεανισκους επ   και παντα νεανισκον επ
αυτην επιστησατε   αυτην επιστησω
      ומי בחור אליה אפקד   ומי בחור אליה אפקד

οτι τις ωσπερ εγω και   οτι τις ωσπερ εγω και
τις αντιστησεται μοι   τις αντιστησεται μοι
      כי מי כמוני ומי יעידני   כי מי כמוני ומי יועדי

και τις ουτος ποιμην ος   και τις ουτος ποιμην ος
στησεται κατα προσωπον   στησεται κατα προσωπον
μου   μου
      ומי זה רעה אשר יעמד לפני   ומי זה רעה אשר יעמד לפני

It will be noted that the Hebrew passages are
identical except for the slight variations אריצנו
49:19//ארוצם 50:44 and יעידני 49:19//יועדני 50:44. The
Greek translations are also very similar, the only
minor variations being the following:

27:44	29:20

απο του Ιορδανου	εκ μεσου του Ιορδανου
εις Αιθαμ	εις τοπον Αιθαμ
οτι ταχεως	οτι ταχυ
και παντα νεανισκον	και τους νεανισκους
επιστησω	επιστησατε

    Whatever the explanation for the above differences
(some may be due to a different Vorlage from our MT), it
is nevertheless the remarkable similarities between the
two passages that demand particular attention for the
moment. It does seem clear that there must be some
intrinsic connection between the similar renderings
other than mere chance. The theory of one and the same
translator being responsible for both passages is one
possible explanation. Yet there is a weakness to this
solution: there is namely no guarantee that a single
translator would render the same passage in identical
fashion twice; in fact, the likelihood is that he
would not, so that where exact reduplication occurs one
is inclined to suspect the intervention of secondary
influences. Deliberate harmonization by the original
translator or a later reviser is a possibility; so also
is cross-consultation by a second translator. The
suggestion that the passage has been affected by
harmonization may find some support in the translation
εκδιωξω αυτους for אריצנו; assuming the same Vorlage
as the MT, the translation αυτους is probably best
explained as harmonization from εκδιωξω αυτους (Heb.
ארוצם) of 27(50):44.

    It is not certain, therefore, that the same trans-
lation equivalents εκδιωκω/הריץ and ανθιστημι/הועיד in
the parallel passages 27(50):44 and 29:20(49:19) demand
a single translator theory for Jer-OG. εκδιωκω is not
an unreasonable translation of הריץ (cf. the translation of רוץ by διωκω in Am 6:13[12], Hab 2:2, Hag. 1:19
and by καταδιωκω in Joel 2:4). As for the equivalence
ανθιστημι/הועיד in the two parallel passages of Jer and
the verse in Job 9:19, it should be observed that these

are the only occurrences of the hiphil of יעד in the MT
and that the translation by ανθιστημι evidently derives
from an association with the root עמד which on several
occasions in the LXX was rendered by ανθιστημι (cf.
Josh 21:42, 23:9, Jud 2:14, Esth 9:2, Ps 75[76]:7, Ob
11, Isa 50:8, Dan LXX 10:13, 11:2,15,16). Also, as Tov
points out, the possibility of a different <u>Vorlage</u> at
MT 49:19 needs to be considered in view of the translation υφιστημι by Aquila and Symmachus.

29:21(49:20)   συμψαω   (II 37, p. 34)

εαν μη συμψησθωσι   אם לא יסחבום
τα ελαχιστα των προβατων   צעירי הצאן

     The verb συμψαω occurs in the LXX 3 times only--
Jer 22:19, 29:21(49:20), 31(48):33--and hence serves as
another example in Tov's list of rare Greek words
common to Jer a' and b'. As with εγχειρεω and ιταμος
above, however, it needs to be pointed out that while
the verb is of rare occurrence in the LXX it is by no
means rare in the Greek language at large. Nor is the
equivalence συμψαω/סחב (both at 22:19 and 29:21[49:20])
at all unreasonable. In fact, in 27(50):45, the parallel passage to 29:21(49:20), where the the LXX renders
סחב by διαφθειρω, Aquila prefers συμψαω. In short, the
appearance of συμψαω in the 3 verses of Jer under consideration need not be viewed as overly significant.

29:22(49:21)   πτωσις   (II 5, p. 25)

οτι απο φωνης πτωσεως αυτων   מקול נפלם
εφοβηθη η γη   רעשה הארץ

     The word πτωσις occurs elsewhere in Jer only at
6:15 in the following context:

δια τουτο πεσουνται   לכן יפלו
εν τη πτωσει αυτων   בנפלים

     In the LXX as a whole, according to HR, πτωσις
occurs 21 times, 9 times as a translation of some form
derived from נפל, 7 times as a translation of a form
derived from נגף, once each as a translation of פגר and
תרעלה, and 3 times with uncertain Hebrew equivalence.

It is true that only in Jer does πτωσις render a form
of the participle נֹפֵל and of the infinitive נְפֹל, but it
seems unwise to read too much into this. After all,
the natural and standard translation of נפל throughout
the LXX is the verb πιπτω (according to dos Santos, 252
times), and it seems a logical extension to employ the
related noun πτωσις for the appropriate form derived
from the root נפל. In itself, therefore, the use of
πτωσις for the participle form in 6:15 and the infinitive in 29:22(49:21) offer minimal support for the
unity of translators in Jer a' and b'.

II. Differences Between Jer a' and b'

In Chs. III and IV Tov turns to a consideration of
the differences between Jer a' and b', traditionally
regarded as the most noteworthy feature of the Greek
style and vocabulary of this LXX book. Tov discerns
two major types of differences between the two halves:
those which he believes betray some revisional tendency
in Jer b' (Ch. III) and those which do not (Ch. IV).
In Ch. III the differences are further subdivided
according to presumed Tendenz discovered: 1) "More
Precise Renditions" (#1-11, pp. 46-52), 2) "Corrections
of Erroneous Renditions" (#12-17, pp. 52-55), 3)
"Stereotyped (literal) Replacing Non-stereotyped (free)
Renditions" (#18-41, pp. 55-68), 4) "Renditions
Reflecting the Heb in a More Consistent Way" (#42-48,
pp. 69-74), and 5) "Other Changes" (#49-51, pp. 74-75).
Ch. IV (pp. 93-106), which contains 24 examples of what
are termed "synonymous renditions," is not subdivided
further in any way. In the discussion below,
differences between Jer a' and b' illustrated by the
oracles against the Philistines and Edom will again be
reviewed according to their sequence of appearance in
the Greek text.

29(47):1 ταδε λεγει κυριος   (III 18, pp. 56-58)

Probably the most arresting difference between the
two halves of Jer is the way the Messenger Formula (MF)
כה אמר יהוה is rendered in the respective parts of the

book. Whereas in the first half the almost unanimous form is ταδε λεγει κυριος, in the second half the dominant rendition is ουτως ειπε κυριος with a few exceptions and hybrid forms in each section (in 14 instances the MF is missing altogether in the LXX, see below p. 213, n.10) /14/. In order to appreciate the significance of these numbers they need to be set in the wider context of the translation of the MF in the rest of the OT (predominately employed with divine name but occasionally with profane name). The relevant statistics are as follows /15/:

	ταδε λεγει deina /16/	ουτως ειπε deina /17/	ουτως λεγει deina /18/
Gen	1	-	1
Ex	11	-	-
Num	2	-	-
Josh	3	-	-
Jud	2	-	1
1-2 Re	6	-	1
3-4 Re	42	-	-
1-2 Chr	7	4	4
2 Esd	-	1	-
MP	44	-	-
Isa	18	4	26
Jer a'	61	-	2
Jer b'	3	71	2
Ez	122	-	-

Miscellaneous variations are ταδε ειπε (1 Re 10:18, 15:2, Jer 29:13 B-S-538), ουτως ελεγεν (2 Re 16:7), ταδε ελεγεν (1 Re 9:9), τοτε ειπε (Jer 19:1), and και ειπε (Am 1:3). The MS evidence for the various forms of the MF in Jer is generally stable, though there are some significant variants, particularly in the O and L recensions /19/.

As can be seen, the most popular translation by far of the MF in the LXX is ταδε λεγει while ουτως ειπε is seldom found outside Jer and ουτως λεγει is confined mainly to Isa. When Thackeray discovered the different renditions of the MF in the two main parts of Jer—not at the beginning but at the end of his investigations (Jewish Worship, p. 35)—he took these as the decisive proof of his multiple translator theory. Tov, however, interprets the phrase ουτως ειπε in Jer b' as

a sign of revision. While the common expression ταδε
λεγει has classical antecedents (cf. LSJ, λεγω III 8),
for Tov ουτως ειπε exemplifies the reviser's tendency
to replace non-stereotyped or free renditions with
stereotyped or literal renditions (outside the MF the
stereotyped rendition of the Hebrew particle כה is
ουτως, while the Hebrew אמר is normally translated by
the aorist ειπε rather than by the present λεγει).

We can readily agree that the Greek ουτως ειπε
represents a more literal translation of the Hebrew כה
אמר than does ταδε λεγει. But this in itself does not
tell us whether the phrase comes from a literally minded
translator or reviser. The absence of any MS evidence
attesting the alleged unrevised form inclines us to
a second translator theory rather than a reviser
theory.

29:(47):3 Omission of the article in the phrase απο
φωνης ορμης αυτου   (III 32b, p. 64)

απο φωνης ορμης αυτου   מקול שעטת

Tov draws attention to one of the conclusions
reached by Ziegler in his excellent study on the use of
the article in Jer-LXX (Beiträge, Ch. 4), namely
the comment that "Der Artikel ist oftmals in der Ier.-
und Thr.-LXX im Anschluss an MT (also besonders beim
Status constructus) nicht gesetzt worden. Er fehlt
häufiger in Ier. II und Thr. als in Ier. I" (p. 167).

By way of illustrating the tendency of Jer b' to
omit the article more frequently than Jer a' in
various syntactical constructions, Tov contrasts the
translation of ברב עונך in 13:22 by δια το πληθος της
αδικιας with the phrase from 29(47):3 cited above (both
constructions being of the type "prep. + double noun").
Tov includes this example in the section "Stereotyped
(literal) Replacing Non-stereotyped (free) Renditions,"
the implication being that Jer b' would frequently
have eliminated the article from the original LXX in
conformity with the Hebrew. But as Ziegler has pointed
out, the determination of the article in Jer-LXX
(and elsewhere) is an extremely complicated business,
the MS evidence seldom being homogeneous. Even
accepting the validity of Ziegler's generalization

regarding the higher rate of omission of the article in Jer b', this does not help much in the resolution of the translator/reviser debate. The phenomenon could be attributed to one or the other. Indeed, one suspects that the use of the article was inconsistent even in the work of a single individual, so that the criterion of the article is probably of minimal value.

29(47):4   απολλυμι   (III 2, pp. 47-48)

του απολεσαι παντας τους αλλοφυλους   לשדוד את כל פלשתים

The Hebrew verb שדד is found 3 times in the oracles against the Philistines and Edom, each time rendered in a different way: 29(47):4 απολλυμι and εξολεθρευω, 29:11(49:10) ολλυμι. For Jer as a whole, the translation pattern for שדד appears as follows /20/:

	Jer a'	Jer b'
ταλαιπωρεω	6	–
ολλυμι	–	6
απολλυμι	–	1
(εξ)ολεθρευω	3	1
πλησσω Q-613 Zi.	–	1
(πιπλημι rel.)		

Related to the above are the translations of שד and שדד which appear 5 times in Jer a' as ταλαιπωρια and 3 times in Jer b' as ολεθρος /21/.

On the basis of the above statistics Tov has concluded in the section entitled "More Precise Renditions" that the root ταλαιπωρ- was revised by Jer-R to the stronger (απ)ολλυμι, since ταλαιπωρ- ('to endure hardship') does not precisely represent שדד ('to devastate', 'to plunder'; generally in passive: 'to be destroyed')" (p. 48). But while it may appear from our vantage point of philological sophistication that (απ)-ολλυμι is a more precise rendition of שדד than ταλαιτωρεω, it is difficult to know how an ancient scribe would have viewed the matter. The fact is that the equivalence ταλαιπωρ-/שדד does enjoy broad based support in the LXX (Ps 11[12]:5, 16[17]:9, 136[137]:8, Job 5:21 [A text], Hos 9:6, 10:2, Am 3:10, 5:9, Mi 2:4(2x), Joel 1:10(2x),15, Hab 1:3, 2:17, Zech 11:2,

3(2x), Isa 16:4 [A text], 33:1, Ez 45:9). It is
also employed freely by Aquila (Jer 4:20, 29:11
[49:10], 30:6[49:28]; see also α'ϑ' ταλαιπωρος/שָׁדוּד,
Jer 4:30). In the light of these facts its seems to us
a moot point whether (απ)ολλυμι and ολεϑρος in Jer b'
can truly be seen as examples of "more precise" renditions in that part of the book. But even if the point
were granted, we have no way of determining whether
these forms derive from a reviser or translator.

29(47):6 μαχαιρα   (IV 21, pp. 101-102)

η μαχαιρα του κυριου   הוי חרב ליהוה

     The common Hebrew noun חרב is rendered in Jer-LXX
as follows /22/:

	Jer a'	Jer b'	Totals
μαχαιρα	36	14	50
ρομφαια	2	12	14

Further analysis of the translation distribution of
these two words yields the interesting observations
that whereas in the first six chapters of Jer μαχαιρα
and ρομφαια are used interchangeably (μαχαιρα: 2:30
4:10 5:12; ρομφαια 5:17 6:25), in the subsequent
chapters μαχαιρα is employed exclusively as far as
41(34):17 while ρομφαια appears exclusively from
45(38):2 to 51(44):28. But since μαχαιρα is predominant in Jer a' while usage is split between the two
words in Jer b', Tov believes it may therefore be
assumed "that in some instances [especially chapters
45-51--n. 30] Jer-R replaced μαχαιρα with ρομφαια." No
translation Tendenz is attributed to this presumed
replacement, the example being one of the "synonymous
renditions" of Ch. IV.

     The term "synonymous renditions" is certainly an
appropriate designation for the two words under consideration. In the rest of the LXX the words consistently
appear side by side much as in the first six chapters
of Jer /23/. Even Aquila seems to have vacillated in
the use of μαχαιρα and ρομφαια as renditions of חו'ב
cf. Reider-Turner, pp. 152-53, 211. What is unique to
Jer is the exclusive use of μαχαιρα in one section of

the book (9:16[15]-41[34]:17) and ρομφαια in another
(45[38]:2-51[44]:28). Unfortunately, however, these
divisions do not correspond to any previous categoriza-
tions of the book of Jer. On a reviser theory we have
to assume the reviser commenced his revision of μαχαιρα
at 45(38):2; on a multiple translator theory we have
to assume that the translator suddenly changed his
previous preference for μαχαιρα at 45(38):2 or that yet
another translator commenced around this point. It is
questionable whether we have sufficient data available
to decide between these or other options. Hence it
seems unlikely that the observed translation patterns
of μαχαιρα and ρομφαια will be of great help in the
search for the elusive revisers or original translators
of Jer-LXX.

29(47):7   εντελλομαι   (IV 22, p. 102)

και κυριος ενετειλατο αυτη   ויהוה צוה לה

     The Hebrew verb צוה is rendered in Jer-LXX as
follows /24/:

	Jer a'	Jer b'
εντελλομαι	16	11
συντασσω	--	8

According to Tov's interpretation of the above statistics, εντελλομαι was changed to συντασσω in Jer b' 8
times, while the 11 occurrences of εντελλομαι in Jer b'
constitute "an unrevised remnant of the OG of that
section."

     On the assumption of a reviser theory, the re-
vision was highly inconsistent at this point; in fact,
the "unrevised remnant" (11x) is larger than the instances of revision (8x). Also, Tov's comment that
συντασσω does not "frequently render צוה in any other
part of the LXX except Ex and Num" is slightly misleading. In addition to Ex and Num it occurs regularly
also in Lev and Josh, occasionally in Gen and Deut and
a few other books. Furthermore, of those Hebrew roots
which συντασσω translates, צוה is by far the most
common, only sporadic instances of other equivalents
being found. Finally, it should be observed that the

interchange of εντελλομαι and συντασσω as found in
Jer b' is not at all unique to that portion. If we
take the Hexateuch as a comparative base, we note that
the two synonyms are used indiscriminately there in
the ratio of 191:74, with which the ratio of 11:8 in
Jer b' may be compared. In conclusion, the usage of
εντελλομαι and συντασσω in Jer b' does not appear to us
unusual or demand the intervention of a reviser; these
words may quite readily be explained as "synonymous
renditions" of a single translator.

29:9(49:8) χρονος (III 10, pp. 51-52)

ηγαγον επ αυτον   הבאתי עליו
εν χρονω ω επεσκεφαμην επ αυτον   עת פקדתיו

     As is well known, Greek has two words for ex-
pressing "time," καιρος and χρονος. Concerning these
it is usually said that the former has the connotation
of "decisive time" or "opportunity" whereas the latter
has to do with "chronological" time. In Jer-LXX καιρος
is found exclusively in Jer a' (29x) while χρονος is
limited to Jer b' (4x). The Hebrew word behind these
translations is usually עת /25/ (26x in Jer a', 3x in
Jer b'), the equivalence χρονος/עת being unique to Jer
b' in the LXX (though it is also found in the VSS of
Aquila and Symmachus at Jer 37[30]:7 and in the
Hexaplaric text of Esth 5:13).

     Tov suggests that καιρος was revised by Jer-R to
χρονος as a less ambiguous translation of עת. However,
it is by no means clear that καιρος would have been
regarded as a "somewhat ambiguous rendition of עת."
After all, this was the standard translation of עת
throughout the LXX, the equivalence χρονος/עת being
unique to Jer b'. Also, in a special study devoted to
the subject of biblical words for time, James Barr
has argued that the distinction that has traditionally
been made in biblical Greek between καιρος as denoting
"opportunity" and χρονος as denoting "chronological"
time is open to serious question (Biblical Words for
Time, 1969, 2nd ed., elaborating a point made by G.B.
Caird in The Apostolic Age, 1955, p. 184, n. 2). With
regard to the LXX, Barr shows that such a hard and fast
distinction simply does not correspond to the facts.
In Jer 45(38):28, for instance, Barr points out that we

might have expected the translation καιρος according to
the usual way of understanding the difference between
καιρος and χρονος (p. 37; cf. also pp. 125-27). If Barr
is right, therefore, it is doubtful that χρονος in Jer
b' could legitimately be considered a revisional feature intended to represent the Hebrew more accurately.
The division between καιρος and χρονος in Jer a' and b'
stands fast; what remains unexplained is the source of
this division.

29:11(49:10)   επιχειρον   (III 4, pp. 48-49)

ωλοντο δια χειρα αδελφου αυτου   שדד זרעו ואחיו

δια χειρα] επιχειρα Rudolph, Ziegler

     Throughout the LXX the Hebrew word זרוע is regu-
larly rendered by βραχιων. This equivalence is also
found in Jer-LXX at 17:5, 21:5 (Jer a') and 39(32):17,
21 (Jer b'). Twice, however, the unusual word επι-
χειρον--nowhere else attested in Greek literature /26/
--is used in Jer b' to translate זרוע (31[48]:25, 34:4
[27:5]). According to Rudolph and Ziegler the MS reading δια χειρα at 29:8 should be emended to επιχειρα
(the Greek translator having misread זרעו for זרוע),
thus giving three instances of this word in Jer b' (for
a discussion of the problems associated with the emendation see above, pp. 147-49).

     Tov's explanation for the appearance of επιχειρον
in Jer b' is that Jer-R apparently considered this
word--possibly coined by him--a more precise rendition
of זרוע than βραχιων, even though he left the latter
twice unrevised. But questions regarding inconsistency
and classification must be raised again. We agree with
Tov (pp. 44-45) that perfect consistency in revision
cannot be insisted upon, yet the degree of inconsistency does become a problem at some point. It would be
hard to fix the point where the problem becomes fatal
to a reviser theory, but the high rate of observed
inconsistencies cannot help but affect our judgement.
With regard to Jer 29:11 there is another inconsistency. If the original translation really was επιχειρον
(or even if it was the MS reading δια χειρα), one might
wonder why a conscientious reviser would not have made
a genuine revision; after all, our Hebrew text says

nothing about "arm" (זרוע) at all, but speaks only of "seed" (זרע)! As for the problem of classification, it is truly difficult to judge whether a reviser or translator would have regarded a word like επιχειρον "more precise" than βραχιων. As an illustration of reviser Tendenz it is of dubious merit.

29:14(49:13) λεγει κυριος   (III 43, pp. 69-70)

λεγει κυριος   נאם יהוה

    Closely related to the translation of the MF כה
אמר יהוה (see above, pp. 167-69) is that of the concluding formulas /27/ נאם יהוה and אמר יהוה, the former
of which is particularly numerous in Jer (175x). Here
the differences between the two halves of Jer are not
as marked as in the case of the כה אמר formula, but
certain significant patterns still emerge. The statistics for the translations of נאם יהוה are as follows /28/:

	Jer a'	Jer b'
λεγει κυριος	75	4
φησι "	--	23
ειπε "	2	6

As in the case of the introductory formulas ταδε λεγει
κυριος and ουτως ειπε κυριος, so here the MS evidence
is reasonably stable though variants do exist in sundry
MSS, but not so as to put many readings in doubt /29/.

    Clearly the overwhelming preference in Jer a' is
for the form λεγει κυριος (also the standard phrase
employed throughout the LXX), while the most popular
rendition in Jer b' is φησι κυριος (found elsewhere
only in 1 Re 2:30, 4 Re 9:26, and 2 Chr 34:27). The
alternate concluding formula אמר יהוה is rendered in
Jer by ειπε κυριος only, once in Jer a' (6:15) and 6
times in Jer b' (29:19, 31:8, 37:3, 40:11,13, 51:26)
/30/.

    Tov interprets these facts as fitting the formula,
"Gk 1 (= Heb 1 + Heb 2) in Jer a' versus Gk 1 (= Heb 1)
and Gk 2 (= Heb 2) in Jer b'," which in effect means
that "Jer-OG used one Greek word to render two

different Hebrew words, while Jer-R tended to employ
two different Greek words." In terms of the expressions נאם יהוה and אמר יהוה this means that whereas
Jer a' normally used only one--namely λεγει--to render
both נאם and אמר, Jer b' (along with The Three, O and
L) preferred to distinguish between נאם and אמר using
φησι for the former and ειπε for the latter.

However, there are some serious exceptions to the
rule as it has been formulated. In addition to the 4
instances of λεγει κυριος which were presumably left
unrevised in Jer b', there are also the 6 occurrences
of ειπε κυριος as translations of נאם יהוה in the same
part; these have to be explained either as remnants of
the OG in Jer b' (contrary, however, to Jer-OG's
regular policy of using λεγει), as representing Hebrew
variants אמר יהוה where MT has נאם יהוה, or as being
Jer b's own rendition (again contrary to his normal
procedure and undermining the validity of the revisional policy which Tov has discerned in the data, cf.
Tov. p. 89, n. 110). The variety of translation equivalents for נאם יהוה in Jer b' is indeed problematic on
any accounting, whether a reviser or second translator
is envisaged. One thing is certain: the data does not
help decide between one or the other.

29:14(49:13) αβατος   (III 1, pp. 46-47)

ειςαβατον   לשמה

The Hebrew words שמה and שממה are represented in
Jer-LXX as follows /31/:

	Jer a'	Jer b'
αφανισμος	18	−
αβατος	3	10
ερημος	2	1
ερημωσις	1	−
εκστασις	1	−
απορια	1	−
απωλεια	−	2

Similarly we have the translations of the verb שמם
/32/:

	Jer a'	Jer b'
αφανιζω	2	-
αβατοω	-	1
ερημος	1	1
εξιστημι	3	-
σκυθρωπαζω	2	-

As can be seen, the most common translation of
שממה/שמה in Jer a' is αφανισμος while in Jer b'
αβατος predominates (cf. also the verb equivalents
αφανιζω/שמם in Jer a' versus αβατοω/שמם in Jer b').
Tov interprets this data to mean that "αφανισμος ('the
act of destroying') has been replaced by Jer-R with
αβατος (literally 'untrodden') because the former does
not precisely represent the Heb," the reviser even
having gone so far as to innovate the verb αβατοω on
the model of ερημοω.

It may truly be said that there is a marked
division of usage between Jer a' and Jer b' in the
occurrences of αφανισμος and αβατος, the former being
characteristic of Jer a' while the latter predominates
in Jer b', though there is some overlap in the case of
αβατος since the latter is found not only as a translation of שממה/שמה in Jer a' but also of שוחה and ערבה
(2:6 and 28[51]:43 respectively). But the interpretation to be placed on these facts remains open ended.
Again there is the question whether the alleged revision really does represent the Hebrew more precisely
than does αφανισμος (the translation equivalence
שממה/שמה//αφανισμος was even used by the scrupulous
minded Aquila; he reserved αβατος for ציה, cf. Reider-
Turner, pp. 1, 37). And as previously stated, there is
in the nature of the evidence no way of knowing whether
the choice of vocabulary equivalents derives from a
reviser or from an independent translator.

29:17(49:16)   καταλυω   (IV 2, p. 94)

ιταμια καρδιας σου	זדון לבך
κατελυσεν τρυμαλιας πετρων	שכני בחגוי הסלע

The verb שכן is translated in Jer-LXX as follows
/33/:

	Jer a'	Jer b'
κατασκηνοω	4	-
καταλυω	-	3
κατοικιζω	2	-
οικεω	-	1

The preference for the equivalence καταλυω/שכן in Jer b' as opposed to κατασκηνοω/שכן in Jer a' is cited by Tov as another example of the reviser replacing an original translation (in this case κατασκηνοω) with a "synonymous rendition."

However, in evaluating this proposal it needs to be remembered that κατασκηνοω and καταλυω are not the only translation equivalents of שכן employed in Jer-LXX. In addition, we find κατοικιζω twice in Jer a' and οικεω once in Jer b'; hence it would be difficult to insist that the "unrevised" form of the word in Jer b' must have been κατασκηνοω. Also open to misinterpretation is Tov's statement to the effect that "Jer-R apparently cherished the root καταλυ-." It is true that in addition to the three translations of שכן by καταλυω we also find the same verb employed in Jer b' at 44(37):13 and 45(38):22 and the nouns καταλυσις and καταλυμα at 29:21(49:20) and 40(33):12 respectively. The point, however, is that the root καταλυ- is also found 5 times in Jer a' (the verb καταλυω at 5:7, 7:34, 16:9, 28[51]:43, and the noun καταλυμα at 14:8), so that as far as preference for the root of this verb is concerned there does not appear to be a dramatic difference between the two parts of Jer. Tov correctly observes that in the LXX the equivalence καταλυω/שכן is "more rare" than κατασκηνοω/שכן (καταλυω/שכן is found elsewhere only four times in Sir while κατασκηνοω/שכן occurs outside Jer 41 times), but this observation in itself is not useful in deciding between a reviser or second translator in Jer /34/.

29:20(49:19) τοπος   (III 48, pp. 73-74)
29:21(49:20) καταλυσις ("   )

In section I of this chapter we have already
looked at two words from 29:20(49:19) which Tov cites
as "distinctive similarities" in Jer a' and b' (cf.
εκδιωκω and ανθιστημι, pp. 164-66 above). It was
pointed out there that 29:20(49:19) forms a parallel
passage to 27(50):44, the corresponding verses being
quoted in full. We noted the remarkable similarities
between the two verses, both in Hebrew and Greek, and
commented briefly upon the possible significance of
these. In the present section we note the <u>differences</u>
between the two parallel verses, observing further that
the parallel passage extends through to v. 22(21) in
the Edom oracle and v. 46 in the Babylon oracle /35/.
Our starting point is the translation of נוה (נָוֶה/נְוֵה),
regularly rendered by νομη in Jer a' but in Jer b'
represented by τοπος, καταλυσις and καταλυμα. In
tabular form the relevant statistics are as follows
/36/:

	Jer a'	Jer b'
νομη	6	–
τοπος	–	2
καταλυσις	–	1
καταλυμα	–	1

The preference for νομη in Jer a' is further reinforced by the use of the same word to translate מרעית
twice (10:21, 23:1), while Jer b' uses yet another
translation option, βοσκημα (32:22[25:36]) for that
word. On the basis of these statistics Tov argues that
the reviser not only chose vocabulary options different
from those of the original translator, but also dis-
tinguished between two different meanings of נוה: habi-
tation/τοπος; abode, pasture / καταλυσις, καταλυμα.

The translations of נוה in Jer are certainly interesting and are best explained by the presence of
different hands in the two parts of the book. Tov's
reviser theory is one way of accounting for the translation distributions of the words in question, but a
multiple translator theory is equally plausible.
Regrettably the data available does not carry us beyond
the documentation of differences to the resolution of
ultimate source.

29:20(49:19) κατα προσωπον   (III 22, p. 59)

και τις ουτος ποιμην   ומי זה רעה
ος στησεται κατα προσωπον μου   אשר יעמד לפני

A glance at the parallel passage 29:20(49:19) //
27(50):44 quoted on p. 164 shows that the Hebrew and
Greek phrase cited above is reproduced verbatim in the
parallel Babylon oracle, including the phrase κατα προσωπον. Yet when we take into account the translation
pattern for לפני in the whole of Jer-LXX, the following
picture emerges /37/:

	Jer a'	Jer b'
κατα προσωπον	5	17
προ ποσσωπον	4	-
εις προσωπον	-	1
εναντιον	6	1
ενωπιον	1	-
προτερος	-	3

With these facts in mind Tov concludes that, "Contrary to Jer-OG, Jer-R for the most part rendered לפני
as κατα προσωπον, which faithfully represents the two
components of the Heb." He also notes that in the
translation of other similar Hebrew words and expressions, Jer b' tends to prefer a more literal rendition
where Jer a' employs a standard Greek such as εναντιον
or ενωπιον.

While there is no doubting the literal character
of the Greek phrase with προσωπον as opposed to the
more natural Greek rendition with εναντιον, it is also
true, as recognized by Tov, that all renditions cited
for Jer occur passim in the LXX. In fact, the literal
translations κατα προσωπον and προ προσωπον outnumber
the more natural renditions 9 : 7 even in Jer a'.
There is no guarantee, therefore, that the use of
κατα/εις προσωπον in Jer b' should be interpreted as
the work of a more literally minded reviser.

29:22(49:21) φοβεομαι   (IV 24, p. 102)

οτι απο φωνης πτωσεως αυτων   מקול נפלם
εφοβηθη η γη   רעשה הארץ

The parallel passages found in 29:20-22(49:19-21) and 27(50):44-46 are by all accounts an enigma in the LXX. Up to the middle of v. 21(20) // v. 45 the Greek and Hebrew match one another almost word for word; but all of a sudden, in the middle of that verse, the spell is broken and we are left with a number of perplexing differences both in the Hebrew and even more so in the Greek translations. These differences may be clearly observed when the two portions are reproduced side by side:

δια τουτο ακουσατε βουλην κυριου	δια τουτο ακουσατε την βουλην κυριου
לכן שמעו עצה יהוה	לכן שמעו עצת יהוה
ην εβουλευσατο επι την Ιδουμαιαν	ην βεβουλευται επι Βαβυλωνα
אשר יען אל אדום	אשר יען אל בבל
και λογισμον αυτου ον ελογισατο	και λογισμους αυτου ους ελογισατο
ומחשבותיו אשר חשב	ומחשבותיו אשר חשב
επι τους κατοικουντας Θαιμαν	επι τους κατοικουντας Χαλδαιους
אל ישבי תימן	אל ארץ כשדים
εαν μη συμφησθωσι τα ελαχιστα των προβατων	εαν μη διαφθαρη τα αρνια των προβατων αυτων
אם לא יסחבום צעירי הצאן	אם לא יסחבום צעירי הצאן
εαν μη αβατωθη επ αυτην καταλυσις αυτων	εαν μη αφανισθη νομη απ αυτων
אם לא ישים עליהם נוהם	אם לא ישים עליהם נוה
v.22(21) οτι απο φωνης πτωσεως αυτων	v. 46 οτι απο φωνης αλωσεως Βαβυλωνος
מקול נפלם	מקול נתפשה בבל
εφοβηθη η γη	σεισθησεται η γη
רעשה הארץ	נרעשה הארץ
και κραυγη θαλασσης ουκ (εν θαλασση Σουφ Zi.) ηκουσθη	και κραυγη εν εθνεσιν ακουσθησεται
צעקה בים סוף נשמע קולה	וזעקה בגוים נשמע

Of the five translation equivalents which are different in the above parallel passages, Tov comments on three (cf. αβατωϑη/αφανισϑη [pp. 176-77 above], καταλυσις/νομη [pp. 178-79], and εφοβηϑη/σεισϑησεται [immediately below]). The equivalence συμψαω/סחב of 29:21(49:20) Tov put forth as an example of the "distinctive similarities" between Jer a' and b' (cf. above, p. 166), but failed to mention the different translation διαφϑειρω of Jer a' at 27(50):45, which neutralizes somewhat the force of the "distinctive similarities" argument. Nor are the different translations τα ελαχιστα / τα αρνια των προβατων for צעירי הצאן discussed in the book (it is interesting to observe that in the latter case it is Jer a' which employs the more literal translation, the choice of Jer b' [αρνια] apparently being influenced by the context).

With regard to the different translations σειω and φοβεομαι of רעש (σειω 8:16, 27[50]:46, 28[51]:29; φοβεομαι 29:22[49:21]), Tov lists these as further examples of "synonymous renditions" in Jer a' and b'. But only by considerably stretching the meaning of "synonymous" can one regard the words in question as equally suitable translations of רעש, σειω definitely being the preferred choice. If the reviser replaced σειω with φοβεομαι, he changed what was already a literal and natural translation to a decidedly more ambiguous one. As Tov points out (p. 93), the study of other revisers such as Symmachus, Origen, Lucian, and Aquila has taught us not to expect consistency. Still, the change from a good rendition to an inferior one (at least "inferior" by our standards) is problematic on the reviser theory.

29:23(49:22) ισχυρος   (III 51, p. 75)

| και εσται η καρδια | והיה לב |
| των ισχυρων της Ιδουμαιας | גבורי אדום |

The renditions of גבור found in Jer-LXX are as follows /38/:

	Jer a'	Jer b'
ισχυρος	4	3
μαχητης	8	-

δυνατος	-	3
ανηρ	1	-

Tov observes that the main rendition of Jer a',
μαχητης does not represent the usual equivalent of the
Hebrew word in the LXX; he suggests that the reviser
preferred instead the two standard renditions of ισχυρος and δυνατος presumably replacing any occurrence of
μαχητης with these.

With the aid of HP and dos Santos we can substan-
tiate the following with regard to the translation of
גבור in the LXX:

--ισχυρος is found distributed more or less evenly
throughout the LXX (23x);

--μαχητης renders גבור 18 times in the LXX; but
apart from one occurrence in the text of Jud and one in
1 Chr the rendition is confined to MP and Jer a' (cf.
Tov VI 7, p. 137);

--δυνατος is the most popular translation equivalence of all (78x), especially in the historical books
from Josh onwards, but seldom found in the prophets;

--ανηρ is one of several miscellaneous translations of גבור found throughout the LXX.

It is true, therefore, as Tov says that "μαχητης
does not represent the usual equivalent of the Heb word
in the LXX" and that the more common renditions are
ισχυρος and δυνατος. But if one translator (Jer a')
could use three words (ισχυρος, μαχητης, ανηρ) in rendering the same Hebrew word, there is no difficulty in
viewing another translator (Jer b') alternating between
ισχυρος and δυνατος. There is surely nothing here to
prefer a reviser theory over a multiple translator
theory.

III. Conclusions

In this section we propose to summarize and
evaluate the success of Tov's challenge to the multiple
translator theory for the book of Jer. · The foregoing

discussion based on material provided by the oracles
against the Philistines and Edom has already indicated
some of the problem areas in the interpretation of the
data; here we will deal in more general terms with
methodological considerations and the relative merits
of the conclusions reached.

       In the absence of any kind of hard core evidence
specifying the intervention either of a second translator or of a reviser at Jer 29, it is recognized by
all that our conclusions on these matters must be
inferential. These inferences are based primarily on
observations of data provided by lexico-statistical
analysis of translation equivalents throughout the
book. Both Thackeray and Tov proceed with essentially
this same methodology and both agree at the outset that
the documented change of style and vocabulary equivalents in the middle of the book testify against its
unity as it now stands and requires some other explanation.

       This conviction regarding the composite nature of
the book is itself, of course, an inference based on
the assumption of consistency in the style and vocabulary choices of a single translator. In introducing
his JTS article on "The Greek Translators of Jeremiah"
(p. 245), Thackeray recognized a potential danger in
employing the criterion of translation variants as an
argument against the unity of a prescribed piece. It
is namely true that the translators for the most part
did not rigidly render each Hebrew word by a single
Greek equivalent but deliberately varied their vocabulary choices with the result that renditions sometimes
differ in the same book and even in the same passage
without any change of translator being involved. The
key to the detection of a different hand, therefore,
must be the degree of consistency with which the same
Hebrew word was rendered in different parts of the same
work. If we find that the same Hebrew word is rendered
"with fair consistency" in one part of a book but
rendered differently in another part, then, according
to Thackeray, we are justified in suspecting the unity
of the work. The assumption seems reasonable enough,
but it does serve as a good reminder of the inferential
reasoning which lies at the heart of the entire enterprise, whether dealing with multiple translators or
revisers. The subjective element in determining what

should be considered "fair consistency" of rendering
and what not, should also be kept in mind. We need to
be alert to the possibility that some of the differences between the two parts may simply be due to the
variation of style of a single translator.

Granted these qualifications and appeals for caution, Thackeray was nonetheless persuaded that the
evidence in Jer was strong enough and consistent enough
to deny the unity of the book. Having discovered 28
examples of Hebrew words and syntactical constructions
which met with his standard of "a fair consistency" of
different rendition in the two parts of the book, this
led him inexorably to a multiple translator for the
book. The only other explanation which might conceivably account for the facts, he reasoned, was that of
Hexaplaric influence (pp. 245, 252). Since the words
in Jer a' generally have some Hexaplaric support whereas those in Jer b' do not, it could be argued that the
LXX text had been revised or corrupted up to a certain
point by the Hexapla. But finding this explanation
untenable he was left with (to him) the only alternative solution of a multiple translator theory.

Employing the same methodology and criterion of
translation consistency, Tov has added to the examples
adduced by Thackeray but has sought to interpret the
data differently by postulating the intervention of a
pre-Hexaplaric reviser. It is interesting to note that
although Tov nowhere makes reference to Thackeray's
brief consideration of a reviser explanation, the possibility of such had not escaped Thackeray's notice
--albeit Thackeray could only conceive of a post-
Hexaplaric revision. Living as we do in the "post-
Barthélemy" era, it is only natural that we should now
explore the hypothesis of a pre-Hexaplaric revision as
a means of accounting for the peculiar distribution of
translation equivalents in Jer. To do this, as we have
seen, Tov emphasizes the similarities between the two
parts of Jer.

In taking this approach, it can be argued that Tov
is simply following the same methodology pursued by
Thackeray elsewhere, viz. in his identification of the
translator of Jer b' with that of Bar 1:1-3:8. However, the difficulty experienced by Thackeray in evaluating the significance of the similarities between

Jer b' and Bar 1:1-3:8 ought to give pause in pronoun-
cing on the relationship between Jer a' and b'. Thackeray's vacillation on this matter can be appreciated
from the following account of his changing views. In
the original JTS article Thackeray noted that others
had previously observed the similarities between Jer
and Bar, the only question being whether this was due
to identity of translators or to imitation (p. 262);
his own investigation of the evidence, however, led him
to the conclusion that the similarities could admit of
but one solution, namely that the translator of Bar was
to be identified with the translator of the second
portion of Jer (p. 265). But some years later he
abandoned this view and now argued that the similarities in the first part of Bar to the style of the
second translator of Jer were more likely due to a
close imitation of the latter's style since the observed phenomena were insufficient to prove translation
by one and the same person (Jewish Worship, p. 87).
Yet later again, when he returned to the subject in his
contribution to the New Commentary on Holy Scripture
(1929) on Bar, Thackeray reverted to his original position, namely that imitation would not account for all
the similarities but pointed instead to identity of
hands (p. 105).

    With regard to the two main parts of Jer, however,
Thackeray never experienced any of the above vacilla-
tiòn on the interpretation of the data. He was indeed
aware of some of the similarities between Jer a' and
b', including several of the words discussed above,
e.g., ιταμια, συμφαω, τρυμαλια ("The Greek Translators
of Jeremiah," pp. 253-54), παντοκρατωρ (Jewish Worship,
p. 33), but was able to accommodate these to his multiple translator theory for Jer. In Tov's scheme, everything depends on the interpretation given to these similarities; for this reason his chapter on this subject
(Ch. II) is absolutely foundational as he himself recognizes in different places /39/. Conversely he also
admits that his interpretation of the differences between Jer a' and b' as revisional is true only if the
proposed explanation of the similarities can be upheld
/40/. In fact, not one of the chapters outside Ch. II
on the similarities contributes anything toward the
argument for the unity of the original translation
/41/.

The question then is, What degree of persuasibility is to be credited to Tov's chapter on the distinctive similarities between Jer a' and b'? In attempting
to answer this question we need to consider two sides
of the issue: first, Tov's critique of Thackeray's
explanation for the appearance of the similarities, and
secondly, the strength of his own examples adduced in
favour of a unity of translation.

Tov summarizes Thackeray's explanations as follows
(p. 20):

"(a) Jer β´ imitated Jer α´ ("Gr.Tr.Jer.", 253-4);

(b) Later redactors or scribes were responsible
for 'a certain amount of mixture of the two styles'
(ib., 254);

(c) The similarities resulted from 'imperfect
collaboration of two workers, the second of whom only
partially followed the lead of the first' (The
Septuagint and Jewish Worship, 35)."

Tov follows this summary with a number of observations which may be paraphrased as follows:

1. Would a second translator possess the recall
capacity to employ Jer a's translation equivalents
without the use of a Hebrew-Greek and Greek-Hebrew
concordance?

2. Some of the similarities cannot be explained
by any of Thackeray's explanations. For instance, 10
of the rare Greek words common to both parts reflect
translations of more than one Hebrew word. It is difficult to understand why anyone would copy a certain
rare Greek word (reflecting a given Heb 1) from one
section to the other as a translation of a different
Hebrew word (Heb 2).

3. It is a priori more likely that differences
were inserted secondarily rather than similarities;
otherwise how would one explain the far greater pro-
portion of remaining differences?

4. The phrase "a mixture of the two styles" to
describe Jer a' and b' is ill-chosen since the observed

correspondences do not represent characteristic features of the "style" of either Jer a' or b' but constitute rather isolated instances of agreement in rare
words and renditions.

5. The suggestion that a given translator imitated the vocabulary of a colleague has no parallel in
the LXX, except perhaps in the case of borrowing from
the Pentateuch which, however, represents a different
Sitz im Leben.

6. The assumption of redactors who welded together the two portions of Jer is unconvincing since
there is no proof for the existence of such redactors,
and even if they had existed they would probably have
chosen to erase the differences between the two sections and introduced more easily recognized similarities.

7. The need for "collaboration" between a pair of
translators would have arisen only in case of lexical
difficulties, an explanation which could apply only to
a few of the examples given.

Some of the above points represent valuable observations and need to be carefully considered; yet
counter-arguments exist for most:

1. It is extremely difficult for us to judge what
the recall factor of an ancient scribe might or might
not have been. It is common knowledge that memory retention in antiquity far surpassed anything considered
normal today. Nor can the possibility of verbal cross-
consultation be dismissed or even consultation of a
previously prepared document.

2. Why Jer b' sometimes employs a rare Greek word
to translate a Hebrew word different from that which it
renders in Jer a' is problematic, but not fatal, to a
multiple translator theory, especially since the LXX
provides abundant examples of the most surprising and
unexpected equivalents. Being conditioned to expect
great diversity in translation variants, the "shock"
value of some unique equivalents is considerably minimized.

3. Thackeray never claimed that "the similarities were inserted or developed secondarily," as though the two halves of Jer were submitted to a thorough revision in order to bring them into greater conformity with each other. He did say that the joint had "ragged edges" and that there was a concentration of similarities to the vocabulary of Jer a' in the first three chapters of Jer b' ("The Greek Translators of Jeremiah," p. 253), perhaps with the implication that there was some attempt to bring a degree of uniformity to the book in the initial chapters of the second half.

4. Thackeray's phrase "a mixture of the two styles" is infelicitous from a technical point of view; on the other hand, his choice of terminology is not to be pressed. From the context, it is clear that he was using the word "style" in a loose rather than in a technical sense as a description of "characteristic features" of Jer a' or b'. The phrase itself occurs in the context of Thackeray's discussion concerning the observed correspondences between Jer a' and Chs. 29-31 of Jer b', and he no doubt would have been happy with the designation of these as "rare renditions and words found in two parts of one book."

5. Thackeray's choice of the term "imitation" to describe the work of Jer b' is also open to criticism. Tov is surely right to object that Jer b' "did not reproduce characteristic elements of Jer. α'", which might legitimately be called "imitation," but at best merely copied some renditions found in Jer a'. The notion of "borrowing," however, may not be as inapplicable to the present situation as Tov suggests. It is true that the known phenomenon of borrowing from the Pentateuch represents a different Sitz im Leben from that of one translator borrowing from a colleague, but this does not rule out an extension of the process of consultation. Studies by P.D.M. Turner on "Intra-Septuagintal Borrowing" suggests that borrowing of this type may have been undertaken on quite a large scale /42/.

6. The objection that there is no proof for the existence of redactors who welded together Jer a' and b' seems out of place in a work which depends entirely for its persuasibility on the assumption of an unknown reviser who reworked the Greek text of this prophecy.

Assumptions of this type seem to be part of the "occu-
pational hazard" associated with textual studies from
antiquity. Nor is Tov's objection to the effect that
alleged redactors would probably have erased differences and introduced easily recognized similarities compelling. As frequently observed, lack of consistency
in translation is a problem whether we are dealing with
Thackeray's translators, Tov's reviser, or other presumed redactors. However, after all of this has been
said, it may yet be true that Thackeray has depended
too much on the role of redactors in accounting for the
observed similarities between Jer a' and b'. Some
similarities may be due to chance, others to familiarity with the work of the first translator.

7. It is not clear to us why collaboration between two translators--if practiced at all--must have
been limited to Hebrew words which caused lexical difficulty. If cross-consultation was practiced to any
degree it would surely be unwise to pronounce on its
possible limits.

We are not persuaded, therefore, that Tov's criti-
cisms have undermined the possibility of a multiple
translator theory to account for the lexical phenomena
of the book of Jer. Nor do his examples of the "distinctive similarities" advanced in defense of the unity
theory significantly alter this evaluation. In the
first part of this chapter we have analyzed in detail
12 of the 45 examples listed by Tov and have found the
arguments in several instances open to challenge and
amenable to other interpretations. Tov has suggested
that perhaps because Thackeray recognized only a small
number of the similarities he was inclined to accord
them a secondary status (p. 20). But it seems to us
that simply a few more of the same type of agreements
as those represented by Jer 29 is insufficient evidence
to bear the weight of the unity theory. For, as re-
peatedly pointed out in the second part of this chapter, the observed differences between Jer a' and b',
including the various types of Tendenz discerned within them, can be explained as readily on the assumption
of a second translator as that of a reviser. In fact,
it seems to us that a more natural and less forced
reading of the evidence inclines in favour of the
former.

We need finally to consider Tov's explanation of how it happens that we have extant only the revised portion of Jer b' rather than that of the whole book. The theory, we recall (p. 154 above, n. 3), is that the original work of revision covered the whole of the text, probably effected on two different scrolls. Sometime between the original translation and the writing of our present MSS a mistake was made in the selection of scrolls for the text that was to become standard for all subsequent recopyings. For some reason, a scroll containing the first half of the text type represented by Jer a' was combined with one of the type represented by Jer b', and this combination became the archetype of the present text of Jer. This explanation further entails the presupposition that the dividing line in both text types occurred at the same point. Tov himself describes the proposed solution as "irrational" (p. 162), but finds no other explanation except the less likely one that the reviser commenced his work with Jer 29.

While Tov's proposed scenario of an accidental combination of two scrolls of different text types, one from the original translation and one from a revised edition, is not inconceivable, especially in the light of our knowledge concerning ancient Buchwesen and also in the light of changes in text-types in the same book (e.g. Reigns) or individual MSS (e.g. 130 in Jer), neither does it appear to have anything more to commend it than an original division of labour among two different translators. Tov's well documented footnote (p. 173, n. 22) affirming the ancient practice of dividing large units into different scrolls is useful but can support a two-translator theory as much the accidental combination of two mismatched MSS.

But what strikes us as particularly damaging to the reviser theory is the lack of any surviving MS evidence either from the presumed revised a' portion or from the hypothetically unrevised b' portion. Were all surviving copies of the former scrolls so completely obliterated as to leave no trace in the extant MS collection? In an appendix to Tov's original thesis (pp. 202-208) he did discuss the possibility of vestiges of the revised and unrevised portions of Jer a' and b' respectively among some of the existing MS variants (e.g. 29:22 εφοβηθη B-S-538] εσ(ε)ισθη rel.,

p. 205), but in the published version of the thesis
(p. 172, n. 17) he admits that none of the examples is
conclusive since all have alternate explanations (e.g.
in the case of εσ(ε)ισθη in 29:22 this word is undoubtedly a revision in A Q V O̲ L̲ C;   cf. Ziegler's remark,
"29:22 ist εφοβηθη als ursprünglich in der Text aufzu-
nehmen . . . . Es ist undenkbar, dass der B-Text die
gewöhnliche Wendung εσεισθη η γη durch εφοβηθη η γη
ersetzt hätte," Ieremias, p. 45).

    In short, we are not persuaded that the last word
has been said on the multiple translator theory of Jer.
Tov has indeed pointed out some problem areas underlying this explanation, and, given the unity hypothesis, has effectively taken the available evidence as
far as it will go. The question is whether it will go
far enough to overturn the two-translator theory /43/.
It is true that in current LXX studies it is commonplace to look for Greek revisions on the basis of a
changing Hebrew Vorlage, and while much points to the
genuine survival of such revisions (e.g. Kaige), it
does not seem to us that the lexical phenomena presented by the book of Jer are of the same order /44/.
For the present, therefore, it seems safest to proceed
with the assumption that our extant archetype text of
Jer b' represents an original translation rather than a
revision. The theory of a lost revised text of Jer a'
and of a prior unrevised stage of Jer b', while stimu-
lating and challenging in its own right, remains un-
proved.

CHAPTER FIVE

THE HEBREW/GREEK PROBLEM:

A CRITIQUE OF J.G. JANZEN'S STUDY

OF THE RELATIONSHIP BETWEEN JER-LXX AND JER-MT

In this chapter we turn from the consideration of inner-Greek problems to an analysis of the relationship between the LXX and MT texts of the book of Jer. A subject of much debate, the differences between the two texts in terms of length and arrangement have usually been explained according to one of four broad theories as outlined in the Introduction (pp. 11-12 above): the "abbreviation" theory, the "editorial" theory, the "expansion" theory, and the "mediating" theory. In a Harvard dissertation published in 1973 under the title Studies in the Text of Jeremiah, J. Gerald Janzen has vigorously challenged both the theory of a deliberately abbreviated Greek translation as well as the scholarly consensus of the mediating position which holds that in cases where the LXX and MT differ, a decision on the "better" reading can be reached only case by case and may not be determined deductively by an appeal to generalizations. Building on the evidence of fragments of a MS from Qumrân exhibiting a Hebrew text akin to that of the shorter LXX, Janzen has instead defended the integrity and priority of the Hebrew Vorlage under-lying the LXX over against that of the MT, the latter being viewed as a later expansion of the original writings.

Our last chapter provides the necessary forum for a constructive critique of Janzen's position. Our procedure will be first of all to examine Janzen's statements on the purpose, scope, and motivation of the study as set forth in the Introduction to the book (pp. 1-9). Since matters discussed there affect the way Janzen's study is prosecuted as well as the conclusions reached, a general review and critique of these pages will help to clarify the issues under consideration.

This review is then followed by a detailed analysis of the author's treatment of the differences ("zero
variants") between the LXX and MT texts as illustrated
in the oracles against the Philistines and Edom and
related passages. A last section draws together the
results of our investigation and seeks briefly to
assess the limits of our present understanding as to
how the two texts relate to each other. The basic
outline for the chapter, therefore, will be as follows:

I.   Critique of Janzen's "Introduction"

II.   Critique of Janzen's Explanation of the "Zero
      Variants" in the Oracles Against the Philis-
      tines and Edom

III. Conclusions

I.   Critique of Janzen's "Introduction"

In this section we shall look in turn at three
points discussed in the book's introductory chapter:
A) The Purpose and Scope of Janzen's Study, B) The
Justification for Janzen's Study, and C) The Leading
Questions Underlying Janzen's Study.

A.   The Purpose and Scope of Janzen's Study

The purpose of Janzen's study as explained on p. 1
of the book is to reopen the debate on the radical di-
vergence in length between the MT and LXX versions of
the book of Jer. The study is therefore limited to the
matter of "omissions" or, as Janzen calls them, "zero
variants." The author recognizes the existence of
other problem areas in the relationship between the two
texts, e.g. qualitative or "content" variants, where
the texts diverge not in length but in meaning, and
transpositions, particularly those relating to the
section of the Oracles Against the Foreign Nations;
however, these matters are qualified as "not directly
relevant" to the study and are consequently left to one
side except for incidental comment.

Question: Is Janzen's limitation valid? That
is, Can "zero variants" legitimately be studied in

isolation from "content variants" and other problem
areas in the book without the evidence becoming vulnerable to distortion? It is easy to sympathize with the
need for imposing some kind of limits on the study of a
book the size of Jer--the present work is a prime
example!--and the limitation actually chosen by Janzen
in favour of quantitative differences seems logical and
defensible enough. However, acceptance of such a limitation should clearly be held in view throughout the
investigation and be allowed to temper the finality of
any conclusions reached. Janzen shows himself aware of
this requirement in his opening statement of Ch. VIII
when he says, "The limitation of this study to the zero
variants makes possible only a partial assessment of
the character of the texts of M and $\mathcal{G}$. Full assessment
will involve detailed examination of the content variants, and of the transpositions. . ." (p. 127). However, we will want to ask whether sufficient notice has
in fact been taken of this precaution throughout the
book or whether the author has not indulged in more
interpretation than is warranted by the self-imposed
limits of the study. We hold that the value of a
limited study such as that undertaken by Janzen lies
more in its descriptive than in its interpretative
side.

B.   The Justification for Janzen's Study

     Following a brief review of previous literature on
the Greek/Hebrew problem of the book of Jer (pp. 2-7),
Janzen next discusses the appropriateness of reopening
the question at this time (pp. 7-8). Three reasons are
cited as justification for a new evaluation of the
data: 1) The existence of improved Greek text critical
tools, 2) The discovery of new Hebrew MS evidence, and
3) The unsatisfactory character of the present-day
approach to the text of Jer.

1.   The Existence of Improved Greek Text Critical
     Tools

     The text critical tool referred to, which, ac-
cording to Janzen, makes possible "a new level of
precision" in the determination of the LXX text, is
that of Ziegler's edition in the Göttingen series.

As has been shown in Ch. III above, Ziegler's text of
Jer, while not faultless, is indeed an excellent edition and does provide a solid basis for comparing the
LXX and MT. Since a prior and fundamental requirement
for any definitive study on the relationship between
the Greek and Hebrew texts is that of a reliable LXX
text, we agree that this need has largely been met in
the Göttingen critical text and apparatus.

2.   The Discovery of New Hebrew MS Evidence

     The single most important factor which in Janzen's
opinion necessitates a reinvestigation of the two texts
of Jer is the discovery of new MS evidence from Qumrân.
The current inventory of this material consists of
several fragments from four Hebrew MSS, namely, 2QJer,
4QJer[a], 4QJer[b], and 4QJer[c]. Of these, only the fragments of 2QJer (27 fragments in all, half of which are
too small to be assigned a verse reference) have been
published in the official series, Discoveries in the
Judaean Desert (Vol. III, 1962; Planches, Textes;
eds. M. Baillet, J.T. Milik, R. de Vaux). The biblical
material from Cave 4 has been notoriously slow in
appearing in an editio princeps, but a preliminary
transcription of twelve fragments of 4QJer[a] and three
fragments of 4QJer[b] can be found in Appendix D of
Janzen's book (pp. 173-84). Apparently none of the
fragments of 4QJer[c] has as yet been published in any
form /1/.

     Of the four MSS named above, three attest a
distinct MT type text: 2QJer, 4QJer[a] , and 4QJer[c] /2/.
This leaves only the three small fragments from 4QJer
which alone attest a text type resembling that of the
LXX /3/. With regard to the significance of the latter
MS, Janzen contends that it "confirms the methodological validity of attempts to move from ℭ by retroversion
to its supposed Hebrew Vorlage" (p. 7), and secondly,
that it calls in question the exegetical approach to
LXX studies which has sought to explain divergencies
between the Greek and Hebrew texts in terms of transmission technique or translator Tendenz" (pp. 7-8).
These two claims for the significance of 4QJer[b] need
to be carefully assessed.

We must ask, first, whether 4QJer^b really does
validate the process of retroversion on the scale that
Janzen envisages. The technique of retroversion, once
in great vogue, has in recent times and for good
reasons been practiced with much greater reserve. As
Goshen-Gottstein has observed: "there is no retroversion without a residual of doubt, and what seems self-
evident to one scholar may look like a house of cards
to his fellow" ("Theory and Practice", p. 132). We are
not suggesting, of course, that Janzen would approve of
a return to the indiscriminate retroversion of former
generations (cf. his critical remarks on Workman,
p. 6), yet he does make considerable use of the
technique in the book.

This may be illustrated with reference to Appendices A, B.2, and [B.4] /4/. In these tables which
document occurrences of proper names and divine names
in both texts, the LXX form of a name is always represented in Hebrew characters. But does 4QJer^b give us
the confidence to assume that wherever the Greek has a
shorter name or formula this was translated from a
Hebrew parent text exactly as found in these lists?
To us this appears to place too much confidence in the
technique of retroversion. Janzen (p. 173) invites us
to extrapolate from the extant fragments of 4QJer^b to a
consideration of what the MS as a whole must have been
like and then decide whether we are not convinced that
this MS is emphatically, even if not perfectly, a
witness to a shorter Hebrew text of the book of Jer.
The program is appealing and the solution apparently
simple, yet who would dare say in any given instance
exactly what 4QJer^b or any other MS may or may not have
read? While we can appreciate the convenience of
representing the Greek by Hebrew characters in the
tables referred to--and elsewhere throughout the book--
the "methodological validity" of so doing has not, in
our opinion, been fully vindicated /5/.

As for the exegetical approach to LXX studies of
which Janzen is so critical, we do not think this ought
be dismissed quite as easily either. We agree that
"the time is past when one could approach the Greek
text primarily as a source for learning the exegetical
method of the translator" (emphasis ours), but this is
quite different from ignoring such considerations altogether. As our subsequent critique will attempt to

show, it is precisely this failure to take account of
other factors besides those of length which constitutes
one of our major concerns with Janzen's work. To take
an example not drawn from the Philistine or Edom oracle: Janzen argues at length (pp. 54-57) that the three
occurrences of the word עבדי with reference to Nebuchadrezzar (MT 25:9, 27:6, 43:10) are all secondary since
in each case the LXX either omits the word in question
or attests a different reading from the Hebrew (LXX
25:9, 34:5, 50:10). Yet the existence of other ways of
interpreting the data, whether by emphasizing theologi-
cal/philological aspects of the Hebrew, or translation
Tendenz in the Greek, have been amply demonstrated by
T.W. Overholt (CBQ 30[1968], 39-48; contra W.E. Lemke,
CBQ 28[1966], 45-50), Z. Zevit (JBL 88[1969], 74-77),
and D. Schmidt (IOSCS Bulletin 8[1975], 17-18). The
discovery of 4QJer[b] does not give us license to disregard such exegetical and contextual considerations;
their merits must be evaluated whether a shorter Hebrew
text exists or not /6/.

3.   The Unsatisfactory Character of the Present-day
      Approach to the Text of Jer

      According to Janzen, the problem with the 20th
century approach to the text of Jer has been the
lack of any systematic treatment of the quantitative
differences between the LXX and MT. Instead, scholars
have been content merely to give summary statements of
earlier studies and to discuss instances of variation
on an ad hoc basis, being reluctant to generalize
on the relative priority of the two texts. We agree
that the time is ripe for an up-to-date and comprehensive review of the LXX variants which could then be
expressed in valid generalizations. The documentation
and attempted classification of these variants is,
therefore, a valuable contribution of Janzen's work
/7/.

      At the end of the day, however, we are unable to
share Janzen's confidence in the interpretation of the
data. Our criticism is simply that in Janzen's legitimate attempt to redress a lack in Jer Forschung, he has
over-reacted and has been too quick to classify each variant as necessarily part of some overriding scheme,
usually a pattern of expansion in the MT. While a full

and systematic treatment of the quantitative differences is a necessary task in itself, it is only one part
of the whole. When exclusive preoccupation with
"omission" patterns inhibits the perception of possible
"translation" patterns, then we must ask whether this
approach is not deficient in some way as well.

C.   The Leading Questions Underlying Janzen's Study

     At the close of the introductory chapter, Janzen
formulates the two leading questions which motivate the
work: 1) "Does the shorter reading of 𝕲 arise from the
tendency of the translator to abridge his text, or does
it reflect a Hebrew Vorlage with the shorter reading?"
and 2) "If 𝕲 reflects a Vorlage with the shorter reading, is this reading superior or inferior to the longer
reading of 𝕸?" (pp. 8-9). It is useful to have the
main issues outlined in this manner; however, we
think it unfortunate that they should be expressed in
terms of such dichotomies.

     With regard to the question whether the LXX
reflects translation abridgement or a shorter Hebrew
Vorlage, Janzen feels that the general absence of a
tendency to condense in the Greek OT coupled with the
discovery of Qumrân specimens of a shorter Hebrew text
have now entirely shifted the burden of proof to those
who would continue to hold a theory of condensation.
But this is surely to assume too much. Arguments for
condensation in other parts of the LXX have certainly
not been wanting, e.g. D.H. Gard, The Exegetical Method
of the Greek Translator of the Book of Job, 1952;
D.W. Gooding, The Account of the Tabernacle: Translation and Textual Problems of the Greek Exodus, 1959.
But whatever the case in other books--and both of the
works mentioned have been submitted to criticism--the
evidence for Jer must be tested on its own merits. It
is axiomatic in LXX research that every book is unique
and must be researched de novo.

     Nor can we accept the proposition that support for
a shorter Hebrew text in the form of 4QJer[b] has finally
settled the condensation/expansion controversy. The
discovery of the few fragments of this MS has indeed
given proof of the real existence at one time of a
shorter Hebrew text than the MT--at least in those

passages attested by the fragments of 4QJer[b] and for
the whole book in so far as it is legitimate to extrapolate from the fragments to the whole--thus directing
more attention to the important pre-history of the
Hebrew Vorlage and exonerating the translators of
much of the blame which had been attached to them by
Graf and others. But this is not the same thing as
saying that the fragments of 4QJer[b] have brought about
a complete volte-face in the study of the textual
problem of Jer or that they have undermined all arguments for deliberate or accidental translator condensation. The purpose of our detailed study of the
LXX omissions in the Philistine and Edom oracles on
pp. 203ff. is to demonstrate that such an argument
cannot be sustained.

With regard to the second question, i.e. whether
the shorter or longer reading is to be regarded as
superior, Janzen realizes that this issue is not to be
settled merely by an appeal to the axiom lectio brevior
potior, since the most common scribal error of all,
haplography, works in the opposite direction; nonetheless, the net effect of the paragraph dealing with this
question is to affirm the principle that "it is a
common tendency for texts to grow in transmission," a
generalization which is supported by a long footnote
(n. 35, pp. 191-192) citing evidence for this tendency
in a variety of ancient literatures. While we have no
quarrel with Janzen's references and do not wish to
dispute the evidence that texts of antiquity often did
grow in the process of transmission, we are obliged
nevertheless to say that the footnote in question does
not give a complete or balanced picture. An appeal to
comparative literatures should also mention those cases
where the opposite phenomenon has been observed. The
following discussion takes account of some of these
examples.

From the literature of the ANE, Janzen quotes
passages cited in the writings of W.F. Albright and
S.N. Kramer which appear to support the general
"tendency of ancient Oriental scribes and compilers to
add rather that to subtract" (Albright, FSAC, p. 80).
Albright's example is that of Egyptian mortuary texts
known as the Book of the Dead which "illustrate this
process of expansion by addition." Kramer wrote concerning the tablet UM 29-13-209 + 29-16-414 of the

Akkadian Epic section Gilgamesh and the Land of the
Living that it "seems to have a much more expanded text
than our reconstructed version" (JCS 1 [1947], 7). But
this tablet represents only one aspect of a much larger
and more complex picture. In a Yale dissertation,
Literary-critical Studies in the Gilgamesh Epic: an
Assyriological Contribution to Biblical Literary
Criticism, 1972, J.H. Tigay has pointed out the existence of different Akkadian Gilgamesh texts varying
among themselves. While some texts expand, others
abbreviate; for instance, there is one example of a
Hittite version of Gilgamesh condensed to about one-
fifth the standard length (see esp. pp. 143ff., 194ff.,
282f.). Similarly, in an unpublished paper, "Literary
History: The Gilgamesh Epic and Flood," A.R. Millard
has compared the Gilgamesh Epic of Tablet XI with the
earlier Epic of Atrahasis. This comparison produced a
number of examples of expansion in the later version
such as the addition of synonyms, synonymous parallels,
descriptive phrases and factual additions, but at the
same time showed instances where the earlier text was
longer. Millard emphasizes the impossibility of determining from one version what the other might have been
like at any given point (see also, W.G. Lambert and
A.R. Millard, Atra-hasis: The Babylonian Story of the
Flood, 1969, p. 38, where the same point is made
regarding the phenomenon of concurrent expansion and
contraction).

    Evidence from other quarters is equally ambivalent.
For instance, although a 7th century Sultanepe ·edition
of the Myth of Nergal and Ereshkigal is longer than a
14th century version of the same story, the editor of
the Sultanepe version suggests the possibility that the
earlier account may represent an abbreviated local
version (O.R. Gurney, AS 10 [1960], 107). Another
example may be taken from the Ras Shamra literature.
D.J. Wiseman has pointed out the existence of a short
text from Ras Shamra which was probably copied from an
earlier Old Babylonian version and which, in Wiseman's
opinion, may be yet another example of several episodes
recorded on a number of different tablets being reduced
to a single brief text. To this Wiseman adds the comment, "This form of literary development (i.e. condensation) appears to exist alongside the so-called
'normal editorial method of expansion' . . . . (JNSL 5
[1977], 83).

In addition to the examples drawn from the ANE, Janzen also cites instances of secondary expansion in the Iliad, the Mahabharata, the OT Samaritan text and the NT Syriac text. But from these fields, too, counter-illustrations exist. In classical studies one who positively disbelieved in the validity of the axiom lectio brevior potior was A.C. Clark. In his text critical work on Cicero (The Descent of Manuscripts, 1918) he demonstrated that scribes were much more prone to omit than to add. When he applied his findings to the Gospels and Acts (The Primitive Text of the Gospels and Acts, 1914; The Acts of the Apostles, 1933), he was virtually rejected by his contemporaries, except for a few like B.H. Streeter who showed himself favourable to some aspects of Clark's theories (The Four Gospels, pp. 131ff.). Recently, however, there have been signs of a re-appraisal of Clark's work, particularly on the question of the shorter and longer texts of Acts where it is argued that some of the longer readings of the "Western" text may after all be original (cf. M. Black in his contribution to the Eugene A. Nida FS, pp. 119–131, and D. Parker in NTS 24 [1977], esp. 153–155). From the field of LXX studies we may refer to Ch. 2 of R. Hanhart's monograph Zum Text des 2. und 3. Makkabäerbuches which, as G.D. Kilpatrick in his review of the book says, contains several examples involving "important modifications of the maxim lectio brevior potior (GGA 215 [1963], 12).

In the light of the foregoing, it should be clear that we cannot come to a text with any pre-determined notions of how it may have fared in the process of transmission. Every possibility illustrated by ancient texts has to be allowed, and care taken to avoid imposing an alien consistency upon the scribes. In his concluding paragraph on Ch. I (p. 9), Janzen seems to reduce the options for explaining the textual phenomena of the book of Jer either to a case of expansion in the MT or to haplography in the LXX. At the very least, the examples adduced above must alert us to the possibility of other and more complex forces also having been at work in the development of the texts that we know today as the LXX and MT versions of the book. The following discussion will seek to reinforce the soundness of this deductive observation and illustrate the need for caution in interpreting the complex data relating to the Greek and Hebrew texts of Jer.

II. Critique of Janzen's Explanations of the "Zero
     Variants" in the Oracles Against the Philistines
     and Edom

        In this section we will deal consecutively with all
of those passages in the oracles against the Philistines
and Edom which contain quantitative differences between
the LXX and MT texts. Our purpose is to view the respective variants in the light of their immediate as
well as their broader contexts (including parallel and
related passages), and to test the validity of Janzen's
explanations for the observed differences. The relevant portion of each passage will be quoted in full
from the LXX and MT texts, the "zero variants" in each
case being underlined.

29:1a(47:1)

                                                אשר היה דבר יהוה
                                                אל ירמיהו הנביא
επι τους αλλοφυλους   אל פלשתים
                                                בטרם יכה פרעה את עזה

επι τους αλλοφυλους] pr. ※ος εγενηθη λογος κυριου
προς ιερεμιαν τον προφητην 88; pr. επι τους αλλοφυλους
λογος κυριου ος εγενηθη προς ιερεμιαν τον προφητην Syh
(επι τους αλλοφ. sub ⸰ et λογος - προφητην sub ※) Arm;
+ (※Ο-Qmg) προ του παταξαι φαραω την γαζαν Ο-Qmg Arm;
+ ος (ως 22c 62) εγενετο λογος κυριου προς ιερεμιαν τον
προφητην (+ επι τους αλλοφυλους 51-62-311-449') προ του
παταξαι φαραω την γαζαν L; om. 106 538txt Bo Arm/p

        This verse introduces us unceremoniously into the
middle of the controversy surrounding the relationship
between the LXX and MT texts of the book of Jer.
Initially we may note three points:

        1. The verse is found in radically different
positions in the two texts: 29:1 in the LXX and 47:1
in the MT. In the LXX, the OAN section comes in the
middle of the book, while in the MT it is found at the
end. In the LXX the Philistine oracle stands fourth in
the list of foreign nations following Elam, Egypt, and
Babylon; in the MT, the Philistine oracle stands
second following Egypt.

2. The introductory heading in the LXX is considerably shorter than that of the MT. In structure, the
LXX heading resembles the superscriptions found in the
oracles against Edom, the Ammonites, Damascus, and Moab
(e.g. τη Ιδουμαια, etc.) except that the Philistine
heading employs the preposition επι, a construction
which is unique among the titles of the OAN section.

3. The Hebrew of the first part of the verse (the
awkward and unattached אשר clause) is of a type found
in OT literature only in Jer-MT 14:1, 46:1, 47:1 and
49:34. The last three of these occurrences all appear
in the OAN section, and two of them at particularly
vital points within this section, namely at MT 46:1
(the general superscription to the entire OAN section)
and at MT 49:34 (the introduction to the Elam oracle,
the oracle which in the Greek order commences the OAN
section). The LXX lacks a corresponding phrase for
each of the אשר היה דבר יהוה אל ירמיהו clauses in the
OAN section, while the introduction employed at 14:1,
και εγενετο λογος κυριου προς Ιερεμιαν is otherwise
the standard Greek rendition of the Hebrew ויהי דבר
יהוה אל ירמיהו.

Janzen deals with the אשר היה דבר יהוה formula
--as well as other introductory headings absent from
the LXX--in the closing part of the fifth chapter,
"Supposed Abridgment in ₲", (esp. pp. 111-115), a
chapter in which the author seeks to refute the popular
notion that the Greek translator for various reasons
deliberately abridged his text. With regard to the
four אשר clauses under consideration, therefore, Janzen
holds that these testify not to deliberate omission on
the part of the translator, but rather to secondary
expansion in the Hebrew text. According to this reconstruction, the formula arose at a late stage in the
transmission process of the book, first at 46:1 and
49:34, subsequently by imitation at 14:1 and 47:1.
These conclusions are in turn directly based on the
author's conviction regarding the priority of the LXX
position and internal order of the OAN section.

In order to evaluate these suggestions adequately,
it will be necessary to set the discussion in a broader
perspective than merely the אשר היה דבר יהוה formula.
As is well known, the editorial framework of the book
of Jer contains many examples of stereotyped

superscriptions and introductions, data which has been
utilized not least in the source critical analysis of
the book (e.g. S. Mowinckel, Zur Komposition des Buches
Jeremia, 1914). Comparison with the Greek shows that
in the majority of cases the LXX follows the MT very
closely /8/, an observation which would tend to favour
the view that the translator sought to render his parent text quite faithfully, and that consequently any
quantitative and/or qualitative difference in the LXX
version of these formulas would therefore reflect a
different Vorlage. While the force of this argument
should not be minimized, nor can absolute translator
fidelity everywhere be assumed. In cases where a different underlying Hebrew seems definitely called for,
one is still faced with the challenge of deciding
between the relative priority of the presumed LXX
Vorlage vis-à-vis the MT. Simply to assume in each
instance that the shorter LXX represents a better
reading seems no more legitimate than everywhere to
take for granted that the MT must represent the
superior reading. To illustrate these points we will
review the principal cases of divergent readings among
the introductory formulas in Jer and evaluate the
Beweiskraft of Janzen's explanation of these.

2:1-2

ויהי דבר יהוה אלי לאמר
הלך וקראת באזני ירושלם
καὶ εἶπε   לאמו

Janzen (p. 113, [a]) thinks it possible that in
this case neither the Greek nor the Hebrew represents
the original. Certainly it is true, as he says, that
the Greek καὶ εἶπε constitutes an abrupt transition
from direct divine speech in the immediately preceding
lines of Ch. 1, and one can hardly believe that this
represents the intended editorial introduction to the
new block of material in Ch. 2 (any more than one can
accept לאמר of MT 3:1 as the original transition to the
content of that chapter). It is less easy to see why
the MT heading to Ch. 2 must also be considered secondary. Janzen suggests that the chapter originally
opened directly with כה אמר יהוה and that the present
introductory clause in MT was later formulated on the
model of 1:4, 11, 13. But such speculation seems

unnecessary. Why must a perfectly normal Hebrew intro‐
duction be called in question by an obviously defective
Greek heading? Apart from a prior judgement against
the MT there seems no reason for abandoning it as
representing the intended redactoral framework at
this point. As for the LXX or (more likely) its
Vorlage, it shows definite signs of having suffered
dislocation or textual damage.

7:1-2a

הדבר אשר היה אל ירמיהו מאת יהוה לאמר
עמד בשער בית יהוה
וקראת שם את הדבר הזה ואמרת

ακουσατε λογον κυριου πασα   שמעו דבר יהוה כל יהודה
η Ιουδαια

    Janzen (p. 36, #9) attributes the longer MT
heading to secondary harmonization from MT 26:2 (sic
--must be 26:1-2). But if so, this constitutes poor
harmonization at best, for the heading at 26:1-2 reads
rather differently: בראשית ממלכות יהויקים בן יאשיהו
מלך יהודה היה הדבר הזה מאת יהוה לאמר כה אמר יהוה--hardly
an exact parallel to 7:1-2. The latter part of the
clause in 7:2 (הבאים בשערים האלה להשתחות ליהוה) Janzen
explains (pp. 36-37) as expansion from the similar (not
exact) constructions of 17:20, 22:2, and 26:2, on the
ground that the phrase does not really fit in 7:2 ("the
sermon was delivered not in the gate[s], but in the
Temple court [26:2]"). Janzen is probably right in
relieving the translator of intentional abbreviation
or omission; nevertheless, a complicated process of
harmonization such as that suggested does not seem
compelling. The editorial heading may indeed have been
missing in the translator's parent text, but must it
therefore be viewed as a better text? It could just as
well be argued that the transition from Ch. 6 and the
actual content of Ch. 7 demands some such introductory
statement as is found in MT 7:1.

16:1

ויהי דבר יהוה אלי לאמר
και συ μη λαβης γυναικα   לא תקח לך אשה
λεγει κυριος ο θεος Ισραηλ

Janzen (p. 113 [c]) thinks it possible that the
LXX of this passage preserves a text which stood one
stage closer than the MT to a poetic form of the passage in which Jer was instructed not to marry. If the
divine command at MT 16:2ff. originally existed in
poetry, then the continuity between this passage and
the divine address in Ch. 15 would seem to be secure;
this, in turn, would tend to support the superfluity of
the MT ויהי formula. But the argument for the secondary character of the MT formula depends entirely on the
hypothesis of Ch. 16 being originally poetry which was
later expanded to prose, a proposition difficult to
prove. Again, it may be that the formula was missing
in the translator's Vorlage, but in itself this would
be insufficient evidence by which to establish LXX
priority. The presence in the LXX of the phrase
λεγει κυριος ο θεος Ισραηλ heightens our suspicion that
the Greek may not be original here. The phrase is
missing in O-233 Arm. Since Origen was very careful
not to eliminate from his fifth column text any
readings found in the LXX but absent from the Hebrew,
it is altogether possible that the phrase λεγει κυριος
ο θεος Ισραηλ in 16:1 was a late Greek insertion.

27(50):1

λογος κυριου ον ελαλησεν   הדבר אשר דבר יהוה
επι βαβυλωνα   אל בבל אל ארץ כשדים
                                      ביד ירמיהו הנביא

If the Greek is translating word for word from its
Vorlage, the latter would presumably have read דבר יהוה
אשר דבר . . . , a form not otherwise attested among the
introductory headings of Jer-MT. Janzen explains the
MT here as expanded partly from the frequent occurrences of כשדים in the Babylon oracle and partly from
MT 51:59 (which, however, is not a particularly close
parallel . . . הדבר אשר צוה ירמיהו הנביא). Faced with
two different forms of introductory headings for the
same oracle we would be hard pressed to choose between
them. Both are clearly the result of an editorial
process which went hand in hand with the growth and
formation of the book. However, simply to assert that
the MT must be expansionistic along the lines laid down
by Janzen exceeds the bounds of our evidence.

29:1a(47:1)

With the foregoing documentation and discussion of
introductory headings in mind, we may finally return to
consider the formula (הנביא) אשר היה דבר יהוה אל ירמיהו
of MT 14:1, 46:1, 47:1, and 49:34, the most problematic
of all introductory headings in the book of Jer. We
have learned that each case of divergent reading must
be tested on its own merits; hence, the shorter or
different Greek versions of the אשר formulas cannot be
judged superior merely on the basis of Greek variations
in other headings. In this case, however, Janzen makes
use of an additional argument to support the claim for
LXX priority, namely the relation of the אשר headings
to the different location and internal order of the
Oracles against the Foreign Nations. The argument here
is that the OAN section first circulated independently
before being introduced into the Jer corpus at 25:13.
But since the new edition of Jer would render obsolete
a number of Jer MSS, the expedient was adopted of sewing
the OAN corpus to the end of existing MSS as a kind of
appendix (the thesis is discussed in an "Excursus" to
Ch. V, pp. 115-16). Presumably a scroll of the latter
type became the basis for the MT tradition, while the
edition with the OAN section in the middle became the
archetype of the Hebrew <u>Vorlage</u> employed by the LXX.

No one would want to underestimate the problems
involved, either in the matter of the location and
order of the OAN section or in that of the strange
introductory formula אשר היה דבר יהוה אל ירמיהו
(הנביא), hence we must be grateful for any attempt
that seeks to unravel the mysteries behind these textual problems. Janzen's appeal to a <u>Buchwesen</u> theory
to account both for the different arrangement of the
OAN section in the LXX and MT texts, as well as for the
origin of the אשר היה דבר יהוה formula, must be given a
fair hearing. <u>A priori</u> the theory seems plausible
enough and has an element of realism about it. Yet
many unsolved problems remain. Here we simply wish to
point out some of the difficulties we experience with
Janzen's reconstruction. The critique takes account of
material discussed on pp. 112-116 of Janzen's book.

1. Commenting (p. 113 [d]) on the introductory
heading אשר היה דבר יהוה אל ירמיהו הנביא על הגוים at MT
46:1 (> LXX), Janzen appears to argue that the "original

heading" for the OAN section was the phrase אשר נבא
ירמיהו על [כל] הגוים at the end of MT 25:13, which the
LXX renders α επροφητευσεν Ιερεμιας επι τα εθνη. However, it is questionable whether this phrase ever con-
stituted a title in the Hebrew. As the phrase now
stands in the MT, it is not a title at all but a relative clause syntactically connected to the previous
construction את כל דברי אשר דברתי עליה את כל הכתוב בספר
הזה. It is true that many commentators regard the
phrase in 25:13bβ as a secondary editorial addition;
however, to consider it a title is something else
again. It is recognized, of course, that with the
addition of the appositive τα Αιλαμ the LXX construes
the phrase α επροφητευσεν Ιερεμιας επι τα εθνη τα Αιλαμ
as a superscription; but this has little bearing on
the original function of the underlying Hebrew.

2. In the same paragraph on p. 113 Janzen further
states, "If, as most commentators agree, the position
of the Oracles at the end of the book is secondary, the
clear likelihood is that 46.1 M was inserted secondarily after the shift, which left the original heading at
25.13." But this statement makes for some confusion,
especially the phrase "after the shift." According to
our understanding of Janzen's account of the origin of
the OAN material (see above), there never was any
"shift" or dislocation of the material to begin with,
only a simultaneous addition of the material at two
different places, one in the middle of the book in new
MSS and one at the end of the book in existing MSS. On
the assumption of such mechanical addition of identical
material one might have expected the oracles to have
been introduced with the same superscription.

3. On a comparison with MT 26:1, 27:1, and 28:1,
Janzen believes that the Greek at 26:1, εν αρχη
βασιλευοντος Σεδεκιου βασιλεως εγενετο ο λογος ουτος
περι Αιλαμ, probably represents the original heading of
the the Elam oracle rather than MT 49:34 אשר היה דבר
יהוה אל ירמיהו הנביא אל עילם בראשית מלכות צדקיה מלך
יהודה. However, in a footnote (n. 85, p. 228) he calls
attention to the unusual fact that the Elam heading
stands at the end of the oracle rather than at the
beginning. It is therefore suggested that the original
superscription to this oracle read τα Αιλαμ, εν αρχη
βασιλευοντος Σεδεκιου βασιλεως εγενετο ο λογος ουτος
περι Αιλαμ, that haplography occurred between the first

and second Αιλαμ, and that a subsequent restoration of
the original heading was inserted at the end of the
oracle. For confirmation of the likely original form
of the superscription we are referred to the heading of
the Egypt oracle of similar construction: τη Αιγυπτω
επι δυναμιν Φαραω Νεχαω βασιλεως Αιγυπτου ος ην . . .
(LXX 26:2). In short, on Janzen's view the heading at
LXX 25:14, α επροφητευσεν Ιερεμιας επι τα εθνη τα Αιλαμ,
consists of two elements: α επροφητευσεν Ιερεμιας επι
τα εθνη as the general heading to the OAN section, and
τα Αιλαμ as the (partial) heading for the Elam oracle.

The view that τα Αιλαμ originally did not belong
with the preceding phrase α επροφητευσεν Ιερεμιας επι
τα εθνη has considerable merit in the light of the
unaesthetic if not ungrammatical juxtaposition τα εθνη
τα Αιλαμ. But whether haplography in a presumed original introduction τα Αιλαμ . . . Αιλαμ(see above) is the
correct explanation is less certain. For one thing, it
is strange that the Elam superscription should have
commenced with the accusative article τα. If anything,
it must have been constructed with the dative, a hypothetical τη Αιλαμ (as in the Egypt oracle and other
oracles, e.g. τη Αιγυπτω). It could just as well be
argued that τα Αιλαμ points to a secondary insertion of
אל עילם which in the Greek was rendered τα Αιλαμ by
attraction to τα εθνη when the phrase α επροφητευσεν
Ιερεμιας επι τα εθνη was taken as a title rather than a
concluding relative clause as in the Hebrew.

Janzen's preference for the LXX form of the Elam
superscription (or postscript) derives from his judgement that "the proper form" (p. 114) for an introduction with בראשית is to be found in MT 26:1, בראשית
ממלכות יהויקים בן יאשיהו מלך יהודה היה הדבר הזה מאת
יהוה, which in the LXX is rendered as εν αρχη βασιλεως
Ιωακιμ υιου Ιωσια εγενηθη ο λογος ουτος παρα κυριου.
(33:1). But surely it is precarious to speculate regarding the "proper form" of an introductory statement,
and even more precarious to assume that the Elam title
was necessarily modelled upon it. That some sort of
dislocation has taken place in the the heading of the
Elam oracle seems beyond question. But as things stand
now, with the major part of the title at the end of the
oracle rather than at the beginning, it is the Greek
text rather than the Hebrew that gives more evidence of
having suffered dislocation.

4. On p. 114 Janzen further asserts that the
shorter heading επι τους αλλοφυλους at LXX 29:1 "has
the appearance of originality, resembling the catch
lines לאדום, לבני עמון, למואב, etc." This statement
appears to suggest that the original heading for the
Philistine oracle would have been constructed with the
ל. But the suggestion, if intended, is quite misleading. It may be admitted that the title επι τους
αλλοφυλους resembles the other headings τη Ιδουμαια,
τους υιους Αμμων, τη Μωαβ in that they are all short;
yet it is virtually certain that the underlying Hebrew
was not לפלשתים on the model of לאדום etc., but אל
פלשתים as in MT. All the superscriptions in the OAN
section commencing with ל are translated in the LXX
with the dative construction (article plus name),
whereas the standard translation of אל (or על) in this
kind of context is επι with accusative, cf. 29(47):5
באה קרחה אל עזה / επι γαζαν.

5. Janzen concludes his discussion of the אשר היה
דבר יהוה formula with the statement, "The formula in
47.1 then would be expansion from these two places
[i.e. from MT 46:1 and 49:34], as would its occurrence
in 14.1, where G Syr read (surely correctly) ויהי דבר
יהוה אל ירמיהו for M אשר היה דבר יהוה אל ירמיהו." But
since we have experienced various difficulties with the
proposed explanation of how this formula arose at MT
46:1 and 49:34, neither can we be very confident about
a theory of tertiary expansion at 14:1 and 47:1.

When all is said and done, it must be admitted
that we still do not know how to account for the appearance of the אשר formula, either at MT 47:1 or in
the other places. The strange form of the unattached
relative clause employed as a superscription, coupled
with the consistently divergent or missing Greek, combine to make its priority in the MT text suspect. But
whatever the literary and transmission history of this
phrase, it is essential to see that conclusions of this
type must be arrived at independently of any general-
ized theory regarding the relationship between the two
texts. As our critique of Janzen's treatment has
shown, while the redactoral framework of the LXX Vorlage probably differed at various points from that of
the MT, this cannot automatically be taken as a sure
guide to a prior or superior structure of the prophet's
oracles.

29:1b(47:2a)

ταδε λεγει κυριος   כה אמר יהוה

Jer-MT is characterized by an abundance of prophetic formulas such as אמר יהוה, נאם יהוה, כה אמר יהוה and by the use of various forms of the divine name in these formulas, e.g. יהוה, יהוה צבאות, יהוה אלהי ישראל יהוה צבאות אלהי ישראל. Often in the LXX these formulas are either missing or the divine name is found in shorter form. In the Philistine and Edom oracles we have six examples of such formulas with divine name, the corresponding Greek and Hebrew of which are as follows:

29:1b:(47:2a)

As above

29:8(49:7)

ταδε λεγει κυριος   כה אמר יהוה צבאות

29:13(49:12)

ταδε λεγει (ειπε B-S-538) κυριος   כה אמר יהוה

29:14(49:13)

λεγει κυριος   נאם יהוה

29:17(49:16)

> LXX   נאם יהוה

29:19(49:18)

ειπε κυριος παντοκρατωρ   אמר יהוה

From the above we observe that in LXX Ch. 29 the formula כה אמר יהוה is attested on each of the three occasions in which it occurs in the MT. The formula נאם/אמר יהוה is attested on two out of three occurrences; the divine name with the כה אמר formula is shorter in v. 8(7), while the divine name with the formula אמר יהוה is longer in the LXX of v. 19(18). These findings in Ch. 29 are typical of the pattern

found throughout Jer-LXX. The formula כה אמר יהוה is
almost always attested in the Greek;   equivalents for
נאם אמר יהוה on the other hand, are frequently missing
in the LXX;   the divine name is usually shorter in the
LXX, though on occasion it is longer. The relevant
statistics for these generalizations are as follows:

Prophetic Formulas

	Frequency In MT	Missing in LXX
. . כה אמר	154 /9/	14 (7 in larger context) /10/
. . . נאם	175 /11/	72 (21 ") /12/
. . . אמר	9 /13/	2 (1 ") /14/

Divine Name in Prophetic Formulas

Form and frequency in MT		Form and frequency in LXX	
יהוה צבאות	19	κυριος	16 /15/
		κυριος παντοκρατωρ	1 /16/
		missing	2 /17/
יהוה אלהי ישראל	14	κυριος	8 /18/
		κυριος ο Θεος Ισραηλ	5 /19/
		missing	1 /20/
יהוה אלהי צבאות	1	κυριος παντοκρατωρ	1 /21/
י' צבאות אלהי ישראל	31	κυριος	17 /22/
		κυριος ο Θεος Ισραηλ	9 /23/
		κυριος παντοκρατωρ	2 /24/
		missing	3 /25/
יהוה אלהי צבאות אלהי ישראל	3	κυριος	? /26/
		κυριος παντοκρατωρ	1 /27/

Especially noteworthy is the "disappearance act" of צבאות whether inside or outside the prophetic formulas. In the MT of Jer this name occurs 82 times (65 times as part of a prophetic formula, 17 times in other contexts), but in the LXX a translation equivalent is found only 11 times /28/.

Janzen's treatment of the prophetic formulas and divine names is found in his fourth chapter, "The Proper Names in Jeremiah," esp. pp. 75-86, together with tabulated statistics in Appendices A and B, pp. 139-159 /29/. In all of these variants, the point of Janzen's discussion is to show that the Greek was translated from a shorter and better <u>Vorlage</u> than the MT.

One is inclined to feel that the case for a shorter <u>Vorlage</u> is at its strongest in the matter of the prophetic formulas and divine names. Whether it is also a superior <u>Vorlage</u> at these points is, however, a moot point. It is true that respect for the deity may have worked in favour of a longer form of the divine name rather than vice versa. But even granting this point, one could not assume the same explanation for all other instances of a shorter text. Discussion of the "zero variants" in the ensuing verses of Ch. 29 will highlight the danger of rigidly applying the same solution to every instance of a shorter LXX text regardless of context.

29(47):4

εν τη ημερα τη ερχομενη	על היום הבא
του απολεσαι παντας τους αλλοφυλους	לשדוד את כל פלשתים
και αφανιω την Τυρον και την Σιδωνα	להכרית לצר ולצידון
και παντας τους καταλοιπους της βοηθειας αυτων	כל שריד עזר
οτι εξολεθρευσει κυριος	כי שדד יהוה את פלשתים
τους καταλοιπους των νησων	שארית אי כפתור

κυριος] + τους αλλοφυλους (+ και 36) O L (= α΄ϑ΄ Qmg, ο΄ 86mg)

νησων] + και καππαδοκιας O L (= α΄ϑ΄ Qmg; cf. οι γ΄ καππαδοκας 86mg)

The "zero variants" in this verse are את פלשתים
and כפתור. According to Janzen (p. 59), both of these
words are secondary expansions from parallel and related contexts, את פלשתים from v. 4a and כפתור (subsequently) from Gen 10:14, Deut 2:23, Am 9:7 and 1 Chr
1:12. In evaluating the hypothesis that the foregoing
words are secondary expansions, it is essential to see
the variants in relation to the whole verse, including
other "content variants." When this is done, it becomes clear that the LXX and MT give quite different
interpretations of the passage. Accordingly, it is
necessary to weigh the internal and contextual fitness
of the variants involved.

We may inquire first whether there is any Hebrew
textual evidence for the LXX omissions in question.
Janzen suggests——and he puts it no stronger than that——
that the omission of את פלשתים may be supported by
2QJer. According to M. Baillet's reconstruction of the
passage (DJD, III, Textes, p. 65), the line in which
את פלשתים occurs (1. 10) has 55 letters. In Janzen's
opinion this "seems over long" in relation to lines 5-9
and lines 11-13 which have 47 49 46 49 35 46 48 46
letters respectively. Without את פלשתים 1. 10 would
have only 46 letters, "a perfect fit." But these
statistics give only a partial picture. Line 1 on the
on the same fragment has 51 letters and the immediately
preceding line of the same passage (on another fragment) has 56 letters. On Baillet's reconstruction,
therefore, the 55 letters in 1. 10 certainly fall well
within the scope of possible line lengths for this MS.
Furthermore, since the two other examples of readings
regarded by Janzen as secondary in the Philistine
oracle (the long introductory formula of v. 1 and
of v. 4b) are both firmly attested by 2QJer, it is not
unreasonable to assume that את פלשתים of v. 4b was also
present in this MS. The presence of כפתור in 2QJer
ought to be decisive for the presence of את פלשתים as
well, since according to Janzen כפתור was a secondary
gloss added subsequent to the intrusion of

2QJer does not, therefore, support the LXX "zero
variants" את פלשתים and כפתור. If the LXX was translated from a Hebrew Vorlage other than the MT, that
Vorlage tradition has been entirely lost to us, at
least for this passage. However, it is to be noted
that in one interesting detail, 2QJer does support a

content variant in the LXX of v. 4, namely in the
reading והכרתי (MT להכרית) which corresponds to LXX
και αφανιω. But what is the significance of this observation? Does 2QJer/LXX witness to a better text
here? Decidedly not. In the MT, להכרית is a perfect
parallel to לשדוד, both infinitives introducing phrases
which complete the formula על היום הבא, as follows:

>". . . on the day that is coming
>to destroy all the Philistines,
>to cut off from Tyre and Sidon
>every remaining ally."

However, the Qumrân reading והכרתי completely breaks
the parallelism of the phrase and introduces a clumsy
change of subject which must be expressed in the form
of an intrusive and quite inexplicable quote: ". . . on
the day that is coming to destroy all the Philistines.
'And I will cut off from Tyre and Sidon every remaining
ally.' For the Lord is destroying the Philistines . . ."
It would be quite unjustified to place the blame for
such an awkward and meaningless interruption on the
author of the original composition. Thus, while και
αφανιω in this instance probably comes from a textual
variant already present in the translator's _Vorlage_, it
must be this _Vorlage_ rather than the MT that is secondary.

     What is true of the LXX και αφανιω is also true
for the continuation of the LXX phrase (την Τυρον και
την Σιδωνα και παντας τους καταλοιπους της βοηθειας
αυτων); it cannot be said to represent a better version
of the oracle than the MT either. By taking the words
לצר ולצידון as direct rather than indirect objects, the
LXX significantly alters the meaning of the passage.
According to the LXX, the prophetic judgement at this
point shifts from the Philistines to Tyre and Sidon
(και αφανιω την Τυρον και την Σιδωνα και παντας τους
καταλοιπους της βοηθειας αυτων, "I will wipe out Tyre
and Sidon and all the rest of their help") whereas in
the MT the focus remains consistently on the Philistines (להכרית לצר ולצידון כל שריד עזר "to cut off from
Tyre and Sidon every remaining ally [i.e. the Philis-
tines]" /30/). In the MT nothing is said concerning
the destruction of Tyre and Sidon; these cities are
introduced only by way of emphasizing the destruction
of the Philistines, the last remaining ally of the

Phoenician cities /31/. The LXX phrase και παντας τους
καταλοιπους της βοηθειας αυτων for MT עזר כל שריד
/32/ suggests either a different <u>Vorlage</u> or a loose
rendering in which שריד was associated with שארית /33/,
MT עזר was read as עזר and the possessive αυτων was
added for stylistic completion. In the absence of firm
evidence for a different <u>Vorlage</u> and in light of the
difficult Hebrew poetry of this section, the second
explanation seems preferable.

This brings us to the last and crucial phrase of
the verse, οτι εξολεθρευσει κυριος τους καταλοιπους των
νησων / כי שדד יהוה את פלשתים שארית אי כפתור. The
omission of any words corresponding to MT את פלשתים and
כפתור in the LXX puts the phrase τους καταλοιπους των
νησων in parallelism with τους καταλοιπους της βοηθειας
αυτων, so that the pattern commenced with και αφανιω
την Τυρον και την Σιδωνα is continued to the end of
the verse, in each instance the object of destruction
being non-Philistine people. In the MT the explicit
mention of פלשתים and כפתור allows for no ambiguity
regarding who is being addressed. If we now inquire
into which of the two versions makes better sense, the
balance continues to lie with the MT as giving the most
coherent and consistent meaning. By shifting the object of destruction from the Philistines to Tyre and
Sidon, the LXX again introduces a change of focus which
can only be regarded as foreign to the structure and as
disturbing to the unity of the original composition.

But is the presence of פלשתים and כפתור in the
MT really necessary to the sense of the passage?
Could it not be that while the LXX has misconstrued the
intention of the original in the matter of Tyre and
Sidon (direct for indirect object), it may still be a
faithful witness to the omission of the פלשתים and
כפתור? We may consider the case of פלשתים first /34/.
If this word were missing in the original, its omission
would have little bearing on the meaning or clarity of
the passage. The residual phrase כי שדד יהוה את שארית
אי כפתור would probably be an adequate reference to
the Philistines, considering their traditional association with Caphtor/Crete. In view of this, it is not
inconceivable that פלשתים might have been introduced
into v. 4b from 4a by a scribe who, already having
copied לשדוד את כל פלשתים once, when he came to the
similar phrase a few words later automatically added

את פלשתים. This is essentially Janzen's suggestion.
Another possibility is that פלשתים may have been a
marginal or interlinear gloss on the phrase שארית
אי כפתור which was later incorporated into the text.
But while such scenarios are certainly conceivable,
they may represent gratuitous speculation.

     In the case of כפתור Janzen contends that it has
entered our text from Gen 10:14, Deut 2:23, Am 9:7
and 1 Chr 1:12 subsequent to the intrusion of את
פלשתים. Thus we are to understand a gloss upon a gloss
--at which point the proposed reconstruction becomes
exceedingly tenuous. A perusal of the actual texts from
which כפתור is said to have derived puts further strain
on the proposal. The texts are as follows:

     Gen 10:14 / 1 Chr 1:12

               ואת כסלחים אשר יצאו משם פלשתים ואת כפתרים

     Deut 2:23

          והעוים הישבים בחצרים עד עזה כפתרים היצאים מכפתור
          השמידם

     Am 9:7

          הלוא את ישראל העליתי מארץ מצרים ופלשתיים מכפתור

     With regard to the above passages we may observe
the following: 1) In Gen 10:14 / 1 Chr 1:12 the אשר
clause as it stands refers not to the כפתרים but to the
כסלחים, though admittedly this order may itself be the
result of a scribal dislocation (cf. C. Westermann,
Genesis, BK, p. 665). 2) The references are widely
scattered, and apart from Deut 2:23 do not come from
sources generally paralleled in Jer. 3) In no case is
there any strong verbal similarity between the Jer
version and the other passages, e.g., nowhere else is
כפתור mentioned in conjunction with coastlands or
islands. The secondary derivation of כפתור in MT 47:4
from the above passages seems, therefore, not
compelling.

In another context (Ch. IV, "The Proper Names in Jeremiah," p. 74) Janzen cites איי כפתור (sic) as an example of the MT making a hypothetically original איים more explicit. But along with the theory of MT expansion one ought also to consider another explanation why כפתור may have been omitted by the translator. Although כפתור was translated by Καππαδοκια in Deut 2:23 and Am 9:7 (also at Jer 29[47]:4 by the Minor VSS), this is probably a mistranslation (cf. BDB on כפתור). In Ch. II above (pp. 50-51), we argued that the Hexaplaric reading των νησων και Καππαδοκιας rather than των νησων Καππαδοκιας as in the Minor VSS may reflect an attempt to avoid the geographical/historical difficulty of associating the Philistines with Capppadocia. Could it be that the LXX translator was equally troubled by the phrase אי כפתור in the context of this verse and decided to resolve the dilemma by simply omitting the כפתור and writing νησων instead /35/? Admittedly speculative, the proposition may be as plausible as the theory that כפתור entered the text as a gloss from far-removed and peripheral passages.

As for the proposition that both פלשתים and כפתור are interpolations, this seems quite unwarranted. In the context of vv. 3-4, a hypothetical phrase כי שדד יהוה את שארית איים would have little meaning. Finally it may be noted that the metrical scansion of the line is quite favourable to the inclusion of פלשתים and כפתור. The line as it stands consists of a 3:3 bicolon, the most common stress pattern in Hebrew poetry.

29(47):5-6

ηκει φαλακρωμα επι Γαζαν	באה קרחה אל עזה
απερριφη Ασκαλων	נדמתה אשקלון
και οι καταλοιποι Ενακιμ	שארית עמקם
(v. 6) εως τινος κοφεις	עד מתי תתגודדי
η μαχαιρα του κυριου	(v.6) הוי חרב ליהוה
εως τινος ουχ ησυχασεις	עד אנה לא תשקטי
αποκατασταθι εις τον κολεον σου	האספי אל תערך
αναπαυσαι και επαρθητι	הרגעי ודמי

κοφεις] κοφης S* 87 alii; κοφεται 407; κοφει 410

εως τινος ουχ ησυχασεις] pr. εως ποτε συστραφησεσθε L Syh/mg Tht. (= σ΄ 86mg)

In the above passage there is only one "zero variant" in the LXX text, namely the omission of a corresponding word for the Hebrew exclamation הוי. This example is cited by Janzen (p. 125) in the short penultimate chapter (Ch. VII), "Miscellaneous Variants," a chapter intended to deal with those zero variants which cannot easily be fitted into well defined categories such as "Double Readings," "Additions from Parallel and Related Contexts," etc., and hence are of more difficult interpretation. After giving extended comment on six such miscellaneous variants, Janzen provides two continuous lists of zero variants, one consisting of Hebrew words (i.e. those absent in the LXX) and one of Greek words (i.e. those absent in the MT). The variant הוי of 47:6 occurs in the former of these lists. The question, then, is whether any reason can be cited for the absence in the LXX of a Greek word corresponding to הוי and whether the LXX possibly attests a better reading than the MT, in which case the latter would have to be regarded as conflate or expansionist.

It is clear that the LXX has divided the Hebrew phrases in question differently from that of the MT, for whereas in the MT the phrase עד מתי תתגודדי is an independent question at the close of v. 5, in the LXX it has been associated with the subsequent Hebrew phrase חרב ליהוה (הוי) resulting in the translation εως τινος κοψεις η μαχαιρα του κυριου (this explains the different verse divisions in the two texts). But it does not appear that this linking of תתגודדי with חרב ליהוה represents a superior division to that of the MT; in fact, the reverse is just as likely the case. That תתגודדי is to be associated with its preceding phrase באה קרחה אל עזה . . . is clear from a comparison of Deut 14:1, Jer 16:6 and Jer 48:37 where in each case, as in Jer 47:5, baldness and acts of self-mutilation are juxtaposed as common features of pagan mourning. The LXX completely misses the point (as does Duane Christensen, [Transformations of the War Oracle in Old Testament Prophecy: Studies in the Oracles Against the Nations, 1975, pp. 212-213] in his emendation of תתגודדי to תתגוררי following 2QJer /36/), hence the wrong association of תתגודדי with חרב ליהוה reflected in the LXX reading εως τινος κοψεις η μαχαιρα του κυριου.

But how then are we to explain the absence of הוי
in the LXX text? Its omission in the translator's
Vorlage is of course a possibility to be reckoned with,
but such omission is not to be insisted upon. Since
עד מתי תתגודדי must stand as an independent question
at the close of v. 5, and since MT v. 6 constitutes an
address to a personified "sword of Yahweh," it is most
appropriate that the address be preceded by a vocative
such as הוי. Without it, the phrase חרב ליהוה עד אנה
לא תשקטי lacks the poetic vigour that is characteristic of the rest of the composition. We regard הוי,
therefore, as very likely integral to the original
poem. Its omission in the LXX is most naturally explained as a deliberate disregard of a word that did
not fit the translator's (false) reading of the text.
It is doubtful that the omission of such a word was
associated with any crisis of conscience on the translator's part, at least not more so than the misren-
dering of the reflexive תתגודדי by the simple κοψεις
or by the strange rendition of דמי by επαρθητι at the
close of the verse. The argument that the translator(s)
of this book had such an inviolable notion of Holy Writ
that they could not possibly have omitted any word that
lay in the Vorlage is not borne out by our analysis
(contra H.M. Orlinsky, "The Septuagint as Holy Writ
and the Philosophy of the Translators," HUCA 46 [1975],
esp. 109-10).

Janzen does not specifically try to explain the
variant הוי in MT 47:6. In the introduction to Ch. VII
(p. 121) he suggests that some of the variants listed
in this section may have arisen through scribal lapse,
others are probably to be taken as glosses, though the
source or reason for these glosses may not be apparent.
A.B. Ehrlich (Randglossen zur Hebräischen Bibel, IV,
1912, p. 356) did indeed think that הוי arose as dittography "aus dem Vorhergehenden," but this is hardly a
credible explanation since there is not much resemblance between הוי and the termination of תתגודדי. Nor
is there any rationale for thinking that הוי might be a
gloss on חרב. In the light of contextual considerations, the variant weighs as heavily against the LXX as
it does in favour of the MT, and we think, therefore,
that the LXX is a witness here neither to a shorter
Vorlage not to a better reading, but to an erroneous
Greek translation and possibly deliberate omission.

29:10(49:9)

οτι τρυγηται ηλθον   אם בצרים באו לך
οι ου καταλειψουσι σοι καταλειμμα   לא ישארו עוללות

ηλθον B-S-106'-538 Q C-613 Co Arab Tht./p] + σοι rel.
= Compl. Rahlfs

       In this verse the LXX apparently has no cor-
responding word for לך following ηλθον. This small
omission is not documented by Janzen but it is doubtful
that it provides support for a shorter Hebrew <u>Vorlage</u>.
The phrase is closely paralleled in Ob 5 where לך, as
expected, is translated by προς σε. Harmonization of
parallel passages in the Hebrew is always a possibility, so that it could be proposed that לך in Jer-MT 49:9
was added at a late stage in conformity with the Ob
passage, the LXX bearing witness to an earlier reading;
however, other examples of the loose handling of the
text by the translator makes such an explanation unnecessary. In addition to the absence of a word for
לך, the LXX of this phrase has two further unusual translation equivalents, οτι for אם and καταλειμμα(-ατα)
for עוללות /37/, as well as two LXX plusses, οἱ and
σοι. Alternative explanations might be that the relative pronoun οἱ is in fact intended to represent לך, or
that the dative personal pronoun σοι originally stood
for לך but has since been dislocated in the LXX from an
original position following ηλθον to its present position following καταλειψουσι /38/. But in spite of such
possibilities, the simplest explanation still seems to
be that the translator has proceeded in a free, quasi-
paraphrastic way in which the Hebrew לך following באה
simply failed to be expressed.

29:13(49:12)

οτι ταδε λεγει κυριος   כי כה אמר יהוה
οις ουκ ην νομος   הנה אשר אין משפטם
πιειν το ποτηριον   לשחות הכוס
επιον   שתו ישתו
και συ αθωωμενη   ואתה הוא נקה תנקה
ου μη αθωωθης   לא תנקה
                                         כי שתה תשתה

οις B-S-538 A-106' C Co Aeth Arab] pr. ιδου rel.

επιον] pr. (※ O) πιοντες O L Arm Tht.

αθωωμενη] + (※ O) αθωωθηση O L/-51-62-449 239 Arm

αθωωθης B-S 106'-538 La/Sg Co Aeth Arab] + οτι πινουσα
πιη L Tht; + οτι πινων (πιων/πιουσα/πινοντι)
πιεσαι rel. = Ald. Compl. Rahlfs

This verse has five "zero variants" in the LXX
text. The words evidently unrepresented in the LXX are
הנה, שתו, הוא, תנקה and the phrase כי שתה תשתה. Of
these Janzen deals with the first (הנה) and the last
(כי שתה תשתה), both of which he asserts to be missing
in the LXX by haplography (p. 118). Janzen does not
presume to judge whether the instances of alleged
haplography occurred already in the Hebrew <u>Vorlage</u> or
later in the transmission of the LXX, though of the two
instances mentioned here he cites the former (הנה) as
an example of a "certain or probable" case of haplography in the Hebrew <u>Vorlage</u>. We will need to evaluate
these suggestions as well as to analyze the other
variants in the verse not mentioned in Janzen's study.

הנה

The particle הנה occurs five times in the MT text
of the Philistine and Edom oracles: vv. 2, 12, 15, 19,
22. By contrast, in the LXX of these oracles it is
attested only three times, namely at vv. 2, 20(19) and
23(22), each time by the familiar translation ιδου; it
is missing in vv. 13(12) and 16(15), in the latter case
as part of the introductory phrase כי הנה absent <u>in</u>
<u>toto</u> in the LXX. As already noted, Janzen proposes
that the הנה of v. 13(12) may have dropped out in the
translator's <u>Vorlage</u> through haplography (יהוה הנה);
he does not comment on the omission of הנה in
v. 16(15).

The rate of omission of הנה in LXX Ch. 29 (40%) is
considerably greater than that found in the rest of the
book. In fact, this little word (with variants הנני
הנך), of such frequent occurrence in the MT text of
Jer (approximately 130x), is represented in the LXX
with surprising consistency, a translation equivalent
for it being absent only some fifteen times /39/ (not
counting those occasions when it is missing as part

of a longer passage absent in the LXX). In the light
of its regular attestation elsewhere, Janzen's suggestion that its omission in LXX 29:13 may be due to
scribal accident in the Hebrew Vorlage gains credibility. The same may be said for the of omission of הנה
at 39(32):17 (cf. Janzen, #26, p. 118).

As for the omission of any corresponding Greek for
the phrase כי הנה at v. 16(15), this is less readily
explained. At least no obvious scribal explanation for
its omission lies close at hand. Hence appeal to a
shorter Hebrew Vorlage is clearly a viable option,
though it is a moot point whether such a Vorlage would
represent a preferable text (cf. the parallel passage
in Ob 2 which commences the sentence with הנה).

הוא

Janzen does not comment on the omission of a Greek
word for the MT הוא in this verse, but Duane Christensen (Transformations of the War Oracle, p. 230, n. h)
regards הוא as a secondary development from an original interrogative particle ה. This view he defends on
the ground that the LXX gives no evidence that the הוא
of MT was present in the text. Along the same lines it
could be theorized that הוא derived from the initial ה
of an original niphal infinitive absolute הנקה, the
form found in the parallel passage of MT 25:29.

Yet such speculation appears unnecessary, especially since deliberate translator intervention is a
strong possibility. The use of the pronoun הוא to
strengthen another pronominal subject is certainly a
well-established characteristic of biblical Hebrew (GK,
141b) and is found elsewhere in Jer (e.g. 14:22). But
a literal equivalent in Greek, συ αυτος, would certainly
have been awkward--probably too barbaric even for our
otherwise stylistically insensitive translator.

שתו ,תנקה ,כי שתה תשתה

The remaining "zero variants" in the LXX of 29:13
(MT 49:12) all have to do with constructions involving
the Hebrew infinitive absolute. These are שתו ישתה,
נקה תנקה, and the phrase כי שתה תשתה. In the first two

of these--not dealt with by Janzen--the LXX has shorter
forms than the MT constructions (επιον and αθωωμενη
respectively); in the last, the entire Hebrew phrase
is without corresponding Greek equivalent in the LXX.
In order to see these renditions of the infinitive
absolute in a broader perspective it will be necessary
1) to look at the way the infinitive absolute is rendered generally throughout the LXX, 2) to compare parallel and related passages to 29:13(49:12), and 3) to
analyze the internal dynamics of 29:13(49:12).

     In the LXX, the Hebrew infinitive absolute plus
finite verb is usually translated in one of two ways:
1) by the juxtaposition of verb and its cognate noun
(usually in the dative, sometimes in the accusative);
2) by the juxtaposition of verb and its corresponding
participle (or the participle of a verb of kindred
meaning). In an article devoted to the subject ("Renderings of the Infinitive Absolute in the LXX", JTS
9 [1907-08], 597-601), Thackeray claimed that whereas
both methods are employed throughout the LXX, the verb-
noun method (an idiom with some precedence in secular
Greek) predominates in the Pentateuch, while the verb-
participle method (which is strictly "translatese")
predominates in most other books, the only exceptions
being Isa, Ez, Mi and the A text of Josh and Jud. For
the book of Jer this assertion can readily be documented: clear cases of participle-verb constructions
outnumber those of noun-verb constructions by 2 to 1
/40/.

     In the continuation of his article Thackeray pro-
ceeds to remark that in several passages (some fifty in
all according to him), the infinitive absolute is not
rendered at all, most of these instances being found in
the Pentateuch and Jer a'. He further suggested that
these omissions were no doubt intentional and not merely due to a difference of texts, since "the translators
of these books showed a greater freedom in their work"
(p. 600). Thackeray does not cite references, but in
the case of Jer, our research fails to bear out his
generalization. That is, the evidence does not support
any pattern of omission of the infinitive absolute on a
grand scale in Jer a' (only four omissions); moreover,
an equal number of omissions are found in Jer b' /41/.
We should not be quick, therefore, to explain the
shorter LXX in 29:13(49:12) by an appeal to a general

tendency in Jer-LXX to shorten or omit the infinitive
absolute constructions as such. In the overwhelming
number of cases the Hebrew infinitive absolute in Jer
is rendered in the Greek by one means or another.

A more profitable line of inquiry is to look at
the important parallel passage to 29:13(49:12), namely
the "Cup of Wrath" pericope in 32:14-15(25:28-29). The
relevant portions read:

ουτως ειπε κυριος[29]	כה אמר יהוה צבאות
πιοντες πιεσθε[30] . . .	שתו תשתו . . .
(v. 15) και υμεις καθαρσει[31]	(v. 29) ואם הנקה תנקו
ου μη καθαρισθητε[32]	לא תנקו

It will be observed that in this passage the first
infinitive absolute, שתו תשתו, is firmly attested in
the LXX and translated exactly according to the normal
participle-verb pattern, πιοντες πιεσθε. Since these
phrases in the Edom oracle and the Cup of Wrath passage
are clearly related, there is good reason for believing
that the infinitive absolute is also original to the
Edom oracle at MT 49:12.

But if this is so, how is the shorter Greek at LXX
29:13 to be explained? Certainly the Vorlage may already have been shorter--though hardly superior for
that reason. Or again, it is not inconceivable that
the expression may have been deliberately shortened by
the translator. According to the LXX, the drinking of
the cup by those for whom it was not appointed was
already a fait accompli, a translation which may have
been facilitated by reading שתו (=επιον) rather than
שתו, the imperfect ישתו being displaced in the process.
But whether we are dealing with a case of translator
Tendenz or shorter Vorlage, the pertinent observation--
as comparison with the parallel passage of 32:14(25:28)
shows--is that it is the LXX and not the MT which is
defective here.

In the case of the next infinitive absolute in the
verse, נקה תנקה, the parallel passage of 32:15(29:29)
is also instructive, though in a different way. In
these parallels it is noteworthy that in both cases the
LXX is shorter than the corresponding MT in identical
fashion, an observation which could point to a different Vorlage. However, the reason for their similarity

may lie elsewhere. The passages read as follows:

29:13(49:12)

καὶ σὺ ἀθωωμένη   ואתה הוא נקה תנקה
οὐ μὴ ἀθωωθῆς   לא תנקה

32:15(25:29)

καὶ ὑμεῖς καθάρσει   ואתם הנקה תנקו
οὐ μὴ καθαρισθῆτε   לא תנקו

In spite of some minor differences between the two
Greek translations /42/, the striking similarity between them is that in both cases the LXX appears to
pass over the first תנקה/-קו and translate as though
the Hebrew read נקה לא תנקה in MT 49:12 and הנקה לא
תנקו in MT 25:29. But by so doing the Greek loses the
emphatic effect of the Hebrew rhetorical question. The
point of the Hebrew in MT 25:29 is to emphasize the
presumption of the nations in thinking that they should
escape punishment when even the people of God's own
city will not escape it; similarly in MT 49:12 the
point emphasized is the presumption of the Edomites in
thinking that they would go unpunished when even the
undeserving nations will not escape punishment. These
contrasts are effectively served by the infinitive
absolute in rhetorical question followed by the emphatic denials, לא תנקה/-קו. To short-circuit the question is to lose the force of the comparisons and the
poetic appeal of the Hebrew. It is possible that the
Greek translator simply did not understand the expressions ואתם הנקה תנקו / ואתה הוא נקה תנקה as questions
and could not make sense of the passage with תנקה/-קו
present. The similar problems may have been resolved
in the same way in both verses.

As for the omission in the LXX of any words corresponding to the last infinitive absolute in the verse,
כי שתה תשתה, Janzen may well be right in proposing
haplography as the reason for this "zero variant." No
other persuasive explanation is immediately available.
Just as לא תנקו in MT 25:29 is followed by a כי clause,
so the same was likely true of MT 49:12. The view of
Rahlfs that the phrase ὅτι πίνων πίεσαι should be
retained as original LXX is not defensible on text
critical grounds (cf. Ch. III, p. 135).

29:14(49:13)

οτι κατ εμαυτου ωμοσα	כי בי נשבעתי
λεγει κυριος	נאם יהוה
οτι εις αβατον και εις ονειδισμον	כי לשמה לחרפה
και εις καταρασιν	<u>לחרב</u> ולקללה
εση εν μεσω αυτης	תהיה בצרה
και πασαι αι πολεις αυτης	וכל עריה
εσονται ερημοι εις αιωνα	תהיינה לחרבות עולם

εις αβατον και εις ονειδισμον και εις καταρασιν] pr.
εις αφανισμον και   86; εις αφανισμον και εις ονειδισμον
και εις αβατον και εις καταρασιν Ο L

    The presence of four rather than three (as in LXX)
coordinated substantives in the MT of this verse (לשמה
לחרפה, לחרב, לקללה / αβατον, ονειδισμον, καταρασιν)
is attributed by Janzen (p. 59) to a "typical filling
out of this series." According to this view, the
reading לחרב is a further example of expansion from
parallel contexts in the MT. The series in question
is one of several such found in the OT. In order to
evaluate the relative merits of the various proposals
which have been put forward to account for the absence
of a Greek word in 29:14(49:13) for MT לחרב, it will
be necessary to review all the occurrences of the
Hebrew series and their Greek counterparts. In formal
structure at least, the series has its prototype in
Deut 28:37. It is employed sparingly in Ki/Chr and Ez,
but is fully exploited in the prose sections of Jer.
The following passages come under consideration:

                1.   Deut 28:37

εν αινιγματι και παραβολη	לשמה למשל
και διηγηματι	ולשנינה

            2.   1 Ki 9:7 (par. 2 Chr 7:20)

Ki: εις αφανισμον και λαλημα	למשל ולשנינה
Chr: εις παραβολην και εις διηγημα	----- " ----

                3.   2 Ki 22:19

εις αφανισμον και εις καταραν	לשמה ולקללה

4. Jer 19:8

εις αφανισμον και εις συριγμον   לשמה ולשרקה

5. Jer 24:9

εις διασκορπισμον   לזועה לרעה

6. Jer 24:9

εις ονειδισμον και εις παραβολην   לחרפה ולמשל
και εις μισος και εις καταραν   לשנינה ולקללה

7. Jer 25:9

εις αφανισμον και εις συριγμον   לשמה ולשרקה
και εις ονειδισμον   ולחרבות

8. Jer 25:11

εις αφανισμον   לחרבה לשמה

9. Jer 29:14(49:13)

εις αβατον και εις ονειδισμον   לשמה לחרפה
και εις καταρασιν   לחרב ולקללה

10. Jer 32:4(25:18)

εις ερημωσιν και εις αβατον   לחרבה לשמה
και εις συριγμον   לשרקה ולקללה

11. Jer 36(29):18

LXX missing vv. 16-20   לאלה ולשמה ולשרקה ולחרפה

12. Jer 49(42):18

εις αβατον και υποχειριοι   לאלה ולשמה
και εις αραν και εις ονειδισμον   ולקללה ולחרפה

13. Jer 51(44):6

εις ερημωσιν και εις αβατον   לחרבה לשממה

14.   Jer 51(44):8

εις καταραν και εις ονειδισμον   לקללה ולחרפה

15.   Jer 51(44):12

εις ονειδισμον και εις απωλειαν   לאלה לשמה
και εις καταραν   ולקללה ולחרפה

16.   Jer 51(44):22

εις ερημωσιν και εις αβατον   לחרבה ולשמה
και εις αραν   ולקללה

17.   Ez 5:14

εις ερημον   לחרבה ולחרפה

18.   Ez 23:46

ταραχην και διαπαργην   לזעוה ולבז

19.   Ez 29:9

απωλεια και ερημος   לשממה וחרבה

20.   2 Chr 29:8

εις εκστασιν και εις αφανισμον   לזועה לשמה
και εις συριγμον   ולשרקה

21.   cf. Mich 6:16

εις αφανισμον . . . και εις συριγμον   לשרקה . . . לשמה ∘
και ονειδη λαων   וחרפת עמי

Observations on the above:

    1. The prototype of Deut 28:37 is most closely
approximated in 1 Ki 9:7 and Jer 24:9. After Jer 24:9
the words משל and שנינה do not occur again in this
series. In fact, שנינה occurs in the OT only in those
passages from Deut, Ki/Chr, and Jer already cited.
On the other hand, the first word of the Deut series,
שמה, becomes the cornerstone of the Jer passages, being
found in all but three (#5, #6, and #14) of the Jer

series, as well as frequently by itself (sometimes in
the form שממה)。 Other terms that occur, listed in
their order of decreasing frequency are: חרבות/חרב(ה)
(8x), חרפה (8x), קללה (8x), שרקה (6x), אלה (3x),
זעור/זועה (3x), רעה (1x), בז (1x).

    2. It is evident that there is no standard length
for the series; it may consist of two, three, or four
terms respectively /43/.

    3. The LXX is shorter than the MT by one term in
five of the Jer passages: (#5, #8, #9, #10, #15), and
once in Ez (#17). On one occasion in Jer (#11), the
entire series is missing as part of a larger passage
absent in the LXX.

Discussion of the five "zero variants" in Jer-LXX:

    In each of the five "zero variants" in the above
series Janzen prefers the shorter Greek as the better
text, the MT according to this interpretation having
suffered conflation through dittography in the case of
לרעה of 24:9, expansion from parallel contexts in the
case of לחרבה of 25:11 (from 25:18) and לקללה of 25:18
(from 24:9), and "typical filling out" of this pejorative series in the case of לאלה of MT 44:12 and לחרב of
49:13.

    A definitive explanation of all the variants in
question may not be possible in our present state of
knowledge. Certainly in a stereotyped formula such
as this, one must entertain the possibility of both
scribal conflation and expansion having taken place, so
that a priori there is no reason for denying that some
of the LXX omissions may well go back to an earlier
stage in the transmission process than that represented
by the MT. By the same token, however, the number of
terms could vary just as easily by virtue of scribal
omission or translator initiative. Only in rare cases
can it be said that the evidence is conclusive one way
or another. Our main criticism of Janzen's handling of
the variants in question, therefore, is the tendency to
see only one kind of explanation as valid, namely
secondary expansion in the MT. When the variants are
analyzed in detail, it becomes apparent that alternative explanations are possible, sometimes even

preferable. We work in the realm of probabilities, but the degree of probability can never be satis- factorily determined until all the evidence is in. Neglect to consider some of the relevant evidence naturally raises question marks over what might otherwise seem obvious solutions.

In the evaluation of the five "zero variants" below we will first quote Janzen's notation in full before proceeding with our critique.

24:9 "ונתתים לזועה לרעה לכל ממלכות הארץ] 𝔊 omits לרעה, which clearly is intrusive here (cf. 15.4, 29.18, 34.17; Dt. 28.25). The addition is best explained as conflation (cf. Ziegler, Beiträge, p. 87), from a manuscript in which לזועה was transcribed as "לרעה (pp. 12-13, #16).

The case for dittography in the above examples is a strong one. The term לרעה does not occur in this series elsewhere, and as for לזועה it always occurs by itself in each of the Jer passages cited (15:4, 29:18, 34:17). Moreover, the transcriptional explanation for the appearance of לרעה is persuasive.

This does not mean, however, that לזועה can never appear in series in the OT. A comprehensive review of the evidence should also note that לזועה/לזעוה does appear in series of two and three terms respectively in Ez 23:46 and 2 Chr 29:8 (לזעוה ולבז and לזועה לשמה ולשרקה), all of which are attested by the LXX, so that in this sense Jer 24:9 with two terms is not anomalous. Furthermore, like לרעה of Jer 24:9, the second term of the Ez passage (לבז) is also unique to the series. In the light of these comparisons, the combination of לזועה לרעה in Jer 24:9 appears less strange. In other respects, however, the Ez and Chr passages do not conform to the pattern of the Deut/Jer formula (cf. the phrase לכל ממלכות הארץ in the latter pair); recogni- tion of this fact minimizes the likelihood that the Ez/Chr passages were determinative in any way for the form of the Jer passage. So we are brought back to the suggestion that לרעה in Jer 24:9 is secondary, perhaps by dittography as Janzen suggests.

25:11 "לחרבה"] om. 𝕲. From verse 18" (p. 45, #57).

The series in this verse consists of two terms,
לשמה לחרבה, the first of which according to Janzen is
intrusive from v. 18 of the same chapter. However, it
should be noted that an exact parallel to the series in
25:11 is found in 51(44):6 where the LXX attests both
terms. While the absence of a conjunction between
the two terms appears to produce an awkward asyndeton
in the Hebrew--thus possibly pointing to the intrusive
nature of לחרבה--the presence or absence of the conjunction in this and similar series appears to follow
no consistent pattern (some Hebrew MSS have the conjunction in both 25:11 and 44:6). In view of the above
considerations, the case for MT expansion is less assured /44/.

32:4(25:18)   "ולקללה כיום הזה] om. 𝕲. ולקללה is from
                  the related series in 24.9 and elsewhere.
                  On כיום הזה as a gloss, see nos. 117,
                  163, 173 [sic: the correct numbers are
                  116, 162, 169], and Brevard S. Childs, 'A
                  Study of the Formula, "Until This Day",'
                  <u>JBL</u> 82 (1963), 279-292" (p. 45, #58).

As observed in Janzen's notation, לקללה (the
fourth and last term of the MT series לחרבה לשמה לשרקה
ולקללה, is part of the larger word complex (ולקללה
כיום הזה) missing in the LXX. Rudolph (<u>HAT</u>, p. 164)
has suggested that the phrase כיום הזה may have been
deliberately omitted in the LXX because it did not
correspond to the historical reality of the translator's day /45/. However, in the article referred to,
Childs argues that the phrase עד היום הזה (with variants) "in the great majority of cases is a formula of
personal testimony added to, and confirming, a received
tradition" (p. 292); on this interpretation the LXX
omission of the phrase could be a pointer to an earlier
form of the Hebrew text. The same may be true of the
omission of a corresponding word for ולקללה, especially
since on every other occasion in which לקללה occurs in
these series (2 Ki 22:19, Jer 24:9, 29:14[49:13],
32:4[25:18], 49[42]:18, 51[44]:8,12,22), it is always
represented in the LXX.

51(44):12   "ולחרפה ולקללה ולשמה לאלה [והיו]"   "From
            42.18, a typical filling out of the
            pejorative series" (p. 58, #166[h]).

     The series in MT 42:18 is identical to MT 44:12 so
that the theory of Hebrew expansion by the addition of
לאלה in 44:12 appears specious at first sight. But in
both verses the Greek translations are fraught with
difficulties. For greater ease in following the
discussion, it will be helpful to reproduce the corresponding texts:

49(42):18

ειϚ αβατον και υποχειριοι   ולשמה לאלה
και ειϚ αραν και ειϚ ονειδισμον   ולחרפה ולקללה

51(44):12

ειϚ ονειδισμον και ειϚ απωλειαν   As above
και ειϚ καταραν

    It will be observed that in both Greek series we
are confronted by anomalous translations and by apparent textual dislocations. As the texts now stand in
49(42):18, ειϚ αβατον seems to correspond to לאלה and
υποχειριοι to לשמה (as indicated in the Hebrew/Greek
equivalence apparatus of HR), but the reverse is
clearly the case (as effectively demonstrated by
T. Muraoka in Textus, 8 [1973], 26, contra Ziegler,
Ieremias, p. 45). The anomalous Greek word in the
series is υποχειριοι, which is odd both in form and
substance (L has ειϚ υποχειριουϚ which at least in
formal structure follows the typical pattern of preposition plus noun; but it is unlikely that this
represents the original reading; it is rather a
stylistic modification typical of the L recension).
The uncharacteristic form without preposition, the
inverted sequence of αβατον/υποχειριοι, and the unique
translation equivalence υποχειριοϚ/אלה are all testi-
monies to a difficult translation problem and/or
complicated transmission history surrounding the word
אלה.

    Turning to 51(44):12, the pairing of Hebrew/Greek
equivalents in this verse is, if anything, even more

problematic. According to present word order, εις
ονειδισμον corresponds to לאלה, εις απωλειαν to לשמה,
εις καταραν to לקללה, leaving לחרפה without equivalence. But since חרפה is consistently rendered by
ονειδισμος, and since απωλεια /46/ and καταρα must
correspond to לשמה and לקללה respectively, it is
necessary again to postulate a textual dislocation
either in the LXX or MT and agree with Janzen that לאלה
is indeed the word without equivalence in the LXX.

But must we also assume, therefore, that לאלה of
MT 44:12 derives from MT 42:18 as a "typical filling
out"? In the light of the textual instability of both
verses, this explanation may be inadequate. Since
the problem-word in both instances appears to be אלה,
we may wonder whether the root cause of the discrepant
Greek texts may not lie in the translator's unfamiliar-
ity with this word. This view receives some support
from the fact that in the only other place where we can
test the translation of אלה in Jer, namely at 23:10, it
was read as אָלָה and translated τουτων (the same Hebrew
word also appears in MT 29:18 but is missing in the LXX
as part of a larger context). In short, the translator
appears to have tried everything: variant vocalization,
wild guess, and omission. These seem to us equally
credible explanations as the assumption of secondary
expansion in the Hebrew.

29:14(49:13) "לחרב] om. ℭ. Typical filling out of
                 this series" (p. 59, #182).

This brings us finally to the passage with which
we began the discussion of these series, the omission
in 29:14(49:13) of a corresponding Greek word for the
Hebrew לחרב. Two reasons have generally been cited in
favour of the shorter LXX at this point. First, the
form of the Hebrew word is anomalous; elsewhere in Jer
it is found in the form חרבה (twice in the plural חרבות
[MT 25:9 and the second occurrence in MT 49:13]), which
corresponds well with the other feminine substantives
all terminating in הָ. Secondly, commentators have felt
that חרב is a somewhat different kind of word in comparison with the other terms in this series which all
express human reactions: אלה, קללה, שמ(מ)ה, חרפה, שרק,
זועה. Thus Rudolph (p. 288), refers to לחרב in MT
49:13 as "Dieser objektive Ausdruck zwischen den

subjektiven," with the implied suggestion that חרב
could not have been part of the original series since
it would be out of character with the rest. Traditionally, therefore, לחרב in MT 49:13 has been explained as
a case of dittography from the preceding לחרפה (so
Ehrlich, p. 87; Rudolph, p. 288; and Ziegler,
Beiträge, p. 87; cf. the apparent confusion of לחרבות
and לחרפה in 25:9 /47/), or even from לחרבות of the
following clause (so Bright, p. 329; Volz, p. 320,
entertains both possibilities). Janzen (p. 25) is
aware of Ziegler's decision in favour of dittography
and considers this explanation "plausible," but adds,
"or M may be just expanding the series, as elsewhere."
His remark on the same passage on p. 59, #182, quoted
above shows that his preference clearly lies in favour
of MT expansion.

     However, we cannot share this preference. If it
had been a case of "filling out," one would have expected to find the same form (חרבה) as used elsewhere.
If the secondary status of לחרב be insisted upon, then
the explanation of scribal dittography seems the best
one available. It may be inquired, however, whether
too much has been made of the difference between חרב
and the other terms employed in the series. Perhaps MT
49:13 could be read in the form

לשמה לחרפה
לחרב ולקללה

where לשמה and לחרב are deliberately balanced by לחרפה
and לקללה, the first pair being taken as representing
concrete, visible results, the second pair as representing abstract, moral states. On this reading לחרב
should not be surrendered too easily. The Hebrew
Vorlage of the LXX could have been short by haplography (if לחרפה and לחרב are similar enough to have
occasioned dittography, the same similarity could
have occasioned haplography). Admittedly the evidence
is inconclusive either way /48/.

Conclusion

     There is no standard number of terms in the series
considered, and a shorter Greek text cannot be taken as
a sure witness to the original length of the series.

Each variant has to be examined on its own merits.
Sometimes this examination yields a preference for the
LXX, sometimes for the MT, sometimes it is impossible
to decide between them. Repeated appeals to expansion
from parallel and related contexts oversimplifies the
nature of the relationship between the two texts. The
data considered in this section does not readily admit
to such broad generalizations.

Other coordinated series in Jer present the same
kind of problems as those found here, e.g. the triad
חרב רעב דבר ("der erstaunlich abweichenden Bezeugung
der Trias im MT im Vergleich mit LXX"--H. Weippert, Die
Prosareden des Jeremiabuches, BZAW 132, 1973, p. 150).
In deciding in favour of the shorter LXX series (where
it occurs), Janzen (pp. 43-44) appeals to "the general
tendency" of the MT to expand. Again, it is precisely
this kind of generalization that we consider ill-
advised and have found inappropriate for describing the
texts of Jer.

29:18(49:17)

και εσται η Ιδουμαια εις αβατον   והיתה אדום לשמה
πας ο παραπορευομενος επ αυτην   כל עבר עליה
συριει   ישם וישרק על כל מכותה

συριει B-S-130-538 A-106' La/Sg . . .] εκστησεται   (pr.
συριει C) και συριει επι (εν 87txt) παση τη πληγη
(πασαν την πληγην Q-239-613) αυτης   rel.

There exist seven close parallels to this verse,
four outside the book of Jer (1 Ki 9:8 // 2 Chr 7:21,
Zeph 3:1[MT 2:15], Lam 2:15) and three within (18:16,
19:8, 27[50]:13). According to Janzen (pp. 59-60,
#183), the readings ישם and על כל מכותה in Jer-MT 49:17
are secondary expansions from 19:8 and 50:13. In order
to evaluate this proposal it will be necessary to
review all the relevant passages.

1 Ki 9:8

και ο οικος ουτος ο υψηλος   והבית הזה יהיה עליון
πας ο διαπορευομενος δι αυτου   כל עבר עליו
εκστησεται και συριει   ישם ושרק

2 Chr 7:21

και ο οικος ουτος ο υψηλος	והבית הזה אשר היה עליון
πας ο διαπορευομενος αυτον	לכל עבר עליו
εκστησεται	ישם

Zeph 3:1(MT 2:15)

πως εγενηθη εις αφανισμον	איך היתה לשמה
νομη θηριων	מרבץ לחיה
πας ο διαπορευομενος δι αυτης	כל עובר עליה
συριει και κινησει τας χειρας αυτου	ישרק יניע ידו

Lam 2:15

εκροτησαν επι σε χειρας	ספקו עליך כפים
παντες οι παραπορευομενοι οδον	כל עברי דרך
εσυρισαν και εκινησαν κεφαλην αυτων	שרקו וינעו ראש
επι την θυγατερα Ιερουσαλημ	על בת ירושלם

Jer 18:16

του ταξαι την γην αυτων εις αφανισμον	לשים ארצם לשמה
και συριγμα αιωνιον	שרוקת עולם
παντες οι διαπορευομενοι δι αυτης	כל עובר עליה
εκστησεται και κινησουσι την κεφαλην αυτων	ישם ויניד בראשו

Jer 19:8

και καταταξω την πολιν ταυτην	ושמתי את העיר הזאת
και αφανισμον και εις συριγμον	לשמה ולשרקה
πας ο παραπορευομενος επ αυτης	כל עבר עליה
σκυθρωπασει και συριει	ישם וישרק
υπερ πασης της πληγης αυτης	על כל מכתה

Jer 29(50):13

και εσται εις αφανισμον πασα	והיתה שממה כלה
και πας ο διοδευων δια βαβυλωνος	כל עבר על בבל
σκυθρωπασει και συριουσιν	ישם וישרק
επι πασαν την πληγην αυτης	על כל מכותיה

It is quite clear that the above passages constitute a stereotyped prophetic saying, the common element
to each being the pivotal כל עבר construction in the
middle of the sentence. In all Hebrew passages except

2 Chr 7:21, the כל עבר phrase is followed by two verbs
expressing horror at the devastation viewed. The verb-
pairs in question are as follows: שרק/שמם (1 Ki 9:8,
Jer 19:8, 49:17, 50:13), נוע/שמם (Jer 18:6), and
נוע/שרק (Zeph 2:15, Lam 2:15). In the MT of Jer 19:8,
49:17, and 50:13, the saying is concluded by the phrase
על כל מכתה. The fact that these three Jer-MT passages
have the same verb-pairs and conclude in identical
fashion is evidence of their close literary connection.

But in Jer 29:18(49:17) the situation is complicated by the omission in the LXX of any word corresponding to the Hebrew verb ישם and the phrase על כל
מכותה, whereas in all other passages the LXX consistently supports the MT. Janzen takes the shorter LXX
of this phrase as the original reading and regards the
literary parallelism existing between MT 49:17 on the
one hand and MT 19:8 and 50:13 on the other hand as a
case of secondary expansion in the former. But this
explanation we find unsatisfactory.

It is virtually certain that the original composition of MT 49:17 must have contained two verbs, not
one, in conformity with all the other Hebrew passages
except 2 Chr 7:21. But the case of the single verb in
2 Chr 7:21 reinforces rather than weakens the priority
of the two-verb pattern, for it is obvious that in this
case it is the Chronicler or his _Vorlage_ that has
shortened the original form as found in 1 Ki 9:8 (see
the discussion of this point by I.L. Seeligman, _VT_ 11
[1961], 205-206). Similarly in Jer 49:17 we must hold
that the original form of the clause contained both
verbs, one of which was omitted by the translator or
was already missing in his _Vorlage_. To put it the
other way around: the presence of ישם in the MT of
49:17 is no more a case of secondary expansion than is
the presence of שרק in 1 Ki 9:8.

In order to support the position that the LXX is
the earlier text at 29:18(49:17), Janzen comments,
"That the cliche כל עבר עליה ישם וישרק may occur with
only one of the verbs is shown by 18.16, Zeph. 2.15"
(p. 60). Certainly it is true that in Jer 18:16 and
Zeph 2:15 only one of the particular verb-pairs
occurs (שמם and שרק respectively); but the point is
quite irrelevant. It remains true that in each case it
is nonetheless verb-pairs that are used, even though the

actual verbs composing these pairs may vary;   this is
the decisive point.

Although no similar concrete evidence is available
by which to judge the lack of a corresponding Greek
phrase for על כל מכונה in 29:18(49:17), one suspects
that the LXX is no more to be trusted here than in the
case of the omission of ישם. Cross-fertilization from
the parallel passages of 19:8 and 50:13 is a possibility to be reckoned with, but since the verb-pairs
employed were originally identical there is no reason
for supposing that they should not have been completed
in the same way by the phrase על כל מכ(ו)תה. Why it
should have been omitted by the translator or was
already missing in his Vorlage exceeds the capabilities
of our critical methodology to determine.

29:22(49:21)

οτι απο φωνης πτωσεως αυτων   מקול נפלם
εφοβηθη η γη   רעשה הארץ
και κραυγη θαλασσης ουκ ηκουσθη נשמע קולה סוף ביב צעקה

ηκουσθη] + η φωνη αυτης (σου Syh/mg) O; + φωνη (pr. η
51-62-311-407-449) σου L Arm

In the LXX of this verse there is no equivalent
for the MT reading קולה. This "zero variant" is not
mentioned by Janzen even though a fairly strong case
can be made for a shorter and better Greek text at this
point /49/. As it stands, the presence of קולה at the
end of the verse makes for uncommonly awkward Hebrew
syntax. Various translations have been attempted to
accommodate the presence of both Hebrew words צעקה and
קולה, the most literal of which (RV) has, "there is a
cry, the noise whereof is heard in the Red Sea."
Others vocalize צעקה as a verb and read, "it cries out,
and the cry is heard at the Red Sea" (NEB, cf. JB).
Yet most commentators are generally agreed that קולה
is to be deleted. In this judgement we concur.

The basis for the deletion of קולה on this occasion is the conjunction of three lines of evidence: the
omission in the LXX of any word corresponding to קולה;
the difficult Hebrew syntax with קולה and the testimony of the parallel passage at 27(50):46, the latter

of which reads as follows:

οτι απο φωνης αλωσεως Βαβυλωνος   מקול נתפשה בבל
σεισθησεται η γη   נרעשה הארץ
και κραυγη εν εθνεσιν ακουσθησεται   וזעקה בגוים נשמע

Although there are some obvious differences between
the two passages both in the Hebrew and Greek versions
(e.g. נפלם / נתפשה בבל ,נרעשה/רעשה ,צעקה בים סוף /
וזעקה בגוים with corresponding Greek differences /50/),
nevertheless they constitute a genuine parallel so that
the absence of קולה in MT 50:46 is telling. How then
did the intrusive word enter the text at MT 49:21? The
most likely explanation is that it began its life as a
textual variant to צעקה; in the process of transmission it was drawn into the text at the end of the
colon. Volz (p. 321) has a somewhat more complicated
explanation, namely that צעקה originally stood where
קולה now stands but that it fell out of the text and
was replaced by קולה; when צעקה was again recovered it
had to give way to the presence of קולה at the end of
the phrase and hence was introduced at the beginning
instead. Such speculation is permissible but probably
superfluous. However, Volz' statement that "Die zwei
Substantiva צעקה und קולה im gleichen Satz vertragen
sich nicht" remains true, and the deletion of קולה
from MT 49:21 (cf. the notation in the text critical
apparatus of BHK) finds genuine support from the
omission of a corresponding word in the LXX /51/.

29:23a(49:22a)

ιδου ωσπερ αετος οφεται   הנה כנשר יעלה וידאה
και εκτενει τας πτερυγας   ויפרש כנפיו
επ οχυρωματα αυτης   על בצרה

οφεται] αναβησεται και επιστησεται (επιπτησεται   51-51s
-62-407-449) L

     In the first line of this verse, the LXX is twice
at odds with the MT: the translation of οφεται for MT
וידאה and the omission of a corresponding Greek word
for יעלה. The former is readily explained as a case of
confusion of the similar letters ד/ר in וידאה /52/,
quite possibly a reading already present in the translator's Vorlage or misread by him, either accidentally

or deliberately (he may not have been familiar with the
rare verb דאה /53/). However, the omission of a word
for יעלה is less easily accounted for.

One argument in favour of the secondary status of
יעלה is the parallel passage of MT 48:40 הנה כנשר ידאה
which is also without the verb יעלה. Thus Bright
(p.330) and Christensen (pp. 239-240) take the two verbs
יעלה and ידאה in MT 49:22 as variant readings which
have been conflated in MT. Ziegler (Beiträge, p. 87)
on the other hand, calls יעלה a doublet of the type
that should have been entered in the apparatus to BH as
"dittogr." Janzen (p. 25, #63) considers this explanation "plausible, but unsure." There is no word
immediately adjacent to יעלה which closely resembles
it, but perhaps Ziegler has in mind dittography from
the somewhat similar but distant phrase in v. 19, הנה
כאריה יעלה. This at least was the suggestion of Hitzig
(p. 369) and Duhm (p. 357), and it may be as plausible
an explanation as any.

A very similar set of problems is encountered in
the MT and LXX versions of the parallel passages
29:9(49:8) and 30:8(49:30), which are set out below:

29:9(49:8)

ηπατηθη ο τοπος αυτων	נסו הפנו
βαθυνατε εις καθισιν	העמיקו לשבת

30:8(49:30)

φευγετε λιαν	נסו נדו מאד
βαθυνατε εις καθισιν	העמיקו לשבת

The inner-Greek textual problem represented by the
difficult rendering ηπατηθη ο τοπος αυτων at 29:9(49:8)
has been discussed in Ch. III above (pp. 145-47), where
it was argued that the original Hebrew read much as we
find it in MT, i.e. נסו הפנו. In the parallel passage
of 30:8(49:30), however, the verbs employed are נסו
נדו, where the LXX omits the second of these. As with
יעלה of MT 49:22, so here Ziegler calls נדו a case of
dittography (Beiträge, p. 87) which Janzen (p. 25) also
assigns to the category of "plausible, but unsure." In
this instance the orthographic similarity of נסו and
נדו strengthens the case for dittography. However,

there is also the possibility that נסו of MT 49:30
could have come from its use earlier in the oracle at
MT 49:8, just as יעלה of MT 49:22 may have derived from
MT 49:19.

In the end we will probably have to plead ignor-
ance on the reason for the discrepant readings discussed in this section. One thing, however, appears
certain, namely that a solution to these individual
problems is not to be found in any general theory
either of expansion or contraction. Such generalizations have not proved helpful in our pursuit of the
earliest recoverable text.

29:23(49:22) // 31(48):40b,41b

In this final section we study the parallel verses
29:23(49:22) and 31(48):40b,41b as examples of the common phenomenon of duplicate passages in Jer.

29:23(49:22)

ιδου ωσπερ αετος οφεται	הנה כנשר יעלה וידאה
και εκτενει τας πτερυγας επ οχυρωματα αυτης	ויפרש כנפיו על בצרה
και εσται η καρδια των ισχυρων της Ιδουμαιας	והיה לב גבורי אדום
εν τη ημερα εκεινη ως καρδια γυναικος ωδινουσης	ביום ההוא כלב אשה מצרה

31(48):40-41

οτι ουτως ειπε κυριος	כי כה אמר יהוה
	הנה כנשר ידאה ופרש כנפיו אל מואב
(v.41) ελημφθη Ακκαρων	נלכדה הקריות
και τα οχυρωματα συνελημφθη	והמצדות נתפשה
	והיה לב גבורי מואב
	ביום ההוא כלב אשה מצרה

κυριος] + (※ O) ιδου ως αετος ορμησει και εκπετασει
χειρας (τας πτερυγας L Tht. = 29:23) αυτου επι μωαβ
O L C Tht. Arm

συνελημφθη] + (※ O) και εσται η καρδια των (> O)
δυνατων μωαβ εν τη ημερα εκεινη ως καρδια γυναικος
ωδινουσης O L C(om. των δυν.) Arm

In the last five verses of the Edom oracle there
are three clear examples of duplicate passages within
Jer: 29:19(49:18) // 27(50):40, 29:20-22(49:19-21) //
27(50):44-46, and the one quoted above. In the first
two pairs the LXX consistently attests the Hebrew of
the MT on each occurrence, but in 29:23(49:22) //
31(48):40b,41b the LXX omits the second occurrence of
the Hebrew duplicate. This pattern of sometimes attesting, sometimes omitting one of the members of a
Hebrew pair is typical of the LXX of this book. Janzen
believes that duplicate passages in Jer unattested by
the LXX are further examples of expansion from parallel contexts (pp. 94-95), though in the case of the
duplicate in MT 48:40b,41b he proposes a special explanation of how the passage from MT 49:22 came to appear
just here, namely as a gloss originally on בצרה in MT
48:24 which was later taken into the wrong column of
the MS with appropriate change of names (p. 59, #179).

The inconsistency of the LXX in attesting the
duplicate passages of Jer has been common knowledge to
students of this text for a long time. In fact, it was
this very observation that inspired the first systematic treatment of the relationship between the LXX and
MT texts of the book, namely that by M.G.L. Spohn in
1794. In the opening pages of his work Spohn identified 25 Hebrew doublets, six or seven of which in their
second occurrence were absent from the LXX. To account
for this phenomenon, Spohn posited the theory that the
translator was a private individual who chose not to
translate a second time what he already had translated
once, even though he was frequently inconsistent in
the execution of his plan.

This theory of the deliberate omission in the LXX
of the second occurrence of a Hebrew duplicate passage
has had popular currency among commentators even till
recent times. Thus Bright (p. cxxiii) remarks that the
LXX habitually omits doublets on their second occurrence" (similarly p. lxxv), and Weiser (p. 401, n. 3)
comments on the LXX omission at 31(48):40b,41b: "Das
Fehlen in G erklärt sich daraus, dass in der Septuaginta 49,22 (=G 29,23) dem Moabspruch (=G Kap. 31)
vorausgeht, und eine Wiederholung in 48,40 vermieden
wurde" (cf. Bright, p. 321). But this theory will not
stand scrutiny.

As Janzen has pointed out (pp. 91ff.), the chief objection to a theory of the deliberate omission of the second occurrence of a duplicate passage is the number of times both parts are in fact attested in the Greek. While it is possible to document the LXX omission of the second occurrence in the following seven doublets, 6:13-15 // 8:10b-12, 7:24-26 (or alternatively 11:3ff.) // 11:7-8, 15:13-14 // 17:3-4, 16:14-15 // 23:7-8 /54/, 24:8-10 // 29:16-18,. 46:27-28 // 30:10-11, 49:22 // 48:40b, 41b /55/, it is noteworthy that on twice as many occasions both occurrences of the doublet are attested /56/. Spohn tried to account for this lack of consistency by the suggestion that sometimes the translator simply forgot what he had already translated once, sometimes the omission of a duplicate passage would seriously disrupt the context and was therefore retained, and at least on one occasion (29:20-21 [49:19-20] // 27[50]:44-45) the second passage may have been rendered by a different translator from the first. But such arguments seem arbitrary and artificial.

In his discussion of the seven passages which are commonly cited as evidence for the theory of deliberate omission, Janzen eliminates two from further consideration on the ground that they can be satisfactorily explained by haplography either in the LXX or in its Hebrew Vorlage, leaving five for more detailed treatment. In each case Janzen seeks to demonstrate that the missing Greek passages were not originally present in the translator's Vorlage but that they were added at a later stage from parallel and related contexts.

The arguments for a shorter Vorlage in these instances are well marshalled. Particular mention may be made of the syntactical arguments against the presence in the Hebrew Vorlage of the duplicates encountered at MT 8:10b-12 (p. 95) and 23:7-8 (pp. 92-93). Also well taken are the remarks on the absence in the Moab oracle, 31(48):40b,41b, of the duplicate passage from the Edom oracle, 29:23(49:22): "We cannot believe that the translator, having translated the couplet already in 49:22, was so concerned to avoid repetition of doublets that he would go to the trouble to ferret the parallel lines from their interwoven context and excise them, only to translate several large doublets and scores of smaller ones, too indifferent or careless in his method to notice that he had already translated them once before." In these cases we accept that it is much easier to believe that the duplicates in question were missing in the translator's <u>Vorlage</u> than that they were deliberately omitted by him.

The significance of the shorter <u>Vorlage</u> at these places is, however, ambiguous. Janzen assumes that wherever we have a shorter <u>Vorlage</u>, this is also a pointer to a superior <u>Vorlage</u> and a secondary MT text. But the difficulty in accounting for the appearance of the MT passages as expansions from parallel passages is illustrated by Janzen's own attempts at such explanations. We refer in particular to his discussion of the MT "interpolations" at 8:10b-12 and 23:7-8, pp. 95-96 and pp. 92-93 respectively. The paragraphs commencing with the phrase "We propose . . ." contain intriguing proposals for reconstructing the original form of the passage in question, not without their own touch of brilliance, but when all is said and done they remain speculative theories beyond evidential control. The same is true concerning the suggestion how the passage from MT 49:22 found its way secondarily into MT 48:40b, 41b, i.e. via a gloss on בצרה at 48:23 which was later taken into the wrong column of the MS with appropriate change in name. What is questionable about these reconstructions is that they all proceed on the same premise, namely that where the LXX omits a duplicate passage this must be a testimony to the primary character of the LXX <u>Vorlage</u>. In certain cases this may well be the case, but it ought to be the result rather than the premise of the discussion. Janzen's conclusions regarding the duplicate passage discussed are based on "the absence of clear evidence that 𝔊 deleted purposely" and "the abundant evidence for the expansionist character of 𝔐" (p. 96). But since we have been unable to endorse either of these conclusions on the scale suggested by Janzen's work, we are inclined not to dismiss too quickly the MT attestation of all duplicates either.

III. Conclusions

In the introductory chapter to Janzen's book we were presented with the two leading questions underlying the study, viz, whether the LXX text bears

witness to a deliberately abbreviated translation or
to an existing shorter Hebrew Vorlage than the MT. The
author's answer to these questions is that, except in
those cases where the LXX is not demonstrably short by
scribal lapse, the LXX goes back to a Hebrew text which
is both shorter and superior to that of the MT (cf.
pp. 128, 135). The hypothesis of translator abridgement, the author believes, should be abandoned once for
all (p. 115), thus closing one long-standing debate
about the text of Jer (p. 128). But not only is the
"abbreviation" theory rejected; also dismissed is the
"mediating" position of scholars like Rudolph, Hyatt,
and Bright who have resisted attempts to generalize
regarding the relative merits of variant readings in
the two texts. By contrast, Janzen affirms that generalizations about the character of the texts are valid,
specifically that the MT consistently represents a
late, developed tradition. In short, Janzen's study
constitutes a determined modern apology on behalf of
the "expansion" theory.

The contemporary context of the work is highlighted in a concluding section where the results are
tentatively accommodated to the larger theory of local
texts initially proposed by W.F. Albright but later
modified and elaborated by Frank M. Cross, according
to which three centres of Jewish learning--Babylonian,
Palestinian, and Egyptian--were predominant in the
preservation of the Hebrew scriptures. On this scheme,
the MT is said to represent the Palestinian tradition
--generally characterized by expansion and conflation--
while the Hebrew underlying Jer-LXX represents the
Egyptian tradition which, having survived in isolation
from ca. 450-350 B.C., had escaped the same degree of
expansion characteristic of the Palestinian text.

While welcoming Janzen's fresh investigation of
the Hebrew/Greek problem and recognizing many points of
value in it, our own review of a specific portion of the
text has failed to provide convincing support for the
broad conclusions advanced by Janzen. Evidence of
various kinds, both direct and indirect, do point to
the existence at one time of a Hebrew text shorter
than the MT, and we can be grateful to Janzen for
having brought this issue into focus. However, the
author is often too quick to generalize and simply to
assume a shorter Vorlage. Failure to take account of

translation phenomena and contextual considerations
undermine the arguments for a ubiquitously shorter
Hebrew _Vorlage_ than the MT. Hence it is doubtful that
the present LXX text is everywhere as reliable a witness to the shorter Hebrew _Vorlage_ as that assumed in
the work under review.

     Another matter has to do with the writer's incli-
nation to assume that wherever an argument can be
advanced for a shorter _Vorlage_ than the MT that this
also represents a superior _Vorlage_ to the MT. The two
questions of length and superiority ought to be held
apart and the issues not blurred. Yet such blurring of
the issues is precisely what we find in the summary
paragraph on p. 128 where evidence for a lack of translator abridgement in the LXX is tacitly taken as evidence for a superior Hebrew text. Yet the one (a
shorter _Vorlage_) does not necessarily imply the other
(a superior _Vorlage_). Here, too, we have not found
that generalizations of the kind proffered by Janzen
can be sustained.

     While one feels the inherent attraction of broad
generalizations that in one sweep can solve a multitude
of textual conundrums, one must resist the temptation
to yield to such generalizations where they do not
stand up to close scrutiny. The temptation must be
resisted even if in the process it makes the task of
the Jer student more rather than less difficult. At
the same time it is important not to lose one's perspective: whether in the longer or shorter version, the
book of Jer still speaks to us with power and conviction which should not be obscured in the course of an
otherwise legitimate and necessary text critical enterprise.

NOTES
BIBLIOGRAPHY

NOTES TO CHAPTER I

/1/ A similar approach is taken by J.C.M. das Neves in
the published work, A Teologia da tradução grega dos Setenta no
livro de Isaías, Lisbon, 1973, where the author employs Ch. 24
as a test case for exploring the theological tendencies of the
LXX version of Isaiah. This kind of "spot" method has also been
utilized in various book reviews, e.g. the review of The Hebrew
Text of the Old Testament, 1973, by L.H. Brockington in BibOr 32
(1975), 84-85, where the reviewer evaluates the book on the
basis of Gen 49.

/2/ Some of these have been documented in the critical
apparatus to Ziegler's text, e.g., 15:19, 17:26, 18:13, 28:44,
30:10, 37:6, and 38:2.

/3/ According to its Introduction, this famous edition
claims to be a faithful representation of Codex Vaticanus.
However, recent investigations have shown that it is essentially
an Aldine text revised according to the Vatican MS. This idea
was first mooted by Paul de Lagarde, Mitteilungen, I, 123, and
has since been supported by the studies of A. Rahlfs, "Die
Abhängigkeit der sixtinischen Septuaginta Ausgabe von der
aldinischen," ZAW 33 (1913), 30-46; M.L. Margolis, "The Aldina
as a Source of the Sixtina," JBL 38 (1919), 51-52; and J.
Ziegler, "Der Text der Aldina im Dodekapropheton," Biblica 26
(1945), 37-51, esp. 49-51.

/4/ For instance, some of the unique readings found in the
Complutensian Polyglot are the following (those underlined):

29:1 και εγενετο ρημα κυριου προς ιερεμιαν τον προφητην
επι τους αλλοφυλους προ του παταξαι φαραω την γαζαν = MT

29:4 τους αλλοφυλους τους καταλοιπους των νησων της
καππαδοκιας = MT

29:13 ιδου οις = MT; ου μη αθωωθηση, οτι πιων πιεσαι = MT

29:16 ιδου μικρον = MT

29:18 εκστησεται και συριει επι πασαν την πληγην αυτης = MT

29:19 om. παντοκρατωρ = MT

29:22 om. οτι = MT; om. και = MT

/5/ For additional background information concerning the
publication history of both the smaller and larger Cambridge
editions see H.B. Swete, The Old Testament in Greek, I, xi;

Introduction to the Old Testament in Greek, 1902, pp. 188-90, as well as the "Prefatory Note to Genesis" in BM, I, 1906, i-v, and "Preface to the Octateuch," I, 1917, v-vii.

/6/ Cf. his remarks in Anmerkungen zur griechischen Übersetzung der Proverbien, p. 3 (cf. Mitt. I, 21); "Noch einmal meine Ausgabe der Septuaginta," (Mitt. III, 230-31), and Librorum Veteris Testamenti canonicorum pars prior Graece, 1883, p. xvi.

/7/ For useful summaries on the history and objectives of the Göttingen series see the articles by W. Kappler, "Ziele und Aufgaben des Göttinger Setpuaginta-Unternehmens," GGA 202 (1940), 115-24; R. Hanhart, "L'edizione dei LXX e la fondazione Gottingense che la perpara," RivStorLettRel 1 (1965), 351-52; idem, "Jüdische Tradition und christliche Interpretation: Zur Geschichte der Septuagintaforschung in Göttingen," Kerygma und Logos, FS Carl Andresen, ed. A.M. Ritter, 1979, pp. 280-97; J.W. Wevers, "The Göttingen Septuagint," IOSCS Bulletin 8 (1975), 19-23; and P. M. Bogaert, "La Septante de Göttingen," Revue Théologique de Louvain 11 (1980), 80-82.

/8/ Ieremias Vates e versione Ioudaeorum Alexandrinorum ac reliquorum interpretum graecorum emendatus notisque criticis illustratus, 2 vols., Leipzig, 1824 ("Tomus 2 post obitum patris edidit, F.G.A. Spohn").

/9/ Das Buch Jeremia griechisch und hebräisch (Nach dem Tode des Herausgebers besorgt von J. Dahse und Erwin Nestle), Stuttgart, 1924.

/10/ In Colligere Fragmenta (FS Alban Dold), eds. B. Fischer and V. Fiala (Texte und Arbeiten 2), 1952, pp. 13-24.

/11/ Historisches Jahrbuch 77 (1958), 347-57.

/12/ The quote comes from M.H. Goshen-Gottstein, "Theory and Practice," Textus 3 (1963), 149, n. 70. Note also the comment by B. Childs in Old Testament Books for Pastor and Teacher, Philadelphia, 1977, pp. 15-16, to the effect that he prefers "the very useful" edition of Swete in favour of "the eclectic text" of Rahlfs.

/13/ See the statement recorded above (p. 6) from the Cambridge University Reporter, 13 March, 1883, particularly the comment that the apparatus of the larger edition would "provide materials for the critical determination of the text." Swete remarks that the collation of HP "promise materials upon which a critical revision of the text may ultimately be based" (Old Testament in Greek, I, ix), and with regard to his own edition he feels that a reliable reproduction of Codex Vaticanus "supplies at least an excellent standard of comparison, . . . until a critical text has been produced (Introduction, p. 190).

According to their "Prefatory Note to Genesis," Brooke and
McLean say that their object is to present "the evidence
available for the reconstruction of the text or texts of the
LXX" (BM, I, 1, i).

/14/ See the remark in "Prefatory Note to Genesis" on
Lagarde: "He alone, if any one, could have 'sustained the
labour,' not only of the preliminary task which has been
entrusted to us, but also of its more important sequel—the
reconstruction of the pre-hexaplaric text of the LXX., so far
as that is now possible" (p. iv). Compare also Swete's remarks
on Lagarde, Introduction, p. 288, and Old Testament in Greek,
I, x.

/15/ Again in the "Prefatory Note to Genesis" note the
statement, "At an early stage of the undertaking it was decided
that it would be premature to attempt to provide a reconstructed
or 'true' text in this edition." Similarly in the "Preface to
the Octateuch" (1917), "No attempt has been made to provide a
reconstructed or 'true' Septuagint text. As Dr Deissmann said
at the Oriental Congress at Hamburg when the plan of our edition
was discussed, 'In the present state of LXX studies an edition
of the LXX in the strict sense of the word is not yet possible.
What however is possible and absolutely necessary is a trustworthy collection of the textual material.' The work originally
undertaken by the Syndics of the Press in 1883 was based on the
same view. In preparing the present volume we have come across
no evidence of any sort which has led us to modify our belief in
its absolute truth." See also Swete on Tischendorf: "It was
plain to him that the time had not come for the construction of
a critical text," Old Testament in Greek, I, ix.

/16/ E.g., G. Lambert, Nouvelle Revue Théologique 80
(1958), 990; B. Botte, Recherches de Théologie Ancienne et
Médiévale 25 (1958), 147-48; R. Tournay, RB 65 (1958), 292;
O. Eissfeldt, TLZ 83 (1958), 22-24; H. Schneider, TRe 65
(1960), 101-06.

/17/ This remains the clearest example of the change of
style in the second half even though the actual phrase ουτος
ειπε κυριος occurs for the first time only in 30:1.

/18/ Already in 1794 M.G.L. Spohn suggested that the different versions of the parallel passages in 29:19-20(49:18-19)
// 27(50):44-45 implied different hands, Ieremias vates
(published 1824), pp. 9-10 (cf. also pp. 17, 20). See also
the remarks by P.F. Frankl (1872), pp. 448-49; A. Scholz
(1875), p. 14; C. Workman (1889), p. xxvii; A.W. Streane
(1896), p. 1, n. 1; and J.J. Kneucker (1879), p. 83, n. 8.
Only E. Kühl (1882) made an explicit statement to the effect
that the translation of Jer was a unity (p. 8).

/19/ "The Greek Translators of Jeremiah," JTS 4 (1902-03), 245-66; Jewish Worship, 1921, pp. 29-37.

/20/ "The Greek Translators of Ezekiel," JTS 4 (1902-03), 398-411; "The Greek Translators of the Prophetical Books," JTS 4 (1902-03), 578-85; "The Greek Translators of the Four Books of Kings," JTS 8 (1906-07), 262-78.

/21/ See for example the contributions by G. Buchanan Gray, "The Greek Version of Isaiah: Is it the Work of a Single Translator?" JTS 12 (1911), 286-93; J. Herrmann and F. Baumgärtel, Beiträge zur Entstehungsgeschichte der Septuaginta, 1923; O.J. Baab, "A Theory of Two Translators for the Greek Genesis," JBL 52 (1933), 239-43; N. Turner, "The Greek Translators of Ezekiel," JTS 7 (1956), 12-24; M.S. Hurwitz, "The Septuagint of Isaiah 36-39 in Relation to that of 1-35, 40-66," HUCA 28 (1957), 75-83; G. Howard, "Some Notes on the Septuagint of Amos," VT 20 (1970), 108-12; T. Muraoka, "A Re-examination of the Two-Translator Theory of a Septuagint Book," unpublished paper read at the IOSCS meeting of the International Congress for OT Studies, 1971; idem, "The Greek Texts of Samuel-Kings: Incomplete Translations or Recensional Activity?" 1972 Proceedings, 1972, 90-107; J.A. Arieti, "The Vocabulary of Septuagint Amos," JBL 93 (1974), 338-47.

/22/ "On the Present State of Proto-Septuagint Studies," JAOS 61 (1941), 88, n. 31. In his article on "The Septuagint as Holy Writ and the Philosophy of the Translators," HUCA 46 (1975), Orlinsky provides a lengthy footnote (n. 2, pp. 89-90) citing numerous works on the subject.

/23/ See for example the critiques by A. Kaminka, Studien zur Septuaginta, 1928, p. 9; J. Ziegler, Untersuchungen zur Septuaginta des Buches Isaias, 1934, pp. 31-46; idem, Die Einheit der Septuaginta zum Zwölfprophetenbuch, 1934-35, pp. 1-16; idem, "Der textkritische Wert der Septuaginta des Buches Job," Miscellanea Biblica, II, 277-96, 1934; A.C. Johnson, H.S. Gehman, E.H. Kase, The John H. Scheide Biblical Papyri: Ezekiel, 1938, pp. 52-73; I.L. Seeligmann, The Septuagint Version of Isaiah, 1948, pp. 39-42; D.W. Gooding, The Account of the Tabernacle, 1959 (the book argues for a unity in the translation of the LXX of Exodus, except for Ex. 38 which is seen to come from a different hand; cf. Chs. 4-7 of the book); T. Muraoka, "Is the Septuagint Amos VIII 12 - IX 10 a Separate Unit?" VT 20 (1970), 496-500; D. Barthélemy, Les Devanciers d'Aquila, 1963, pp. 91ff.

/24/ Some representative examples are the following: E. Duval, "Le texte grec de Jérémie d'après une étude récente," RB 12 (1903), 394-404; L. Köhler, "Beobachtungen am hebräischen und griechischen Text von Jeremia Kap. 1-9," ZAW 29 (1909), 1-39, esp. p. 5. n. 4; W.W. Graf von Baudissin, Kyrios als Gottesname im Judentum und seine Stelle in der Religionsgeschichte, 1929,

I, 191, n.1; R.A. Martin, The Syntax of the Greek of Jeremiah,
Part I, 1957, p. 7; W. Rudolph, Jeremia, (HAT 12), 1968,
p. xxiii; E. Würthwein, Der Text des Alten Testaments, 1966,
p. 53, n. 1.

/25/ Ziegler says, "Bei der Untersuchung des Übersetzungs
charakters ist zu beachten, dass die Ier. LXX nicht einheitlich
ist. Dies haben schon ältere Textkritiker bemerkt, so Spohn.
Thackeray nimmt zwei Übersetzer an . . . . Mann muss Thack.
zustimmen . . . ." Ieremias, p. 128, n. 1. In Beiträge he speaks
for instance of "dem zweiten Ier. Übersetzer," pp. 28-29 and
passim.

/26/ The Minuses and Pluses of the LXX Translation of Jeremiah
as Compared with the Massoretic Text, unpublished dissertation,
Jerusalem, 1977, p. 159. Since the days of K.H. Graf (1862,
pp. xlff.) and F. Giesebrecht (1907, pp. xxvff.) it has been
commonplace to say that the the LXX text is shorter than the MT
by 2700 words or 1/8 the total of the Hebrew text. These
figures now need to be corrected by the computer aided counts of
Min. For a list of the major LXX omissions see, for instance,
A. Gelin, Dictionnaire de la Bible, IV, col. 857ff.

/27/ MT order: Egypt, Philistines, Moab, Ammonites, Edom,
Damascus, Kedar, Elam, Babylon. LXX order: Elam, Egypt, Babylon,
Philistines, Edom, Ammonites, Kedar, Damascus, Moab.

/28/ Prologue to Jeremiah, PL 24, col. 679.

/29/ Dissertatio de variis vitiis LXX. interpretum versioni
ante B. Origenis aevum illatis, Oxford, 1710, p. 12.

/30/ E.g. HTR 57 (1964), esp. 287 (n. 28), 298-99; IEJ
16 (1966), esp. 82 (n. 6), 84-85, 92-93 (n. 36), 94; "The
Evolution of a Theory of Local Texts," QHBT, esp. pp. 308-09.

/31/ Relevant studies by Tov are the following: "L'incidence
de la critique textuelle sur la critique littéraire dans le livre
de Jérémie," RB 79 (1972), 189-99; "Exegetical Notes on the
Hebrew Vorlage of the LXX of Jeremiah 27(34)," ZAW 91 (1979),
73-93; "Some Aspects of the Textual and Literary History of the
Book of Jeremiah," in P. M. Bogaert (ed.), Le Livre de Jérémie
(BETL 54), 1981, pp. 145-67. For the work of Min see above,
n. 26.

/32/ E.g. RB 81 (1974), 631 (F.L.); CBQ 38 (1976), 109-10
(R.W. Klein); JJS 28 (1977), 198 (P. Wernberg-Møller); SOTS
Book List, 1975, pp. 35-36 (W. McKane). Two extended reviews--
both critical--are those by G.F. Hasel in BibOr 32 (1975), 236-
38, and M. Dahood in Biblica 56 (1975), 429-31.

NOTES TO CHAPTER II

/1/   A number of MSS listed by Ziegler (Ieremias, pp. 8-10)
are incomplete or fragmentary and do not contain Ch. 29; these
are 147, 198, 231, 393, 445, 449, 456, 567, 951, 966, 980.

An additional nine MSS exist which do contain the text of
Jer 29 but have not been collated for this study; they are 97,
228, 420, 430, 435, 461, 501, 568, 684. These late and less
important minuscules were among those not collated for the
Göttingen edition of Jer; they were therefore not included in
the Unternehmen's photograph/microfilm collection and consequently were unavailable to me there. MSS 97 (known in HP and
Nestle-Dahse by the number 33) and 228 were collated by HP (from
whence they were taken over by Nestle-Dahse). These two, along
with 430, 435, and 568 are "Catena" MSS and contain the same
type of text as that described below in the section on the C
group (pp. 76-81). MSS 420 and 501 are dependent on 631 and 36
respectively, both of which have been collated for this study.

Ziegler (p. 11) also lists MSS 349, 533, and 573 as containing Jer texts but this information is incorrect according to
Rahlfs' Verzeichnis. The MSS in question are indeed Catena
texts as noted by Ziegler, but they do not contain the book of
Jer (cf. Rahlfs, Verzeichnis, p. 26, pp. 186-7, p. 205).

Another MS collated by HP (followed by Nestle-Dahse) is 41,
but this MS according to Rahlfs' Verzeichnis is one of those
which is "vorschollen."

/2/   In the collation of HP this codex is cited by the
abbreviation "Alex" (for a MS reading included in the main text
of Grabe's edition of Alexandrinus) and by the Roman numeral III
(for a MS reading not incorporated into Grabe's text). Tischendorf used the symbol "Ax" in his critical apparatus.

/3/   A page reference followed by an asterisk (e.g.,
p. 347*) indicates the back side of a codex leaf.

/4/   Symbol in HP: XII. In the collation of Field this MS
is known both as "Cod. XII" and "Cod. Jes.," the latter name
coming from Montfaucon's designation of it as "Ms. Jes[uitarum].

/5/   The alternative and more common symbol for this MS--at
least in NT studies--has been the Hebrew letter א, but typing
and printing expediency favours the use of the letter S.

/6/   Symbol in HP: 23.

/7/   Those oracles with different page number for the

Philistine and Edom oracles follow the Hebrew arrangement of the text. An exception is MS 106 which has a special order (see below, p. 89).

/8/ In Field's collation this MS is designated 87*.

/9/ In Field's collation this MS is designated 87. MS 88 in Field has reference to a collation by Bernardo Stephanopoli of a not very accurate copy of the original codex executed by Leo Allatius (d. 1669).

/10/ This MS is one of the few which contains both Old and New Testaments; in BM it is referred to by the letter "p."

/11/ Designated 144 in HP and Nestle-Dahse.

/12/ This papyrus, containing fragmentary verses from Chs. 28-32, was one of five papyri unavailable to Ziegler at the time of his publication (the others--which do not contain Jer 29-- are 804, 817, 837, and 984). However, the yield of attested text from Jer 29 in 986 is not great: only the two end letters -υς from the definite article τους in 29:11!

/13/ There exist at least three further Latin allusions to the text of the Philistine and Edom oracles (Biblia Patristica, Vol. 2):

1) Origen, in his commentary on Matthew (GCS, Origenes XI, p. 7), is thought indirectly to hint at 29(47):4 in the following remark: ". . . quomodo et visio Tyri vel quaecumque prophetantur de Tyro vel de principe Tyri, quomodo etiam visio quadrupedum in deserto apud Esaiam pendent in duobus istis mandatis."

2) Pseudo-Cyprian in Adversus Iudaeos (CCL 4, p. 273; also in the edition of D. van Damme, Freiburg, 1969, p. 127) may have 29:19(49:18) in mind in the phrase "et ad solitudinem Sodomae patriam eorum redegit."

3) Victorinus Poetovionensis in In Apocalypsim (CSEL 49, p. 52) may allude to 29:23(49:22) // MT 48:40 in the phrase "et quod morte devicta ascenderit in caelis extendens alas suas."

However, these allusions are so remote and secondary that they have not been taken up in the collation.

/14/ Walton made no attempt to correlate the MT and LXX sequence of oracles; as a result, LXX Ch. 29 (and daughter VSS) is found opposite MT Ch. 29, Jeremiah's letter to the exiles!

/15/ The term preferred by Ernest C. Colwell ("Method in Classifying and Evaluating Variant Readings," pp. 96-97). For

Colwell a "variation unit" is defined as a certain length of
text "wherein our manuscripts present at least two variant
forms; it is that passage in which differences occur." By this
concept Colwell wished to avoid the impression of giving special
recognition to a collation text over against which "variants"
are plotted (see also the article by E.J. Epp, "Toward the
Clarification of the Term 'Textual Variant'," in the George
D. Kilpatrick FS, esp. pp. 156-157). One can appreciate
the misunderstanding Colwell is trying to avoid, but the fact
remains that the only practical way to proceed is to use one
particular text against which to plot other readings. It
only needs to be emphasized again that this collation text is
entirely neutral and that no value judgement on the "variants"
to that text is intended at this stage.

/16/ Even earlier, groupings of MSS had already been
noticed by Holmes and Parson in the process of their collations
(cf. the comments in the preface to Vol. I on the peculiar text
represented by MSS 19, 108, 118 in the Pentateuch).

/17/ Exceptions to the principle of extension have to do
with MSS that change text type in mid-course; e.g., 130 is
under influence of the L group in Chs. 1-9, similarly 538 in
Chs. 17-20, 37-38, 48-49 (cf. Ziegler, Ieremias, p. 83).

/18/ By the term "recension" in this discussion is to be
understood a text that has been subjected to consistent and
deliberate revision, as opposed to one that has been formed by
accidental or ad hoc scribal change.

/19/ Previous scholars (e.g. Thackeray, Grammar, p. 4;
Soisalon-Soininen, Der Charakter der asterisierten Zuzätze in
der Septuaginta, p. 1; D.W. Gooding, Recensions of the LXX
Pentateuch, p. 5) have pointed to the Origenic recension as the
place to start in the work of LXX text restoration, and my
research confirms the methodological validity of this approach.

/20/ Greek text in GCS, Origenes X, p. 388. English
translation taken mainly from M.F. Wiles, "Origen as a Biblical
Scholar," CHB I, p. 457.

/21/ Other references by Origen to his use of the critical
signs can be found in Epistula ad Africanus, PG 11, cols. 56-60;
Johannescommentar, GCS, Origenes IV, p. 410; Die Schrift vom
Gebet, GCS, Origenes II, p. 332.

The traditional view that Origen took over the Αρισταρχεια
σηματα from the Alexandrian grammarians in his work on the
Hexapla is well presented by Swete, Introduction, pp. 69ff. In
more recent times the question has been raised by P. Kahle
whether these signs were ever present in the Hexapla at all
("The Greek Bible Manuscripts Used by Origen," JBL 79 [1960],
116). It is true that Origen nowhere explicitly states that

he employed these signs in the Hexapla itself. As Jellicoe has
observed (SMS, p. 124), such use is something we infer from his
writings but the inference may be quite incorrect. For our
present purposes, however, the question is purely academic. The
relevant point is that Origen on his own testimony--and this
can hardly be controverted--did use these signs somewhere.
Jellicoe suggests in response to Kahle's challenge that Origen
some time after the completion of the Hexapla may have composed
a separate recension of the LXX with the signs included, but
this is pure speculation and has no more merit than the traditional view. Notwithstanding the absence of the signs in
Mercati's Hexaplaric fragment of the Psalms (a phenomenon which
may be open to other explanations, cf. Bo Johnson, Die Hexa-
plarische Rezension des 1. Samuelbuches der Septuaginta, pp.
14-15), it still seems in order to speak of the fifth column
text of the Hexapla as containing the LXX recension of Origen
replete with the critical signs.

/22/ It goes without saying that not every asterized
reading in our MSS is uncritically to be attributed to Origen.
The question of the reliability of the signs is a problem that
must be dealt with case by case. This will be demonstrated in
the analysis below.

/23/ In Ziegler's text referred to by the italicized O.

/24/ Critical signs are occasionally found in other MSS
besides those mentioned here, e.g. at 29:4 in MSS 449-770 (see
below, p. 51).

/25/ Other forms of the obelus attested elsewhere are
— ⊤ ÷ (cf. Field, I, lv-lvi). The sign ⟵ is of infrequent
occurrence and is unique to Syh. Field devoted a special
section to a discussion of this sign (I, lxiv-lxvii) and
concluded that it is merely a different form of the obelus.
Ziegler agrees with this in regard to its use in Jer (Ieremias,
pp. 78-79), but in Isa (Isaias, p. 59, n. 1) and in Ez
(Ezechiel, pp. 42-43) he thinks it is used rather as a kind of
index to point out a reading present in Syh but absent in 88.

/26/ The mechanics of typing the present MS singlespaced
on a micro-printer has made the use of conventional superscripts
difficult to incorporate, hence the form "86mg" (cf. above,
p. 23).

/27/ See below, p. 53, n. 30 for a discussion of the
reliability of Hexaplaric signs on double readings.

/28/ Compare the comment by Margolis, "The principle of
expressing the Hebrew nota accusativi was present to the mind of
Origen when he started his work of revision; where he failed to
live up to it in the earlier edition he made up for the omission
in the subsequent recension" (Margolis is speaking of the

Hexapla and the Tetrapla editions respectively), "Textual
Criticism of the Greek Old Testament," Proceedings of the
American Philosophical Society 67 (1928), 194.

/29/ This view was defended by Wevers in his article, "A
Study in the Textual History of Codex Vaticanus in the Books of
Kings," ZAW 64 (1952), 189. S.P. Brock came to a negative
conclusion on this subject in his study of The Recensions of
the Septuagint Version of I Samuel, 1966, p. 55.

/30/ The same pattern of new reading asterized, old reading no sign may be observed in 88-Syh on eleven occasions elsewhere in Jer (3:19, 5:5, 6:12, 31:30, 31:31, 34:7, 36:2, 38:8,
12, 39:8, 51:28). On eight occasions in 88-Syh both elements of
a double reading are marked (new reading asterized, old reading
obelized: 2:6, 4:20, 6:2, 31:36, 37:6, 38:13,14, 45:9). Six
times in 88-Syh neither part of a double reading has preserved a
sign (29:14, 33:17, 38:12, 48:9, 49:1, 51:23, cf. Ziegler, Ieremias, p. 79). These statistics point to the inconsistency with
which Origen's critical signs have been preserved even in our
primary Hexaplaric witnesses. A similar conclusion was reached
by C.T. Fritsch in his article, "The Treatment of the Hexaplaric
Signs in the Syro-Hexaplar of Proverbs," JBL 72 (1953), 169-81.

/31/ An alternative explanation might be that επιπτησεται
was intended to translate יעלה (cf. the translation πτεροφυη-
σουσιν for יעלו in Isa 40:31), but this seems less likely.
According to 86mg and Syh/mg, both Aquila and Symmachus sub-
stituted αναβησεται for επιπτησεται (αναβαινω is the standard
translation of עלה both in Aquila and in the LXX), while the
reading και επιπτησεται of Symmachus in 86mg is definitely sub
asterisco indicating an addition; also the presence of the
conjunction with επιπτησεται suggests that this verb corresponds
to the Hebrew וידאה rather than יעלה.

/32/ Where it is assumed, but cannot be proved because of
the nature of the Syriac language, that Syh attests the same
reading as 88, this is indicated by Syh being placed in paren-
thesis thus, 88(-Syh).

/33/ In the case of the asterized addition of τους
αλλοφυλους in 29:4, Ziegler is of the opinion that it should be
attributed to α'θ' (as in Qmg) rather than ο' (as in 86mg), cf.
the notation in the second apparatus of the Göttingen edition.

/34/ Jerome's words are: "vix enim unus aut alter in-
venietur liber, qui ista [i.e. additamenta hexaplaris] non
habeat" (CSEL 55, p. 389).

/35/ For example, Ziegler has determined that 233 is a MS
heavily influenced by the Hexaplaric recension and wherever
possible associates it with the O group. There is no evidence
in Jer 29 which would in itself lead to this conclusion and the

matter can be decided only on the basis of a study of the entire
book. In fact, it will be argued below (p. 102) that 233 is not
Hexaplaric either in these oracles or in the entire OAN section.

/36/ This is the same methodology as that employed by S.P.
Brock in his unpublished Oxford dissertation, The Recensions of
the Septuagint Version of I Samuel, cf. p. ix.

/37/ Again this symbol differs from the italicized L employed by Ziegler; in the latter's text the joint attestation
of the sub-groups L + l is marked L'. In the critique of
Ziegler's text (Ch. III), this study employs Ziegler's italicized
symbols in the case of a direct quote from his apparatus (e.g.
p. 101 below); elsewhere, the unitalicized forms are used.

/38/ MSS which deviate from a group are best indicated by
a superscript thus, 51⁻⁵¹⁻⁶²⁻⁴⁴⁹' Again, the mechanics of typing
this particular MS has necessitated an adjustment in notation.
In our documentation, deviating MSS follow the slash thus, L/-51
-62-449' (cf. p. 23 above).

/39/ An unintentional scribal change from π to σ is also
theoretically possible.

/40/ ιω' = Ιωσιππος, a new translator whose readings are
attested approximately 100 times in Jer (cf. Ziegler, Ieremias,
pp. 102, 106). In Jer 29 we have additional examples of his
translation in vv. 3(2x), 4, 9, and 20.

/41/ In the majority text the phrase reads ΟΤΙΤΑΧΥΕΚΔΙΩΣΩ.
In the hypothetically faulty uncial, the middle arm of the ε
may have been missing and hence the letter might have been read
as a sigma (ς). To make sense of the resultant text,
ΟΤΙΤΑΧΥΕΚΔΙΩΣΩ, the first part was read as ΟΤΙ ΤΑΧΥς, followed
by full stop. The Κ was then taken for conjunction ΚΑΙ, and the
latter part read ΚΑΙ ΔΙΩΣΩ (cf. the remark by Ziegler, Ieremias,
p. 81 that several erroneous readings show that L goes back to
an uncial "codex archetypus").

/42/ The notation "Tht./p" signifies that only some (p =
pars) of the Theodoret MSS have this reading.

/43/ The incidence of Chr./Tht. readings in this section
would probably have been higher still had the whole of the
chapter been extant in Chr./Tht. For it should be understood
that when Chr./Tht. fail to support a reading from O/L (or L
alone) this is more often due to the fact that the reading in
question is not quoted by Chr./Tht. than to the fact that they
have a different reading.

/44/ There are a total of six double readings in the L
recension of Jer 29. They are brought together in the following
list:

29:6   εως τινος κοφεις / εως ποτε συστραφησεσθε

29:10   σου/ου

29:11   (το) σπερμα αυτου / δια χειρα

29:12   ινα σωθωσιν / και εγω αυτους διασωσω

29:14   βοσορ / εν μεσω μερους

29:20   και τους νεανισκους επ αυτην επιστησατε /
        και τις εκλεκτος προς αυτην επισκεφομαι

/45/ The omission in v. 8 of ωχετο σοφια αυτων in L/-51
-407-449') is undoubtedly due to scribal parablepsis: συνετων
ωχετο σοφια αυτων.

/46/ "Constantinopilis usque Antiochiam Luciani martyris
exemplaria probat," Praefatio Hieronymi in librum Paralipomenon,
PL 28, col. 1392.

/47/ See the works of Ceriani ("Le recensioni dei LXX e la
versione latina detta Itala," p. 1, R. Istituto Lombardo,
1866); Field (Origenis Hexaplorum quae supersunt . . .
fragmenta, I, 1875, pp. lxxxiv-xciv; II, pp. 428-29); Lagarde
(Ankündigung, p. 22; Pars Prior, pp. xiii-xv; Mitteilungen,
I, 175), Rahlfs (Septuaginta-Studien, III) and G.F. Moore ("The
Antiochian Recension of the Septuagint," The American Journal of
Semitic Languages 29 [1912-13], 37).

/48/ See "La prétendue 'recension lucianique'" in Les
Devanciers d'Aquila, 1963, pp. 126-27, and especially his "Post-
Scriptum: la 'recension lucianique'," an appendix to the article
"Les problèmes textuels de 2 Sam 11,2 - 1 Rois 2,11 reconsidérés
a la lumière de certaines critiques des 'Devanciers d'Aquila',"
in 1972 Proceedings (Septuagint and Cognate Studies 2), 1972,
pp. 64-89. Barthélemy proposes that the term "recension" be
reserved for a text that gives evidence of deliberate approximation towards the Hebrew ("Post-Scriptum," pp. 72-74). But this
requirement vis-à-vis the Hebrew seems too limiting. Normally
the term has been used with reference to a text that has undergone conscious revision according to certain discernible guide-
line--whatever the direction of the revision. According to the
latter definition, the L group of Jer certainly qualifies as a
"recension." Cf. above n. 18, p. 256.

/49/ The situation which obtains in Jer is therefore quite
different from the text commonly labeled Lucianic in Sam where
Wellhausen already showed that it contained many valuable ancient readings lost elsewhere in the Greek tradition.

/50/ According to Rahlfs' Verzeichnis there exist another
four Catena MSS of Jer, namely 97, 430, 435, 567 (fragmentary),

and 568. Contra Ziegler's assertion that MSS 349, 533, and 573
are also Catena MSS containing the book of Jer, see p. 14, n. 1
above; contra Ziegler's contention that MS 68 is dependent on
the Catena text, see below, p. 93, n. 60.

/51/ The plus sign at the end of an entry such as Q-V+ has
reference to the collection of minuscules normally associated
with the Q group, e.g. 26-46-86'-(130)-233-(239)-534-544-(613).

/52/ C readings have not been documented in these lists.

/53/ The discovery of pre-Hexaplaric revisions or recensions is nothing new; cf. the earlier discussions by D.W.
Gooding, "The Argument for a Pre-Origenic Recension," pp. 88-89
in his Cambridge thesis, The Greek Deuteronomy (1954), G. Zuntz,
"Der Antinoe Papyrus der Proverbia und das Prophetologion,"
ZAW 68 (1956), 124-84, and P. Katz, "Frühe hebräisierende
Rezensionen der Septuaginta und die Hexapla," ZAW 69 (1957),
77-84. Most recently one thinks of the Kaige recension discovered by Barthélemy. My conclusions on the character of the Q
text--which were reached quite independently--correspond to
those of Ziegler (Ieremias, p. 63) and thus tend to confirm the
soundness of his interpretation (contra R. Tournay, RB 65
[1958], 292, in a review of Ziegler's Jer text).

/54/ Compare the very similar textual phenomena in the
recensions of 1 Sam were readings attested within the limits of
O/D + L/E are likely to be Hexaplaric, whereas those with wider
support or those without the support of O/D are less likely so
(Brock, Recensions, pp. 127ff.).

/55/ "Le recensioni dei LXX de la versione latina detta
Itala," 1886, p. 106; De Codice Marchaliano seu Vaticano graeco
2125 Prophetarum, 1890, pp. 48ff., 105ff.

/56/ R.R. Ottley, Isaiah According to the Septuagint, I,
1904, pp. 6ff., 14ff.; II, 1906, pp. xff., xxxiff; Handbook to
the Septuagint pp. 91ff; W.O.E. Oesterley, Studies in the Greek
and Latin Versions of the Book of Amos, 1902, p. 2 ("That Q
contains the Hesychian text is universally admitted"); F.C.
Burkitt, EB, IV, 1903, col. 5021 ("the Hesychian text is best
represented by the first hand of Codex Marchalianus");
W. Grossouw, The Coptic Versions of the Minor Prophets, 1938,
p. 16; A. Vaccari, "The Hesychian Recension of the Septuagint,"
Biblica 46 (1965), 60-66; H.S. Gehman, JBL 48 (1929), 329-32,
and HSDB, 1963, p. 351; J.W. Wevers, IDB, IV, 1962, p. 275.

/57/ Rahlfs was skeptical about being able to trace the
Hesychian text, cf. Septuaginta, I, p. xxxi, even though in his
earlier Septuaginta Studien, II, 1907, pp. 183-97, he had
identified the Hesychian recension with the Lower Egyptian text
in Psalms. Ziegler has been negative throughout, cf. Isaias,
p. 23, Ezechiel, p. 29, n. 3, Daniel, p. 47, n. 1. Others have

tried to identify it with the B text, e.g., Grabe, Letter to Mill, 1705; this proposition has recently been revived by Jellicoe, JBL 88 (1963), 409-18.

/58/ Ceriani, De codice Marchaliano, pp. 34-35; Swete, Introduction, p. 144.

/59/ Those listed are the more significant A readings; there are of course other unique A readings which are merely clerical and orthographic.

/60/ Another pair of minuscules that belong to this group are 68 and 122, but these are near identical copies of B, at least in Jer. Ziegler describes 68 as a Catena text (Ieremias, p. 11), but this is definitely not so, at least not in Jer. Some examples from Jer 29 that prove the dependence of 68 and 122 on B are the following:

29:3   εφ B S 68 122 130] επι rel.

29:4   επερχομενη B 68 122] ερχομενη rel.

29:9   δαιδαμ B 68 122] δεδαν 407 538 544; δεδανω 534; δαιδαν rel.

29:10   ως B S 68 122] ωσπερ A-106-410 C-613; ωσει rel.

29:11   om. και B S 68 122 130

29:13   ειπε(ν) B S 68 122 538] λεγει rel.

29:21   αυτην B S* 68 122 106 410 130 538] αυτη A; αυτης S* 26; αυτους rel.

29:22   εφοβηθη B S 68 122 538] εσ(ε)ισθη rel.

/1/ See the variants listed above p. 5, n. 4.

/2/ A comparative chart of selected readings from Jer 29 illustrates the kind of trivial modifications found in various editions of the LXX <u>textus</u> <u>receptus</u> (in the chart c = Bc, * = B*):

B	Six.	Maius	Bagster	Tisch.	Swete
29:4 εξολεθρευσει (εξολο. Bc)	c	c	c	c	*
29:5 απεριφη (απερρ. Bc)	c	*		c	c	*
29:5 Ενακειμ	-κιμ	*	-κιμ	-κιμ	*
29:6 ουκ (ουχ Bc)	c	c	c	c	c
29:10 καταλιψουσιν (καταλειψ. Bc)	c	c	c	c	c
29:10 καταλιμμα (καταλει. Bc)	c	c	c	c	*
29:10 επιθησουσιν	-σι	*	-σι	-σι	*
29:12 υπολιπεσθαι (υπολειπ. Bc)	c	c	c	c	*
29:12 ζησεται (ζηση. Bc)	c	c	c	c	*
29:12 χηραι	αι χ.	*	αι χ.	αι χ.	*
29:13 αθοωμενη (αθωω. Bc)	c	c	c	c	c
29:17 νοσσειαν (νοσσι. Bc)	c	c	c	c	c
29:19 καθιση	-σει	*	-σει	-σει	*
29:19 ενοικησει	κατοι.	*	κατοι.	κατοι.	*
29:20 στησται (στησε. Bc)	c	c	c	c	c

29:21 συνφηθωσιν   *   * *
  (συμφηθωσι Bc)   c c   c   c c   c c

29:21 αυτην   -τους   *   -τους   -τους   *

29:23 εκτεινει   *
  (εκτεν. Bc)   c   c   c   c

/3/ Cf. above, pp. 7-8. He was, of course, aided by a
great deal of scholarship that had already been devoted to the
study of Jer-LXX (cf. his remark, "Die notierte Literatur zeigt,
dass bereits in ausgiebiger Weise die LXX von Ier. Thr. Bar.
untersucht worden ist," Beiträge, p. 6).

/4/ Note that Lagarde listed the witnesses in this order,
"Noch einmal," pp. 230-31.

/5/ One wonders whether the subdivisions in some of the
other editions have become overly refined, e.g. in Isaias L''' =
1I + 1II + 1III, and C'' = cI + cII.

/6/ See his comments in Duodecim Prophetae, pp. 138-39;
however, in Isaias the explanatory sheet "Erklärung der Zeichen
und Abkurzungen" contains an extensive list of "codices mixti."

/7/ Cf. above the discussion on the sub-divisions within L,
pp. 72-74.

/8/ For example, why in 29:15 are 106 239 538 not joined
by hyphens in attesting the reading παραγινεσθε, especially
since earlier in the same verse V-239-538 are joined by hyphens
in attesting the reading τα εθνη (106 is also one of the minuscules which sometimes joins the Q group, cf. Ieremias, p. 60)?

/9/ These extraordinary omissions are as follows:

In Isa

15:1	106 538txt 109 91txt-490txt	
17:1	106 538txt	
19:1	106 538txt 407 736txt	
21:1	106 538txt 301	
21:11	106 538txt 393	
22:1	106 538txt 763txt	
23:1	106 538txt 763txt 407txt 456	

In Jer

26(46):13		106 538txt
27(50):1		106 538txt
29(47):1		106 538txt Bo Arm/p
29:8(49:7)	46	106 538txt
30(49):1	46	106 538txt Arm/p

30:6(49:28)   106 538txt
30:12(49:23)   106 538txt 763txt Arm/p

/10/ For example, for the reading ιδου μικρον at 29:16 Ziegler cites all the supporting and non-supporting evidence; why he made an exception in this case is not entirely clear.

/11/ Ziegler's comment to the effect that this calculation "ist nicht allzu schwierig" (Ieremias, p. 138) is not entirely fair. For someone familiar with the MS evidence for a particular book such calculations may not be too difficult, but for the occasional reader who quickly needs to know the supporting evidence for a particular reading the process is less simple.

/12/ Additions to the first apparatus in the 1976 reprint (those in bold print):

29:2   γην] pr. την   449* 538

29:6   αναπαυσαι] pr. και C'-613

29:9   Δεδαν 407 538 544

29:14   εις αιωνα] εις αιωνος O 51 449

29:15   απεστειλε] εξαπεστειλε(ν) c 613 534

29:17   ενεχειρησε] ενεχειρισε(ν) O L'/ 62 87 et al.

29:23   οψεται] αναβησεται και επιστησεται (επιπτησεται 62 407 449 = 1)

Deletions:

29:2   αλαλαξουσιν] ολολυξουσι (λυζ. 22* 48* 449)

29:8 9 αυτων, ηπατηθη το προσωπον αυτων] om. αυτων‾αυτων 87 106

Further recommended additions are the following:

29:1   επι τους αλλοφυλους] + ος (ως 22c-62)

29:2   κεκραξονται] κραξονται   S* 62 86c

29:11   ωλοντο] ωλετο   O(sub ※)-Qmg-86mg

29:14   καταρασιν] επικαταρασιν   L' Chr. Tht.

29:14   εση] > 710 Chr.

29:16   εδωκα σε εν] εδωκας εν   239 534

29:17   τρυμαλιας] εν τρυμαλιαις 88-Syh/mg L/-51-62-407

29:17   υψωσεν] εαν υψωσης (-σεις A 26 239 86mg)

29:19   αι] οι 88 613

Suggestions for deletions:

29:11   τα κρυπτα] om. τα Tht.

/13/ Hence S.P. Brock's remark in the SOTS Book List,
1978, p. 46, to the effect that the new edition "is evidently a
straight reprint of the 1957 edition . . . without any alterations" remains essentially true with the exception of the
apparatus to Jer 29.

/14/ The term "contemporary" approach is mine rather than
Walters'. Walters employed no parallel term to the adjectives
"traditional" and "documentary" used to describe the first two
alternatives.

/15/ A couple of minor differences may, however, be noted.
In the case of the movable nu Ziegler follows the "school rule"
(cf. his comment Duodecim Prophetae, p. 118), whereas Rahlfs
always inserts the nu whether the following word beings with a
vowel or consonant. In the Edom oracle compare the following
spellings:

	Rahlfs		Ziegler
30:3	καταλειφουσιν	29:10	-ουσι
	επιθησουσιν		-ουσι
30:6	ειπεν	29:13	ειπε
30:8	απεστειλεν	29:15	-λε
30:10	ενεχειρησεν	29:17	-σε
30:12	ειπεν	29:19	ειπε
30:14	συμφησθωσιν	29:21	-σι

By contrast Ziegler appears always to employ the final
sigma for ουτως where Rahlfs occasionally omits it, cf. 13:9,
35:6.

/16/ See the comment by G.D. Kilpatrick in his review of
R. Hanhart's Zum Text des 2. und 3. Makkabäerbuches (1960): "It
is quite clear from these pages [i.e. Ch. 1] how much students
of the Greek Bible owe to Dr. P. Katz, but we have to distinguish
between what our authors wrote and what is philologically
correct," GGA 215 (1963), 12. See also a comment to the same
effect by T. Muraoka in his review of Walters' Text, JSS 19
(1974), 307.

/17/ W. Kappler, "Ziele und Aufgaben des Göttinger Septuaginta Unternehmens," GGA 202 (1940), 115-24.

/18/ The most common Hebrew equivalence is, as might be expected, שארית (Gen 45:7, 2 Re 14:7, 4 Re 19:31, Isa 14:30, Jer 27[50]:26, 47[40]:11) or שאר (Isa 10:22, 14:22), but it is also used to translate שריד in Jud 5:13, 4 Re 10:11, ניר in 3 Re 15:4, יתר in Job 22:20, and possibly שחים in Isa 37:30.

/19/ The interpretation of the phrase is complicated by the uncertainty regarding the reading δια χερα at the commencement of the verse which Ziegler emends to επιχειρα. But on the basis of the MS reading, the sentence ωλοντο δια χειρα αδελφου και γειτονος μου might be translated, "they have perished each by the hand of his brother and his neighbour," which seems preferable to ωλοντο δια χειρα αδελφου αυτου γειτονος μου, "they have perished each by the hand of his brother, my neighbour," where the deity seems to speak of Israel as "my neighbour."

/20/ The same kind of reasoning lies behind Ziegler's choice of the "concluding formula" λεγει/ειπε/φησι κυριος. In 1:19 and 2:3 Ziegler opts for the form λεγει κυριος on the basis of translation pattern (see below, p. 175, n. 28) against that of the main MS evidence (cf. his explanation in Beiträge, p. 38).

/21/ For a sampling of Kilpatrick's method applied to the LXX see his review of W. Kappler and R. Hanhart's editions of 1, 2, and 3 Maccabees in GGA 215 (1963), 10-22. A real desideratum for LXX scholarship would be a comprehensive analysis and critique of the craft of textual criticism as formerly and currently practiced in the editing of LXX texts --the same kind of analysis taking place in the field of NT textual criticism (e.g., the Kilpatrick FS, Studies in New Testament Language and Text [1976]; J.E. Epp, JBL 93 [1974], 386-414; idem, HTR 69 [1976], 211-57; D. Parker, NTS 24 [1977], 149-62).

/22/ "Diese Ausführungen zeigen, dass eine v o l l e Gewähr für die Ursprünglichkeit verschiedener Lesarten nicht immer geboten werden kann . . . . Die fortschreitende Forschung mag manche Lesarten, die im App. stehen, in den text aufnehmen und umgekehrt," Duodecim Prophetae, p. 133.

/23/ See the statistics given by B. Metzger, The Text of the New Testament, pp. 184-85.

/24/ Cf. K. Lake, The Text of the New Testament, pp. 9-10. For a review of the arguments advanced against the practice of emendation in the NT in a paper advocating a return to this practice, see the lively article, written with wit reminiscent of A.E. Houseman, by John Strungnell, "A Plea for Conjectural Emendation in the New Testament," CBQ 36 (1974), 543-58.

/25/ The lexicons distinguish between אביר* and אביר, the

former found only in the construct form אֲבִיר with יעקב (5x) or
ישראל (1x) referring to the deity, the latter in all other contexts. For the purpose of this review, no such distinction is
necessary.

/26/ The same tendency simply to employ the root meaning
of אביר is characteristic of the Minor Greek VSS. Thus Aquila,
where attested, almost uniformly uses δυναστης (Isa 34:7, 46:12,
Ps 21[22]:13, 49[50]:13, 77[78]:25, 131[132]:2), or δυνατος (Isa
10:33), except 1 Sam 21:7(8) αρχων (MS 57 sub σ') and Lam 1:15
υπερμεγεθης (probably reading אדיר). The other VSS were more
free but still stayed close to the base meaning, e.g. Symmachus
has δυναστης (Isa 49:26), δυνατος (Isa 10:33), κραταιος
(Isa 34:7), σκληρος (Isa 46:12), ταυρος (Ps 21[22]:13--acc. to
Field, citing Montfaucon), παμμεγας (Ps 67[68]:31), υπερηφανος
(Ps 75[76]:6), μεγαλος (Ps 77[78]:25), μεγιστανες (Lam 1:15);
Theodotion has δυναστης (Ps 77[78]:25), ισχυρος (Isa 34:7), and
κρατος (Isa 10:33).

Among the English VSS the RV tends in the same direction,
cf., Jud 5:22 "strong ones," and similarly Jer 8:16, 26(46):15.

/27/ The equivalence ταυρος/אביר (not always a correct
equivalence) was facilitated in each instance by the association
of אביר with some other animal, e.g. in Jer 27(50):11 ταυρος/
אביר is parallel to βοιδιον/עגלה. The English VSS agree that
the correct translation there is "strong horses" (RV) or "stallions" (RSV, NEB, JB). The LXX (mis)translation βοιδιον has
occasioned the further mistranslation of צהל by κερατιζω; צהל/
מצהלה is otherwise correctly and uniformly rendered in Jer by
χρεμετιζω/χρεμετισμος (cf. 5:8, 8:16, 13:27, 38[31]:7). The
important point to note, however, is that the meaning βοιδιον
was derived from the immediate context.

/28/ The majority of MSS have the reading ιππασιας ιππων
but this is undoubtedly a double reading, as recognized by
Giesebrecht (p. 231), Köhler (p. 16), Streane (p. 111), Rudolph
(ZAW, p. 279), and Ziegler (Beiträge, p. 99). That ιππασιας and
not ιππων was the original reading is made virtually certain by
the following considerations: it is inexplicable why the reading
ιππασιας should have been added to ιππων since the addition
would make a clear reading more difficult and would not correspond to the Hebrew; on the other hand, it is easy to see that
ιππων could have been added later to give sense to the Greek,
cf. the omission of ιππων in V-46-86-198-239-544 O-233 and some
of the VSS. Possibly ιππων was at one time a marginal gloss on
ιππασιας which was later incorporated into the text. Origen
probably found only ιππασιας in his Vorlage, otherwise he would
also have included ιππων, placing one of the words under the
obelus. Ziegler correctly prints only ιππασιας in the text.

/29/ All the MSS read ο μοσχος ο εκλεκτος but again
it is possible that we have here another double reading (so

Giesebrecht, p. 231; Köhler, p. 21; and Streane, p. 263).
Ziegler is also convinced that the pair forms a double reading
but is less certain which of the two words was original and
which was added later. In his discussion of this lectio duplex
(Beiträge, p. 96) he seems to prefer εκλεκτος as the original,
though he admits that μοσχος could also be right, in which case
εκλεκτος is a later approximation to the Hebrew. The ambiva-
lence is carried over into the body of the text where both words
are printed but o εκλεκτος is put in square brackets. Whether
μοσχος or εκλεκτος or even o μοσχος o εκλεκτος was the original
Greek, it is clear that the translation was derived from the
immediate context as a parallel to the Egyptian bull-god Apis (a
translation based in turn on the reading נס חף "Apis has fled"
versus MT נסחף "swept away").

/30/ These could represent different Vorlagen (for 1 Sam
21:8 cf. Lagarde's suggestion that the LXX testifies to a
reading אֹבִיל הָעֲיָרִים but see the remark by S.R. Driver, Notes,
p. 176; for Ps 75(76):6 BHS proposes כָּל-בַּעֲרֵי; for Isa 46:12
BHS suggests אֹבְדֵי), or they may be desperate attempts by the
translators to make sense of the Hebrew that for one reason or
another was difficult to understand (cf., for instance, the
various translations of אביר in the English VSS of Isa 46:12).
The Hebrew and Greek of Job is notoriously difficult to correlate and in the case of αδυνατος we cannot even be sure that
this was intended as a translation of אביר (cf. the question
marks in HR).

/31/ According to the researches of H.J.M. Milne and T.C.
Skeat (Scribes and Correctors of the Codex Sinaiticus, London,
1938, pp. 54-55), the book of Jer (along with Isa, Lam, MP, and
ShepHer) was copied by Scribe B. Milne and Skeat find it hard
to describe the careless habits of this copyist in moderate
language and are utterly amazed that he could have been chosen
for such an important job. They write, "He [i.e. Scribe B]
seems to have had no firm visual impression of Greek, so barbarous and grotesque are the forms which his misspellings can
present to the eye, and with such utter inconsistency does he
sway from correct to incorrect. . . . Pure blunders, like
telescoping of words and omission of letters or syllables, are
incredibly common. . . ; more curious is the wrong insertion
of the consonant in the middle of the word, as in π(ρ)οιηση
(Jer 37:24), δορ(μ)ατα (Jer 26:4), σα(ν)ρκαν (Jer 51:35).
Another frequent error is produced by metathesis, σεται for
εσται (Isa 35:6), διαμιεν for διαμενει (Jer 3:5). . . ." In the
light of this testimony it is not difficult to see how the οτ of
ο τοπος could have been inverted by metathesis to το, or how a
ρ might suddenly have appeared between π and ο of πος to yield
προς (cf. π(ρ)οιηση Jer 37:24).

/32/ If το προσωπον αυτων corresponds to הפנו this
presumably means that the translator read פנו as a collective
for פניו.

/33/ According to Ziegler (Beiträge, p. 68), Grabe proposed και κραυγη θαλασσης Σουφ; but this needs correction. The statement in the "Prolegomena" clearly reads, "pro θαλασσης ουκ in Rom. Co. legendum ist εν θαλασση Σουφ, juxta heb. ברים סוף."

/34/ This translation is found in Ex 10:19, 13:18, 15:4, 22, 23:31, Num 14:25, 21:4, 33:10,11, Deut 1:40, 2:1, 11:4, Josh 2:10, 4:23, 24:6, Jud 11:16(A text), Ps 105(106):7,9,22, 135(136):13,15, Neh 9:9. In 3 Re 9:26 the translation is της εσχατης.

/35/ According to Streane, the addition of the negative is found in 2:3(2x), 5:2, 9:5(4), 23:32, 28(51):58, 29:22(49:21), 38:35(31:37). The omission occurs in 2:25, 4:1, 5:3,10, 18:18, 28(51):3, 43(36):25. Streane also refers to Wellhausen, Der Text der Bücher Samuelis, p. 26, for evidence of the same phenomenon happening in 1 and 2 Re. Along the same lines one can compare the article by M.L. Klein, "Converse Translation: A Targumic Technique," Biblica 57 (1976), 515-37, esp. the section on the "Addition or Deletion of the Negative Particle," pp. 516-29).

/36/ Compare the device employed in the current Peshitta project, The Old Testament in Syriac, "General Preface," 1972, p. viii.

/37/ Compare J. Barr's review of Walters' The Text of the Septuagint, particularly his comment, "Walters seems to have belonged to an age which accepted the emendation of the text more readily than the present generation of scholars does," HJ 26 (1975), 61-63.

/38/ For some examples of conjectured readings that have been vindicated by papyri discoveries in Ezekiel, see Ziegler, Beiträge, p. 17.

NOTES TO CHAPTER IV

/1/ Thackeray actually delineated three translation units in the book, the third being the "Historical Appendix," Ch. 52, which he designated "Jeremiah γ"; however, he adduced only scant support for the third translator and seemed less sure of his case in this matter (cf. "The Greek Translators of Jeremiah," pp. 246, 260).

/2/ Ziegler's treatment of the multiple translator problem in Jer is in fact ambiguous and unsatisfactory. Several times he distinguishes between "Ier. I" and Ier. II" and refers to them as "der erste Ier.-Übersetzer" (Beiträge, p. 127) and "der zweite Ier.-Übers." (Beiträge, p. 49). This distinction then becomes the basis for text critical decisions, e.g., in the preference for the form λεγει κυριος at 1:19 and 2:3 where the majority of MSS have ειπε(ν) κυριος and φησι(ν) κυριος respectively (cf. Beiträge, pp. 37-38; Ieremias, p. 44). On other occasions he simply speaks of "der Übersetzer" apparently with reference to the whole book and makes decisions on the basis of the unity of the translation, e.g. his preference for the word καλαμηματα at 29:10 (i.e. in Jer b') versus the majority text reading καταλειμμα(-ατα) on the precedent of the translation καλαμασθε for עולל at 6:9 (i.e. in Jer a') (Beiträge, p. 48).

/3/ For elaboration of this part of Tov's argument see pp. 6, 42, 135 of the book, and particularly the appendix, "Why is Jer-R's Revision Preserved Only in Jer b'?" pp. 162-65.

/4/ Cf. LSJ. Usually the context is one of joy, exultation or victory rather than one of pain or grief, but the latter sense certainly is attested, including the NT usage at Mk 5:38.

/5/ Rahlfs. Jer a' 1:18 5:19 16:10 18:23 19:15 23:8

Jer b' 29:2 33:2,2 36:1 39:23 43:11,16,32 47:5 48:12 51:1

Elsewhere: Gen 19:4 Lev 6:15 Deut 22:19,29 Josh 6:13,20 2 Re 3:25 3 Re 2:26 12:24t 13:11 1 Chr 10:11 16:43 17:10 Esth 8:12x 9:28 Ps 21:24 Prov 25:4 Am 7:10 Zech 7:5 Ez 38:8

/6/ Ziegler. Jer a' 18:23 19:15 23:8

Jer b' 29:2 33:2,2 39:23 48:12 51:1

/7/ The same rendition in Hos and Ob is cited as evidence of the close relationship existing between Jer-LXX (especially Jer a' but sometimes, as here, Jer a'b') and the MP (Tov, p. 141).

/8/ Tov believes that the readings το υψος σου (from רמיתי
or רמיכי versus MT דמיתי) in 6:2 and επαρθητι in 29(47):6 (from
רמי versus MT דמי) are additional examples of the same deliberate attempt to avoid the roots דמס/דמה. Zlotowitz (p. 83)
argues against a confusion of ד and ר in the passages under
consideration.

/9/ Not 29(49):7 as in Tov, p. 31.

/10/ The totals include all occurrences of the translated
name in question whether or not a corresponding צבאות is found
in the MT. My totals do not always coincide with those of Tov.
For instance, in the case of σαβαωθ his total of 58 for Isa and
8 elsewhere seems to be based on the aggregate sums as found in
HR. My totals, where possible, are based on Ziegler's critical
texts. In the case of Jer we both record 7 occurrences of παντοκρατωρ in Jer b', but Tov obtains this figure by including
37(30):3 attested by SAVC but rejected by Ziegler, while he
fails to mention 38:36(31:35), a firmly attested occurrence of
παντοκρατωρ. Tov's reference to παντοκρατωρ in Jer 29:29 should
be corrected to 29:19.

/11/ σαβαωθ

        Josh 6:16(17)   1 Re 1:3,11,20 15:2 17:45
1 Esd 9:46   Isa 1:9,24   2:12 3:1 5:7,9,16,24,25 6:3,5 7:7
8:18 9:7(6) 10:16,24,33 13:4,13 14:22,24,27 17:4 18:7,7
19:4,12,16,25 21:10 22:5,12,14,15,17,25 23:9,11 25:6
28:5,22,29 29:6 31:4 37:16,32 39:5 44:6 45:13,14 47:4
48:2 51:15 54:5

/12/ παντοκρατωρ

        2 Re 5:10 7:8,25(H 26),27   3 Re 19:10,14
1 Chr 11:9 17:7,24   Sir 42:17   Hos 12:5   Am 3:13 4:13
5:14,15,16,27 9:5   Mi 4:4   Na 2:14 3:5   Hab 2:13
Zeph 2:10   Hag 1:2,5,7,9,14   2:4,6,7,8,9,9,11,23,23
Zech 1:3,4,6,12,14,16,17 2:8,9,11(H 12,13,15) 3:7,9,10 4:6,9
5:4 6:12,15 7:3,9,12,12,13 8:1,2,3,4,6,6,7,9,9,11,14,14,18,
19,20,21,22,23 9:15 10:3 11:4 12:5 13:7 14:16,17,21,21
Mal 1:4,6,8,9,10,11,12,14,17 4:1,3 (H 3:19,21)

        Jer a' 3:19 5:14 15:16 23:16 27(50):34
28(51):5,57

        Jer b' 29:15(45:18) 32:13(25:27) 38:36(31:35)
39(32):14,19 40(33):11 51(44):7   Bar 3:1,4

/13/ των δυναμεων

        Josh 5:13(H 14 צבא)   2 Re 6:2,18   3 Re 17:1 18:15
4 Re 3:14 19:20,31   Ps 23(24):10 45(46):8,12 47(48):9
58(59):6 68(69):7 79(80):5,8,15,20 83(84):2,4,9,13 88(89):9

/14/ One of the anomalies of the two translator/reviser problem in Jer is the fact that the most striking example of the differences between the two halves of the book, namely the form ουτως ειπε κυριος in Jer b' versus ταδε λεγει κυριος in Jer a', does not emerge until <u>after</u> Ch. 29, a chapter which in other respects is proved to be the watershed between the two halves. ταδε λεγει is found at 29:1,8 while the hybrid form ταδε ειπεν occurs in B-S-538 at 29:13 (cf. above p. 139). With reason Thackeray said that the joint had "ragged edges" (<u>The Septuagint and Jewish Worship</u>, p. 37; in "The Greek Translators of Jeremiah," p. 247, he spoke of "a certain mixture of the two vocabularies" in the opening chapters [29-31] of the b' portion).

/15/ These totals are based on Ziegler's text which means that for the purpose of statistics at least we accept the elimination of ταδε at 9:17, ουτως at 21:7, while reading λεγει rather than ειπεν at 29:13.

Comparison with Tov's numbers (p. 57) and mine reveals some discrepancies, but since Tov does not give references for most of his totals it is impossible to check one against the other. His total of 49 instances of ταδε λεγει in Re may include the formula at 1 Re 14:7 which, however, is found in a passage attested only by the A text among the uncials. For 2 Chr I count 6 rather than 5 occurrences of ταδε λεγει, while for MP I find 44 rather than 43. Where Tov does give references these are found to be incorrect in the following places: The translation of כה אמר יהוה by ταδε λεγει κυριος occurs in Jer 61 times not 58 times as stated by Tov, pp. 21,56,57. Tov's list on p. 56 fails to note the occurrences of ταδε λεγει at 2:2,5 and 28:36. The totals for ουτως ειπε in Jer b' are 71 not 69; Tov fails to mention 34:13, 40:12 and 41:2 (second occurrence), while his list includes Bar 2:21 (Bar references are not incorporated in my lists). Tov's total of 3 for ουτως λεγει includes 21:7 where, however, the ουτως is eliminated by Ziegler.

/16/ ταδε λεγει

      Gen 45:9   Ex 4:22 5:1,10 7:17 8:1(7:26)
8:20(16) 9:1,13 10:3 11:4 32:27   Num 20:14 22:16
Josh 7:13 22:16 24:2   Jud 6:8 11:15

      1 Re 2:27   2 Re 7:5,8 12:7,11 24:12
3 Re 2:30 11:31 12:24 13:2,21 17:14 20(21):19,19 21:2(3),
5,13,14,28,42 22:11   4 Re 1:4,6,11,16 2:21 3:16,17 4:43
7:1 9:3,6,12,18,19 18:19,29,31 19:36,20,32 20:1,5 21:12
22:15,16,18   1 Chr 17:7   2 Chr 11:4 18:10 20:15 21:12
24:20 36:23

      Am 1:6,9,11,13 2:1,4,6 3:11,12 5:3,4,16 7:11,17
Mi 2:3 3:5   Ob 1   Na 1:12   Hag 1:2,5,7 2:6,11
Zech 1:3,4,14,16,17 2:8(12) 3:7 6:12 7:9 8:2,3,4,6,7,9,14,
19,20,23 11:4   Mal 1:4

Isa 7:7   10:24   22:15   29:22   36:4,14,16   37:3,6,21
38:1,5   52:3   56:1,4   57:15   65:13   66:12

Jer a'   2:2,5,31   4:3,27   5:14   6:6,9,16,21,22   7:3,
20,21   8:4   9:7,15,23(6,14,22)   10:2,18   11:3,11,21   12:14
13:1,8,13   14:15   15:2,19   16:3,5,9   17:19,21   18:13   19:3,11,15
20:4   21:4,8,12   22:1,3,6,11,18   23:2,15,38   24:5,8   25:15(49:35)
27(50):18,33   28(51):1,33,36,58

Jer b'   29:1(47:2)   29:8,13(49:7,12;   but see above,
p. 139, for discussion of the variant ταδε ειπεν at 29:13[49:12]
in B-S-538)

Ez 2:4   3:11,27   5:5,7,8   6:3,11   7:2,5   11:5,7,16,17
12:10,19,23,28   13:3,8,13,18,20   14:4,6,21   15:6   16:3,36,59
17:3,9,19,22   20:3,5,27,30,39,47(21:3)   21:9,24,26,28(14,29,31,
33)   22:3,19,28   23:22,28,32,35,46   24:3,6,9,21   25:3,6,8,12,13,
15,16   26:3,7,15,19   27:3   28:2,6,12,22,25   29:3,8,13,19   30:2,
10,13,22   31:10,15   32:3,11   33:27   34:2,10,11,17,20   35:3,14
36:2,3,4,5,6,13,22,33,37   37:5,9,12,19,21   38:3,10,14,17
39:1,17,25   43:18   44:6,9   45:9,18   46:1,16   47:13

/17/   ουτως ειπε

1 Chr 17:4   2 Chr 12:5   18:26   34:23   2 Esd 1:2
Isa 18:4   21:6,16   31:4

Jer b'   30:1,6(49:1,28)   31(48):1,40   32:1,13,14,18
(25:15,27,28,32)   33(26):2,4,18   43:1,3,13,16(27:2,4,16,19)
35(28):2,11,13,14,16   36(29):4,8,10,21,31,32   37(30):2,5,12,18
38(31):2,7,15,16,23,36(35)   39(32):3,14,15,28,36,42   40(33):2,4,
10,12   41(34):2,2,13,17   42(35):17,18   43(36):29,30   44(37):7,9
45(38):2,3,17   46(39):16   49(42):9,15,18   50(43):10   51(44):2,7,
11,25,30   51:32,34(45:2,4)

/18/   ουτως λεγει

Gen 32:4(5)   Jud 11:15   1 Chr 21:10,11
2 Chr 34:24,26

Isa 8:11   28:16   30:12,15   37:33   42:5   43:1,14,16
44:2,6,24   45:1,11,14,18   48:17   49:7,8,22,25   50:1   51:22   52:4
65:8   66:1

Jer a'   14:10   23:16 (also 21:7, but this is
eliminated by Ziegler as a lectio duplex).

Jer b'   41(34):4   42(35):13

/19/   The following is a list of the textual variants for
the messenger formulas as found in Ziegler's apparatus:

Variants for ταδε λεγει: 4:3 ουτως λεγει S*;

13:1 ουτως ειπε(ν) L = οι γ';   17:19 ουτως ειπε(ν) L-198-538;
29:13 ταδε ειπεν B-S-538

          Variants for ουτως λεγει: 14:10 ταδε λεγει 86mg
710;   23:16 ουτως ειπε(ν) O-233 L;   41:4 ουτως ειπε(ν) O-86mg
-233 L;   42:13 ουτως ειπε(ν) O-233 L

          Variants for ουτως ειπε:

          The form ταδε λεγει is found in the L group (or part
thereof) at 31:40 32:13,18 35:2,14 36:8,21 37:18 38:7,16
39:14,28,42 41:2,17 43:29 44:7,9 45:3 49:15,18 51:11,25.

          The form ουτως λεγει is found in miscellaneous
MSS (indicated in the parentheses) at 35:2(233) 36:8(233)
36:22(534) 37:12(A 613) 38:16(233) 39:14(233) 40:12(Q-V+
OLC) 43:29(87txt) 51:7(239).

          Where the MF is missing in the LXX it has been sup-
plied in O/L by ταδε λεγει at 11:22 13:12 17:5 22:30 34:21
36:16,17,25 40:17,20,25 38:35 42:19 and by ουτως λεγει at
18:11.

          The most common variant in the above lists is the
change in the L recension from the anomalous form ουτως ειπε
to the standard usage ταδε λεγει, a change in keeping with the
tendency of that recension to prefer a more natural Greek.
However, the opposite change from ταδε/ουτως λεγει to ουτως
ειπε is found in 13:1 17:19 23:16 41:4 42:13.

     /20/ ταλαιπωρεω   4:13,20,20 9:19(18) 10:20 12:12

          ολλυμι   29:11(49:10) 30(49):3 31(48):1,15,
18,20 (Tov also includes 38[31]:2 where MT has שרידי).

          απολλυμι   29(47):4

          (εξ)ολεθρευω   5:6 28(51):53,55 29(47):4

          πλησσω Q-613   30:6(49:28)

     /21/ ταλαιπωρια   6:7,26 15:8 20:8 28(51):56

          ολεθρος   31(48):3,8,32

     /22/ μαχαιρα   Jer a'   2:30 4:10 5:12 9:16(15) 11:22
12:12 14:12,13,15,16,18 15:2,2,3,9 16:4 18:21,21 19:7
20:4,4 21:7,7,9 24:10 25:17(49:37) 26(46):10,14,16
27(50):16,21,35,36,36,37,37

          Jer b' 29(47):6 31(48):2,10 32:2,13,15,17,24
(25:16,27,29,31,38) 33(26):23 34:6(27:8) 38(31):2 39(32):24,36
41(34):17

ρομφαια   Jer a'   5:17   6:25

Jer b'   45(38):2   46(39):18   49(42):16,17,22
50(43):11,11   51(44):12,13,18,27,28

/23/   Compare, for example, the following mixtures of
μαχαιρα and ρομφαια in the Hexateuch and Ezekiel:

μαχαιρα   Gen 22:6,10   27:40   31:26   34:25,26   48:22
Ex 15:9   17:13   22:24(23)   Lev 26:8,25,33   Num 14:43
21:24   22:29,31   Deut 13:15(16)   20:13   32:25,41,42   33:29
Josh 5:2,3   10:11   19:47   21:42d   24:30a

ρομφαια   Gen 3:24   Ex 5:21   32:27   Num 22:23
31:8   Josh 5:12(13)   6:20(21)   8:24   24:12

μαχαιρα   Ez 5:2,12   26:6,8,9,11,15   28:7,23
30:4,5,6,11,17,21,22   31:17,18   32:12,19,21,23,23,24,26,27,28,
29,30,31,32   33:27   35:5,8   38:4,8,21   39:23

ρομφαια   Ez 5:1,2,12,17   6:3,8,11,12   7:15   11:8,10
12:14,16   14:17,21   21:9,11,12,14,15,19,20,28   23:10,25   24:21
29:8,10   30:24,25   30:10,11   33:2,3,4,6

/24/   εντελλομαι   1:7,17   7:22,23,23,31   11:4,4   13:5,6
14:14   17:22   19:5   23:32   27(50):21   28(51):59   29(47):7
39(32):23   42(35):6,10,14,18   43(36):5,8,26   45(38):10,27

συντασσω   33(26):2,8   34(27):3(4)   36(29):23
39(32):13,35   41(34):22   44(37):21

/25/   καιρος/ny   2:27,28   3:17   4:11   5:24   6:15   8:1,7,15
10:15   11:12,14,14(H 12)   14:8,19   15:11,11   18:23   26(46):21
27(50):4,16,20,27,31   28(51):6,18

χρονος/ny   29:9(49:8)   37(30):7   38(31):1

/26/   Origen tried to guess at the meaning of the word:
επιχειρον η το σκηπτρον παριστησιν η τους υπο την αρχην η τους
μισθωτους, επιχειρα γαρ ο μισθος   (Ghisler II 841 [not 481 as in
Schleusner, and Tov p. 83, n. 30]).

/27/   We call these "concluding formulas" because this
is their main, though certainly not their only function, cf.
R. Rendorff, ZAW 66 (1954), 28.

/28/   Again the statistics are based on Ziegler's text
which means reading λεγει at 1:19 and 2:3 (against the majority
text witnesses in both cases), taking 21:7 as a concluding
formula by eliminating ουτως and considering λεγει κυριος at
23:29 a double reading. The totals include all occurrences of
the Greek formula whether or not a corresponding formula is
found in the MT.

As often, my figures differ slightly from those of Tov. He
lists a total of 71 references for λεγει κυριος; my total is 75
(Tov omits the second occurrence of the formula at 2:19, 3:12
and 38[31]:35; also he neglects to mention the occurrences at
8:13 and 25:19). Under the reference for φησι κυριος Tov fails
to mention 34:12. There are also discrepancies between the
totals given here and those in Ziegler, Beiträge, p. 38, but
Ziegler does not give references. Somewhat surprisingly,
however, his statistics do not appear to be based.on his own
critical text, cf. the reference to φησι κυριος at 2:3 whereas
the text prints λεγει κυριος (this last example should have
been included with the other instances [1:19, 19:12] of readings
mentioned by Ziegler as differing from Rahlfs on the basis of
translation pattern).

         λεγει κυριος Jer a' 1:8,15,17,19 2:2,3,9,12,17,19,
19,22,29 3:1,12,12,13,14,16,20 4:1,9,17 5:1,9,15,18,22,29
6:12 7:11,19,30,32 8:1,13 9:9,24,25(8,23,24) 13:14,25 15:3,6
16:1,11,14,16 17:24 19:6,12 21:7 22:5,16,24 23:4,5,23,24,
30,33,7 25:19(49:39) 26(46):5,18,23,28 27(50):20,21,31
28(51):24,26,39,52,53,57   Jer b' 29:14(49:13) 32:17(25:31)
34:18(27:22) 51:35(45:5)

         φησι κυριος 30(49):2,15 31(48):12,35,38
34:12(27:15) 36(29):23 37(30):3,17,21 38(31):20,27,28,31,
32,33,35,35,37(37,37,36),38 41(34):22 46(39):18 49(42):11

         ειπε κυριος Jer a' 27(50):30,40   Jer b' 30:5,10
(49:5,32) 34:6(27:8) 37(30):8 38(31):1 41(34):5

/29/ φησι is found instead of λεγει in some MSS at 2:3
3:16 22:16 25:19 28:26 34:18. The form ειπε(ν) is found in
some MSS at 1:8,17,19 19:12 27:31.

         λεγει is found instead of φησι in various MSS at
30:2,15 31:12 36:23 37:3,21 38:27,31,32,35,37,38 49:11.
The form ειπε is found at 41:22.

         λεγει is found instead of ειπε in some MSS at 27:30
34:6 37:8 41:5. The form φησι(ν) is found at 27:30 30:10.

         When the formula נאם יהוה is missing in the LXX (as
it frequently is), it is usually added in the O and L recensions
(sometimes in conjunction with a few other MSS). The most common form of the addition by far is φησι(ν) κυριος (65 times:
3:10 5:11 7:16 8:17 9:3,6 12:17 13:11 15:9,20 16:15 18:6
21:10,13,14 23:1,2,11,12,28,31,32,32 25:7,9,12,17,18 27:4,20,
35 28:48 29:17 30:2,5,8,9 31:15,25,30,43,44,47 32:15 34:9
35:4 36:9,11,14,14,19,19 37:11 38:14,16,17,34 39:5,30,44
40:14 41:17 42:13 46:17 51:29); sometimes we find the form
λεγει κυριος (7 times: 8:3 15:21 23:29 27:10 28:25,48
36:32); and occasionally even ειπε(ν) κυριος (3 times: 8:12
26:25 38:14).

/30/ Tov neglects to mention 29:19 and 40:11.

/31/ αφανισμος   9:11(10) 10:22 12:11,11 18:16 19:8
25:9,11,12 26(46):19 27(50):3,13,23 28(51):26,29,37,41,62

αβατος   Jer a' 6:8 12:10 28(51):43

Jer b' 29:14,18(49:13,17) 30:11(49:33)
31(48):9 32:4,24(25:18,38) 39(32):43 49(42):18 51(44):6,22.
Cf. also 30(49):2 (לתל שממה)

ερημος   Jer a' 2:15 4:27

Jer b' 41(34):22

ερημωσις   4:7

εκστασις   5:30

απορια   8:21

απωλεια   30(49):2 51(44):12

/32/ αφανιζω   12:11 27(50):45

αβατοω   29:21(49:20)

ερημοω   10:25 40(33):10

εξιστημι   2:12 4:9 18:16

σκυθρωπαζω   19:8 27(50):13

/33/ κατασκηνοω   7:12 17:6 23:6 28(51):13

καταλυω   29:17(49:16) 30:9(49:31) 32:10(25:24)

κατοικιζω   7:3,7

οικεω   31(48):28

/34/ There is a further difficulty in considering καταλυω
a "synonymous rendition" to κατασκηνοω in 29:17(49:16). The
sense demanded for καταλυω in the context of 29:17 is that of
"destroy" or "demolish" (Bagster: "burst"), rather than that of
"lodge" as in the Hebrew. Is it reasonable to assume that a
reviser, anxious to bring the Greek text into better conformity
with the Hebrew, would replace a perfectly logical translation
choice (κατασκηνοω) with another word (καταλυω) which in the
syntax of the sentence gave it a meaning quite different from
that of the Hebrew?

/35/ It was, in fact, this passage which Spohn already in 1794 pointed to as indicating different translators (Ieremias vates, p. 9).

/36/ νομη   10:25 23:3,10 27(50):7,19,45

      τοπος   29:20(49:19) 32:16(25:30)

      καταλυσις   29:21(49:20)

      καταλυμα   40(33):12

/37/ κατα προσωπον   Jer a' 18:17,20 24:1 27(50):8,44

                          Jer b' 29:20(49:19) 33(26):4
37(30):20 38:37(31:36) 41(34):15,18 42(35):5,19 43(36):7,
9,22 44(37):20 47(40):10 49(42):2 51(44):10 52:12,33

      προ προσωπον   9:13(12) 15:1,19 21:8

      εις προσωπον   30(49):5

      εναντιον   Jer a' 1:17 2:22 15:9 18:23 19:7
25:17(49:37)
                          Jer b' 47(40):10

      ενωπιον   7:10

      προτερος   35(28):8,8 41(34):5

/38/ ισχυρος   Jer a' 5:16 9:23(22) 26(46):5,6

                          Jer b' 29:23(49:22) 31(48):14 39(32):12

      μαχητης   20:11 26(46):9,12,12 27(50):9,36
28(51):30,56

      δυνατος   48(41):16 50(43):6 51(44):20

      ανηρ   14:9

/39/ On p. 5 and p. 20 Tov states that the reviser theory must be correct "by implication" if it can be shown that Thackeray's explanation of the agreements between Jer a' and b' is incorrect.

On p. 6: "It seems to us that the agreements between the two sections of Jer (chapter II) are of such a nature that the two-translator theory cannot be sustained."

On p. 42: "We have attempted to demonstrate in the preceding chapter that Jer a' and b' exhibit many important agreements which make a two-translator theory untenable."

On p. 45: "We suggest our working hypothesis in spite of the mentioned difficulties because the agreements discussed in ch. II do not seem to leave any other possible explanation of the differences between Jer a' and b'."

/40/ See his remark on p. 8: "While the examples of chapter III are supposed to demonstrate that Jer b' has been revised, the examples of chapter IV can also be taken as proof of a two-translator theory. However . . . the data provided in this chapter can be accommodated to our working hypothesis."

/41/ On Ch. V, p. 112: "It should be pointed out that this chapter provides no additional proof that Jer b' is a revision rather than a second translation."

On Ch. VI, p. 135: "Although the majority of the new translation equivalents of Jer-R are revisional, the examples themselves do not provide additional proof that the second part of Jer contains a revision rather than a different translation."

/42/ See the note, "ANOIKODOMEIN and Intra-Septuagintal Borrowing," VT 27 (1977), 492-93, as well as other unpublished studies by her along the same lines (e.g. "Unravelling the Internal History of the Septuagint: A New Method Exemplified," a paper read at the Old Testament Seminar, Cambridge University, February, 1977).

/43/ Tov is forthright about the limitations inherent in his study. For instance, he says, "Our explanations of these difficulties may or may not be correct. In any event, we prefer the uneasy assumption outlined above over the 'easy' two translator theory suggested by Thackeray" (p. 6). Similarly, "We cannot claim that our suggestion is without difficulty. There are too many gaps in our knowledge. However, if we pause for a moment and assume that the theory is correct . . . ." (p. 168). Such remarks exemplify the best of academic integrity.

/44/ Nor is the case similar to our argument for a pre-Hexaplaric revision underlying the Q text since in the latter instance the argument proceeds entirely from extant MS readings.

/1/ While still awaiting publication of the Cave 4 material in the official series, <u>Discoveries in the Judean Desert</u>, corrections to Janzen's preliminary transcriptions are promised for the forthcoming edition of Jer in the Hebrew University Bible Project (cf. E. Tov, "Some Aspects of the Textual and Literary History of the Book of Jeremiah," <u>Le Livre de Jérémie</u>, ed. P.-M. Bogaert, [1981], p. 146, n. 2).

/2/ On 2QJer see <u>DJD</u>, III, 62-69. On 4QJer[a] and 4QJer[c] Cross comments that they contain a text "with virtually no significant deviations from the traditional text," <u>QHBT</u>, p. 308, a statement which may be verified at least with regard to 4QJer[a] in Janzen's Appendix, pp. 174-81. For a discussion of the date (c. 200 B.C.) and orthographic features of 4QJer[a] , see Cross, <u>JBL</u> 74(1955), esp. 162-64, <u>BANE</u>, pp. 145-53, <u>QHBT</u>, p. 316, n. 8. See also D.N. Freedman, <u>Textus</u> 2 (1962), 87-102.

/3/ The attention of the scholarly community at large was first alerted to the existence of this MS, together with a preliminary publication of part of one fragment in Cross' book, <u>The Ancient Library of Qumran</u>, 1958, p. 139, n. 38 (2nd ed. 1961, p. 187, n. 38). The MS is of slightly later date (the Hasmonean period) than 4QJer[a] (<u>QHBT</u>, p. 308).

/4/ There is actually no Table B.4 in Appendix B, but the omission is surely due to "scribal error." Internal considera-tion make it clear that the table on p. 159 should be understood as B.4 with the title "יהוה נאם and אמר יהוה In Jeremiah" (cf. n. 29 below).

/5/ It is recognized, of course, that 4QJer[b] is not an isolated phenomenon in the entire range of LXX-Qumrân studies. The Samuel scrolls from Qumrân in particular have furnished evidence for a Hebrew text with many LXX-type readings. By analogy, this would tend to increase our confidence in extrapo-lating from the small fragments of Jeremiah, but arguments from analogy in these cases have to be handled with caution, as Goshen-Gottstein has reminded us (<u>The Book of Isaiah: Sample Edition</u>, 1965, p. 14). Even in Sam we have to consider not only the similarities between 4QSam[a] and the LXX but also the several significant differences (cf. Tov, "The Textual Affiliations of 4QSam[a] ," <u>JSOT</u> 14 [1979], 51; <u>idem</u>, "A Modern Textual Outlook," <u>HUCA</u> 53 [1982], 21). Also, D.W. Gooding has made the point that, depending on whether the Hebrew <u>Vorlage</u> of Jer-LXX and 4QJer[b] are regarded as members of a close-knit Family or merely of a broad text-type, the range in possible agreements between the LXX 4QJer[b] had it survived in full could easily vary anywhere from as high as 95% to, say, 60% (<u>JSS</u> 21 [1976], 23-24).

/6/ For counter-arguments to the positions of Overholt and
Zevit see Tov, "Exegetical Notes on the Hebrew Vorlage of the
LXX of Jeremiah 27(34)," ZAW 91 (1979), esp. 83-84.

/7/ An even more comprehensive, computer-aided classification is now available in the unpublished thesis of Y-J. Min (see
above, p. 11, n. 26).

/8/ Greek renditions of the main introductory formulas:

a) הדבר אשר היה אל ירמיהו מאת יהוה

This formula is rendered literally ο λογος ο γενομενος προς
Ιερεμιαν παρα κυριου in 37(30):1, 41(34):1,8, 42(35):1, also in
11:1, 18:1, 21:1, 39(32):1, 47(40):1, but in the latter instances with προς Ιερεμιαν/παρα κυριου inverted. On two occasions the same formula is found without מאת יהוה and the LXX
follows suit in 25:1 and 51(44):1. On one occasion (7:1), the
formula is entirely missing in the LXX along with most of the
following verse (for discussion see p. 206).

b) ויהי דבר יהוה אלי

The construction is rendered literally και εγενετο/εγενηθη
λογος κυριου προς με in 1:11,13, 13:8, 18:5, and 24:4. At 1:4
the LXX reads προς αυτον instead of προς με. For the omission
of the formula in 2:1 and 16:1 see the discussion below,
pp. 205-7.

c) ויהי דבר יהוה אל ירמיהו

This formula is identical with the foregoing except that it
replaces אלי with אל ירמיהו. The normal Greek translation, as
expected, is και εγενετο/εγενηθη λογος κυριου προς Ιερεμιαν
35(28):12, 36(29):30, 40(33):1, 41(34):2 (MT adds מאת יהוה
which LXX omits), 43(36):27, 44(37):6 (MT adds הנביא om. LXX),
49(42):7. On two occasions the LXX has προς με instead of προς
Ιερεμιαν,39(32):26, 42(35):12. The formulas in MT 33:19,23 are
missing in the LXX as part of the long passage vv. 14-26 absent
from Jer-LXX Ch. 40.

d) ויאמר יהוה אלי

This formula is consistently rendered και ειπε κυριος προς
με in 1:12,14, 3:6,11, 11:6,9, 13:6, 14:11,14, 15:1, and 24:3.

e) הדבר אשר דבר/צוה . . .

This formula is found in four places in the OAN section of
the book: 26(46):13, 27(50):1, 28(51):59 and 51:31(45:1), but
only in the latter instance does the Greek follow the Hebrew
exactly.

f)   היה הדבר הזה (אל ירמיהו) מאת יהוה

There are three closely related headings which contain this phrase: 33(26):1, 34(27):1 and 43(36):1. The LXX omits the formula in 34(27):1 while it attests minor variants in the other two verses. The omission of the introduction in 34(27):1 may be related to the problematic mention of יהויקם in MT 27:1 which contradicts the content of the succeeding verses dealing with Zedekiah. The usual approach has been to emend Jehoiakim to Zedekiah (with some Hebrew MSS, the Syriac and Arabic), but Janzen regards MT 27:1 secondary from MT 26:1 (p. 14, #24).

g)   Miscellaneous introductory headings are found in 36(29):1, 37(30):4 and 46(39):15 where the LXX follows the MT exactly; in 1:1-2 and 39(32):6 the LXX diverges more significantly.

/9/   For the Greek translation of these see Ch. IV, pp. 167-69, notes 16, 17, 18.

/10/   Missing on its own: 11:22 13:12 18:11 22:30 36(29):25 38:35(31:37) 42(35):19

Missing as part of a larger context: 17:5 34(27):21 36(29):16,17 40(33):17,20,25

/11/   This figure includes the expression כה נאם יהוה of MT 9:21. For Greek translations see the preceding chapter, p. 175, n. 28.

/12/   Missing on its own: 3:10 5:11 7:13 8:3,17 9:3(2), 6(5) 12:17 13:11 15:9,20 18:6 21:10,13 23:1,2,11,12,24,28, 29,31,32,32 25:17,18(49:37,38) 27(50):4,10,35 28(51):25 29:17(49:16) 30:5,8,9(49:6,30,31) 31(48):25,30,43,44 32:15(25:29) 34:9(27:11) 36(29):9,11 38(31):14,16,17,34 39(32):44 41(34):17 42(35):13 46(39):17 51(44):29

Missing as part of a phrase: 9:22(21) 16:5 21:14 25:7,9,12 35(28):4 36(29):14,14,32 39(32):5,30

Missing as part of verses unrepresented in the LXX: (MT references) 29:19,19 30:10,11 33:14 46:26 48:47 49:6 51:48

/13/   Translated by ειπε κυριος in 6:15 29:19(49:18)+παν-τοκρατωρ 31(48):8 37(30):3 40(33):11,13 51(44):26

/14/   Missing on its own in 30(49):2 and as part of a larger context in 8:12.

/15/   6:6,9 9:6,16 19:11 23:15 25:8,28,32 26:18 27:19 33:12 49:7,35 50:33 51:58

/16/   23:16

/17/ 11:22 29:17(49:16)

/18/ 21:4 23:2 40(33):4 49(42):9 41(34):2,13
51:(32(45:2) 44(37):7

/19/ 11:3 24:5 32:1(25:15) 37(30):2 39(32):36

/20/ 13:22

/21/ 5:14

/22/ 7:21 19:15 27(50):18 28(51):33 31(48):1
35(28):2,14 36(29):8,21 38(31):23 39(32):15 42(35):13,18
49(42):15,18 51(43):10 51(44):11

/23/ 7:3 9:15 16:9 19:3 34:3(27:4) 36(29):4
46(39):16 51(44):2,25

/24/ 32:13(25:27) 39(32):14

/25/ 34(27):21 36(29):25 42(35):19

/26/ 42(35):17 45(38):17

/27/ 51(44):7

/28/ 5:14 15:16 23:16 27(50):34 28(51):5,57
32:13(25:27) 38:36(31:35) 39(32):14 40(33):11 51(44):7

/29/ Janzen's statistics in these tables are generally
reliable though it is to be regretted that references are seldom
provided, thus making verification difficult. Some corrections
that need to be made are the following:

In Table B.1, in the column labeled "Other":

for 1 Isa	כה אמר אדני קדש ישראל	read	כה אמר אדני יהוה קדש ישראל
for Ez	כה שמר האל יהוה	read	כה אמר האל יהוה
for 2 Isa	כה אמר מלך ישראל	read	כה אמר יהוה מלך ישראל
for 2 Isa	כה אמר אדניך יהוה אלהיך	read	כה אמר אדניך יהוה ואלהיך

In Table B.3, in the column labeled "Other":

for 2 Isa	אמר רחמך יהוה	read	אמר מרחמך יהוה

On p. 159 in the column labeled "Other":

for ταδε λεγει κυρ. ο θεος read λεγει κυρ. ο θεος

Also on p. 159 there are 9 (not 8) occurrences of the
formula אמר יהוה in Jer-MT (6:15, 8:12, 29:19[49:18], 30[49]:2,
31[48]:8, 37[30]:3, 40[33]:11,13, 51[44]:26), represented by a
Greek translation in Jer-LXX 6 (not 5) times (6:15, 31[48:8],
37[30]:3, 40[33]:11,13, 51[44]:26).

According to Janzen's remark on p. 78, the statistics for
the divine name are given in Tables B.3, B.4 and B.5. But no
tables B.4 and B.5 are found. It seems clear that a title is
missing at the top of p. 159 which should read "Table B.4, נאם
יהוה and אמר יהוה in Jeremiah" (cf. B.3 "נאם יהוה and אמר יהוה
Outside Jeremiah"). As for Table B.5 there is nothing in
Appendix B corresponding to this.

/30/ All the English VSS consulted--except NEB--translate
the -ל construction לצר ולצידון in the normal way as an indirect
object of the infinitive construction להכרית. NEB, however,
takes this as a direct object, ". . . because the day is upon
them when Philistia will be despoiled and Tyre and Sidon destroyed to the last defender." It is difficult to defend the
NEB in this rendering. Not only is it out of character with
normal classical Hebrew usage but, like the LXX, it breaks the
unity of the composition by deflecting the poem from its otherwise singleminded preoccupation with the Philistines.

/31/ Such an alliance after 605 B.C. is not otherwise
known in historical sources, but its existence is quite plausible (cf. Bright, AB, p. 310).

/32/ The Hebrew is admittedly difficult. Literally it
translates, "every survivor, helper." By taking עזר in the
sense of "escapee" ("Entronnener") instead of "survivor," Duhm
(p. 344) declared the phrase "blanker Unsinn," but this verdict
is surely extreme. Volz (p. 302) is much more sober in his es-
timate that in a passage which is poetically terse, the expression can be taken as a case of asyndetic apposition (cf. GK,
131b,c) and hence proposes the translation "jeden Übrigen,
nämlich Bundesgenossen." The RSV translation "every remaining
ally" reflects this reasonable interpretation.

/33/ Compare the frequent use of καταλοιποι in vv. 4-7.
In v. 4b and v. 5 it translates שארית; in v. 7 the Greek phrase
επι τους καταλοιπους επεγερθηναι mysteriously represents MT שם
יעדה, suggesting again a very free use of καταλοιποι.

/34/ It has commonly been regarded as a gloss by the
commentators, cf. Movers (p. 22), Fried. Delitzsch (Lese und
Schreibfehler, p. 137), Schwally (p. 195, n. 3), Giesebrecht
(p. 234), Streane (p. 267), Duhm (p. 344), and Cornill (p. 460).

/35/ This was essentially the suggestion of Giesebrecht,
p. 234.

/36/ By means of this emendation Christensen translates
"How long will you whirl about, O sword of Yahweh?", omitting
הוי with the LXX. But this emendation following 2QJer must be
rejected; it fails to take into consideration the parallels
cited from Deut 14:1, Jer 16:6, 48:37. Moreover, 2QJer does not
endorse the linking of תתגוררי with חרב ליהוה since הוי חרב is
firmly attested by that MS. תתגוררי is undoubtedly secondary in
2QJer (cf. the variant יתגוררו [text יתגודדו] in some Hebrew MSS
at 5:7). The example is one of many such emendations proposed
by Christensen on the basis of meter (e.g. in MT 49:3 he emends
the Hebrew in the opposite direction: MT בגרות --→ בגדדות,
p. 225). On this issue contrast the more cautious approach
recommended by D.K. Stuart in Studies in Early Hebrew Meter,
1976, p. 22: "Emendations may rarely be attempted metri causa
alone."

/37/ For a discussion of the inner-Greek textual problems
associated with the word καταλειμμα(-ατα), see p. 137 above.

/38/ Rahlfs' retention of σου following ηλθον in the body
of the text is indefensible on text critical grounds (cf. p. 137
above).

/39/ 3:22[but Ziegler emends this text to ουδε] 4:24
8:8,9 24:1   25:15(49:35) 27(50):12 29:13,16(49:12,15)
32:15(25:29) 37(30):23 39(32):17,24,27 41(34):2

/40/ Participle-verb constructions (26 occurrences): 3:1
4:10 5:11 6:15 7:5,5 10:5 12:16 13:12 14:19 22:4
26(46):28 28(51):58 32:14(25:28) 33(26):15 33(26):19
38(31):18,20 43(36):16,29 44(37):9 45(38):3,17 46(39):18
48(42):10 49(42):19 51(44):17

Noun-verb constructions (13 occurrences): 9:4(3) 17:24
22:10 23:32 26(46):5 27(50):34? 28(51):56? 31(48):9
33(26):8 39(32):4 41(34):3 45(38):15 47(40):14

/41/ Jer α: 11:12 20:15(LXX has the participle only)
23:17,39

Jer β: 29:13(49:12) 32:15(25:29) 48(41):6,15

In addition to the preceding verses where the LXX attests
only half of the Hebrew inf. abs. constructions, there are also
two occasions where the Greek omits the entire construction:
13:17 and 49(42):22. Then, of course, there are those occasions where the Greek construction is missing as part of a
larger context absent in the LXX: 6:15, 11:7, 28(51):57,
37(30):11, 51(44):29. On yet other occasions the Greek translates in anomalous ways, e.g. 6:9,29, 8:13, 25:30(32:16),
51(44):25(3x). The last mentioned verse has 3 examples of the
Greek infinitive with finite verb, the closest approximation
possible to the MT but the worst possible Greek (these examples

should be added to the lone instance of this phenomenon discovered by Thackeray in Josh 18:13, "Renderings of the Infinitive
Absolute in the LXX," p. 600; Grammar, p. 47). Finally, there
are those occasions where the LXX attests a typical construction
associated with a Hebrew inf. abs. but where the latter is
missing in the MT: 3:1, 12:11, 22:24, 28(51):57, 39(32):28,
41(34):2.

/42/ Compare the different vocabulary αθωοω/καθαριζω and
the different constructions, participle-verb / noun-verb.

/43/ Since a series implies more than one, only those
passages of two or more terms are included in the above list.
However, there are also numerous instances where the same
construction is used with only one term, לשמה being the most
popular. In the Edom oracle cf. 29:14(49:13) ερημου/לחרבות and
29:18(49:17) εις αβατον/לשמה. Even where the Hebrew is lacking
the ל prefix, the Greek often translates as though it were
present nonetheless, e.g. 9:11(10) εις αφανισμον/שממה. On
occasion a Greek series is created even where none exists in
the MT, e.g. 30(49):2 εις αβατον και εις απωλειαν / לתל שממה.

/44/ If לחרבה is to be regarded as secondary, perhaps the
source of the reading is not 25:18--which is after all subsequent to 25:11--but rather the very similar phrase in 7:34 כי
(cf. 25:11 לחרבה לשמה לחרבה כל הארץ והיתה) לחרבה תהיה הארץ.

/45/ For another example of the translator's awareness of
the contemporary situation, see the discussion on the omission
of כפתור in 29(47):4, pp. 51-52 above. However, the argument
from Tendenz is admittedly vulnerable here (i.e in 32:4[25:18]),
since in the very similar passage of 51(44):22, the LXX does
attest the translation of ולקללה.

/46/ The rendition of שמה by απωλεια is irregular since
the normal Greek equivalent for שמה in Jer b' is αβατος (Jer a'
αφανισμος). The word is indeed found once elsewhere, 30(49):2,
apparently as a translation for שממה but the passage is unclear.

/47/ This is the simplest explanation for the LXX reading
εις ονειδισμον in this verse.

/48/ Taking the approach that "Das Nomen חרב(ה) [Jer 25:9,
11,18 44:22 49:13] ist in diesem Zusammenhang auffälling; denn
es lässt sich thematisch nur schwer mit den anderen Begriffen
zusammenbringen," H. Weippert (p. 189, n. 364) thinks this is
the reason why the LXX omitted the verb in 25:11 and why it read
חרפת instead of חרבות in 25:9. She does not comment on the LXX
omission of חרב in MT 49:13, but presumably would apply a
similar explanation. As has been pointed out, however, it is
questionable whether the distinction between חרב(ה) and the
other terms is as radical as Weippert suggests, and even if this
were the case, it is doubtful that the translator would have

been alert to it. חרבה is well attested in Jer both on its own as well as in series and relates without great difficulty to the other terms, so that an explanation from <u>Tendenz</u> as reason for the omission in the Greek does not seem persuasive in these cases.

/49/ For a discussion of the textual problems connected with the B-S reading θαλασσης ουκ see above, pp. 149-51.

/50/ For discussion of the different Greek equivalents εφοβηθη/σεισθησεται, see above pp. 180-82.

/51/ Zlotowitz (pp. 24-25) comes to the same conclusion following an extended review of the LXX treatment of קול in Jer-LXX.

/52/ Compare the interchange of ד and ר in the parallel passages, Ps 18:11 (וידא) and 2 Sam 22:11 (וירא), as well as in the Samaritan variant יראה to Deut 28:49 (in the LXX rendered ορημα).

/53/ The verb דאה* occurs only four times in the OT: Deut 28:49, Ps 18:11 and the parallel passages of Jer 48:40//49:22. In Deut 28:49 it was translated ορημα (see previous note), in Ps 17(18):11 by πετομαι, simply repeating the translation of the previous verb עוף.

/54/ In the LXX the verses are not to be found in their MT position within the chapter (i.e. following v. 6), but do appear at the end of the chapter.

/55/ On account of the different chapter arrangement in the two texts, the omitted portion of the last two doublets cited is the second member of the pair when read in the Greek text only.

/56/ Janzen cites 8 examples only, but he surely intends these to be representative rather than exhaustive. Other examples of larger duplicates that might easily be added are 7:31-32//19:5-6, 16:14-15//23:7-8, 23:5-6//33:15-16, 39:1-10//52:4-16. For useful lists giving most examples of duplicates in Jer, large and small, see Kuenan, p. 253 and Driver, <u>ILOT</u>, p. 259.

BIBLIOGRAPHY OF WORKS CITED

Aland, K. Repertorium der Griechischen Christlichen Papyri:
    I, Biblische Papyri (Patristische Texte und Studien),
    Berlin/New York, 1976.

Albright, W.F. From Stone Age to Christianity, New York, 2nd
    ed. 1957.

_____. "New Light on Early Recensions of the Hebrew Bible,"
    BASOR 140 (Dec. 1955), 27-33 (= QHAT, 140-46).

Allen, L.C. The Greek Chronicles: The Relation of the Septuagint
    of I and II Chronicles to the Massoretic Text (SupVT 25/27),
    1974.

Arieti, J.A. "The Vocabulary of Septuagint Amos," JBL 93 (1974),
    338-47.

Baab, O.J. "A Theory of Two Translators for the Greek Genesis,"
    JBL 52 (1933), 239-43.

Baillet, M., Milik, J.T., de Vaux, R., eds. Les "Petites Grottes"
    de Qumran: Textes/Planches (DJD 3), Oxford, 1962.

Barr, J. Biblical Words for Time (Studies in Biblical Theology,
    First Series 33), 2nd ed., London, 1969.

_____. Review of P. Walters' The Text of the Septuagint, in
    HJ 26 (1975), 61-63; also VT 25 (1975), 247-54.

Barthélemy, D. "Bulletin," RB 59 (1952), 605-10 (= Études,
    pp. 32-37).

_____. "Redécouverte d'un chaînon manquant de l'histoire
    de la Septante," RB 60 (1953), 18-29 (= Jellicoe, Studies,
    pp. 226-38; QHBT, pp. 127-39; Études, pp. 38-50).

_____. Les Devanciers d'Aquila (SupVT 10), 1963.

_____. "Les problèmes textuels de 2 Sam 11,2 - 1 Rois 2:11
    reconsidérés à la lumière de certaines critiques des
    'Devanciers d'Aquila'," 1972 Proceedings (Septuagint and
    Cognate Studies 2), ed. R.A. Kraft, Missoula, Montana,
    1972, pp. 16-89 (= Études, pp. 218-54).

_____. Études d'histoire du texte de l'Ancien Testament
    (Orbis Biblicus et Orientalis 21), 1978.

von Baudissin, W.W.G. Kyrios als Gottesname im Judentum und seine Stelle in der Religionsgeschichte, 4 vols., Giessen, 1926-29.

Baumgärtel, F. "Zu den Gottesnamen in den Büchern Jeremia und Ezechiel," Verbannung und Heimkehr (FS W. Rudolph), ed. A. Kuschke, Tübingen, 1961, pp. 1-29.

Bertholdt, L. Historisch-kritische Einleitung in sämmtliche kanonische und apokryphische Schriften des Alten und Neuen Testaments, Erlangen, 1812-19.

Biblia Patristica: Index des Citations et Allusions Bibliques dans la Littérature Patristique (Centre d'Analyse et de Documentation Patristiques), Paris, 1975/77.

Black, M. "Notes on the Longer and the Shorter Text of Acts," On Language, Culture, and Religion: In Honor of Eugene A. Nida, eds. M. Black and W.A. Smalley, The Hague/Paris, 1974, pp. 119-31.

Bogaert, P.-M. "La Septante de Göttingen," Revue Théologique de Louvain 11 (1980), 80-82.

Botte, B. Review of J. Ziegler's critical text, Ieremias, in Recherches de Théologie Ancienne et Médiévale 25 (1958), 147-48.

Bright, J. Jeremiah (Anchor Bible), New York, 1965.

Brock, S.P. The Recensions of the Septuagint Version of I Samuel. Unpublished thesis, Oxford, 1966.

Brockington, L.H. The Hebrew Text of the Old Testament: The Readings Adopted by the Translators of the New English Bible, Oxford/Cambridge, 1973.

Brooke, A.E. and McLean, N. (from 1927 also Thackeray, H.St.J.). The Old Testament in Greek, Cambridge, 1906-40.

Burkitt, F.C. "The S. Gallen Fragment of Jeremiah," Texts and Studies 4 (1896), 79-82.

_____. "Text and Versions: Old Testament," EB, IV, 1903, cols. 5011-31.

Caird, G.B. The Apostolic Age, London, 1955.

Ceriani, A.M. Monumenta Sacra et Profana, ex codicibus praesertim bibliotheca Ambrosiane, I-III, Milan, 1861-63.

_____. "Le recensioni dei LXX e la versione latina detta Itala," Rendiconti del Reale Istituto Lombardo de Scienze e Lettere, II, 19.4, Milan, 1886.

_____. Codex Syro-hexaplaris Ambrosianus photographice editus (Monumenta Sacra et Profana VII), Milan, 1874.

_____. De Codice Marchaliano seu Vaticano graeco 2125 Prophetarum, phototypice repraesentato commentatio, Rome, 1890.

Childs, B. "A Study of the Formula, 'Until This Day'," JBL 82, (1963), 279-92.

_____. Old Testament Books for Pastor and Teacher, Philadelphia, 1977.

Christensen, D.L. Transformations of the War Oracle in Old Testment Prophecy: Studies in the Oracles Against the Nations (Harvard Theological Review: Harvard Dissertations in Religion 3), Missoula, Montana, 1975.

Clark, A.C. The Primitive Text of the Gospels and Acts, Oxford, 1914.

_____. The Descent of Manuscripts, Oxford, 1918.

_____. The Acts of the Apostles: A Critical Edition with Introduction and Notes on Selected Passages, Oxford, 1933.

Colwell, E.C. "Method of Grouping New Testament Manuscripts," Studies in Methodology in Textual Criticism of the New Testament (New Testament Tools and Studies 9), Leiden, 1969, pp. 1-25. Originally published under the title, "The Significance of Grouping of New Testament Manuscripts," NTS 4 (1958), 73-92.

_____. "Method in Classifying and Evaluating Variant Readings," Studies in Methodology in Textual Criticism of the New Testament (New Testament Tools and Studies 9), Leiden, 1969, pp. 96-105.

Condamin, A. Le Livre de Jérémie (Études Bibliques), Paris, 1936.

Cornill, C.H. Das Buch Jeremia, Leipzig, 1905.

Coste, E. Die Weissagungen des Propheten Jeremias wider die fremden Völker, Leipzig, 1895.

Cross, F.M. "The Oldest Manuscripts from Qumran," JBL 74 (1955), 147-72 (= QHBT, 147-76).

_____. The Ancient Library of Qumran and Modern Biblical Studies, 2nd ed., New York, 1961.

_____. "The Development of the Jewish Scripts," BANE, pp. 133-202.

_____. "The History of the Biblical Text in the Light of Discoveries in the Judaean Desert," HTR 57 (1964), 281-99 (= QHBT, pp. 177-95).

_____. "The Contribution of the Qumrân Discoveries to the Study of the Biblical Text," IEJ 16 (1966), 81-95 (= QHBT, pp. 278-92).

_____. "The Evolution of a Theory of Local Texts," QHBT, pp. 306-20.

Cross, F.M. and Talmon, S., eds. Qumran and the History of the Biblical Text (= QHBT), Cambridge, Mass., 1975.

Dahood, M. Review of J.G. Janzen's Studies in the Text of Jeremiah, in Biblica 56 (1975), 429-31.

Driver, S.R. "The Double Text of Jeremiah," Expositor 9 (1889), 321-37.

_____. The Book of the Prophet Jeremiah, London, 1906.

_____. Introduction to the Literature of the Old Testament, Edinburgh, rev. ed. 1913.

_____. Notes on the Hebrew Text and the Topography of the Books of Samuel, 2nd ed., Oxford, 1913.

Duhm, B. Das Buch Jeremia (Kurzer Hand-Commentar zum Alten Testament), Tubingen/Leipzig, 1901.

Duval, E. "Le texte grec de Jérémie d'après une étude récente," RB 12 (1903), 394-404.

Ehrlich, A.B. Randglossen zur Hebräischen Bibel, IV, Leipzig, 1912.

Eichhorn, J.G. Einleitung in das Alte Testament, III, 3rd ed., Leipzig, 1803.

Eissfeldt, O. Review of Ziegler's edition Ieremias in TLZ 83 (1958), 22-24.

Elliott, J.K., ed. Studies in New Testament Language and Text: Essays in Honour of George D. Kilpatrick on the Occasion of his Sixty-fifth Birthday (NovTSup 44), Leiden, 1976.

Epp, E.J. "The Twentieth Century Interlude in New Testament
     Textual Criticism," JBL 93 (1974), 386-414.

_____. "The Eclectic Method in New Testament Textual
     Criticism: Solution or Symptom?" HTR 69 (1976), 211-57.

_____. "Toward the Clarification of the Term 'Textual
     Variant'," Studies in New Testament Language and Text (FS
     George D. Kilpatrick), ed. J.K. Elliott (NovTSup 44), 1976,
     153-73.

Faulhaber, M. Die Propheten-Catenen nach römischen Handschriften
     (Bibl. Studien IV, 2-3), Freiburg in Breslau, 1889.

Field, F. Origenis Hexaplorum quae supersunt . . . fragmenta, 2
     vols., Oxford, 1875.

Frankl, P.F. "Studien über die Septuaginta und Peschito zu
     Jeremia," Monatsschrift für Geschichte und Wissenschaft des
     Judentums 21 (1872), 444-56, 497-509, 545-57.

Freedman, D.N. "The Massoretic Text and Qumran Scrolls: A Study
     in Orthography," Textus 2 (1962), 87-102 (= QHBT, pp. 196-
     211).

Fritsch, C.T. "The Treatment of the Hexaplaric Signs in the
     Syro-Hexaplar of Proverbs," JBL 72 (1953), 169-81
     (= Jellicoe, Studies, pp. 356-68).

Gard, D.H. The Exegetical Method of the Greek Translator of the
     Book of Job (JBL Monograph Series 8), Philadelphia, 1952.

Gehman, H.S. "The Hesychian Influence in the Versions of Daniel,"
     JBL 48 (1929), 329-32.

_____. "Some Types of Errors of Transmission in the LXX,"
     VT 3 (1953), 397-400.

_____. "Greek Versions of the OT," HSDB, 1963, 347-54.

Gelin, A. "Jérémie," Supplement à Dictionnaire de la Bible, IV,
     1949, cols. 857-89.

Ghisler, M. In Ieremiam Prophetam Commentarii, vols. 1-3,
     Lugundi, 1623.

Giesebrecht, F. Das Buch Jeremia (Handkommentar zum Alten
     Testament), Göttingen, 2nd ed., 1907.

Gooding, D.W. The Greek Deuteronomy. Unpublished thesis,
     Cambridge, 1954.

_____. Recensions of the LXX Pentateuch, London, 1955.

_____. The Account of the Tabernacle: Translation and
    Textual Problems of the Greek Exodus (Texts and Studies 6),
    Cambridge, 1959.

_____. "An Appeal for a Stricter Terminology in the
    Textual Criticism of the Old Testament," JSS 21 (1976),
    15-25.

Goshen-Gottstein, M.H. "Theory and Practice of Textual
    Criticism: The Text-critical Use of the Septuagint,"
    Textus 3 (1963), 130-58.

_____. The Text of Isaiah: Sample Edition with
    Introduction, Jerusalem, 1965.

Grabe, J.E. Letter to Mill, 1705.

_____ et al. Septuaginta Interpretum, vols. 1-4,
    1707-20.

_____. Dissertatio de variis vitiis LXX. versioni ante B.
    Origenis aevum illatis, Oxford, 1710.

Graf, K.H. Der Prophet Jeremia, Leipzig, 1862.

Gray, G.B. "The Greek Version of Isaiah: Is it the Work of a
    Single Translator?" JTS 12 (1911), 286-93.

Grossouw, W. The Coptic Versions of the Minor Prophets: A
    Contribution to the Study of the Septuagint (Monumenta
    Biblica et Ecclesiastica 3), Rome, 1938.

Gurney, O.R. "The Sultantepe Tablets. VII. The Myth of Nergal
    and Ereshkigal," AS 10 (1960), 105-31.

Hanhart, R. "L'edizione dei LXX e la fondazione Gottingense che
    la prepara," RivStorLettRel 1 (1965), 351-52.

_____. "Jüdische Tradition und christliche Interpretation:
    Zur Geschichte der Septuagintaforschung in Göttingen,"
    Kerygma und Logos (FS Carl Andresen), ed. A.M. Ritter,
    Gottingen, 1979, pp. 280-97.

Hasel, G.F. Review of J.G. Janzen's book, Studies in the Text
    of Jeremiah, in BibOr 32 (1975), 236-38.

Hastoupis, A.P. The Septuagint Text of the Book of Jeremiah
    (Chs. 1-25). Unpublished thesis, Northwestern University,
    Evanston, Illinois, 1950.

Herrmann, J. and Baumgärtel, F. Beiträge zur Entstehungsgeschichte der Septuaginta (BWAT 5), Stuttgart, 1923.

Hitzig, F. Der Prophet Jeremia (Kurzgefasstes Exegetisches
Handbuch zum Alten Testament), Leipzig, 2nd ed. 1866.

Holmes, R. and Parsons, J. Vetus Testamentum Graecum cum variis
lectionibus, Vols. 1-5, Oxford, 1798-1827.

Howard, G. "Some Notes on the Septuagint of Amos," VT 20
(1970), 108-12.

Hurwitz, M.S. "The Septuagint of Isaiah 36-39 in Relation to
that of 1-35, 40-66," HUCA 28 (1957), 75-83.

Janzen, J.G. "Double Readings in the Text of Jeremiah," HTR 60
(1967), 433-77.

_____. Studies in the Text of Jeremiah (HSM 6),
Cambridge, Mass., 1973.

Jellicoe, S. "The Hesychian Recension Reconsidered," JBL 82
(1963), 409-18.

Jellicoe, S. The Septuagint and Modern Study, Oxford, 1968.

_____, ed. Studies in the Septuagint: Origins, Recensions
and Interpretations (Library of Biblical Studies), New
York, 1974.

Johnson, A.C., Gehman, H.S., and Kase, E.H. The John H. Scheide
Biblical Papyri: Ezekiel (Princeton University Studies in
Papyrology 3), Princeton, 1938.

Johnson, B. Die Hexaplarishce Rezension des 1. Samuelbuches der
Septuaginta (Studia Theologica Lundensia 22), Lund, 1963.

Kahle, P.E. The Cairo Geniza, 2nd ed., Oxford, 1959.

_____. "The Greek Bible Manuscripts Used by Origen," JBL
79 (1960), 111-18.

Kaminka, A. Studien zur Septuaginta an der Hand der Zwölf
Kleinen Prophetenbucher, Frankfurt, 1928.

Kappler, W. "Ziele und Aufgaben des Göttinger Septuaginta-
Unternehmens," GGA 202 (1940), 115-24.

Katz, P. Review of A. Rahlfs' Septuaginta, 1935, in TLZ 61
(1936), 265-87.

_____. "Frühe hebräisierende Rezensionen der Septuaginta und
die Hexapla," ZAW 69 (1957), 77-84.

Kedar-Kopfstein, B. "Textual Gleanings from the Vulgate to Jeremiah," Textus 7 (1969), 36-58.

Keil, C.F. The Prophecies of Jeremiah, 2 vols., trans. D. Patrick, Edinburgh, 1880.

Kilpatrick, G.D. Review of the Göttingen editions of 1, 2 and 3 Maccabees and R. Hanhart's Zum Text des 2. und 3. Makkabäerbuches in GGA 215 (1963), 10-22 (= Jellicoe, Studies, pp. 418-30).

Klein, M.L. "Converse Translation: A Targumic Technique," Biblica 57 (1976), 515-37.

Klein, R.W. Textual Criticism of the Old Testament: The Septuagint after Qumran (Guides to Biblical Scholarship), Philadelphia, 1974.

_____. Review of J.G. Janzen's book, Studies in the Text of Jeremiah, in CBQ 38 (1976), 109-10.

Kneucker, J.J. Das Buch Baruch, Leipzig, 1879.

Köhler, L. "Beobachtungen am hebräischen und griechischen Text von Jeremia Kap. 1-9," ZAW 29 (1909), 1-39.

Kuenan, A. Historisch-kritische Einleitung in die Bücher des Alten Testaments, 2 vols., Leipzig, 1892.

Kühl, E. Das Verhältnis der Massora zur Septuaginta im Jeremia, Halle, 1882.

de Lagarde, Paul. Anmerkungen zur griechischen Übersetzung der Proverbien, Leipzig, 1863 (summary in Mitteilungen, I, 19-26).

_____. Ankündigung einer neuen Ausgabe der griechischen Übersetzung des Alten Testaments, Göttingen, 1882 (summary in Mitteilungen I, 122-23).

_____. Librorum Veteris Testamenti canonicorum pars prior Graece, Göttingen, 1883.

_____. Mitteilungen, 4 vols., Göttingen, 1884-91.

_____. "Noch einmal meine Ausgabe der Septuaginta," Mitteilungen, III, 1889, 229-56.

Lake, K. The Text of the New Testament, rev. S. New, London, 1928.

Lambert, W. G. Review of J. Ziegler's Ieremias in Nouvelle Revue Théologique 80 (1958), 990.

Lambert, W.G. and Millard, A.R. Atra-ḫasīs: The Babylonian
    Story of the Flood, Oxford, 1969.

Lemke, W.E. "Nebuchadrezzar, my Servant," CBQ 28 (1966), 45-50.

Maas, P. Textual Criticism, trans. B. Flower, Oxford, 1958.

Margolis, M.L. "The Aldina as a Source of the Sixtina," JBL 38
    (1919), 51-52.

_____. "Textual Criticism of the Greek Old Testament,"
    Proceedings of the American Philosophical Society 67
    (1928), 187-97.

Martin, R.A. The Syntax of the Greek of Jeremiah, Part I:
    The Noun, Pronoun and Prepostions in their Case
    Constructions. Unpublished thesis, Princeton, 1957.

Maspero, G. Fragments de la version thébaine de l'Ancien
    Testament (Mémoires publiés par les membres de la Mission
    archéolgoique française au Caire, VI, 1.2), Paris, 1892.

Mayser, E. Grammatik der Griechischen Papyri aus der Ptolemäer-
    zeit, Berlin/Leipzig, 1926-38.

McKane, W. Review of J. G. Janzen's book, Studies in the Text
    of Jeremiah, in SOTS Book List, 1975, pp. 35-36.

Metzger, B.M. The Text of the New Testament: Its Transmission,
    Corruption, and Restoration, 2nd ed., Oxford, 1968.

Millard, A.R. "Literary History: The Gilgamesh Epic and the
    Flood." Unpublished paper read to the Old Testament Study
    Group of the Tyndale Fellowship for Biblical Reserach,
    Cambridge, July, 1976.

Milne, H.J.M. and Skeat, T.C. Scribes and Correctors of the
    Codex Sinaiticus, London, 1938.

Min, Y-J. The Minuses and Pluses of the LXX Translation of
    Jeremiah as Compared with the Massoretic Text: Their
    Classification and Possible Origins. Unpublished thesis,
    Hebrew University, Jerusalem, 1977.

Moore, G.F. "The Antiochian Recension of the Septuagint," The
    American Journal of Semitic Languages 29 (1912-13), 37-62.

Movers, F.C. De utriusque recensionis vaticiniorum Ieremiae,
    Hamburg, 1837.

Mowinckel, S. Zur Komposition des Buches Jeremia (Videnskaps-
    selskapets Skrifter, II, Hist.-Filos. Klasse 5), Kristiana,
    1914.

Muraoka, T. "Is the Septuagint Amos VIII 12 - IX 10 a Separate
     Unit?" VT 20 (1970), 496-500.

_____. "The Greek Texts of Samuel-Kings: Incomplete
     Translations or Recensional Activity?" 1972 Proceedings
     (Septuagint and Cognate Studies 2), ed., R.A. Kraft,
     Missoula, Montana, 1972, pp. 90-107.

_____. "Literary Device in the Septuagint," Textus 8
     (1973), 20-30.

_____. "A Re-examination of the Two-Translator Theory of
     a Septuagint Book." Unpublished paper read at the IOSCS
     meeting of the International Congress for Old Testament
     Studies, Uppsala, 1971.

_____. Review of P. Walters' book, The Text of the
     Septuagint, in JSS 19 (1974), 305-09.

Nestle, Eb. Das Buch Jeremia griechisch und hebräisch (Nach dem
     Tode des Herausgebers besorgt von J. Dahse und Erwin Nestle),
     Stuttgart, 1924.

das Neves, J.C.M. A teologia da tradução grega dos Setenta no
     livro de Isaías (Cap. 24 de Isaías), Lisbon, 1973.

Nicholson, E.W. The Book of the Prophet Jeremiah (The Cambridge
     Bible Commentary), 2 vols., 1973/5.

Norberg, M. Codex Syriaco-Hexaplaris Ambrosiano-Mediolanensis,
     London/Gothenborg, 1787.

O'Connell, K.G. Review of R. Hanhart's book, Esdrae liber I,
     Text und Textgeschichte des 1. Esrabuches, and of J.
     Wever's, Genesis and Text History of the Greek Genesis in
     CBQ 39 (1977), 119-25.

_____. The Theodotionic Revision of the Book of Exodus:
     A Contribution to the Study of the Early History of the
     Transmission of the Old Testament Greek (HSM 3),
     Cambridge, Mass., 1972.

Oesterley, W.O.E. Studies in the Greek and Latin Versions of
     the Book of Amos, Cambridge, 1902.

von Orelli, C. The Prophecies of Jeremiah, trans. J.S. Banks,
     Edinburgh, 1889.

Orlinsky, H.M. "On the Present State of Proto-Septuagint
     Studies," JAOS 61 (1941), 81-91 (= Jellicoe, Studies,
     pp. 78-109).

_____. "The Septuagint: Its Use in Textual Criticism," BA 9 (1946), 22-34.

_____. "Current Progress and Problems in Septuagint Research," The Study of the Bible Today and Tomorrow, ed. H.R. Willoughby, Chicago, 1947, pp. 144-61 (= Jellicoe, Studies, pp. 3-20).

_____. "The Septuagint as Holy Writ and the Philosophy of the Translators," HUCA 46 (1975), 89-114.

Ottley, R.R.   The Book of Isaiah According to the Septuagint (Codex A), 2 vols., London/Cambridge, 1904/06.

_____. A Handbook to the Septuagint, London, 1920.

Overholt, T.W.   "King Nebuchadnezzar in the Jeremiah Tradition," CBQ 30 (1968), 39-48.

Parker, D.   "The Development of Textual Criticism since B.H. Streeter," NTS 24 (1977), 149-62.

Rahlfs, A.   Septuaginta-Studien, I-III, Göttingen, 1904-11.

_____. "Die Abhängigkeit der sixtinischen Septuaginta-Ausgabe von der aldinischen," ZAW 33 (1913), 30-46.

_____. Verzeichnis der griechischen Handschriften des Alten Testaments (MSU 2), Berlin, 1914.

_____. Septuaginta, 2 vols., Stuttgart, 1935.

Redpath, H.A.   "A Contribution Towards Settling the Dates of the Translation of the Various Books of the Septuagint," JTS 7 (1906), 606-15.

Reider, J.   Prolegomena to a Greek-Hebrew and Hebrew-Greek Index to Aquila, Philadelphia, 1916.

_____. and Turner N.   An Index to Aquila (SupVT 12), Leiden, 1966.

Rendorff, R.   "Zum Gebrauch der Formel neʾum jahwe im Jeremiabuch," ZAW 66 (1954), 27-37.

Rudolph, W.   "Zum Text des Jeremia," ZAW 48 (1930), 272-86.

_____. Jeremia (HAT), 3rd ed., Tübingen, 1968.

Schleusner, J.F.   Novus Thesaurus Philolgico-Criticus sive Lexicon in LXX, London, 1829.

Schmidt, D. "Servant-Sensitivity in the LXX of Jeremiah: A
    Significant Translation Problem," IOSCS Bulletin 8 (1975),
    17-18.

Schneider, H. Review of J. Ziegler's Ieremias in TRe 65 (1960),
    101-06.

Scholz, A. Der masorethische Text und die Septuaginta Über-
    setzung des Buches Jeremias, Regensburg, 1875.

Schulz, C. De Ieremiae textus hebraici masorethici et graeci
    Alexandrini discrepantica, Treptow, 1861.

Schulze, J.L. Theodoreti Opera Omnia, II, Halle, 1770.

Seeligman, I.L. The Septuagint Version of Isaiah: A Discussion
    of its Problems, Leiden, 1948.

_____. "Indications of Editorial Alteration and Adaptation
    in the Massoretic Text and the Septuagint," VT 11 (1961),
    201-21.

van Selms, A. "Telescoped Discussion as a Literary Device in
    Jeremiah," VT 26 (1976), 99-112.

Soisalon-Soininen, I. Der Charakter der asterisierten Zusätze
    in der Septuaginta (AASF B 114), Helsinki, 1959.

Spohn, M.G.L. Ieremias Vates e versione Ioudaeorum
    Alexandrinorum ac reliquorum interpretum graecorum
    emendatus notisque criticis illustratus, 2 vols., Leipzig,
    1824 ("Tomus 2 post obitum patris edidit, F.G.A. Spohn").

Stone, M.E. "The Old Armenian Version of Isaiah: Towards the
    Choice of the Base Text for an Edition," Textus 8 (1973),
    107-23.

Streane, A.W. The Double Text of Jeremiah, Cambridge, 1896.

Streeter, B.H. The Four Gospels: A Study of Origins, London,
    1936.

Strungnell, J. "A Plea for Conjectural Emendation in the New
    Testament, With a Coda on 1 Cor 4:6," CBQ 36 (1974),
    543-58.

Stuart, D.K. Studies in Early Hebrew Meter (HSM 13),
    Missoula, Montana, 1976.

Swete, H.B. The Old Testament in Greek, 3 vols., 1887-94.

_____. An Introduction to the Old Testament in Greek,
    2nd ed., Cambridge, 1902; rev. R.R. Ottley, 1914.

Tattam, H. Prophetae majores, in linguae aegyptiacae memphitica
    seu coptica, Oxford, 1852.

Thackeray, H.St.J. "The Greek Translators of Ezekiel," JTS 4
    (1902-03), 398-411.

_____. "The Greek Translators of Jeremiah," JTS 4 (1902-
    03), 245-66.

_____. "The Greek Translators of the Prophetical Books,"
    JTS 4 (1902-03), 578-85.

_____. "The Greek Translators of the Four Books of
    Kings," JTS 8 (1906-07), 262-78.

_____. "The Bisection of Books in Primitive Septuagint
    MSS," JTS 9 (1907-08), 88-98 (= Jellicoe, Studies,
    pp. 459-69).

_____. "Renderings of the Infinitive Absolute in the LXX,"
    JTS 9 (1907-08), 597-601.

_____. A Grammar of the Old Testament in Greek,
    According to the Septuagint, Cambridge, 1909.

_____. The Septuagint and Jewish Worship: A Study in
    Origins (Schweich Lectures 1920), London, 1921.

_____. "Septuagint," ISBE, 1929, pp. 2722-32.

Thompson, J.A. The Book of Jeremiah (The New International
    Commentary on the Old Testament), Grand Rapids, Mich., 1980.

Tigay, J.H. Literary-Critical Studies in the Gilgamesh Epic:
    An Assyriological Contribution to Biblical Literary
    Criticism. Unpublished thesis, Yale, 1971.

Tischendorf, C. Vetus Testamentum Graece iuxta LXX Interpretes,
    ed. Eb. Nestle, 7th ed., Leipzig, 1887.

Tournay, R. Review of J. Ziegler's Ieremias in RB 65 (1958),
    292.

Tov, E. "L'incidence de la critique textuelle sur la critique
    littéraire dans le livre de Jérémie," RB 79 (1972), 189-99.

_____. "On 'Pseudo-Variants' Reflected in the Septuagint,"
    JSS 20 (1975), 165-77.

_____. The Septuagint Translation of Jeremiah and Baruch:
    A Discussion of an Early Revision of the LXX of Jeremiah
    29-52 and Baruch 1:1-3:8 (HSM 8), Missoula, Montana, 1976.

_____. "The Nature of the Hebrew Text Underlying the LXX: A Survey of the Problems," JSOT 7 (1978), 53-68.

_____. "Exegetical Notes on the Hebrew Vorlage of the LXX of Jeremiah 27(34)," ZAW 91 (1979), 73-93.

_____. "The Textual Affiliations of 4QSam^a," JSOT 14 (1979), 37-53.

_____. "Some Aspects of the Textual and Literary History of the Book of Jeremiah," in Le Livre de Jérémie (BETL 54), ed. P.M. Bogaert, 1981, pp. 145-67.

_____. "A Modern Textual Outlook Based on the Qumran Scrolls," HUCA 53 (1982), 11-27.

_____. The Text-Critical Use of the Septuagint in Biblical Research (Jerusalem Biblical Studies 3), 1981.

Turner, N. "The Greek Translators of Ezekiel," JTS 7 (1956), 12-24.

Turner, P.D.M. "Unravelling the Internal History of the Septuagint: A New Method Exemplified." Paper read at the Old Testament Seminar, Cambridge University, February, 1977.

_____. "ANOIKODOMEIN and Intra-Septuagintal Borrowing," VT 27 (1977), 492-93.

Vaccari, A. "The Hesychian Recension of the Septuagint," Biblic 46 (1965), 60-66 (= Jellicoe, Studies, pp. 336-42).

Volz, P. Studien zum Text des Jeremia (BWAT 25), Leipzig, 1920.

_____. Der Prophet Jeremia (Kommentar zum Alten Testament), Leipzig, 1922.

Wahl, O. Die Prophetenzitate der Sacra Parallela in ihren Verhältnis zur Septuaginta-Textüberlieferung, 2 vols. (Studien zum Alten und Neuen Testament 13), Munich, 1965.

Walters (formerly Katz), P. The Text of the Septuagint: Its Corruptions and Their Emendation, ed. D.W. Gooding, Cambridge, 1973.

Weippert, H. Die Prosareden des Jeremiabuches (BZAW 132), Berlin/New York, 1973.

Weiser, A. Das Buch des Prophten Jeremia (Das Alte Testament Deutsch), 4th ed., Göttingen, 1960.

Wellhausen, J. Der Text der Bücher Samuelis, Göttingen 1871.

Wernberg-Møller, P. Review of J.G. Janzen's book, Studies in the Text of Jeremiah, in JJS 28 (1977), 198.

Wessely, C. Griechische und Koptische Texte, theologoischen Inhalts, IV (Studien zur Paläeographie und Papyruskunde XV), Leipzig, 1914.

Westermann, C. Genesis 1-11 (BK), Neukirchen-Vluyn, 1974.

Wevers, J.W. "A Study in the Textual History of Codex Vaticanus in the Books of Kings," ZAW 64 (1952), 178-89.

_____. "Septuagint," IDB, IV, 1962,

_____. Septuaginta, Vetus Testamentum Graecum (Auctoritate Academiae Scientarum Gottingensis editum): Vol. 1, Genesis, 1974.

_____. "The Göttingen Septuagint," ISOCS Bulletin 8 (1975), 19-23.

Wichelhaus, J. De Jeremiae versione alexandrina, Halle, 1847.

Wiles, M.F. "Origen as a Biblical Scholar," CHB I, 454-89.

Wiseman, D.J. "Israel's Literary Neighbours in the 13th Century B.C.," JNSL 5 (1977), 77-91.

Workman, G.C. The Text of Jeremiah, Edinburgh, 1889.

Würthwein, E. Der Text des Alten Testaments: Eine Einführung in die Biblia Hebraica, 3rd ed., Stuttgart, 1966.

Wutz, F. Die Transkriptionen von der Septuaginta bis zu Hieronymus (BWAT 9), Stuttgart, 1925-33.

Zevit, Z. "The Use of עֶבֶד as a Diplomatic Term in Jeremiah," JBL 88 (1969), 74-77.

Ziegler, J. Septuaginta. Vetus Testamentum Graecum (Auctoritate Academiae Scientiarum Gottingensis editum): Vol 13, Duo decim Prophetae, 1943, 2nd ed., 1967; Vol. 14, Isaias, 1939, 3rd ed., 1983; Vol. 15, Ieremias, Baruch, Threni, Epistula Ieremiae, 1957, 2nd ed., 1976; Vol 16, Ezechiel, 1952, 2nd ed. 1967.

Ziegler, J. Untersuchungen zur Septuaginta des Buches Isaias (Alttestamentliche Abhandlungen 12,3), Münster, 1934.

_____. "Der textkritische Wert der Septuaginta des Buches Job," Miscellanea Biblica Scripta Pontificii Instituti Biblici, II, Rome, 1934, pp. 277-96.

_____ . Die Einheit der Septuaginta zum Zwölfprophetenbuch
(Beilage zum Vorlesungsverzeichnis der staatlichen Akademie
zu Braunsberg), 1934-35 (= Sylloge, pp. 29-42).

_____ . "Der Text der Aldina im Dodekapropheton," Biblica
26 (1945), 37-51 (= Sylloge, pp. 306-20).

_____ . "Die Septuaginta Hieronymi im Buch des Propheten
Jeremias," in Colligere Fragmenta (FS Alban Dold), ed.
B. Fischer and V. Fiala (Texte und Arbeiten 2), Beuron,
1952, pp. 13-24 (= Sylloge, pp. 345-56).

_____ . "Zur Textgestaltung der Ezechiel-Septuaginta,"
Biblica 34 (1953), 435-55 (= Sylloge, pp. 394-414).

_____ . "Jeremias-Zitate in Väter-Schriften," Historisches
Jahrbuch 77 (1958), 347-57 (= Sylloge, pp. 439-49).

_____ . Beiträge zur Ieremias-Septuaginta (NAWG, Phil.-
Hist. Kl., 2, MSU 6), Göttingen, 1958.

_____ . Sylloge: Gesammelte Aufsatze zur Septuaginta (MSU
10), Göttingen, 1971.

Zlotowitz, B.M. The Septuagint Translation of the Hebrew Terms
in Relation to God in the Book of Jeremiah, New York, 1981.

Zuntz, G. "Der Antinoe Papyrus der Proverbia und das Prophto-
logion," ZAW 68 (1956), 124-84.

JOURNAL FOR THE STUDY OF THE OLD TESTAMENT

Supplement Series